# a century SUMMERS

## 100 YEARS CRICKET
## OF SHEFFIELD SHIELD

**IRONBARK PRESS**

# a century of SUMMERS

## 100 YEARS
## CRICKET
## OF SHEFFIELD SHIELD

By Geoff Armstrong

**IRONBARK PRESS**

Front cover (left to right): David Hookes, the leading rungetter in the Shield's first 100 years; Simon O'Donnell, Victoria's winning captain in 1990–91; Sir Donald Bradman, the greatest batsman in the competition's history.
Back cover: Mike Veletta (left) and captain Geoff Marsh after Western Australia had won the 1991–92 final.
Title page: The NSW team that played South Australia in Adelaide in December 1899.

Published in 1992 by Ironbark Press
Level 1, 175 Alison Road, Randwick NSW 2031

© Geoff Armstrong

National Library of Australia
Cataloguing-in-Publication

Armstrong, Geoff.
A Century of Summers: 100 Years of Sheffield Shield Cricket.

ISBN 1875471 20 0

1. Sheffield Shield Competition — Anecdotes. 2. Cricket–Tournaments — Australia — Anecdotes. I. Title

796.358630994

Editor: Ian Heads
Design Concept: Scott Rigney
Finished Art: Character & Caps
Printed by: Globe Press, Mulgrave, Victoria

AUTHOR'S THANKS

Of all the people who pushed *A Century of Summers* to its fruition, I am especially grateful for the support of three people.

For the past 12 months, Ian Heads has been my guide, giving me the advantage of his experience and knowledge as this book crept towards its conclusion. Without his encouragement the project would not have been completed. I am also indebted to my good friend Ian Russell, and not just because of comprehensive statistics that feature in this book. Ian took the time to check the accuracy of every word I wrote, and spent countless hours answering a multitude of questions I threw at him. And also thanks to the man who designed the book, Scott Rigney, for his skill and his patience.

Special thanks to Sir Donald Bradman, Alan McGilvray, Richie Benaud and David Hookes for their superb contributions, which have added so much to the final product.

And also thanks to: Deborah Wood, Linda Carini, Lorraine Bonnet, Tony Greig, Alan Crompton, David Middleton, Geoff Greenwood, John Palmer, Shirlene Yap, Murray Lembit, Ern McQuillan, Greg Purcell, Andrew Hall, Rose Toohey, Helen Simpson, Paul Thomas and Norm Tasker; to the many others who assisted in the book's development; to my parents, who gave me Jack Pollard's *Cricket the Australian Way* in 1968, and set me on the way; and to my uncle, who took an impressionable nine-year-old to the SCG to see Barry Richards bat in January 1971. That was when this book really started.

PICTORIAL MATERIAL

The photographs in *A Century of Summers* were gained from a variety of sources, including the superb collection of Sydney-based photographer Ern McQuillan, the libraries of *The Sydney Morning Herald* and the Adelaide *Advertiser*, and PBL Marketing. The publishers would like to thank the following newspaper photographers whose work appears in this book: Kevin Berry, Frank Burke, Steve Christo, Stephen Holland, Viv Jenkins, Quentin Jones, Paul Lakatos, Gary McLean, Paul Matthews, Peter Moxham, John O'Gready, Robert Pearce, Steven Siewert, Colin Townsend, Nicholas Wilson and Paul Wright.

ABOUT THE AUTHOR

Geoff Armstrong is one of Australia's leading sports researchers, and has worked on a number of recently published books, including *True Blue: the Story of the NSW Rugby League*, and *The Kangaroos*, both by Ian Heads, *Backpage of Cricket* by Alan McGilvray, *Great Days of Australian Golf* by Phil Tresidder, and *The Moose* that Roared by Rex Mossop. In 1991 he compiled the best-selling *The Greatest Game*, an anthology on Australian rugby league. During Sydney summers he plays cricket with the Burwood Briars in the NSWCA Municipalities and Shires competition.

# Contents

Foreword by Alan Crompton, ACB Chairman   6

Introduction   8

THE GOLDEN AGE

Introduction by M.A. Noble   10

1. The Grace of Lord Sheffield   12
2. The Australasian Cricket Council   17
3. First Blood to Victoria   21
4. South Australia's Dr Grace   25
5. The Blackham Incident   28
6. The Original Fast Man   33
7. Mighty Clem   36
8. Thrown Out — The Tragedy of Jack Marsh   40
9. Tom Hastings — The One Game Wonder   43
10. Catch of a Lifetime   46
11. Charlie Macartney's First Season   48
12. The 1906 Dispute   51
13. A Leader of Men   53
14. Glorious Uncertainty   56
15. Algy Gehrs' Amazing Hundred   60
16. Victor Trumper   63

BETWEEN THE WARS

Introduction by Alan McGilvray   70

17. End of the Shield?   72
18. The First Draw   74
19. The Murder of Claude Tozer   77
20. Colossus of Melbourne   78
21. The Run Machine   82
22. The Brief Career of Dr Harry Rock   85
23. Stormy Days in Victorian Cricket   88
24. Queensland Makes the Grade   91
25. Long Live Victoria!   94
26. The Coming of Bradman and Jackson   97
27. The Kippax-Hooker Last Wicket Miracle   101
28. Clarrie Grimmett   104
29. They Can't Be All Out, I'm One Of Them!   107
30. Fast Eddie Gilbert   109
31. Tim Wall Gets The Lot   112
32. Bradman   116
33. The Genius of Fleetwood-Smith   120
34. The Tiger   123
35. From Bundaberg to the Big-time   126
36. A Pocket Edition Hero   129

TOWARDS THE TELEVISION AGE

Introduction by Richie Benaud   134

37. The Brilliance of Keith Miller   136
38. Slammin' Sam   138
39. The Fifth State   140
40. Farewell to the Don   143
41. A Tense Afternoon at the Gabba   145
42. Cup Day   147
43. South Australia All Out 27   149
44. The Return of Bodyline   151
45. The First Tie   153
46. Proving a Point   156
47. Another Bradman?   159
48. Simpson v the Rest   162
49. Richie Benaud   164
50. When 613 Was Not Enough   168
51. Dazzling Doug   171
52. Two More Ten-Fors   175
53. Winning the Les Favell Way   177
54. A Gentleman From Surrey   180
55. John Benaud's Boots   183

THE MODERN ERA

Introduction by David Hookes   188

56. Springbok Sensation   190
57. Building a Dynasty   192
58. Greg Chappell, Queenslander   195
59. Sam! Sam! Sam!   200
60. A State on Strike   201
61. Lillee and Marsh   204
62. Hurricane Hookes   208
63. Allan Border and the Great Split   210
64. Flat Jack   213
65. Straight Hit   217
66. End of an Era   218
67. The Closest Final   221
68. Being a Commentator Isn't Easy   224
69. King of the Adelaide Oval   227
70. Boon and Marsh Inc.   229
71. Cyclone Craig   232
72. Twin Peaks   238
73. A Comeback of the Bravest Kind   242
74. A Modern Miracle   246
75. Henry Lawson   248

Epilogue by Sir Donald Bradman   257

Statistics   264
Bibliography   280

# Foreword

## by Alan Crompton, O.A.M.
## Chairman of the Australian Cricket Board

A *Century of Summers* is a magnificent tribute to the heart and soul of Australian cricket — the Sheffield Shield competition.

As we celebrate the centenary of the Shield competition this summer, it is interesting to ponder whether Lord Sheffield could ever have envisaged that his donation of 150 pounds for the development of Australian cricket would have such a far reaching impact on the game.

The 46in x 30in Shield trophy the Australasian Cricket Council had commissioned with the assistance of the Lord's pounds, has become the symbol of the competitive spirit which is the hallmark of the Australian way of playing.

The Sheffield Shield competition is not only the nursery for grooming players for the international arena, as members of the Australian team, but is also widely acclaimed as the highest standard competition in the world outside of Test cricket.

There is an old saying: "When the standard of the Shield competition is high and even, the strength of the Australian team is high."

Ever since South Australia and New South Wales played the first match in 1892–93, the scene has been set for hard-fought interstate rivalry.

It's very apt that these same two States will clash in Adelaide from December 18–21, 1992, with a special centenary celebration to be held on December 19.

Since those early days, some of the greatest names in world cricket have honed their skills in the Sheffield Shield competition, players regarded by their peers as the best ever, including Sir Donald Bradman and Bill O'Reilly.

For me the Shield has always had a special place in my heart as I recall the excitement I experienced at the SCG as a young lad in short pants in the mid-50s marvelling at the consummate skills of Keith Miller, Les Favell, Neil Harvey, Ken Meuleman, Richie Benaud, Colin Pinch, Peter Burge, Alan Davidson, Graeme Hole and so many others — and worrying the life out of them for autographs.

I particularly remember as if it were yesterday, the explosive power of Norm O'Neill plundering many Shield attacks in the absence of the Australian team in South Africa in 1957.

I recall vividly (in longer pants this time) the tensions and the pressures of several of the Sheffield Shield finals played throughout the '80s, culminating most recently in the pulsating final of last season between NSW and WA in Perth.

With so many Test tours and one-day-internationals being played in modern-day cricket, the Shield competition no longer attracts big crowds.

However, public interest flourishes. All the arm-chair selectors can quickly tell you who is performing well for their state, who should be in the Australian team.

The interest remains because of the importance of the competition in developing players for the international scene.

And the parochial interstate rivalry is still as fierce as ever. Why else would Queensland go into mourning at the end of each season as its first shield title remains elusive? Why would team-mates in the Australian team become fierce opponents when they represent their states?

As this book will prove, the Sheffield Shield competition is rich with stories of famous matches and outstanding individual performances and records.

It is perhaps fitting that on the eve of the centenary South Australia, the state that won the historic first match against NSW by 57 runs, has produced the new Shield record holder in David Hookes.

The dashing former South Australian captain and Test batsman retired from first-class cricket at the end of the 1991–92 season after becoming the highest-scoring batsman in Shield history with a total of 9,364 runs.

Hookes produced some memorable performances during his 120 Shield matches, including a century off 34 balls in 43 minutes in Victoria in 1982–83, and a mammoth innings of 306 to create a record Australian first-class partnership of 462 with Wayne Phillips against Tasmania in 1987.

This book brings the Shield's abundant colour to life with features by Sir Donald Bradman, Richie Benaud, M.A. Noble, Alan McGilvray and David Hookes and profiles on all the great players.

It traces the story from Lord Sheffield and the first Shield season, to Clem Hill and Victor Trumper in "The Golden Age" to "Between the Wars" and the rise of Bradman and Jackson, Tiger O'Reilly, Clarrie Grimmett and Don Tallon.

Then it's on through the days of Keith Miller, Sam Loxton, Neil Harvey, Bob Simpson, Les Favell and Doug Walters to the modern era of Ian and Greg Chappell, Dennis Lillee, Rod Marsh to the present day Waugh twins, David Boon and Geoff Marsh – including of course, the Allan Border years.

The Sheffield Shield will always hold a special, and important, place in Australian cricket.

It is to the men who gave the competition such great tradition over 100 years that *A Century of Summers* pays such a fitting tribute, in a commemorative book that is a "must" for all cricket enthusiasts.

# Introduction

A *Century of Summers* is not a complete historical record of the first 100 years of the Sheffield Shield. That was never the intention. Instead the aim was to tell the stories of many of the remarkable, fantastic and unlikely moments that have occurred during the competition's history. In the pages that follow inspiring cricketing moments are juxtaposed with the controversial, the champions sit next to the obscure.

The Shield has developed some of Australia's most celebrated sporting champions, men such as Victor Trumper, Allan Border, Bill O'Reilly and Keith Miller, plus, of course, the greatest of them all, Sir Donald Bradman. It has also conjured some of Australian cricket's most memorable games and miraculous performances, such as the Alan Kippax-Hal Hooker world record 10th-wicket partnership of 307 compiled in December 1928, and the effort of the South Australians of 1992 to score 506 in the fourth innings, to win a match long-thought lost.

With these heroes and heroics go the tradesmen, the players who battled for seasons without ever taking the step to a secure Test spot. Men such as Algy Gehrs, Phil Ridings, Sam Trimble and Peter Sleep — all had their moments in the Sheffield Shield. So too did some others, long forgotten, such as a wicket-keeper from Victoria, called Tom Hastings, whose first-class career extended for over 20 seasons, but who played just nine times in the Shield. His one moment of glory came in January 1903, when he scored 106, batting number 11 against South Australia, the only time he went past 25 in a first-class match, and the only time the last man in has scored a century in a first-class match in Australia. Then there was the terribly unlucky Dr. Harold Rock, who played only four Shield games, and was twice dropped after scoring a century. And so the cavalcade goes on...

*A Century of Summers* has been divided into four eras, and each of them is introduced by a man who played his cricket during that time. The M.A. Noble essay that precedes "The Golden Age" was adapted from a series of articles Noble wrote for the *Sydney Mail* in the 1920s. The contributions of Alan McGilvray, Richie Benaud and David Hookes were commissioned especially for this book, and reveal much of the cricket and the cricketers of their day. The book closes with a brilliant and incisive epilogue by Sir Donald Bradman, in which the Great Man looks back at the 100 years of cricket played since the first Shield match, and gives his views on the directions the game is taking in the 1990s.

In the summers up to the second World War, the Shield was often the main event in the Australian cricket season. Times have changed. Not since 1961–62 has a Test match featuring Australia not been played between a Shield season's opening and closing contests. Only rarely nowadays do the nation's major players enjoy the chance to take their places in a majority of Shield matches. This has, to some degree, lessened the quality of the cricket played in the competition, but not its importance.

The Sheffield Shield is as much a part of the Australian cricket scene in the 1990s as the bat, the ball, and compulsory field placements in the first 15 overs. The Shield is still an ever-changing production line, developing, as it has for 100 years, the quality and character of the Australian Test team. It remains an absorbing struggle, highly competitive, often unpredictable, and continues to earn the sporting public's respect and interest, if not, sadly, the public's money through the turnstile.

It is not the job of Sheffield Shield cricket to compete with the excitement of one-day internationals, or the glamour and traditions of the Test matches. It has its own place in the game's pacy, aggressive computer age. The Shield needs to do no more than continue to produce the quality of cricket and cricketers it has done over the past 100 seasons to be a part of the sport for many years to come.

Geoff Armstrong
October 1992

# THE GOLDEN AGE

# Introduction by M. A. Noble

Memories will crowd upon the "old hands" who occupy a place in the pavilion. We have had our innings. Poor Victor Trumper and Reg Duff, who together opened the batting in many of our matches, have gone. With them went genius for the game in the one, and a grim determination that nothing could dismay in the other. I know the glorious heights reached by Victor. He was peerless on wickets that were doing a bit and against bowlers who could take advantage of any condition that was against the batsman. In real genius for the game no-one has ever compared with Victor. "Tibby" Cotter died a soldier — one often pictures him. To look upon the Sydney Cricket Ground is to see again in a sort of vision the forms of these and other comrades in past battles. Hugh Trumble, Clem Hill and I will meet again, no doubt, and recall the old times. When old players get together there is plenty to recall.

The first century I scored against Victoria was in 1897 at the Sydney Cricket Ground. I made 71 in the first innings, and was 99 in the second. Bill Howell, the last batsman for New South Wales, had just come in. Harry Graham was fielding at extra cover. I played the ball towards him and, not knowing the game so well as I did later on, I called out: "Come on, Bill!"

Off we went, Bill as anxious as I was, I believe, that I should get my hundred, and neither of us looking at Graham, who had quietly come in a few yards after I had glanced around the field and fixed my gaze intently on the bowler. Harry picked up the ball like the great fieldsman he was and (oh, sublime luck!) sent it hard and high right over the wicketkeeper's head to the fence, giving me five for the stroke, while Bill Howell was not much more than halfway down the wicket.

It was a costly mistake for Victoria. Bill and I, exhilarated by the good fortune, kept going, our scores being 48 and 152 respectively. So I made an error of judgement and did not pay for it, whereas Graham made an error and his side paid heavily. The moral of it is: Don't make errors, but if you do, have luck on your side.

I recall a match between New South Wales and Victoria, and Vernon Ransford came in when I was bowling. I sent up eight overs for no runs. My object was to bowl at the leg stump and worry him into making a risky stroke. I had a man at mid-on

fairly wide, a man at square leg behind and deeper than the umpire, and a man at fine leg. I thought I could get him caught at deep short-leg.

Ransford, seeing the man there, would not make the shot; but I kept him at that end all the time, and in the ninth over there was one with a little extra bounce in it, and he turned and sent it straight to the man at deep short-leg. I thought my strategy had worked, but instead of getting the ball safe in his hands, the fieldsman let the ball hit him right on the forehead, and it bounced off and fell on the ground.

Ransford went on to make 180 runs. There was no hope of working the same trick on him again. No first-class batsman is ever trapped twice the same way in one innings. Reg Duff was in the match and when the fellows were crossing over at the end of the over he said to our erring brother: "You know you're in the game, old man." This did not tend to make him any happier.

The Victorian match can always be relied upon to create big public interest, largely due, one imagines, to the many stirring and hard-fought battles of former years and to the known capacity of the players to fight to the last ditch in order to snatch a victory.

One match stands out in the memories of all who saw it, when on the last day, Victoria had to make about 330 runs to win, and did it — some performance in those days. The closing stages are vividly impressed upon my mind. When Jack Saunders, the last man, came in, about 12 runs were needed. Seven of these were obtained, when Saunders played a ball to Tom Howard. Saunders ran down the pitch, and getting halfway, was sent back by his partner, Peter McAlister. Howard, seeing the probability of an easy run out, threw the ball very gently and accurately to Arthur McBeath, who had backed up the wicket.

It was all so simple; he only had to take it and knock the bails off, and the game was ours. So sure were we that several of us started for the pavilion while the ball was on its journey; but alas! for optimism, McBeath missed the catch, and Saunders scrambled home. The extra five runs were soon made, and Victoria gained a fine victory. This is just a reminder that our Victorian brothers are never beaten until the last ball is bowled.

These matches, at times, have provided some of the best, most exciting and keenly fought games, either international or interstate, that have ever taken place, and have supplied the necessary training for our representative players for the sterner and more significant contests with England. When we remember the great players who at different periods have opposed one another for Sheffield Shield supremecy, the high standard of cricket associated with these games, the hard fought and splendidly conducted contests, the brilliantly conceived strategy, and the tactics so excellently carried out by players of great ability, it is easy to understand why public interest has been maintained during all those years, and why the contests have become perhaps the greatest instrument in educating the national mind to a proper appreciation and approval of good, clean, healthy sport.

*(Adapted from articles written for the Sydney Mail in the 1920s.)*

*Montague Alfred Noble, a central figure in many of the great and controversial events of Australian cricket's Golden Age.*

# 1

# THE GRACE OF LORD SHEFFIELD

In 1891 Australian cricket was in deep depression — as was the economy of the time. The national XI had been humiliated in England the previous year, losing 16 of 38 matches, including both Tests. Attendances at major matches, so buoyant in the early '80s, were in sharp decline. The waning interest in big-time cricket was reflected at club level, where public support was minimal.

On February 18, 1891, the Sydney sporting weekly *The Referee* commented:

"The colonial press of late years has very frequently deplored the apathy displayed by the public in all things connected with our most favourite pastime. At important meetings, such as the banquetting or reception of visitors from other colonies, this regrettable fact has been dolefully spoken of, and many apparently inadequate schemes have been at various periods devised whereby to revive that long lost enthusiasm, only to invariably have their fatality proved beyond question."

Three days later a cable was received in Melbourne from a cricket loving aristocrat from Sussex in England, Lord Sheffield, bringing the news that it had been decided to organise an English cricket team to visit Australia in the season 1891–92. The concept had been spoken of throughout February, but had received only lukewarm support in Australian cricket's boardrooms and press columns.

Eton educated, Lord Sheffield was then 59. At various stages in an interesting life he was or had been a diplomat, politician, land-holder and philanthropist. His property, Sheffield Park, East Sussex, extended for 2400 hectares, and had hosted countless cricket matches of varying qualities. Lord Sheffield had been the President of the Sussex County Cricket Club since 1879, a post that had been held by his father when the club was first formed in 1839.

Without Lord Sheffield's patronage it is unlikely a tour by an English team would have taken place in 1891–92. The Australian cricket community was wary of the damage to local competitions caused by successive English tours. The perception was that teams were constantly arriving from Britain chasing no more than a handsome profit, with less than enough concern for the welfare of Australian cricket. And these teams were labelling themselves as representatives of "All England", but in most cases fell well below the reality of a fully representative or full-strength English side.

Lord Sheffield's charitable reputation was such that any team under his control was unlikely to be tagged mercenary. His masterstroke was to sign the most complete player in world cricket, Dr W.G. Grace, for the trip — a move which at once authenticated the quality of this English side.

Grace was 43 then, weighing more than 114 kg, but still one of the great players of the English game. One Sydney scribe wrote of him in 1891: "Mr Grace represents and typifies cricket to us just as the Archbishop of Canterbury may be said to represent theology." His records, even today, are extraordinary, far and away superior to any of his contemporaries. Lord Sheffield guaranteed him 3000 pounds, and also provided transport and accommodation for his wife and two of his children. Grace, it should be remembered, was an amateur.

On March 23, 1891, the NSW Cricket Association granted its patronage for the tour, on the condition that all expenses incidental to the matches be borne by the tourists. The decision came almost a month after the Victorian Cricketers' Association had moved that they would "grant patronage to Lord Sheffield in the event of his deciding to bring a team of English cricketers to Australia."

At the meeting the VCA gave the tour its support, one delegate expressed the view that patronage would have been refused had the team been purely professional. In both Melbourne and Sydney memories were still vivid of the two, coincidental, English cricket tours of 1887–88, which had been financial disasters for the local cricket associations.

Later in 1891, the Melbourne *Argus* would write: "But for the fact that the English team is organised

*In late November, 1891, the* Australasian *published this caricature of Lord Sheffield. The Earl did not enjoy having his photograph taken, and this drawing is the only pictorial record of his historic tour of Australia.*

upon the most genuinely sportsmanlike lines by Lord Sheffield and accompanied by W.G. Grace, it is a matter of certainty that the Victorian cricketing authorities at least would have discouraged the visit of the team."

In the Melbourne *Leader*, a letter was published from Lord Sheffield in which he stated: "I was very much afraid you might find that a visit of English cricketers would do much to dislocate local cricket, but the Australian clubs have most generously waived all objections, for which I am deeply grateful..."

On August 19, J.C. Davis, the *Referee's* leading cricket writer, struck an optimistic chord: "Experience has taught us that the engagements of the English teams in the metropolis have at all times had a most deleterious effect on club matches...The visit of Lord Sheffield's team might, however, be the means of reviving deadened public interest, as the appearance of the famous Dr W.G. Grace alone will create a revulsion of feeling which must operate beneficially on the game..."

Davis went on to call Lord Sheffield's side "the most formidable that has left the shores of England for an extended tour." Suspicions continued however as to the financial motivations of the tour.

Davis cynically pointed out the NSWCA would "not get a fig" out of Lord Sheffield's tour. He continued, "the English teams come out here, crush all our club engagements, reduce our intercolonial program, monopolise all the choice dates on the Association Ground, provide for themselves the patronage of the Association, procure all the proceeds leaving us the bald and empty honour of having had them in our midst."

In late August, the NSWCA received a letter from the Victorian, Mr Frank Illingworth, Lord Sheffield's agent in Australia. The letter stated that no member of the side would have any financial interest in the tour, and that should any surplus after expenses be achieved it was Lord Sheffield's intention "to dispose of it in some satisfactory manner, so that no individual will reap any benefit."

The English side arrived in Western Australia on November 6, 1891. They quickly sailed on to Adelaide, arriving at the South Australian capital on November 9. On that day South Australia was amassing a huge total in the intercolonial match against the visiting Victorians. The champion local allrounder George Giffen scored 271, and South Australia ended the Monday (the second day of the match) at 7 for 519.

The following day the Adelaide *Advertiser* published an extended interview with Lord Sheffield, who they described as "a typical English county squire". The first question asked of him concerned the financial aspects of the trip. The paper's correspondent wrote: "He explained that as he had organised the tour the whole of any surplus accruing — though of this he seemed far from sanguine — would remain in his hands to be disposed of as might be thought best. Whether, however, it will be divided among the professional members of the team or be handed to public charities has not yet been decided upon. Indeed his lordship, wholly unconcerned as to the commercial success of the tour, did not appear to have given this point any particular consideration..."

Frank Illingworth had been forced to terminate his duties as Lord Sheffield's agent owing to ill health. His responsibilities were taken up by Major Ben Wardill of the Melbourne Cricket Club. Wardill had been in Adelaide to finalise preparations for the Englishmen's first visit to Melbourne, which was to follow the opening match of the tour, in Adelaide starting on November 20.

In his book *The History of the Sheffield Shield* Chris Harte reproduced a letter, dated November 20, 1891, from Wardill to the secretary of the NSWCA, John Portus. In it Wardill stated that "Lord Sheffield asked me if the (NSW Cricket) Association would accept a trophy of the value of 150 pounds or thereabouts for competition by the three colonies in any way agreed upon by them."

It is interesting that Lord Sheffield was most concerned that the NSW Cricket Association would accept such an offer. Criticism of the tour, specifically its negative impact on local cricket, had been loudest in NSW. The first mention of Lord Sheffield's offer in the Australian press occurred on November 24. Significantly the information was released in Sydney, and was reproduced in the Melbourne and Adelaide papers as cabled news from the NSW capital.

If Lord Sheffield had chosen to donate the trophy before he arrived in Australia, it is surprising that he did not reveal that fact in his first interview with the Adelaide *Advertiser* on November 9, or at the mayoral reception the next morning. It appears the trophy concept, which would eventually crystallise into the reality of the Sheffield Shield, was a reaction to concerns in the Australian, and most specifically the Sydney cricket community as to the financial motives of the touring team. Later Lord Sheffield would indicate he was not worried if the 150 pounds was split between the three major cricket associations, perhaps a further indication that his motivation was strictly to allieviate any oppostion to the potential profits of the tour, rather than to foster a genuine intercolonial cricket competition.

The cricket side of the tour was a major success for the Englishmen, except for the three-Test series, where Australia triumphed with victories in the first two matches, in Melbourne and Sydney. The matches attracted large crowds, mainly it seems because of the presence of Dr Grace.

*The powerful Australian side that toured England in 1902. The central figure is Major B.J. (Ben) Wardill. In 1891–92, Wardill acted as Lord Sheffield's agent in Australia, and played a significant role in the negotiations that led to the creation of the Sheffield Shield.*

For Grace personally, the tour was a moderate personal success and a complete public relations disaster. He scored just one first-class century, a glorious unbeaten 159, opening up, against Victoria in late November. But he consistently made the headlines with his boorish and arrogant behaviour. One writer claimed Grace had "differences" with opponents or umpires in nearly every game he had played.

In a non-first-class match played on the outskirts of Sydney, at Parramatta, Grace refused to participate against the 20 local players unless his side was permitted to bat 12, instead of the originally agreed 11. At another time, he was publically critical of the dress sense of one of Sydney's leading umpires. In Tasmania, he refused to bowl his front-line bowlers in a bizarre protest at the actions of the local groundsman, who had apparently illegally watered the pitch.

Grace also refused to allow the Australian captain Jack Blackham to toss his lucky penny at the start of the third Test. The doctor spun it himself, and won his first toss of the series. However the English captain's most publicised dispute came in Sydney during the return match with NSW in February, when he reacted to a not out decision in such a manner that the local umpire, Ted Briscoe refused to continue. Press reports claimed Grace had suggested the umpire was blind, though the English fieldsman Bobby Abel thought that Grace had said to Briscoe nothing worse than: "You really must pay more attention to the game!"

Grace was severly censured in the papers, especially in Sydney where, although he attracted large crowds, it appears he was almost universally disliked. The Sydney *Truth* on January 31, 1892 wrote: "His behaviour on the cricket field, not to mention his demeanour in private, has been caddish, snobbish, or anything else you like, except gentlemanly." The paper then went on to reproduce a letter published after Grace's first trip to Australia in 1873–74, which was signed "W.G.G.", but not written by the doctor. It was also printed in the Sydney *Daily Telgraph*. The tone of that bogus letter is summed up by the beginning of the final paragraph, which read:

"A good deal was said about my stopping away from the lunch at various places. My reason was that I didn't want to fraternise with the tinkers, tailors, and snobs who are the great guns in your cricket world. To take their money was a fair thing in return for work done, but to hob-nob with a lot of scum was a far different thing. Fancy the chance of a greasy butcher on his travels walking up to me one day at Lord's with 'How d'ye do, Mr G.; I lunched with you in Australia.' My dear fellow, as far as I can see, colonial society is low, shockingly low."

This letter, though patently a fraud, reflects the Australian public's perception of the English captain. Grace had genuine correspondence published in the *The Sydney Morning Herald* on February 3 and the *Telegraph* a day later, denying authorship of the despicable letter. But by then his image was beyond repair, and the acrimony that continued until the tour's end established Grace as one of the most vilified of all sporting champions to visit Australia.

It is extremely ironic that the very popular Lord Sheffield needed the very unpopular Dr Grace on this most important of tours for the tour to be a profitable venture.

At a meeting of the NSWCA on December 14, 1891, the Association voted to thank Lord Sheffield for his "generous offer" of 150 pounds for a trophy for intercolonial cricket, and elected a committee of three to confer with the other two states on the proposal. Although such communications did take place, nothing was resolved for four months.

The NSW authorities seemed much keener to create an intercolonial competition than their Victorian counterparts. The South Australians, who had not met Victoria on equal terms before 1880, and had not played NSW in an intercolonial match at all before February, 1890, were obliged to wait and discover what the two major cricketing states decided for them.

In Melbourne, the VCA appeared to prefer splitting the 150 pounds between the three states. However in April, 1892, they agreed to leave the final decision to the proposed Australasian Cricket Council, which at that stage did not exist but which would conduct its inaugural meeting in September of that year.

At that first meeting, after much haggling and debate, the Sheffield Shield competition was created. The story of that decision is told in the following chapter.

Lord Sheffield left a 150 pound legacy that remains a symbol of one of the most competitive sporting competitions in the world. But perhaps even more important than the trophy that lives to this day, he, Dr Grace and the rest of the English team revived public interest in the game of cricket in Australia. The first Shield matches of 1892–93 were played in an atmosphere more positive than had existed in Australian cricket for many years.

Lord Sheffield died in 1909, aged 77, a cricket lover until the end. Dr Grace went on, scoring runs and raising tempers until his retirement in 1908. He died in 1915, just months after the death of Australia's greatest pre-World War I champion, the incomparable Victor Trumper. The names of Lord Sheffield and

"WG" remain as well-known as any in the international cricket world — Grace through the runs he accumulated and the records he established, Lord Sheffield because of the cricket competition that will always bear his name.

# 2

# THE AUSTRALASIAN CRICKET COUNCIL

The creation of the Sheffield Shield competition was the single worthy contribution of the Australasian Cricket Council — the first attempt by administrators to organise a national body to control Australian cricket. The Council was formed in September, 1892, largely through the initiative of officials from the NSW Cricket Association, whose primary motive appeared to be enthusiasm for a slice of the substantial profits that could be made by Australian cricket teams touring England.

At that time such tours were private affairs, with the profits being shared by organisers and players. The Association's logic was that such profits should be used to benefit the game in Australia, rather than the bank balances of a select group of individuals. The players understandably did not agree, and the lust for control of these tours would create an undercurrent of animosity between officials and players that eventually led to the suspension of the entire NSW team in 1906, and the absence of six of Australia's finest players from the tour of England in 1912.

Cricket officials from NSW, Victoria and South Australia had met as early as 1887 to discuss the establishment of a national administrative body. Nearly three years passed before the matter was raised again at a NSWCA Executive Committee meeting, which led to a sub-committee being formed, and letters being sent to the other major associations suggesting a cricket council be formed — "without delay". Another sub-committee was created to produce a draft constitution, which was finally submitted to the NSWCA on November 16, 1891.

Four weeks later a NSWCA monthly meeting decided the draft constitution should be sent to the associations of Victoria, Tasmania, South Australia and Queensland. A conference was scheduled for Adelaide in late March, 1892, for officials from the three major cricket associations to further discuss the creation of a Cricket Council. The conference was held on the Friday of the third Test between Australia and Lord Sheffield's team and it was decided a Council would be formed.

On April 20, J.C. Davis wrote in *The Referee*: "It is highly probable that one of the first duties to devolve upon the Australian (sic) Cricket Council after its formation will be the disposal of the 150 pound donated by Lord Sheffield for the encouragement of the game in the colonies. On the face of it this might seem a task very easily accomplished, but the Council will find it rather perplexing, inasmuch as the whole of the colonies are concerned in it. Doubtless various suggestions for its disposal wll be offered, some of a novel and ludicrous character."

The inaugural meeting of the Australasian Cricket Council was held in Sydney on Tuesday, September 13, 1892. One of the NSWCA delegates was to have been the Association's president George Reid, but he resigned as a delegate 24 hours before the meeting. Reid, a tough politician and then leader of the NSW Opposition, was instigating a no confidence motion against the Government on the Wednesday afternoon. Four delegates arrived from Victoria (R.W. Best, D.A. Madden, H.H. Budd and W. Kelleher) and two from South Australia (A.F. Robinson and G. Mostyn Evan), while the Queensland and Tasmanian associations sent formal acceptence of the constitution, but no representatives. Evan held proxy votes for the two other South Australian delegates who were unable to attend (G.O. Whitridge and John Creswell). One of the four NSW delegates, Richard Teece, was elected Chairman, and another, the NSWCA secretary John Portus, secretary. The other NSW delegates were Victor Cohen and J.M. Gibson.

The first matter dealt with was the timing of the next Australian tour of England. This was the major issue in the minds of the delegates. Victor Cohen was at that time in the process of organising a tour and after much discussion he received the sanction of the Council to manage a trip in 1893.

The next matter on the agenda was Lord Sheffield's 150 pounds.

Before the meeting the Victorians had made it clear they believed the money should be split between NSW, Victoria and South Australia. Immediately they made their move, their senior delegate, Mr Best, putting forward the motion: "That the sum of money given by Lord Sheffield be divided equally amongst the associations of Victoria, New South Wales and South Australia, to be devoted in a manner that each governing body may determine."

The motion was seconded by the South Australian delegate, G. Mostyn Evan. But the South Australians were not operating as a bloc. The other SACA representative, Mr Robinson, moved, as an amendment: "That the money be devoted to the purchase of a premiership shield, to be held by the premier colony for the year, and that a sub-committee, consisting of Messrs Cohen, Robinson and Kelleher, be appointed to draft the necessary rules."

That amendment was carried, by a vote of 6 to 5, Evan voting with the four Victorians against the decision.

The sub-committee brought their draft rules back to the delegates the following day, when the meeting was resumed during a cruise of Sydney Harbour. These rules were:

*1. That the donation be devoted to the purchase of a silver shield to be called the Sheffield Shield and to be given for competition between the three colonies named.*

*2. That the competition be confined to intercolonial matches.*

*3. That the first competition for the possession of the Shield be held on the occasion of the next intercolonial match between any two of the three colonies named and that the colony winning the match hold the Shield until it suffer a defeat in an intercolonial match, upon the happening of which event the Shield shall pass into the possession of the colony inflicting defeat; similarly for all succeeding contests.*

*4. In the event of a tie the Shield shall remain in the possession of the colony holding it at the commencement of the match resulting in the tie.*

*5. The representatives of the colony holding the Shield (providing they have played in not less than two matches in any one season) shall each be awarded a badge to be worn on coat or cap, such badge to be of suitable design. Subject to the permission of the Earl of Sheffield, it is suggested that the design shall be the Sheffield coronet and the figures representing the year to which the badge is applicable.*

Clause 3 did not satisfy the majority of delegates, who contended that the Shield should be won by the season's most successful colony. *The Sydney Morning Herald* wrote of the Council's second day: "Mr Teece occupied the chair, all members being in attendance. With reference to the Sheffield Shield to be given for competition at intercolonial matches, the chairman moved that the winning colony should hold the Shield for the season."

The original rules should have been amended before the meeting closed, but were not. This oversight perhaps reflects the significance delegates placed on the Shield debate. The rules, as initially drafted, remained in place. Consequently the winners of the first intercolonial match of 1892–93 would be the Sheffield Shield holders.

Later on the cruise Evan moved: "That in the opinion of the council it is desirable that the three colonies shall meet each other an equal number of times in every season for the Sheffield Shield." This was carried, a minor triumph for the South Australians, who had had some difficulty getting matches with Victoria and especially NSW in previous years.

At the first Victorian Cricketers' Association meeting held after the inaugural ACC meeting, Best reported to his members that the Shield would be held "by the colony having the best average of wins for the season". (Best also expressed grave disappointment at the decision to spend all of Lord Sheffield's donation on the Shield.) Clearly he believed the Shield rules defined the winning colony as that which possessed the best season record.

As the rules stood, Best was wrong. The first Sheffield Shield match was the South Australia-NSW match in Adelaide in December, 1892. The local's victory gave them first ownership of the trophy (although at that point no Shield existed).

The shortcomings of the rules became obvious to Victorians after the next two intercolonial matches of 1892–93. Their side defeated NSW (in what was effectively a "non-Shield" match) and then South Australia (to "win" the Shield). After the defeat of South Australia, Victoria were just one win away from achieving an unbeatable record for the season, yet, as the rules stood, victory in either of their return fixtures would not be sufficient to guarantee possession of the Shield until 1893–94.

In the *Argus* of January 5, 1893 "Observer" wrote:

*Two prominent players in the early years of the Shield.
Left: The champion Victorian bowler, Hugh Trumble, a
stalwart for his state from before the Shield's first
season until 1903–04. Above: South Australia's first
Shield wicketkeeper, A.H. "Affie" Jarvis.*

"As cricketers are aware, the intercolonial matches of this season are being played for the possession of the Sheffield Shield, but unless a mistake has been made in drafting the conditions under which the trophy is to be held they appear altogether unsatisfactory, since the latest victor of each season, and not the best team on points will hold the Shield until the following summer. Surely some mistake has been made. Should Victoria, for example, beat New South Wales in the return match and South Australia suffer defeat in Sydney, the latter team would still become the holders of the Sheffield Shield by beating Victoria in

Adelaide, and would, with the shield, it is presumed, take also the badges for the players...The fairest method would certainly be some such system of points as that in force for pennant matches in Victoria. As it is the cricket council have either drafted foolish conditions, or their intentions have not been carried into effect in the rules."

Five days later, the matter was raised at the monthly VCA meeting. The *Argus* reported the following exchanges:

"Mr P. KNUCKEY asked whether it was true, as stated in the press, that the Sheffield Shield would be held by the colony winning the last match of the season instead of the greatest number of matches.

Mr H.H. BUDD said that the statements in the newspapers to that effect could not be accepted as reliable.

The SECRETARY (E.D. Heather) read the recommendations of the cricket council, which showed that in the event of the colony holding the shield being beaten by any other colony in the last match of the year, the colony so winning held the shield unitl the following season.

Mr KNUCKEY — I consider that arrangement pure rubbish.

Mr D. SCOTT pointed out that under such an arrangement the premier colony on all matches played for the season may not hold the shield.

Mr KELLEHER said that when these conditions were drafted the Victorian Association was averse to playing home-and-home matches with South Australia, and hence the difficulty. Unquestionably the present arrangement was not satisfactory, and now that each of the three colonies would play each other twice, he would bring the matter before the cricket council, which would probably meet in Sydney about January 30, with the object of having fresh conditions drafted."

The proposal of the VCA at the January 30 ACC meeting was unanimously accepted. The new clause read:

"That the first competition for the possession of the Shield be held on the occasion of the next intercolonial match between any two of the three colonies named, and that the colony winning the larger percentage of intercolonial matches during the season to be the holders of the Shield. In the event of a tie then the position of each colony to be determined by the best batting and bowling averages for the season in such matches."

Interestingly, this change was not mentioned in press reports of the meeting. All the available space was devoted to the animated discussions concerning the makeup of the side to tour England later that year. The selectors, all of whom were prominent Test players, had put their final choices before the Council for approval. The press reports clearly show that most delegates wanted some of the selections altered, but that the Council did not have the power to make any changes. That the Council's hands were tied in this way frustrated many commentators, and J.C. Davis wrote: "This action of the Council will not serve to strengthen it in the estimation of the public. In fact, unless the alterations in the rules proposed by Mr Gibson be carried out, the usefulness of the Council in the future will have vanished as completely as daylight does before darkness."

Gibson had proposed "that the selection of all Australian teams should be rested in this Council."

Although the decision to create a Sheffield Shield had been made in September, 1892, nothing more than letter writing was done about getting the trophy designed and crafted until July 1893, when advertisements were placed in papers in Sydney, Melbourne and Adelaide, seeking tenders "for the manufacture and supply in silver of the 'Sheffield Shield'". A further advertisement was placed in early October, apparently because the initial applications were unsatisfactory.

The applications were culled down to 16 designs, which were considered by the ACC delegates, and, at a meeting on December 28, 1893, the tender of P. Blashki of Melbourne was accepted. Blashki was a Pole, who had migrated to Australia in 1858 and started a jewellery business in Melbourne in 1875. *The Referee* wrote that the "design is very elaborate, including a representation of Lord Sheffield's cricket ground, the Sheffield and Australian arms, and a bust of the donor. The Shield will consist of 200oz of Australian silver, several ounces of gold and the arms will be enamelled. The trophy, which will be the most highly prized that has ever been competed for in Australia, is to measure 43in by 30in."

The final product changed little from the original design, though strangely Lord Sheffield's bust was replaced by a statuette of the goddess "Victory". The production of the Shield was not completed until mid 1894, and not presented to South Australia, the 1893–94 champions, until July, 1894.

The Australasian Cricket Council was wound up in 1900, its major objective — to gain control of Australian tours of England — unachieved. For most of its brief life the ACC was seen as very much the toothless tiger. The players resented the Council's intrusions, and delegates seemed more concerned with the administrative hassles of their own colonies.

But the pot of gold represented by the profits of England tours remained out of reach, and in 1905 the Australian Cricket Board of Control was established, with wider powers and greater resolve. That body gained a grip on the management of overseas tours, but only after the cream of Australia's playing strength fully tested the administrators' claims on authority.

In the history of Australian cricket, the Australasian Cricket Council is chronicled as little more than an ineffective forerunner to the Board of Control, which evolved into the Australian Cricket Board in 1973. Its one significant decision was the creation of an intercolonial competition, where the teams involved met each other an equal number of times, and played for an elaborate and prized trophy. This decision, made on a tight 6–5 vote, remains one of the most inspired administrative acts in Australian cricket. That it was made by an administrative body totally lacking in inspiration and endeavour remains one of Australian cricket's great ironies.

# 3

# FIRST BLOOD TO VICTORIA

Jack Worrall was one of the most notable figures in Australian sport before the First World War. With the Victorian Football League club Carlton, he was the first recognised football "coach", introducing a more disciplined and professional approach to Melbourne's premier winter sport. Formerly a champion rover with Fitzroy in the Victorian Football Association, Worrall also coached successfully at Fitzroy and Essendon, winning six VFL premierships between 1902 and 1922.

For the last 20 years of the 19th century, if Worrall wasn't winning football matches, he was scoring runs. He was a brave cricketer for Victoria for 18 years from 1884, and for Australia in 11 Tests between 1885 and 1899, twice touring England. Thickset, strong and aggressive, he amassed 417 runs, out of 922, for Carlton against Melbourne University in 1896, then the highest known individual score at any level of Australian cricket. He later became a respected sportswriter, frequently quoted in the Sydney, as well as Melbourne newspapers, and also a noted cricket coach.

Worrall was Victoria's first captain in Sheffield Shield cricket. Strangely, in a season where the Victorians sailed through their four Shield matches undefeated, Worrall was one of four leaders — Dr John Barrett, Jack Blackham and Harry Trott being the others. It was perhaps fortunate no Shield had been crafted at this stage. One wonders who would have been asked to make the acceptance speech.

In the first Victorian Shield match, Worrall led his state to an eight wicket victory in the traditional Christmas game against NSW at the MCG. Barrett and Trott both played, but Blackham, the champion wicketkeeper and then Australian captain, was unavailable owing to an injured finger. Worrall was one of three Victorian selectors (as was Blackham), but the ballot among the players to decide the captaincy was a tight one, Worrall winning over Barrett by a reported two votes. How the margin could be two votes was not explained. Perhaps the 12th man was involved, or did one team member vote twice, informally, or abstain?

This match was not the first of the Shield season, NSW having already fallen in Adelaide, despite forcing the South Australians to follow on. In that match, the NSW batsman Harry Donnan had scored the first Sheffield Shield century (bowled Ernie Jones for 120) after his captain, the renowned left-handed opener Harry Moses, had been bowled by George Giffen for 99. Giffen, the record breaker, became the first man to take five wickets in a Shield innings (6–133), but was beaten to the first ten wicket match haul by Michael Pierce, the NSW right-hand leg breaker, who took 13 wickets on his first-class debut.

As was outlined in chapter two, under the Shield rules existing at that time the victory gave South Australia the "Shield", and meant that when the New South Welshmen took on the Victorians three days later, no trophy was at stake. This situation was certainly not publicised, and the former Australian captain Tom Horan, writing in *The Australasian*, knew nothing of it:

"Through the generosity of Lord Sheffield, a magnificent trophy has been presented for competition and it is hardly necessary to state that the interest attached to the triangular intercolonial contest has been enhanced by his lordship's gracious gift in a measure that must be very pleasing to this patron of cricket patrons."

The Victorian defeat of NSW was decisive. Worrall lost the toss, but his bowlers, spearheaded by the medium-paced Bob McLeod, kept NSW to a meagre 197. Victoria's reply was led by the top order. The brilliant left-hander William Bruce scored 128, and was well supported by his opening partner Barrett (who was also left-handed), and Trott, the stylish number three. Jack Worrall, batting four, scored 31 and was out trying to force the pace, skying Pierce to long off. The NSW outcricket was heavily criticised. Horan called the bowling (which lacked the celebrated Charlie Turner), "some of the weakest bowling I have ever seen in an intercolonial match between Victoria and New South Wales, or in any other inter-colonial match for that matter." Of the fielding he wrote: "Their fielding was about the poorest I have ever witnessed."

New South Wales, 178 behind on the first innings, battled back, and managed to set the locals 187 to win, a target the Victorians comfortably reached for the loss of only Bruce and Barrett. Trott remained 70 not out. After the match the NSW umpire, the former champion bat Charlie Bannerman, commented on the fairness and good humour of the crowd. Apparently the MCC president had delivered a stinging rebuke to members at the previous annual meeting, and this had had much effect.

Sitting amid the members on the final day was the South Australian side, in Melbourne for their first Shield match against Victoria. For this game the Victorians made three changes, and Barrett won the cap-taincy, by six votes to three. There had been only token criticism from the press of Worrall's leadership against NSW, and the result had been the right one, but only the Melbourne Cricket Club members, Bruce, McLeod and Hugh Trumble, supported Worrall, who had clearly upset someone.

Barrett was luckier at the toss than Worrall had been and, after consulting with team-mates, sent South Australia in. That rare and brave move was justified by Trumble, Bruce and John Carlton who bowled the visitors out for a miserable 73. The wicket was wet and dangerous, the weather overcast, and the batting desperate. George Giffen, opening up, made 32, and Jones slogged the final 13 runs, but the innings was over in less than an hour and a half.

Barrett amended his batting order, opening with himself and Trott, and keeping Bruce for when the wicket improved. The strategy made little difference. Captain Barrett and former captain Worrall were both out in the early overs, and Bruce, batting five, made only 9. The unlikely Victorian hero was their doughty second-string wicketkeeper, Percy Lewis, who came out to smash the innings of the match. He made 85, out of 180, in 126 minutes, and managed, unlike his team-mates, to get at Giffen — by continually swing-ing the great bowler to the largely unmanned leg side.

The pitch was much less temperamental on the second day and South Australia improved in the sedate conditions, reaching 6–296 by stumps. For Barrett the day was a nightmare. His own fielding was dreadful, while Worrall was outstanding, and the local barrackers took delight in highlighting the contrast. Barrett, a doctor by profession and dour stonewaller at the batting crease, was not always popular with the working class members of the outer. On the third day the crowd was also unmerciful on Giffen, a peculiar attitude for which Victorian officials, and Barrett, later apologised to the South Australian champion.

Although the crowds were rowdy, they were substantial in numbers. Attendance figures at the two matches in Melbourne were unprecedented for intercolonial cricket, and the boom extended to Sydney and Adelaide. By the end of the season, cricket followers could look back on the most competitive season of intercolonial matches, while the treasurers of the cricket associations of all three colonies were basking in the dividends of Lord Sheffield's revival of the game in Australia.

The match ended on the fourth morning, Victoria winning by six wickets on the back of a fine partner-ship between a revitalised Barrett and the 22-year-old Harry Graham. The pair had come together at 4–108 (Worrall 39), chasing 241, and turned the game, with Barrett defending and Graham superb. The youngster finished with 86, and his captain was proudly unconquered on 68.

Victoria could now call themselves the Shield holders, although criticism was becoming evident of the existing Shield rules. South Australia ventured to Sydney where they were destroyed by an innings. The NSW key was Turner, star of many an intercolonial match, who belted 62 with the bat, and then took ten wickets as South Australia crumbled for 183 and 92. Giffen's obscure second innings experiment with the batting order did not help at all. Parkin, who batted 10 in the first innings, opened up with Hiscock (the first innings number five), but both made ducks. Delaney was promoted from eight to first wicket and made 18, and the top scorer was the keeper "Affie" Jarvis, who scored 28 batting nine, after being run out

*C.T.B. (Charlie) Turner, considered by all to be NSW's leading bowler in 1892–93. Turner missed his state's first two matches, in Adelaide and Melbourne, but returned to dominate the home match against South Australia with a superb all-round performance.*

*The NSW team that played South Australia in the first ever Sheffield Shield match in December 1892. The photograph was taken in the Adelaide botanical gardens. Standing (left to right): A. Newell, M. Pierce, S. Jones, S. Callaway, unidentified scorer; Seated: S. Gregory (with hat on right knee), A. Bannerman, H. Moses, H. Donnan, F. Iredale; At front: I. Wales, G. Youill.*

early on as an opener in the first innings. Why Giffen dismantled the batting order was a mystery. This was NSW's first win in a first-class match for 23 months.

Jack Blackham was fit, and captain, when the Victorians caught the train to Sydney two weeks later for their third Shield match of the season. He took with him his lucky penny which had so infuriated Dr Grace the season before. The coin worked once more, Victoria batted first and reached 331, with Blackham batting last and topscoring with a belligerent, undefeated 64. Dr Barrett made 55, Worrall 38 and Graham 39. The gate from the more-than-14,000 crowd on the first day was a record for an intercolonial match in Sydney, and 10,000 watched the third day — but the match was a great disappointment for the Sydney patrons, who saw their side disintegrate on the fourth day, bowled out for 99, when 332 was the target.

The match had a bizarre finish. Turner had batted three in the NSW second innings, but had to retire hurt after being hit on the finger by a fast one from Trumble. When the ninth wicket fell just before the scheduled 6 o'clock finish, Turner could not be found, having left the ground for treatment. He was not to know his team-mates would bat so feebly. Blackham could have claimed the game, but instead suggested that stumps be drawn, which they were, and his side had a relaxing night on Sydney town before dismissing Turner with the third ball of the following day.

The decision on January 31 of the Australasian Cricket Council to change the rules as to how the Sheffield Shield would be awarded meant that Victoria did not need to defeat South Australia in Adelaide to confirm their champion status. For Blackham, Trott, Trumble, Bruce, Graham and McLeod, there was the extra glory of selection in the touring team for England, though there was much sympathy for Barrett, who most suggested would have been a much wiser choice than the South Australian Walter Giffen.

For the final Shield match of the year, Victoria were without, for various reasons, Blackham, Barrett, Worrall, Bruce and Trumble, but still won comfortably by five wickets, despite George Giffen taking nine wickets in an innings for the fourth time in a first-class match in Australia, and scoring 181 in his side's second innings. Giffen would finish decisively clear at the top of the batting and bowling aggregates for this first Shield season. For the Victorians the highlight was a match-winning eighth-wicket stand of 198 between centurions Bob McLeod and Frank Laver.

The Shield season was over, but there was still room on the cricket calendar for the first-class debuts of Queensland and Western Australia. For the men from the west, their initiation was a tough one, thrashed by South Australia and then humiliated by a much under-strength Victoria. Tom Horan wrote of that match: "I hope a time may arrive when a win against the west will be regarded as something worth recording." However the defeat was an education, and the demoralised players were heartened by news that the WA Governor had decided to provide 14 acres for a cricket ground in Perth with a prepared turf wicket. No longer would they be forced to learn their trade on matting wickets. For Queensland there was joy, a low-scoring 14-run win over a weakened NSW. The two colonies had clashed eight times since the time 22 of Queensland had played a NSW XI in June 1864, but this was the first time eleven had played eleven.

Jack Worrall missed the Victoria-Western Australia mismatch. For him, the season was a disappointment. At Christmas he was the Victorian skipper and a candidate for selection for the tour to England. The captaincy was shortlived, and a mediocre batting average ultimately had him out of the running for the Australian squad. In the end all he had was a Shield winner's medal and another football season to look forward to.

In the years to come he would never be more than an occasional performer for his country. But once in a while in the Shield he would produce something special, such as a gallant 103 in Sydney in January 1898, when he opened up on a spiteful wicket, and was last out with his team's total on 187. Two more centuries the following season, including a remarkably brave 109 on a diabolical MCG pitch against NSW which won Victoria the match and, as events turned out, the Shield, led to an elusive second England tour. The trip was a personal success and he opened the batting in the last four Tests, but it was also the end of his spasmodic international career.

For two years, 1900–01 and 1901–02, Worrall was the undisputed Victorian captain, and in the first of these seasons he led his state to the title. Assessing his career, it is fair to label him as no more than a quality Shield cricketer, but as that, he was a very fine player. His commitment to Victoria and Victorian cricket was unquestioned. In the years that followed there were many cricketers with as much, or in some cases much more, ability, but only Jack Worrall could say he was the original Victorian Sheffield Shield captain.

# 4

# SOUTH AUSTRALIA'S DR GRACE

On the day Lord Sheffield's English team arrived in Adelaide in November, 1891, the renowned South Australian cricketer George Giffen completed a massive double century against Victoria. This was Giffen's highest score in intercolonial or Sheffield Shield cricket, but only one part of a unique all-round achievement performed by the champion South Australian during the match.

The innings, 271 runs in more than nine hours (of a total of 562), must have impressed the tourists, who saw Giffen as the colonial rival to their great captain W.G. Grace. Giffen followed up his batting marathon with an extraordinary bowling performance, taking 16 wickets for 166 (off 76 overs) as the Victorians were bowled out for 233 and 163. No other cricketer in the game's first-class history has come close to taking 16 wickets and scoring more than 250 runs in the same match. But this was the second time in 1891 Giffen had scored a double century and taken more than ten wickets in a match against Victoria. *Wisden* of 1892 noted that in the last seven innings against the unfortunate Victorians, Giffen had scored 921 runs.

In May 1891, six months before Grace arrived in Australia, J.C. Davis, in the *Referee*, said of Giffen: "If one was to judge by consistency of form and style — and I know of no other possible standard by which a batsman's capabilities may be gauged — George Giffen is undisputedly the champion bat of Australia, and possibly the world."

After seeing Giffen in action in Adelaide Grace described him as, "the best man in Australia, and one of the best all-round men in the world." When Giffen played in Sydney or Melbourne promoters made a point of advertising his appearance. The clash between Grace and Giffen in 1891–92 was to be one of the highlights of the tour. Ironically both had disappointing Test series, Grace averaging a mediocre (for him) 32.8 with the bat, and Giffen just 15.5. Giffen did take 10 wickets in the second Test, his one significant contribution, while Grace rarely bowled.

George Giffen's intercolonial cricket career had begun in the match against Tasmania, in Adelaide in November, 1877. This was the inaugural first-class cricket match played in South Australia, and the first eleven-a-side match involving a South Australian representative side. Giffen batted three and scored 27 in his side's only innings, and took 4–16 and 2–40.

Giffen's next foray into first-class cricket came in South Australia's next first-class match — all of three years later, against Victoria in Melbourne. This was the first time eleven of Victoria had been opposed to just eleven of South Australia. Giffen scored 3 and 63, and took two wickets.

Through the 1880s Giffen dominated his state's performances against Victoria (South Australia did not meet NSW until 1890). In March, 1886, he took 17 Victorian wickets for 201 runs, having earlier scored 20 and 82. In eight matches between 1885 and 1891 Giffen took at least ten wickets in all but one of those games (in the other he captured eight). In four of the last five of those matches Giffen scored a century, the lowest 135, the highest 271.

Giffen was clearly the most important player during South Australia's early Sheffield Shield seasons. In 1892–93 he took 33 wickets in four games, and scored 468 runs, including the inevitable century against Victoria. The next year, when South Australia won the Shield, Giffen took "only" 17 wickets, but scored 526 runs, including another century in Melbourne and a double-hundred against NSW at the Adelaide Oval.

Giffen was 5ft 11in (180cm) tall, and weighed around 13 stone (82.5kg). He was a man of extraordinary stamina, much fitter than most of his cricketing generation. Tom Horan, wrote of Giffen after his first wondrous allround performance of 1891: "You only have to look at the man to see that he is simply in the pink of condition. Note his vigour of movement in the field, and the strong flexure of his joints. See his splendid muscles rise and fall with the slightest action of the arm, and you will allow that he is just the man to last as long as you like ..."

The renowned Australian cricket writer, commentator and historian A.G. "Johnnie" Moyes described Giffen the bowler as being: "about average height, and with good chest and shoulders, he had a short, springy run to the wicket, and he seemed to have the ball on a string. Bowling at medium pace, he could hold the ball back just a little more than the batsmen expected, and the number of young players he trapped, either caught-and-bowled or leg-before-wicket, was legion. He was crafty, shrewd, persistent, and a superb stayer."

Of Giffen's batting, Moyes wrote: "In his youthful days Giffen was inclined to rashness, but later he settled down to more sedate methods...he had style, text-book orthodoxy, strokes and courage."

Giffen scored the Shield's first double century — 205 against NSW in Adelaide in the opening match of the 1893–94 season — after the two teams' combined first innings had totalled 224. The next season, against Victoria, he scored an unbeaten 94 and took 12 wickets. In the following month he took 16 NSW wickets for 186 runs, bowling 91.3 of his team's 189.3 overs. This remains the best match bowling figures in the history of the competition. For a period in the 1890s it appeared the only way of preventing Giffen taking ten wickets in a match was to achieve an innings victory.

Giffen was Johnnie Moyes' first cricket hero, and inevitably the hero of all other young South Australian sporting fans. Without him it is doubtful his state side would have been treated seriously by Victoria and NSW. He was the first link in a cricketing chain that extended through Darling, Hill, Richardson, Grimmett, Bradman, Favell, the Chappells, and David Hookes.

But what of Giffen the man? Many a story has been told of his reluctance to take himself off when bowling, though it must be acknowledged that through much of his career with South Australia he was clearly the best bowler in the side. He could be infuriatingly obstinant, but was also extremely loyal, and more than once showed more faith in a colleague than the situation, or his fellow selectors, suggested.

In his first Test as captain, the second of the 1894–95 Ashes series, Giffen bowled 78.2 six-ball overs (of 202.2) in the second innings. At one stage, after Giffen had seemed to be bowling for ever, vice-captain Hugh Trumble approached his skipper and suggested a change. "Yes, I think I'll go on at the other end," Giffen shot back. He did, and ended with six wickets, though England won the match by 94 runs.

He could be an angry, ill-tempered man, and was not popular with all his team-mates — which could explain why it took so long for him to captain his country. In 1893 his participation in a proposed trip to England was seen as crucial to the tour's financial success. He agreed to tour on the bizarre condition that

*The incomparable George Giffen, the greatest all-rounder of his day, perhaps of any day.*

his brother (a regular, but moderate Shield player) was also selected, despite the superior claims of batsmen such as Barrett, Iredale, Reedman and Donnan. That tour was riddled with dissension and controversy. The manager, Victor Cohen from NSW, blamed it on "the South Australians". On his return the champion NSW bowler Charlie Turner said of Giffen: "Well, you know when a man is too conceited and plays for himself instead of his side he does a lot of harm, and that was undeniably Giffen's great fault."

The Queensland fast bowler Arthur Coningham said of the tour: "Sometimes it would look like a Victoria match through the preference given to the Melbourne men. The result was at one match Giffen went up to Blackham on the field and said 'You are not treating us fairly.' Blackham starting arguing and Trumble had to go between them." Blackham, like Giffen, was not a placid man.

On his death in 1927, *Wisden* recalled that Giffen was once called the "W.G. Grace of Australia". It also fondly recalled his final remarkable achievement. In February 1903, Giffen returned for one last fling at his old rivals, the Victorians. He had not scored a 50 against them since late 1894, and had missed the previous two South Australia-Victoria matches.

Giffen, a month short of his 44th birthday, trained passionately for the match, and then dominated it. He scored 81 and an unbeaten 97, and took 15 wickets for 185, an amazing performance of skill and endurance. With Joe Travers he added 101 for the last South Australian partnership of the match, when 137 would have brought an unlikely victory.

The final word on Giffen is left to Johnnie Moyes, who summed him up this way: "What a cricketer he was, superb as batsman and bowler, a bit cantankerous and wayward at times perhaps, but when one studies the history of South Australian cricket as it applied to his times, then one can only marvel at his achievements, and forgive him any foibles."

# 5

# THE BLACKHAM INCIDENT

John McCarthy Blackham was the first great wicketkeeper of Australian cricket. He was behind the stumps in the first ever Test match in March, 1877, and remained Australia's Test keeper for more than 17 years. For Victoria he was a stalwart, arguably its finest cricketer of the 19th century.

Blackham was reputed to be the first Australian to keep wicket without a long stop and set a standard in wicketkeeping that remained beyond his death in 1933. Undisputably a champion cricketer and respected leader, he could be a surly man and was prone to disputes with administrators, umpires and opponents. During his career he confronted some of NSW's leading umpires, including the former brilliant batsman (and Blackham's former Australian teammate) Charlie Bannerman. In January, 1894, after the NSW-Victoria match in Sydney, Blackham questioned the umpiring standards in NSW, and created a rift between the NSW and Victorian Cricket Associations that threatened the very future of the fledgling Sheffield Shield competition.

NSW won the controversial match by 19 runs, after Victoria fell short chasing 191 for victory on a damp wicket. This was an era without pitch covers, when the hot sun on a wet pitch could create a bowlers' paradise. The arguments arose over NSW umpire Jack Tooher's decision to delay the start of play on the final day, a ruling disputed by the Victorian captain Blackham, and the Victorian umpire Tom Flynn.

Tooher was a former NSW cricketer, and Test umpire. He contended the wicket was too wet to play, but Blackham felt that, as the weather improved, the batting conditions were deteriorating rather than improving. Where there was disagreement, the status quo prevailed, and the teams stayed off the field for 48 significant minutes.

The match was sensational from the start, when Blackham, who was celebrating his 20th season in intercolonial cricket, won the toss and stunned the local crowd by sending NSW into bat. The pitch was wet and the weather overcast. The great veteran Billy Murdoch went out with Syd Callaway, and the pair

*The Victorians in 1893–94. Back row (left to right): J. Worrall, F. Laver, H. Trumble, C. McLeod, H. Stuckey; Seated: H. Trott, W. Bruce, J. Blackham, H. Graham, J. Harry; Front: J. Carlton.*

defied the bowling for 30 minutes, Callaway blazing and Murdoch stonewalling. Then Murdoch was bowled for two, and soon after Callaway caught at point for 38.

The local captain Harry Moses took over Callaway's aggressive role, and raced to 24 before he was caught at slip off Charlie McLeod soon after lunch. During the interval the sun had come out, and the wicket, difficult at the start, was now treacherous. The innings disintegrated, the last eight wickets disappearing for 55. McLeod finished with six wickets.

Blackham's gamble at the toss now backfired, as the Victorians found themselves batting on a dreadful pitch. They collapsed to 7 for 48, as the local champion Charlie Turner took command. Hugh Trumble joined his captain in a face saving 27-run stand, but the innings ended at 88, with Turner, perhaps the best wet wicket bowler Australia ever produced, bowling unchanged for 6 for 51.

The Victorian innings had lasted just 83 minutes, and NSW had to go in again on the still kicking turf. In 35 minutes before stumps they slogged 45 runs, but lost three wickets. With the prospect of a less frightening batting surface the next day, the match was evenly poised.

But the rain continued — so heavily that the second day, the Saturday, was washed out completely. Sunday was brighter, and on the Monday, play began scarcely late, on a slow, but very playable pitch. NSW inched to a respectable score, thanks almost entirely to Callaway, who Moses had held back from the dangers of the Friday evening, and Turner, who had been sent in late on the first day as a nightwatchman.

Another storm soon after one o'clock soaked the wicket once more, but still Callaway went on to the game's only half century. Harry Donnan, held back to number nine, was left stranded, 13 not out. The innings ended at 151, and the Victorians went in 190 behind on an improving wicket.

Blackham thought his side was beaten — "We had a good chance until that last shower of rain came, but I'm afraid that has settled us" — but Frank Walters and Jack Harry added 60 for the first wicket. Then, in perhaps the best batting conditions of the match, five wickets fell for 31, including the key wicket of

Harry Trott for 19. At stumps it was 5 for 106. Harry Graham, the "Little Dasher", remained on 16 — the great Victorian hope.

The final day began with the highly publicised pitch dispute. Blackham was said to be "exceedingly angry" at the delay. When play did not begin on time at midday he suggested the match be abandoned.

One correspondent described the pitch as being "quite wet and sodden, and the water oozed up with the slightest pressure." The players went out around 12.45, and the batsmen made no attempt to disguise their intentions by beating the fieldsmen out to the middle. Harry Graham was even seen clapping at the umpires, exhorting them to get to the square just that little bit quicker.

At the start the pitch was slow, and the bowlers could not get a foothold. Moses started with the right-arm medium pace of Andrew Newell and the left-handed fast bowler Arthur Coningham, holding back Turner until the wicket was at its worst. Graham and McLeod, wasted no time, pushing the score to 136 by lunch. Moses was forced to bring on his champion bowler earlier than he wanted, for Graham was superb, driving, cutting and pulling at every opportunity.

The weather, like the home crowd, had been gloomy but during the lunch break the sun came out to slowly dry the pitch. Graham and McLeod came back, poised to win the game for Victoria, but were soon in trouble, as the ball began misbehaving once more. McLeod was in terrible trouble against Turner's breakbacks, and Billie Moore, the NSW keeper, was struck in the face by a lifter from Coningham. Even Graham was in difficulty, and was fortunate when driving hopefully at Turner he saw little Syd Gregory, the best fieldsman in the country, drop a sitter at mid-off.

Graham had been dropped twice before lunch, once in the deep and once at the wicket. The crowd was convinced he was the luckiest batsman alive. Nobody could remember the last time Syd Gregory had put such a chance down. Then Graham drove hard again, this time at Coningham, and Gregory dived to his left and grabbed the catch. It was much more difficult than the opportunity missed. Graham, out for 45, had played the innings of the match. Victoria were 6 for 148.

Five minutes later McLeod was gone as well, bowled by a savage Turner breakback. Turner was just about unplayable, Coningham dangerous, and the pair harassed Blackham and Trumble until the latter swung frantically at Coningham and skied a catch to third man — 8 for 159. Frank Laver, the 24-year-old all-rounder in his second season of big cricket, joined his captain, and the pair added nine desperate runs before Turner bowled Laver with an impossible one.

Left-handed specialist batsman Harry Stuckey had been kept back to last by Blackham. Stuckey was a good enough player to score three Shield centuries in 33 matches for Victoria. He strode out confidently, but was soon jumping and weaving as the ball performed its spiteful tricks. A single was fluked off Coningham, then another off Turner, before Coningham knocked Stuckey's leg stump out of the ground. The crowd could hardly control its excitement, and umbrellas, hats and canes flew into the air. The NSW team, led by Turner and Coningham, came off to vigorous applause.

Twenty three thousand people had watched the match, 14,000 of them on the first day. They had witnessed all the excitement, but missed the angry slanging match that followed at the post-match function. And they could only read in amazement of the acrimony of the next eight months, that threatened the future of such matches as the one they had attended.

After the game, the president of the NSW Cricket Association, Mr George Reid, then Premier of NSW and later an Australian Prime Minister, proposed a toast to the Victorians, saying it was something to beat a side captained by Blackham, as that was like playing against 12 men.

Blackham in reply, thanked Reid for his words, and then launched a heated verbal assault on the NSW umpire, Tooher.

"I do not think the Victorians have been properly treated in the match," Blackham said. "No doubt it was a mistake, but still it was very unfair to the Victorian Eleven that they were not allowed to start at noon, when the wicket was not a bit worse than it had been at other stages of the match. We were kept off the wicket by the umpire until it got sticky."

Blackham's voice was drowned out by dissenting voices from the floor. Reid stood up and asked Blackham if he thought the umpire had made a mistake.

"I do not think, I am sure of it!" the Victorian captain angrily spat back. He was then cut off by the Victorian team manager, Mr Gooch, who rose and proposed a toast to the NSW team.

Harry Moses responded by criticising Blackham for his remarks. Later umpire Tooher explained he had acted throughout the match purely in the interests of fair play. He suggested the appointment of professional umpires in future, as he did not think amateurs should be subjected to the insults he had received. He announced he would not umpire a cricket match again.

*Two major players in one of the most bitter days in Victoria-NSW cricket. Left: The celebrated Victorian and Australian keeper and captain, Jack Blackham. Above: The "Little Dasher" Harry Graham.*

Blackham apparently made further remarks in the Victorian dressing room that were overheard by members of the NSWCA. On his return to Melbourne, he repeated his opinion that his side was harshly treated. He was joined by the Victorian umpire Flynn, who informed everyone he agreed with Blackham, and not his fellow official Tooher.

Tom Horan, in the *Australasian*, criticised Blackham, a former teammate writing: "I feel sure that in his calmer moments J. Blackham will regret having used words calculated to cast a severe imputation upon so thoroughly conscientious an umpire as J. Tooher. I would recall to Blackham the condition of the Melbourne Cricket Club ground at Christmas, when W.L. Murdoch and others declared it unfit for play. Yet J. Tooher decided that it was fit, and it is beyond question that to his decision on that occasion was chiefly due the win gained by Victoria. I am very sorry that this unpleasantness has occured, especially as all the colonies concerned appeared to be sailing along grandly under the flag of fair play."

Within two weeks the NSWCA was writing to his Victorian counterpart requesting an inquiry into remarks made by Blackham and Flynn against umpire Tooher. The Association also unaminously supported a motion that:

"This Association places on record its very deep regret that Mr J. Blackham should have so far forgotten himself as to state publicly that his team had been beaten by the umpire."

The VCA did not reply until late May. Umpire Flynn by this stage was denying he had said anything at all. Blackham denied making any public comments outside of his reply at the post-match function, but stood by what he had said then. The NSWCA considered the Victorian captain's explanation, "evasive and unsatisfactory", and also regretted that the VCA "have not seen fit to express its displeasure at his admittedly offensive remarks."

The VCA met again in the last week of August. At that meeting it did not directly approach the Blackham affair, but did decide that the appointment of intercolonial umpires demanded attention, and that the VCA should move immediately to remedy "a growing lack of confidence in the umpiring of other colonies".

In Sydney, one NSWCA delegate saw the VCA's indifference as "a very notable sample of this spirit of fair play from the Victorian Cricket Association in connection with the Blackham incident, and their treatment of the communications relative thereto from the Association of this colony. Perhaps our good cabbage-garden cousins would like to bring two umpires with them next they visit us, or perhaps even better still they might desire to play both matches on the Melbourne Cricket Ground, in front of the most one-sided lot of cricket followers in all Australia."

The NSWCA felt they and their umpire deserved an apology, and that they had waited long enough to get one. At a meeting on September 17, a motion not to play the Victorians until Blackham's remarks were withdrawn was carried with only one dissenter.

The majority of the Sydney press thought such a boycott was too severe. The future of NSW-Victoria matches was in real jeopardy. *The Sydney Morning Herald* felt Blackham had never questioned Tooher's honesty, and as such his post match comments should not have aroused the subsequent furore. The VCA used the *Herald's* viewpoint to support their own. The *Sydney Mail* cricket correspondent thought it inevitable the VCA would support Blackham to the end:

"In their eyes he is the man whose judgement and generalship have snatched many a hopeless match out of the fire for them, who has led them to victory time after time, who has been in their ranks for 20 years and revolutionised cricket even in the old country by showing the Englishmen how to keep wickets without a longstop. Is it likely now that the Victorians will abandon Blackham with such service to look back upon and with public opinion in Victoria strongly in his favour? It is not probable."

The attendance at the NSWCA meeting of October 15 was one of the largest on record. A communication from the VCA was read, in which they suggested the remarks made by Blackham had been misinterpreted. Three motions were put forward, two suggesting the matter be closed, and a third that the September 17 resolution be adhered to. The three motions were ruled out of order by George Reid, although it appears that the third, which had much support, should not have been. Had that motion been voted on, it is very possible NSW-Victoria matches would not have been played in 1894–95.

The Sydney sporting weekly, *The Referee* commented: "No doubt Mr Reid thought it very judicious not to pass such a motion in the interests of the game, and as matter of expedience he thought it desirable to put the matter off. But matters of expedience cannot, or rather, should not be allowed to over-ride rules."

A special meeting of the NSWCA, devoted to the Blackham affair, was scheduled for October 22. There the matter was resolved, but only after Reid informed the gathering of a series of communications between himself and the VCA president, and between himself and umpire Tooher.

Reid had wired his Victorian counterpart Mr Best asking him to see Blackham regarding his comments back in late January. Best's reply stated that Blackham had no intention of accusing umpire Tooher of cheating, but rather of an error of judgement. On receiving that reply, Reid approached Tooher, who wrote to the NSWCA president:

*Dear Mr Reid,*

*Although I deeply resented at the time what I thought, and still think, to be the very unjust remarks of Mr Blackham at the end of the last Victorian match, I am very anxious that the harmony that has prevailed so long between the cricketers of the two colonies should not be disturbed. I would not value a forced apology from any man. It is therefore very pleasing to hear from you, on the authority of the president of the Victorian Association, that Mr Blackham did not intend to impute dishonesty or unfairness to me, but only an error of judgement. I earnestly trust that the NSW Cricket Association will, on that assurance, see its way to let the matter drop.*

*Yours faithfully,*
*John A Tooher.*

After discussion, a motion was put that the September 17 motion be rescinded, but that the Association's disapproval of Blackham's remarks and the VCA's subsequent disinterest be recorded. This was carried, with three dissenters.

So the saga ended. It appears the controversy's smooth conclusion owed much to the common sense and good politics of George Reid. Victoria and NSW did play in 1894–95, and ironically in Sydney, NSW lost after having to bat last on a poor wicket. But though the cricket continued, there were still some in the NSW cricket hierarchy who believed such a match should not have been played.

With hindsight, it seems extraordinary the affair went on for so long. The *Sydney Mail* blamed it on "the cheap patriotism which unfortunately always makes itself objectionably prominent in connection with such matters."

One is reminded of a story told by the "Demon" Fred Spofforth, about an incident during the trip to England of the first Australian team in 1878:

"While we were coasting along New Zealand, we were caught by a terrible storm, and being in a very small steamer, we were in considerable danger. Charles Bannerman, who was an expert swimmer, was very frightened and refused to go into his cabin, and said that if he ever reached dry land again he would never leave it as long as he lived.

"Well," I said, "Suppose we are wrecked. What will you do?"

"First," he said, "I'll save Alec (his brother), then Murdoch, then you."

"Well, what about the Victorians?" I asked.

"Let them drown," he replied. "Do you think I'm going to risk my life for them?"

# 6

# THE ORIGINAL FAST MAN

South Australia's Ernie Jones was Australia's first genuine fast bowler, a pace apart from the medium and medium-fast champions such as Spofforth, Boyle, Turner and Ferris who had preceded him in Australian cricket.

Jones made his first-class cricket debut in the first Sheffield Shield match played, against NSW in Adelaide in December, 1892. He bowled with great pace, sprayed the ball around, and took three renowned wickets — Harry Moses, Sam Jones and Alec Bannerman — for 49 runs in the second innings. "Affie" Jarvis, the South Australian keeper, stood up to the new recruit in that match, but never again.

Ernie Jones was not a tall man, but he was powerfully built. He wore the nickname "Jonah" throughout his career. With the decline of George Giffen, he emerged to carry the South Australian bowling attack. Jones bowled right-handed, off a short run, and could make the ball kick angrily if in the mood, which he usually was. For years, any Shield bowler who came on the scene was compared to Jones for speed, especially after the 1896 Ashes tour on which many Englishmen found him too quick to cope with. Ranjitsinji, the champion Surrey and England batsman, referred to him as "Slinger", because of his bowling action, which was something akin to those of Jeff Thomson or Wayne Holdsworth of later years. Another famous Englishman, F.S. Jackson, wrote in 1944 that Jones was the finest Australian fast bowler he ever saw.

*The South Australian Ernest Jones, first in the long line of champion Australian fast bowlers.*

Jones cracked Jackson's ribs in the first match of Australia's 1896 tour, leaving the Englishman incapacitated for three weeks. Jackson remembered Jones then as a wild bowler who concentrated on "short bumpy stuff", but the Australian captain, Harry Trott from Victoria, took hold of the South Australian and made a great fast bowler of him. Trott convinced Jones that reducing his run-up would not diminish his pace and, as Jackson put it, "taught him the value of length and control."

In Shield cricket Jones took 209 wickets in 39 matches, a tally exceeded by only three South Australians, the spinners Clarrie Grimmett, Ashley Mallett and Peter Sleep. In February, 1896 he, with opening partner Fred Jarvis, bowled out Victoria for just 43, Jones taking 6–15 off 12 overs. On 19 occasions he took five wickets in a Shield innings and four times ten wickets in a match — his best innings figures being 8–157 fighting a losing cause against NSW in January, 1897.

Johnnie Moyes wrote of Jones: "He could stay all day, loved bowling fast, could make the ball lift nastily, and didn't hesitate to do it because he could bring it up from what was a good length for a man of his pace. I remember as a small boy watching him bowling on the Adelaide Oval, and my chief recollection is of feeling that it just was not fair for any bowler to make the ball fly over the batsman's head…. he was an express, not a goods train camouflaged to look like one."

Jones was also an outstanding fieldsman (M.A. Noble called him "the best mid-off I ever saw"), and an extraordinary working-class character. Perhaps the most famous anecdote told of him concerns a fierce bouncer that sailed through Dr. Grace's beard. "Sorry doc, she slipped!" he is reputed to have said. Another story told of an English gentleman at Lords sidling up to Jones and asking if the great fast bowler had gone to Adelaide University. Jones confirmed this but when pressed admitted it was only to collect the rubbish.

The fiery fast bowler was a crowd favourite at Adelaide. In his classic 1898 book *With Bat and Ball* George Giffen, recalling the Shield match against Victoria at the Adelaide Oval in March 1894, wrote:

"Adelaide crowds as a rule are very quiet, and one does not hear one tithe of the barracking which is indulged in in Melbourne and Sydney, but the appearance of Jones with the bat was always the signal for a chorus of yells in which the one word distinguishable was 'Jonah'. When he lashed out, and his wicket fell for 'nowt' as it did twice in this game, the good humoured commiseration he received was most amusing. No harm was intended by the crowd; as a matter of fact Jones was, and still is, one of their idols…."

Jonah dominated the final day of that match, which South Australia won by 58 runs. Victoria, seeking 371, began the morning session chasing another 141 with seven wickets in hand. South Australia needed to win the match to take the Shield. A successful run chase by Victoria would have given the title to NSW on percentages. Fred Jarvis bowled the opening over, conceded a single, and then Jones blasted out three wickets with his first four balls.

Frank Laver was the first, yorked by a rapid loosener, then Charlie McLeod was too late on a fast full toss. Frank Walters survived the hat trick, but then missed a good length flier which sent the leg stump back spinning out of the ground. The Adelaide *Advertiser* commented wryly: "6–230 was rather different from 3 for 229."

The two Victorian survivors, Bob McLeod and Percy Lewis withstood the Jones volcano, and took Victoria to 308 before another burst from the fast bowler after lunch changed the game again. Lewis was late on a straight one, and then John Carlton was bowled by what the *Advertiser* correspondent called "a regular clinker". Four runs later the match was over. McLeod drove Giffen, but Jones, diving gallantly, stopped the ball, and the bowler grabbed at the rebound to run out Bob Mitchell. Straight away McLeod lofted a catch to the ubiquitous Jones at mid-on, ending the match to hearty cheers from all around the oval.

The *Advertiser* wrote of Jones' bowling: "Some of his balls — especially at the start — were sent down with lightning-like velocity, and the only wonder is that the batsmen stopped as many of them as they did." After the match, Sir Edwin Smith, a great benefactor of South Australian cricket, enthusistically proposed a toast to the health of Lord Sheffield. He suggested a cablegram be sent to his lordship "informing him that his challenge shield has been won this year by South Australia." Sir Edwin was sure this news would please Lord Sheffield.

The toast was received "with cheers and musical honours".

A collection was organised among the members, to reward the weary Jones for his mighty efforts. He received five guineas, and also an umbrella — a token of appreciation from one supporter for the fast man's grand fielding.

Jones is one of only three men to be given out handled the ball in Sheffield Shield cricket (Peter Burge, batting for Queensland against Victoria in 1958–59, and Rob Gartrell, for Tasmania against Victoria in 1986–87, are the others). In February 1895, Victoria had all but defeated South Australia in Melbourne. In distressingly hot conditions, the home side had made 348 (captain Harry Trott 152), and South Australia

118 (A.E. Trott 4–24) and 9 for 245 (Jack Lyons 135). Tom Horan in the *Australasian* described the controversial dismissal:

"F. Jarvis batted capitally for 14 not out and Jones shaped well for nine. The latter had a rent in his shirt, and the ball got in there and stopped. Jones, forgetting the rule, touched the ball with his hand and (wicketkeeper) Lewis straightaway appealed. The umpire Fisher had, of course, to give the batsman out, but Harry Trott regretted that an appeal was made…"

Jones' intention was to hand the ball to Lewis, but the Victorians played it hard in those days. Giffen wrote later that the spectators were much amused. One could not imagine Jonah sharing the joke. Or the Victorian opening batsmen, who were obliged to survive the angry fast bowler and score the 16 runs needed for victory (which they safely did).

Following his death, at 74 in November 1943, *Wisden* called Jones "the best fast bowler ever produced by Australia". Despite this rating, he is strangely in many ways a forgotten figure, given the legendary status of contemporaries such as Giffen, Trumper, Hill and Noble. But he was the first of his kind, the Shield's first truly fast bowler and a worthy trailblazer for the likes of Gregory, Lindwall, Lillee, Thomson and McDermott.

# 7

# MIGHTY CLEM

Of all the left-handed batsmen who played in the Sheffield Shield's first 100 years, four stand out: two post war Australian champions, Neil Harvey and Allan Border, the remarkable Barbadian Garfield Sobers, and the great South Australian of cricket's first Golden Age — Clem Hill.

Hill was a schoolboy prodigy, born while the original Test match was being played in Melbourne, and first acclaimed following a massive innings of 360 for Prince Alfred College in their annual match against St Peters College in 1893. Hill was from good cricketing stock. His father, John (who sired 16 children), scored the first ever century on the Adelaide Oval, in 1878. That feat was overwhelmed by Clem, who ended with 45 first-class centuries, seven in Test cricket, and 18 in the Sheffield Shield.

Hill was famous for his hook shot, a stroke the Australian public may never have seen but for the intervention of the champion George Giffen. The story goes that when Hill was 13, his sportsmaster had warned that the precocious left-hander would be left out of any future school elevens if he persisted in blazing across the line. Giffen was coaching at the school at the time, and was amazed at the talents of the youngster who was hooking his best deliveries. "Sonny, you're going to be a world's batsman," Giffen is reputed to have said. "That's the shot of a champion." He then went over to the sportsmaster to ensure Hill was in the school side.

M.A. Noble wrote of Hill at the crease: "Some hold it (the bat handle) with one hand on top and the other at the bottom of the handle. Clem Hill was noted for this. He had to place his feet wide apart, with the bat between them, to get down properly and work his body into an easy position. It gave him the appearance of crouching, but this position was only assumed because it was the easiest for him at the moment. He was never seen in the same attitude when actually playing the ball."

Like Harvey and Border, Hill was short, powerful and quick on his feet. The fastest bowling scarcely worried him and, in the manner of all great players, he was at his most valuable in a crisis. Perhaps his most celebrated Test innings was played early in his career — a defiant 188 against England in the Fourth Test of the 1897–98 series, when he led an Australian fightback after six more experienced wickets had fallen for just 58. As did Border many years later he had his critics as a captain, but more importantly, the respect of his men.

Johnnie Moyes wrote of Hill: "His late and square cutting, his powerful off-side shots, and his facility in getting the ball away on the on-side were features of his batting which raised him to the highest

*The magnificent Clem Hill, the greatest left-hand batsman produced by South Australia.*

*Clem Hill standing in front of the Adelaide Oval scoreboard after his greatest day in the Shield, against NSW in December 1900. Only Bill Ponsford and Don Bradman have made bigger scores in the competition's history.*

level...It was a thrill to see his name go on the scoreboard, a joy and a privilege to take the field under his leadership. As long as he was there we felt that everything would turn out right."

Clem Hill's Shield debut came on November 30, 1894, when he batted nine and scored 21 against Victoria. This appearance came 21 months after his first-class debut, as a 16-year-old wicketkeeper. After Hill's first appearance at a Shield batting crease, the Victorian captain, crafty old Jack Blackham, declared the teenager South Australia's next great batsman — an extraordinary but precise assessment.

Hill's first great Shield innings was played in March 1896 — 206 not out in Sydney, after Jack Lyons, Ernest Leak and captain Giffen had fallen for 34 on the first morning. With Joe Darling (121) he added 169 for the fourth wicket. Without him, Hill slammed 154 of the last 197 runs scored, his last run breaking his skipper's record for the highest score in Shield cricket. That innings, and a subsequent second innings 74 for "The Rest" against an Australian XI, won Hill a place on the 1896 tour of England.

Hill's most famous Shield hundred occurred in December, 1900 against a powerful NSW XI in Adelaide, 365 not out, scored in 515 minutes out of an innings total of 576, at that time the second largest score made in first-class cricket, behind A.C. McLaren's 424 for Lancashire against Somerset in 1895. Hill became the third Australian, after Murdoch and Trumper, to score a triple century in first-class cricket, and the first to do so in a Sheffield Shield match.

The Adelaide *Advertiser* had ended their summary of the opening day of that match, which saw NSW all out 279, in the following pessimistic tone: "The attendance was not as good as might have been expected, and the popular idea that South Australia was outmatched probably had something to do with this fact."

The mood hadn't changed the next morning, especially when Hill, batting first wicket, had to come to the crease as early as the third over, after Leak was bowled by NSW's new fast bowling discovery, Jack Marsh. If Trumper, Duff, Gregory and company could be bowled out for less than 300 what terrors lay ahead facing the likes of Marsh, M.A. Noble and Bill Howell.

The champion left-hander struggled early and at 19 was dropped at slip by Marsh off Noble. A run later he might have been run out had Reggie Duff's throw from short cover been more accurate. But thereafter Hill dominated, despite losing Fred Hack (bowled Marsh 12) at 43, Giffen (caught and bowled Howell 7) at 65, and Alfred Jarvis (caught Howell bowled Hopkins 9) at 88.

The fourth wicket fell just after lunch, bringing the local captain Jack Reedman out to join Hill. The wicket had quietened, and Hill was now in classic form. His skipper was a tough old campaigner, capped by Australia in 1894–95, and ably equipped for the battle at hand. Noble had strained his side, but Marsh and Howell persisted and Reedman defended while Hill attacked. First gradually, and then rapidly, South Australia headed towards a first innings lead.

Hill was renowned as a player of the fastest bowling, and this day he added to his reputation. "Marsh was as good as a feast to Hill, who drove his fastest balls with the greatest of ease," boasted the *Advertiser*. "He made his runs by as fine an exhibition as he has ever given at the Adelaide Oval."

Before tea Hill had his hundred, and the century partnership for the fifth wicket came soon after. In the final session Hill slaughtered NSW, pouncing to slay anything wide or short. Just before the close the gallant Reedman, on 71, edged the weary Howell to slip. Bill Stuart was promptly bowled. At stumps Hill was 176, South Australia 6 for 311.

NSW needed wickets the next morning, and they got them. After Jack Matthews had helped Hill add 30 runs, Marsh bowled Matthews and Affie Jarvis with successive balls. South Australia 8–341, Marsh on a hat-trick bowling to Hill, the match, despite Hill's massive score, evenly poised. The hat-trick ball, as fast as Marsh could bowl, went faster for four, for Hill's two hundred, and changed the mood of the game. While number 10 Edgar Walkley held up an end, Hill went about breaking records, and ruining the contest. Two hundred and fifty came and went. The record score by a South Australian, Giffen's famous 271 against Victoria in 1891, was passed, and then the 300.

Billy Murdoch's Australian record 321, set in 1882, was gone with a flourish. Next to fall was the world record ninth-wicket stand of 193 set by Grace and Kitcat for Gloucestershire v Sussex in 1896. The carnage continued to 575 when Walkley missed a good one from Marsh. The final wicket, left-hand opening bowler Joe Travers, fell one run later, leaving Hill unbeaten, and triumphant. Had the rules allowed he might have batted forever.

Hill had reached his 300 with an eight — four all run and four overthrows, and his 350 with a five, all run after a long drive to the Southern scoreboard. He also struck 35 boundaries. The benevolent New South Welshmen provided three tired cheers for their Test colleague as he strode off, and the patriots in the stands gave Hill a resounding ovation. Never before had a team made more than 500 gainst NSW.

Acclaim for the innings was universal. In Sydney J.C. Davis wrote : "If South Australia has not a champion team, the team includes a champion in Clem Hill. The left-hander's latest exploit in compiling 365 not out at the expense of the New South Wales bowlers bears out the reputation he has gained of being the greatest bat Australia has ever produced."

Tom Horan described Hill as the "Coriolanus" of cricket. "Clem has done many notable deeds in cricket, but this stands alone."

The punchline to Clem Hill's amazing innings, and South Australia's eventual emphatic innings victory, came just three weeks later in Sydney, when the South Australian's had to field through a NSW innings of 918 that included five personal centuries. Marsh took ten wickets in the match as vengeance was got by an innings and 605 runs. Hill managed 55 and 20, and fell to Marsh in both innings. Reedman made 1 and 6, Walkley 0 and 17.

Clem Hill went on to play many more big Shield innings for his home state. In the 15 years up to the first world war, he dominated his state's batting order in a manner matched in later eras only by Ponsford for Victoria, Bradman for NSW and South Australia and Greg Chappell for Queensland. His greatest Shield year was in 1909–10, when in his only four innings he scored 176, 205, 185 and 43, and led South Australia to a second Shield success. Hill masterminded another triumph in 1912–13, a year after his captaincy had been heavily criticised by Board of Control officials during the 1911–12 Ashes series.

Although he announced his retirement from big cricket in 1914, Hill's first-class career did not end until the opening match of the 1924–25 season, a testimonial match for Bill Howell. When cricket resumed after the Great War, Hill was there to guide his beloved South Australia back into the first-class scene. He captained his state in their one interstate match in 1918, a non-Shield match versus Victoria, retired again, but made another comeback in February 1923, to take part in South Australia's Shield match with Victoria, which doubled as a benefit match to George Giffen. A month short of 46 years old, captain Hill scored 66 and 39.

His Shield aggregate of 6274 was unbeaten until the emergence of Don Bradman, but his status as Australia's greatest left-hand batsman has perhaps never been lost. In retirement he became a handicapper with the South Australian Jockey Club, the Victorian Amateur Turf Club, and finally the Geelong Racing Club. Clem Hill died in Melbourne in 1945, following a long illness that resulted from injuries sustained in a fall from a tram in Collins St. A proud South Australian to the end, his body was returned to its rightful resting place, the scene of his most memorable triumphs, the city of Adelaide.

# 8
# THROWN OUT —
# THE TRAGEDY OF JACK MARSH

The aboriginal Jack Marsh was born at Yugilbar, on the Clarence River in Northern NSW, in 1874. Before his first-class cricket debut, Marsh was one of NSW's best professional sprinters. Unfortunately he appeared too late to take advantage of the pro-running boom of the late 1880s and early 1890s, but in 1898 he was described in *The Referee* as: "a marvellous runner over shorter distances; in fact it is doubtful if we have ever had a better."

His cricket career blossomed in 1899–90, when he took 30 wickets at 9.86, bowling fast for South Sydney in Sydney first grade cricket. A successful start to the following season won him selection in a Colts XV that played a NSW XI at the SCG in November 1900. In his opening over of that match, Marsh yorked the acclaimed Victor Trumper, but two overs later was no-balled three times by square-leg umpire Curran for throwing.

Marsh's unusual, whippy delivery had caused comment ever since he began dismissing some of Sydney's finest batsmen in grade cricket. However he had never been called until this confrontation with umpire Curran. The hiccup did not worry him, and before the end of his first spell he had added the worthy scalps of proven Test players Frank Iredale and Bert Hopkins. Curran was barracked from the Hill, even more so after he again called Marsh for throwing when the fast man bowled from his end.

Curran's action led to one of the more unusual incidents in NSW cricket history. The *Sydney Mail* described the story this way:

*"Marsh, the aboriginal bowler, was much upset over his being no-balled…. Getting a few leading cricketers together he suggested a test to prove he did not throw the ball, and the means adopted was to fasten a bit of wood tightly along the elbow in such a position as to absolutely prevent the joint being bent. An order was then placed with a maker of such things, and a splint was prepared. There was, however, something in this arrangement which did not please the umpire, W. Curran, who declined to further officiate unless the bandages were discarded, or that he be allowed to tie the splint. But he proposed to cover up the wrist as well as the elbow, to which, of course, the darkie objected. Marsh wore the splint, the umpire stood on his dignity, and refused to go out."*

Curran was replaced by the former international batsman Sam Jones, best remembered for being controversially run out by W.G. Grace in the Ashes Test at The Oval in 1882. Jones thought Marsh's action to be legitimate, with or without a splint.

Marsh finished with seven wickets for the match, six in the first innings, enough to win him selection for NSW's first Shield match of the season, against South Australia at the Adelaide Oval.

This was the match in which Clem Hill scored his famous 365, but initially it was the appearance of the aboriginal fast bowler that captured most attention. The Adelaide *Advertiser's* correspondent at the match wrote of Marsh: "He takes a very long run with great swinging strides, but does not appear to have as much pace as the fast South Australian (Ernie Jones)…Marsh sends in an occasional very fast one which even the accomplished (NSW wicketkeeper Jim) Kelly finds exceedingly difficult to take."

Kelly spent his first day keeping to Marsh right up to the stumps. The experience was expensive, and painful, and the next day Kelly went back some distance to take the fast bowler's fliers. All told he conceded 23 byes in the innings, most of them off Marsh.

The *Advertiser* also noted comments by various spectators about the legality of Marsh's bowling action. Their cricket writer commented:

"There were not wanting those who questioned the fairness of the aboriginal's delivery...I do not feel called on to pass an opinion beyond saying that occasionally his action looked a little doubtful."

From Adelaide, Marsh, and NSW, journeyed to Melbourne for the Christmas match with Victoria. The NSW bowlers had a receptive wicket (and no Clem Hill to contend with), and bowled their side back into the game after NSW were all out for just 153 on the first day. Victoria were at one stage 3 for 2, and on the second day scraped together a one run first innings lead. Marsh took three wickets and impressed Tom Horan with his pace and endeavour.

"Marsh has a curious sort of wobble in going up to the crease," Horan wrote, "and so far as I saw, no objection could reasonably be urged against his delivery. He mixes his pace, and is very smart and active in his movements."

Victorian captain Jack Worrall was more reserved: "He has a most peculiar zig-zag run — something like the movement of a snake. His fast ball has a lot of pace in it, though a long way behind Jones' top. He sent down a lot of fine balls, but on the whole is inclined to be erratic."

NSW collapsed again for 135 in their second innings (including a six by Marsh's new-ball partner Bill Howell clean out of the MCG), but then Marsh and Noble attacked the Victorian top order and the home side ended the second day 5 for 45, still 90 runs from victory.

The two not out Victorian batsmen, Trumble and Stuckey needed 80 minutes on the third day to win the match. In the context of the low scoring match, their partnership was remarkable, though it had much to do with a crucial umpiring decision by local umpire Bob Crockett, who, from the bowler's end, no-balled Marsh for throwing a delivery that clean bowled Stuckey.

Crockett had called Marsh twice previously in the match, but this decision rattled the fast bowler, and his bowling clearly suffered. In a post-match interview Marsh commented: "It so happened that I was expected to do great things with the ball in this match and it so happened that I didn't". This was a harsh self-assessment. His six wickets for 91 compared admirably with the efforts of the established Test bowlers Howell, Hugh Trumble, Monty Noble and Frank Laver.

NSW returned to Sydney for the return match with South Australia a week later. When the first day's play was due to start at noon Marsh was nowhere to be seen, and did not arrrive until 12.20. He then

*The Bathurst team that played against the 1903–04 touring Englishmen. The controversial fast bowler, Jack Marsh, is seated at the far right of the middle row. Two years earlier an English team captained by A.C. MacLaren had refused to play a match against a Bathurst team that included Marsh, because they believed the aboriginal was a chucker. Two places to Marsh's right is Austin Diamond, who two seasons later scored 164 for NSW on his Shield debut.*

complained to NSW officials that he was too ill to play. Perhaps he was sick of the sight of Clem Hill, but he need not have worried, as the visitors collapsed for only 157.

NSW replied with a collosal 918. Iredale, Noble, Syd Gregory, Duff and Poidevin all scored hundreds and Victor Trumper made 70. At stumps on day one NSW were 1 for 224, having scored their runs in two hours on the same pitch that South Australia had struggled on. Trumper and Iredale had started the innings by reaching 50 in 22 minutes and 100 in 54 minutes. 499 runs were scored on the second day, and the entire innings occupied just nine hours and 20 minutes — establishing a new world record for a single innings in first-class cricket.

Marsh captured 5–34 in the first South Australian innings, and he took five more (for 54) when they batted again. His victims included Hill in both innings. The champion left-hander played a lone hand of 55 in the first innings, including three fours in Marsh's first over, before top edging an attempted hook to short leg. In the second innings he sliced to point when 20.

J.C. Davis would later recall that, in the summer of 1900–01, Marsh was, with Trumper, the most popular cricketer in the state. A long career for NSW seemed assured for Marsh and international honours beckoned, as did a tour to England in 1902.

None of it came about. In fact Marsh played just one more Shield match.

The start of the return NSW-Victoria match was delayed a week owing to the death of Queen Victoria. NSW won the toss, batted, and were bowled out for a miserable 170. Victoria's reply began sensationally. The Victorian captain Worrall was partnered by Warwick Armstrong. Marsh was no-balled by the visiting umpire Crockett for throwing three times in his first over, and twice more in his second. In his third over he beat Armstrong twice and then bowled him, to the unrestrained joy of the patrons in the outer, who had been barracking Crockett unmercifully.

Marsh was no-balled by Crockett eight times on day one and strangely it was Marsh's slower ball that the umpire objected to. Tom Howard, the NSW part-time off spinner, was also called. Just after lunch on the second day, Marsh was called by Crockett once again, and lost his temper, hurling the ball at the Victorian batsman Frank Laver. In all he was called 19 times, each time by Crockett, as Victoria built a lead of 109 runs.

NSW's second innings was dominated by a superb 230 by Trumper, carved out in oppressive heat, and scored in just 293 minutes. Davis thought it Trumper's greatest innings in Australia to that time, and it provided Victoria with a target of 344 to win.

This they achieved, but only just, winning by a single wicket after Peter McAlister and last man Jack Saunders added 10 runs amid great tension to get the visitors home. The win gave Victoria a perfect record for the Shield season — four wins from four games — and the Shield for the fifth time.

Marsh's bowling in the Victorian second innings was dreadful, his first innings' experience having ruined his control. After 16 overs Victoria had scored 60, and 55 had come from Marsh's bowling. In all he bowled 23 overs for 104, and one wicket, and NSW captain Syd Gregory was heavily criticised for perservering with him. In a match as tight as this, Marsh's 19 first innings no-balls proved crucial. In fact, in the match NSW scored 611 runs off the bat, to the Victorians' 567.

Marsh was not called in the second innings. Subsequent reaction to his treatment by Crockett was mixed. Tom Horan, writing in Melbourne wrote: "With regard to the constant no-balling of Marsh by Crockett, I have nothing to say, but if Marsh didn't chuck any more than he chucked in Melbourne then he didn't chuck very often."

J.C Davis wrote: "That Crockett, or anyone else, should call a certain ball Marsh bowls is not surprising to me. But it never did strike me that Marsh's real fast ball, delivered straight over, was anything but an absolutely fair ball. Accordingly when this ball was once called on Monday I was rather surprised. It was the calling of that particular ball which so disturbed the serenity of the bowler."

Throwing was the major topic in English cricket in 1900. The actions of a number of prominent county bowlers had been questioned, and some no-balled. Australian sporting editors had given the issue many columns in their papers, reporting on various British and occasional Australian opinions as to what defined a throw, and what needed to be done to rid the game of the chuckers. The issue had snowballed through 1900, and in December of that year, a meeting of the first-class county captains in London banned a number of British bowlers whose actions were regarded with suspicion.

Marsh was the first bowler no-balled for throwing in Sheffield Shield cricket (Ernie Jones had been called by the English team's umpire Jim Phillips in Adelaide in 1897, and by Phillips again in the second Test in 1897–98). It appears Marsh was unlucky he appeared on the scene at a time when Australian cricket needed a scapegoat. English cricket was in the process of cleaning its game of all throwers, and it was important that Australia was seen to be doing the same.

Crockett was Australia's most repected umpire, and he took it upon himself to lead Australia's assault on illegal bowlers. Crockett was not a dishonest umpire, nor in all likelihood, was he a racist one. But in 1900–01 his definition of a throw tightened considerably, and Marsh, with his unusual, whippy action, became his celebrated target.

By the end of 1901, the throwing controversy that had bedevilled English cricket had died, the victim of a concerted umpiring campaign led by Jim Phillips, and a hard-line letter from the MCC to all the counties suggesting any persistent offenders should be banished from the game.

In Australia, Jack Marsh retreated to grade cricket, where he topped the bowling averages for three straight seasons from 1901–02. He was never chosen for NSW in the Shield again, but made more headlines in February, 1902, when the touring English captain A.C. McLaren refused to play against a Bathurst team including Marsh, on the grounds that Marsh, as a chucker, would endanger the welfare of the touring batsmen.

Marsh's death on May 26, 1916 was the final, tragic episode in his unfortunate life. The former fast bowler was the victim of a sinister incident in the NSW country town of Orange, which led to a local bookmaker and his assistant being charged with murder. Much of the evidence given at the trial was damning, but the jury found the different eyewitness accounts contradictory and the two men were acquitted.

Marsh was apparently drunk, and in a brawling mood at the time of his death, but it appears he was the victim of a cowardly assault, being brutally kicked about the head while he lay injured on one of Orange's main streets. It was suggested Marsh was originally felled by a billiard ball thrown by one of the two accused, a terrible irony if true, considering the way he was thrown out of first-class cricket.

In a tribute in the June 7, 1916 *Referee* J.C. Davis wrote of Marsh: "Many held that he threw. I am sure he did so at times in his early career, but later, when he was even more deadly, his delivery struck me as being not against the rules. This, of course, is a matter of opinion and with a man of his particular powers there will always be some doubt on the point, especially among those who did not take take the trouble to look closely into his action...If he had been able to win a place in Test match cricket I believe his bowling would have established a fresh standard of hard wicket excellence and created a new type, differing altogether from anything ever known before. But fate decreed that his bowling should not come into Test matches."

# 9

# TOM HASTINGS —
# THE ONE GAME WONDER

In the period between a match against Arthur Shrewsbury's English team in December 1887 and the home Shield game against South Australia in the first week of 1909, Victorian selectors chose 14 different wicketkeepers for first-class fixtures.

The 14 included internationals Jack Blackham, Fred Burton, Jack Harry, Alf Johns and Barlow Carkeek. Also among them was Thomas John Hastings, a cricketer of limited means, whose first-class career spanned this 21-year period. In that time he played just 15 first-class matches, and a meagre nine Sheffield Shield games.

And yet, like many other obscure Australian cricketers, he had his one moment of Shield glory. It came in January 1903, against South Australia in Melbourne, when Tom Hastings, batting eleven, scored his one first-class innings of more than 25 — 106 not out! It was the only instance of an Australian cricketer scoring a first-class century from the lowliest position in the batting order.

Hastings was born on January 16, 1865 in Melbourne. His debut in 1887 was a miserable one, scores of 4 and 10, and just one catch, as Shrewsbury's team slaughtered the Victorians by an innings and 456 runs. He was forced to miss the second day of the carnage because of illness, and wasn't selected again for nearly ten years.

## Mr. Fosbery, Inspector of Police.

### A JUBILEE OF SERVICE AND INTENDED RETIREMENT.

On the 6th proximo Mr. Fosbery completes the 50th year of his connection with the police of Australia. On the next day he enters on his 70th year of life. Of the 50 years service in the police, 41 were in New South Wales. Since 1874 Mr. Fosbery has ably filled the important office of Inspector-General. More than this, he has also held, and is holding, several positions in which grave responsibilities have been and are involved. His work has been increased latterly by the alteration in the traffic laws, which now places the control of the metropolitan traffic entirely in his hands. This was previously administered by the Metropolitan Transit Commission. Mr. Fosbery is also the senior member of the Board of Health, he being one of the original appointees nearly 30 years ago. He is a member of the board which administers the Old-age Pensions Act, besides being chairman of the Public Service Tender and Supply Board. The Inspector-General has always taken a keen interest in the aborigines, and since its formation, about 20 years ago, he has occupied the position of chairman of the Aborigines' Protection Board. Another post he fills is that of vice-president of the Savings Bank of New South Wales. But apart from his many official engagements, Mr. Fosbery has also found time to take an active interest in the management of various benevolent societies.

Can it be wondered that Mr. Fosbery would welcome relief from his arduous work—a rest which he, by the rules of the service might have demanded many years ago.

In recognition of his long and honourable period of service Mr. Fosbery, it will be remembered, was made a C.M.G. by his Majesty the King last June, and when the distinction was announced it was generally regarded as an honour richly earned and well deserved.

### A Modern Solomon.

A Paris commissaire of police, M. Brunet, solved a case brought before him in a manner not unworthy of Solomon. A workman, named Jacques Meraud, lately missed half a dozen fine pigeons. He blamed an individual named Marcel Boucheux living near by. Both men asserted that the pigeons belonged to them. At last the commissaire ordered the cage containing the birds to be taken to the police station, and to the leg of each pigeon he attached a small piece of sealing-wax for the purpose of identification. He then liberated the birds, and while his secretary went with M. Boucheux the commissaire accompanied M. Meraud. The six pigeons were soon found in the workman's pigeon house. The experiment was considered a convincing one, and M. Boucheux was taken into custody and charged with the theft.

FIRST INNINGS, VICTORIA.—GRAHAM AND ARMSTRONG AT THE WICKETS.

SOME MEMBERS OF THE VICTORIAN TEAM.
Back Row—Reading from Left to Right: T. Hastings, F. Collins, S. M'Michael (Manager), P. M'Alister, B. Tuckwell. Front Row: R. Mailer, F. Laver (Captain), M. Ellis, D. Noonan.

Inter-State Cricket, Victoria v. N.S.W. SYDNEY CRICKET GROUND. JANUARY 24, 1903.

His return came against Tasmania in January, 1897. A month later, Hastings made his Shield debut in Adelaide, where he took two catches, including Clem Hill for 95 (the first of many first-class nineties for the great left-hander), and scored 0 not out and 0 as Victoria crashed to their first innings defeat in the Shield.

Hastings did not play again in the Shield until December 1901, when he was a member of the Victorian side that lost by 42 runs to NSW at the MCG. Hastings scored 0 and 12 (equal third highest score as the locals crashed to 110 all out chasing 153 for victory) and completed one catch and one stumping. He was involved in an intriguing incident at the end of the second day's play, when the NSW umpire Callaway allowed Monty Noble an extra delivery in the final over of the day, and Hastings was bowled by it.

He kept his place for the return match in Sydney, and was promoted in the batting order, to number nine, from where he managed 11 and 5. Jack Woodford was preferred as keeper for a match against McLaren's Englishmen in February, but Hastings was back for the first Shield game of the 1902–03 season, the Christmas match at home to NSW.

This match started under a cloud, after Jack Worrall was forced to withdraw from the Victorian side. Worrall, via the columns of a London newspaper, had questioned the legality of Jack Saunders' and Warwick Armstrong's bowling actions, and the two bowlers reacted by refusing to play in the same side as their accuser. The VCA supported Saunders and Armstrong, and effectively ended the former Victorian captain's first-class career.

The match was dominated by the superb bowling of NSW left-hander Bill Howell, who won the game for the visitors when he took 9 for 52 in Victoria's second innings. One of Howell's victims was Tom Hastings, LBW for 0, completing the hapless wicketkeeper's only pair in first-class cricket.

Hastings was fortunate to keep his place for the Victorians next Shield match, at home to South Australia, starting on New Year's day. His first-class batting average was a dreadful 8.07 (121 runs in 17 innings, 2 not outs, highest score 23). His Shield average was worse — precisely four runs per innings, including four ducks, from seven completed innings. Victorian captain Frank Laver, after winning the toss, wrote Hastings' name down at number 11, where he was perfectly entitled to be.

The South Australians, spearheaded by the warhorse Ernie Jones, supported by the left-hand medium-fast Jack Travers and the right hand medium pace of Norrie Claxton, kept labouring all day on a wicket Tom Horan called "as true as a billiard table". They had their reward after tea, when the Victorians crashed from 5–233 (Peter McAlister 68) to 9–261. Hastings came to the wicket to join Fitzroy's Mathew Ellis, a top order batsman who was making his Shield debut. Ellis had originally been selected as 12th man, but was at the wicket because Jack Saunders had arrived at the ground that morning too ill to play. Ellis would open the Victorian second innings, but for the moment, he had to bat down the order, at number nine.

Ellis had been responsible for all but two of the runs scored since he arrived at 7–244. The *Age* commented: "Fitzroy was evidently well represented in the outer circle of spectators, who lustily cheered every scoring stroke made by Ellis, and he well deserved the applause."

Last wicket partnerships have a habit of sneaking up on opposing captains, and this one was no different. While the South Australian opening batsmen were planning their early overs in the late afternoon, the two unheralded Victorians pushed their team's total towards 300, and then beyond.

On 14, Hastings was dropped by Claxton in the slips off Jones. A tough chance, not at the time considered a crucial one, but suddenly it dawned that the batsmen were entrenched. Ellis drove Jones to the fence so hard he could arrogantly stand defiant at the batting crease. Clem Hill rung the changes, but his tired attack wilted as Ellis and, wonder of wonders, Hastings attacked the bowling. The 300 was brought up in 255 minutes, after Ellis crashed Claxton over mid-wicket for four. Then Hastings repeated the stroke, to applause that had the *Argus* correspondent thinking of the football season.

Hill tried the googly bowler Harry Kirkwood, but his length was poor, and Travers was soon back to try to stop the tide. Jack Reedman tried to tie up the other end, but Hastings smashed him through the covers. At stumps Ellis was 60, scored in 78 minutes, while Hastings was 40, in five minutes less than the hour. The score was 9–348.

The crowd on the opening day had been 7000, mediocre for a holiday, the poor figured blamed on what Jack Worrall called the "pulseless batting" of the Victorians against NSW . On the second day, most of that number were back, dreaming that the last-wicket sensations might continue. Hill played his trumps, Jones and Travers, at the start, but the batsmen prevailed, and soon Claxton was on for Jones. Then Jones for Travers, and Travers for Claxton. The century stand was the first milestone of the morning, then Hastings' 50.

The 400, scored in 328 minutes, came up through a Hastings' edge off Jones to third man. The *Argus* commented: "The crowd had found their voices, but not for satire as in the match against New South Wales." Ellis was lucky when Jones slipped when he might have reached a miscued drive, and then Hastings went to 69, the second highest score of the innings.

Soon afterwards Ellis had his century — the third Victorian to reach three figures on his Shield debut. He had been batting 148 minutes. At lunch he was 107, Hastings 84 and the home side 9–439.

Hastings had never scored a century in any level of cricket, but his nerves were eased by the South Australian Algy Gehrs, who twice slipped and allowed fours to Hastings soon after the interval. Ellis hit Kirkwood over the fence at long on for five (to score six the ball had to be hit out of the ground), and then Hastings grabbed a single for the 200 stand. The *Age* described what happened next:

"A single to Ellis brought Hastings opposite Reedman, who had replaced Travers at the pavilion end, and the Carlton wicketkeeper brought the coveted century opposite his name by glancing Reedman for a couple."

Soon after Ellis was stumped, charging unsuccessfully at Reedman. The innings ended at 472, the partnership of 211 just 19 short of the then tenth-wicket first-class record. Ellis had batted for 185 minutes for 118, Hastings 157 minutes for an undefeated 106. "He played in an attractive style, and never seemed liked getting out," Tom Horan wrote proudly of the Victorian keeper.

Despite a typical Clem Hill century, Victoria eventually won the match by 179 runs. Hastings, back in the real world, had a poor match with the gloves, twice missing Hill, and then was caught in the deep for 9 when batting number 10 in the Victorian second innings.

In Sydney in the last week of January 1903, Victoria lost by five wickets. Hastings achieved his second highest score in first-class cricket, caught and bowled Trumper 25, but was hit on the head while keeping and forced to miss most of the NSW first innings. He then went to Brisbane and played in the first eleven-a-side match between Victoria and Queensland

Jack Monfries was preferred as keeper for the match against South Australia in March. Hastings was not selected again until the November 1908 Shield match in Adelaide. He scored 1 and 11 and completed one catch. Back at the MCG, Hastings opened the batting against NSW and scored 13, as his side defeated the eventual Shield champions by an innings and 47 runs. Back at number 10 less than a week later, Hastings scored 9 and 0 against South Australia in what proved to be his final Shield and first-class appearance.

Mat Ellis' cricket career never scaled the heights his Shield debut suggested. He scored just one Shield fifty to go with his famous century, playing in only five more Shield games between 1903 and 1907.

Both Hastings and Ellis rely on their extraordinary innings to sustain their name in cricket folklore. Their stand ranks with Kippax and Hooker's famous partnership of 307 in 1928 as the most freakish and unexpected in Australian cricket. But the Hastings-Ellis alliance has one feature not even Kippax and Hooker can match. The two Victorians were not established Shield players, rather journeymen cricketers playing out their one moment of personal glory.

Especially for Tom Hastings, 21 years a first-class wicketkeeper but never a regular selection, it is his obscurity and relative mediocrity that makes his achievement of scoring a century from number 11 as remarkable as any feat performed in the long history of the Sheffield Shield.

# 10

# CATCH OF A LIFETIME

Mat Ellis was the man at the other end to Tom Hastings' remarkable "number 11" century against South Australia in 1902–03. Soon after that game the pair travelled to Sydney for a Shield encounter with New South Wales — a contest the home side won easily, after Victoria had the worst of a rain-affected wicket.

For Ellis, the match was a mixture of good and not so good. In the first innings he made a neat 23 out of his side's lacklustre 207. In the second he battled hard in a losing cause for 53, before being run out by

*Frank Laver, the Victorian captain in 1902–03.*

Reggie Duff, after a mix-up with, of all people, Tom Hastings. For the doughty keeper Hastings, the match was a disaster after the glory of his hundred, and he spent most of the third day in his team's hotel, after a ball from his teammate, opening bowler Fred Collins, had struck him on the forehead.

The match was most memorable for a brilliant catch Mat Ellis managed from a lofted hit to the outfield by the immortal Victor Trumper. It was a catch Warwick Armstrong remembered whenever he was asked to recall the best catches he had seen. Trumper was 100 not out, in full, glorious cry, and, with Duff, had already passed 200 for the opening wicket. Despite the remarkable nature of the catch, it was a moment that Ellis could only recall in later years with a wry smile, and a resigned shake of the head.

Armstrong was the bowler, and Trumper skied him to the deep, where Ellis, stationed near the bike track that surrounded the SCG until 1920, backpeddled to get under the swirling ball. Ellis continued back until his feet touched the asphalt. Realising that a catch on the bike track was not out, Ellis jumped forward as the catch finally arrived, and as he did so knocked the ball forward back out into the field of play.

The ball was all but out of reach, but Ellis would not be denied, and with a desperate lunge had his left hand under it, completing a catch the likes of which the Sydney patrons had never seen. His stunned teammate, Danny Noonan, raced towards him, and Ellis, as he jumped to his feet, threw him the ball. Together the pair celebrated the amazing end of a famous partnership.

But something was wrong. Trumper and Duff were madly running between the wickets, and teammates were screaming for the ball to be returned. Umpire Crockett had ruled not out, and Ellis, incensed, ignored his colleagues and ran at the umpire, yelling that his catch had been cleanly taken.

Ellis could not be quietened. When Crockett finally got a word in, it was all he could do to explain that his ruling was correct. Ellis was incredulous. How could his great moment be taken from him. He started again, and none of Armstrong, Crockett or Victorian captain Frank Laver could comfort or restrain him.

The crowd, estimated at around 8,000, were screaming for play to continue. The cricket had started late, and dark clouds were gathering in the distance. Ellis pleaded, arms waving, that an injustice was being done. Trumper, ever the diplomat, leaned back on his bat, and quietly grinned as Duff chortled. After the pantomine had lasted for what Armstrong later claimed was three minutes, Crockett was finally able to explain that it had been a no-ball, and suggested it was just about time play was allowed to continue.

Ellis bowed his head, and crept slowly towards the ever-closer jeers of the crowd. Two runs had been scored while Ellis and Noonan had played their celebratory little game in the outfield. As Armstrong put it: "Ellis walked back to his place, a sadder but wiser man."

"But," Armstrong always added, "it was a magnificent catch."

# 11

# CHARLIE MACARTNEY'S FIRST SEASON

Charlie Macartney was one of the greatest of all New South Wales cricketers. His first-class career spanned 22 seasons; he first entered the Shield arena in 1905 as a bowling all-rounder and departed as Australia's finest batsman. He was known for most of his career as "The Governor-General", a title reflecting a grand, almost arrogant, demeanour. It was given to him by the English batsman K.L. Hutchings in 1907–08, adopted by his admirers on the Sydney Hill, and remained appropriate throughout Macartney's celebrated career.

Charles George Macartney was born in West Maitland on June 27, 1886. His grandfather, George Moore, had played against the English touring teams of Stephenson, Parr and W.G. Grace. Grandson Charlie did not tour England until 1909, the year after Grace's retirement, thus narrowly missing a rare family double. His grandfather's brother, James, had also played against Stephenson's side in 1862, and James's sons Billie and Leon both played interstate cricket.

Macartney's family came to live in Sydney's Eastern Suburbs in 1898, then moved again, to

Chatswood, on the North Shore, two years later. His schoolmates at Chatswood included the son of Australia's first Test captain, Dave Gregory, and the nephew of M.A. Noble. Once, Noble visited the school to give a coaching clinic, and later praised Macartney's talents in a local paper.

Macartney left school at 15, to work at a produce market in Sussex Street, in the city centre. Three years later he was playing first grade cricket for North Sydney, after a two-and-half-season apprenticeship in the lower grades. Selected in first grade originally as a replacement for Reggie Duff, who was touring New Zealand with an Australian side, Macartney finished the season with a batting average of 131. He never played lower grade cricket again.

He joined the newly-formed Gordon club for the 1905–06 season, scoring the club's inaugural first grade century, and in November was selected for a Queensland tour with a below-strength NSW side. There he scored an unbeaten 57 and took three wickets, sufficient to get him into the state side for the trip to Adelaide. In a series of articles for the Sydney weekly newspaper the *Sunday News* in 1928–29, Macartney looked back on that tour, and other incidents in his first Shield season. He remembered his first meeting with Victor Trumper, who, for "business reasons", was unable for the trip:

"It was just before the team left for Adelaide that M.A. Noble introduced me to the great Victor Trumper. I had never met him or seen him before, excepting once in the distance at the Sydney Cricket

*Below: The Australian team that toured England in 1909, the first of four such trips for Charlie Macartney.*
*Back Row (left to right): V. Ransford, W. Bardsley, H. Carter;*
*Standing: W. Whitty, P. McAlister, A. Cotter, R. Hartigan, J. O'Connor; Seated: V. Trumper, A. Hopkins, M.A. Noble (capt), F. Laver, W. Armstrong; At front: S. Gregory, C. Macartney, W. Carkeek.*
*Right: Macartney after the War, practising the off-drive.*

Ground when he was batting against Maclaren's team in 1901, and I was a boy spectator. I was to discover very shortly that no better sportsman or batsman ever lived, and his generosity and unselfishness were on par with his ability."

Against South Australia, Macartney scored an unbeaten 70 as NSW won by an innings and 82 runs. For South Australia, Clem Hill hit another Shield century, a powerhouse 146, before he was bowled by Noble. Macartney recalled that innings:

"His leg glancing and on-side play generally, as well as his hefty drives through the covers, will always live in my memory. After he had made 146, and looked like going on for another 365, Noble bowled him with a fast ball which took the middle stump clean out of the ground, beating the batsman in the pace absolutely. Clem's remark: 'Where did you get that one from, Tommy?' was proof of that."

Macartney said of the Adelaide Oval: "I was immensely struck with the quality of the wicket on the Adelaide Oval. It was like a sheet of glass....During my first few trips to Adelaide the far ends were roped off for some ten or twenty yards, but in later years the fence was erected closer in."

The NSW side caught the train to Melbourne for their annual Christmas match against Victoria. Macartney remembered his first sight of the famous MCG:

"Noble took me down to the Melbourne Cricket Ground on the afternoon of our arrival in the city and I was amazed when I first saw the ground. It was the first occasion that I had seen a cricket ground not built on the level. 'Fancy bowling up hill,' I said to Noble, to which he replied that it was not quite as bad as it might appear...The wicket in Melbourne was a beauty, but it struck me then, as it has done ever since, that the ball always rose higher off the pitch than anywhere else I have ever played."

In the match against Victoria, NSW amassed 805. Noble scored 281 and "Sunny" Jim Mackay 194. Macartney, who came to the wicket after Noble's dismissal, was out first ball, the only one of the top eight NSW batsmen not to get past 40. Late in the innings, the NSW fast bowler Albert "Tibby" Cotter, who bashed 68 in 35 minutes, slammed 26 off one six-ball over of Jack Saunders.

Back in Sydney, NSW defeated South Australia by nine wickets, with the prolific Mackay scoring a hundred in each innings. The second century caused a dispute between Noble and the visiting captain, Joe Darling:

"NSW had only about 170 runs to obtain to win," recalled Macartney, "and when Mackay required two or three runs for his double, the side required only four runs to win. Noble, who was batting at the other end, leg glanced a ball, but the batsmen did not run. Had the ball gone to the boundary the game would have been over; leaving Mackay a few short. However Sunny Jim got there, but Joe Darling was very incensed over the happening, declaring that it was not right to place the individual before the side and the game. There is no doubt Darling's expressions were merited, but it is difficult at times to escape from sentiment, all the same."

In the final game of Macartney's debut Shield season, NSW overcame Victoria, despite batting first on a poor SCG pitch. The match was tagged the "Jubilee Match", a celebration of 50 years of cricket between the two states. The difference between the two sides was Trumper, who scored a remarkable 101, dominating the otherwise triumphant Saunders, who took seven wickets in the innings. Trumper hit his 101 out of 139 in three minutes less than an hour. In 1916, *Wisden* called the masterpiece, "perhaps the most brilliant display of his career."

"Victor Trumper made such a magnificent hundred on a sticky wicket that it was worth being in the side for that alone," remembered Charlie Macartney. "Laver and Saunders were a pretty rich pair to bat against on a wicket of that kind.

"Saunders nearly bowled Trumper with the first ball, but Vic, after remarking that he would just as soon be caught off him as bowled, set about the job properly, and with beautifully executed strokes belted every bowler into every quarter of the Sydney Cricket Ground.

"Trumper brought off the best big hit I have ever seen. A yorker from Frank Laver was the ball he selected for the hit, and with no apparent effort, he seemed to pick it up with the bat, and it finished up on the roof of the northern pavilion. I have seen bigger hits made by lunging, but this was a fast footed one, which it had to be from the pitch of the ball."

Macartney finished his first Shield season with a modest 80 runs (from 4 completed innings) and seven wickets at a fraction more than 30. The glory days were still to come. Within two seasons he was in the Test side, and his career continued until 1926–27, the season before Don Bradman made his Sheffield Shield debut.

# 12
## THE 1906 DISPUTE

Despite the disintegration of the Australasian Cricket Council in 1900, many cricket administrators in Sydney and Melbourne yearned for a national body of cricket control. This was especially so of the officials of the NSW Cricket Association, who deplored the status and workings of the Melbourne Cricket Club and the influence some players held through their relationship with that club.

For many years the Melbourne Cricket Club was the body that backed cricket tours of English teams to Australia. It was intended that this would change from January 9, 1905, when, at the instigation of the VCA, representatives of the Victorian, NSW and South Australian cricket associations met in Sydney and supported a resolution to form a Board of Control. This Board had its first meeting in Melbourne on May 6, 1905.

While the Queensland Cricket Association gave its support to the new body, and was granted representation, the South Australian Association chose not to be involved after questioning late changes to clauses in the constitution relating to the financing of overseas tours.

In the Sydney *Daily Telegraph* of July 5, 1906, the origins of a dispute that would rock Australian cricket were revealed. When the Australian team was in England in 1905, the players became aware of the proposed constitution of the newly formed board. As they understood these rules, the intention was to give the Board absolute authority over the financing of teams sent to England. The players understood this would lead to the Board appointing the manager of future touring teams, and that his duties would be to collect all revenue, pay all travelling and other expenses and also pay the players a small sum per week as compensation for loss of time from their regular employment. What would become of tour profits they were not sure. From newspaper reports they gathered they would not be represented on the Board of Control.

The players resolved to stand together in opposing a Board created on these terms. The matter was discussed with members of the Melbourne club and an alliance formed between the Australian players and the club.

In September 1905, the Melbourne club held a meeting with VCA and NSWCA representatives, seeking a seat on the Board of Control, but were knocked back. In the same month the Australian captain in England, the South Australian Joe Darling, cabled the SACA secretary, telling him that the Marylebone Cricket Club would not recognise a Board of Control without South Australia on it, and that the Australian players did not agree with the existing Board constitution. Four months later, the Melbourne Cricket Club, apparently with the knowledge of the SACA, secretly approached 11 of NSW's finest players and gained a written undertaking that they would be available to play against a touring English team, sponsored by the Melbourne Club, in 1906–07 — in short a rebel tour. The NSW players were some of the finest in the land, the backbone of the team that had won the Sheffield Shield each season since 1901–02: the captain M.A. Noble, Victor Trumper, Reg Duff, Albert Cotter, Jim Mackay, Hanson Carter, Bert Hopkins, Rev. E.F. Waddy, George Garnsey, Jack O'Connor and Austin Diamond.

The deal was kept secret for four months. When it finally emerged that these players had effectively shunned their own association, the NSWCA reacted with scarcely concealed rage. Its anger was not lessened when it announced that no matches would be played in NSW — only for the SCG Trust, which was in dispute with the Association, to provocatively and subsequently announce that it, the Trust, and not the NSWCA, hired out the ground.

The 11 players were brought before the Association's executive committee, and then banned indefinitely from playing in the state, unless they agreed to break their contract with the Melbourne Club. Only Waddy announced he would withdraw from the agreement, the remainder were suspended, effectively leaving NSW minus almost its entire team for the coming season. It was thought that many of the suspended players would transfer to Melbourne. This, the *Daily Telegraph* suggested, would not necessarily be a bad thing. "The games with Victoria, the next strongest state, in recent years have been altogether too one-sided," thought the paper.

In the Sydney press, Noble pleaded for the players to be granted representation on the Board. He also suggested that the Melbourne club and the SCG Trust should be included. In Melbourne, the former Australian captain, Harry Trott, described the state associations as a "meddling, wrangling lot of old ladies", who had "already done more harm to the good old game than they can ever expect to remedy." Major Ben

Wardill, the secretary of the Melbourne club and a significant figure in Lord Sheffield's English tour of 15 seasons earlier, remarked that his club was not seeking control of Australian cricket, but merely sought a representation on the Board of Control that went further than the NSW and Victorian associations.

The dispute dragged on until August — a battle between the battalions of the Board, the VCA and the NSWCA on one side — and those of the leading players, the Melbourne Club, the SACA, and the SCG Trust on the other. After a three month saga the Melbourne club was finally guaranteed one of the three Victorian delegate's positions on the board. The SACA then applied for, and was granted, admission to the Board.

Soon afterwards, following the intervention of the old political warhorse George Reid, the NSWCA agreed to rescind the suspensions of its star players —although in what was seen as a petty parting shot, it banned the ten rebels from holding office in the Association for three years. This embargo was aimed directly at Noble, who had been a delegate for the Paddington club, and was the chief marshall of the players' revolt. Later in the year, Noble lost the right to decide the final make-up of the NSW team on tour. Instead he was obliged to wait for a telegram from the NSWCA, telling him what his final eleven would be.

The events of 1906 brought into the open the enmity that had engulfed the relationship between leading players and the officials of the NSW and Victorian associations. Two senior officials, William McElhone in Sydney and Ernest Bean in Melbourne, became the key figures in their respective associations' tussle to control the game. As it was these men who dominated the Board of Control, it was inevitable that a major clash between the players and the Board would occur. It came in 1912, when the Board, as the players had feared all along, appointed their own manager and brought on a dispute that led to Trumper, Carter, Cotter, the Victorians Warwick Armstrong and Vernon Ransford, and the Australian and South Australian captain Clem Hill declining invitations to tour England that year. The bitterness of this split was still apparent after the War, especially in Victoria where Armstrong was frequently in dispute with

*Members of the Australian Cricket Board of Control, in 1906. Back row (left to right): G.M. Colledge, F.A. Iredale, H.R. Rush; Front row: A.W. Green (treasurer), E.E. Bean (chairman), W.P. McElhone (secretary).*

Bean and the VCA.

The withdrawal of the suspensions before the commencement of the 1906–07 season meant the affair had little direct impact on the Sheffield Shield at that time. Ten of the eleven players participated in the Shield in 1906–07, though O'Connor went to South Australia and Trumper played for NSW only in the final match against Victoria. The one player missing was "Sunny" Jim Mackay.

Mackay was close to the leading Australian batsman of this time. After missing selection in the 1905 tour of England, he had dominated the 1905–06 Australian domestic season, putting Trumper, Hill, Noble and company very much in the background. His scores in NSW's four Shield matches were: 90, 194, 105, 102 not out, 18 and 50. An aggregate of 559 runs at 111.80.

Critics used superlatives that had previously been reserved for Trumper and Charlie Bannerman, the champion bat of the 1870s. In 1919, J.C. Davis wrote of Mackay: "Like Trumper, Mackay made his strokes with marvellous accuracy, the timing and snap all round the wicket being of a character rarely seen. Though Trumper was without peer in style among Australians, I always rank Mackay with him as a batsman."

On the eve of the 1906–07 season, Mackay announced he was leaving Sydney for South Africa, where he had accepted a job related to the operation of a diamond mine. Philip Derriman, in *True to the Blue*, states that Mackay's primary motivation for leaving Australia was to get away from the hostility of the dispute with the NSWCA. In his adopted country he soon found his best run-scoring form, but a motor cycle accident in May 1907 cost him his health and he was never the same cricketer from this point. He returned to Australia in 1907, first to Melbourne where he took a coaching job with the Melbourne club, and then to Sydney, but the accident had ruined his sight and he could not find the runs that had once flowed so freely. He played his last game in Sydney in January 1909.

Despite their troubled off-season NSW won the Shield again in 1906–7, in magnificently emphatic fashion. Three of their four matches were won by an innings. Only in Melbourne were they pressed, winning by just two wickets after a mad scramble to get 186 in the fourth innings. Macartney, ironically not one of the eleven rebels, was the all-round star, scoring 405 runs and taking 30 wickets during the summer. Diamond and Hopkins both topped 500 runs for the season, Garnsey took 32 wickets and Noble was Noble, always superb. Even without Trumper and Mackay they were an all-conquering team, a combination that must rank with any of the great sides that have dominated the Sheffield Shield.

# 13

# A LEADER OF MEN

Australian cricket has produced many celebrated team captains. At international level, the Australian team has been led by men such as Joe Darling, Warwick Armstrong, Bill Woodfull, Don Bradman, Richie Benaud, Ian Chappell and Allan Border. In the Sheffield Shield these champions have had to match wits with innovative and inspiring leaders such as Jack Worrall, Vic Richardson, Keith Carmody, Les Favell, John Inverarity, David Hookes and Geoff Lawson.

Alongside them all stands the imposing figure of Montague Alfred Noble. To most of his friends he was Monty, to some Alf, occasionally Tommy, to most cricket historians M.A. Noble. To all that played with or against him a respected, feared and formidable cricketer, the most effective captain of the pre-World War I era.

Noble was a tall man, an inch over six feet (185cm), and powerfully built. He had huge feet to support his commanding physique, but was still an agile man both in the field and at the crease. With the bat in his hands, Noble could defend or attack, depending on the situation. His bat was always close to his pad, and his approach inevitably correct, befitting a student of the game.

Noble first played Shield cricket in 1894–95, selected after he managed an unbeaten 152 for a NSW Colts XVIII against A.E. Stoddart's Englishmen. Chosen purely as a batsman, he was hastily dropped after a discouraging debut, but returned in December 1896 with a hard-fought second innings 69 against South Australia. His career was on its way. A month later he scored 71 and 153 not out against Victoria, and finished the season with a batting average of almost 69, the best of those with 200 or more runs for the season.

Noble made his international debut in the second Test of the 1897–98 series. He scored 17, and took 6–49, bowling third change, in England's second innings. His bowling anaylsis is remarkable, considering his career Shield bowling figures to that time amounted to 2–115 from 41.4 overs. When originally selected for Test cricket, just prior to the start of the NSW-Victoria match that preceded the second Test, Noble did not have a Shield wicket to his name.

Yet he demoralised the tourists with a new concept to slow-medium off-spin bowling — the swerve ball. He developed it after seeing visiting American baseball pitchers gripping the ball in a way Test cricketers did not, and married his new innovation to his lengthy run-up, perfect control, and shrewd change of pace. It was a delivery the Englishmen had not seen before, and Noble took 15 wickets in his first two Tests before his opponents came somewhere closer to coping. Noble, it seemed, kept handing out lessons throughout his career. The great Englishman, Sydney Barnes, said he learnt to bowl the outward swing from watching Noble at work.

*Below: Two of the Shield's most powerful figures, M.A. Noble (left) and Warwick Armstrong.*
*Right: The younger Noble, in his Australian cap.*

Noble's Sheffield Shield statistics are quite remarkable. His career batting average suggests he was a 19.64 runs per innings better batsman than Victor Trumper, and 15.72 runs per innings better than Clem Hill. His Shield bowling average is slightly inferior to Hugh Trumble, but superior to Ernie Jones, Bill Howell, Warwick Armstrong and Jack Saunders.

Outstanding performances abound in his story. He scored four successive Shield centuries in 1899, in four matches. In two of those games he also took eight wickets. Against Victoria in January 1900, he scored a crucial 155 in NSW's second innings, and then captured 6–91 as NSW won by 111 runs. In December 1901 he snared 10–82 for the match in Melbourne, including 7–44 in the first innings. In four seasons, 1902–03 to 1905–06 he scored seven Shield centuries, including 230 against South Australia in December 1903, and 281 against Victoria in December 1905. In 1908–09, his farewell season, he averaged 104.5 with the bat, scoring 213 in Adelaide and 213 and 69 not out in his final Shield match, a NSW victory over Victoria at the SCG.

Yet for all this achievment with bat and ball, it is for his inspired and ruthless leadership that he is best remembered. Macartney rated him: "The best captain it has been my pleasure to play under", a huge compliment considering Macartney also scored centuries for Hill, Trumper, Armstrong and Herbert Collins.

Arthur Mailey labelled Noble: "The best captain I ever played under, and the most convincing captain to whom I ever listened." He thought him a better leader than Woodfull, Bradman or Benaud. Johnnie Moyes also ranked Noble highly:

"Harry Trott was a grand leader who could command the allegiance of his troops. Those who played under Darling loved and admired him. Yet Noble probably excelled both in shrewd, tactical excellence. He too had the respect and affection of his team-mates, and some of them were very strong, and even obstinate, characters, who knew cricket and had minds of their own."

Noble, more so than any Australian before him, gave great credence to field placements. He was the first master of getting the angles right, of offering batsmen the narrowest gaps to the fence. There was logic in the exact position of each fieldsman, and Noble, a keen disciplinarian, deplored men who strayed from their assigned mark. He was renowned for his firm approach, and demanded no more than the best from his men. He was also acutely fair, and a story is told of him rebuking a colleague who jumped the fence to take part in a run chase, rather than entering the field through the pavilion gate.

Off the field he was friendly, sociable man, but he knew what time stumps was, and kept the affability and charity for after 6 o'clock. The famous South Australian umpire, George Hele, who considered Noble a marginally better captain than Bradman and Benaud, told this story of a Shield match between NSW and

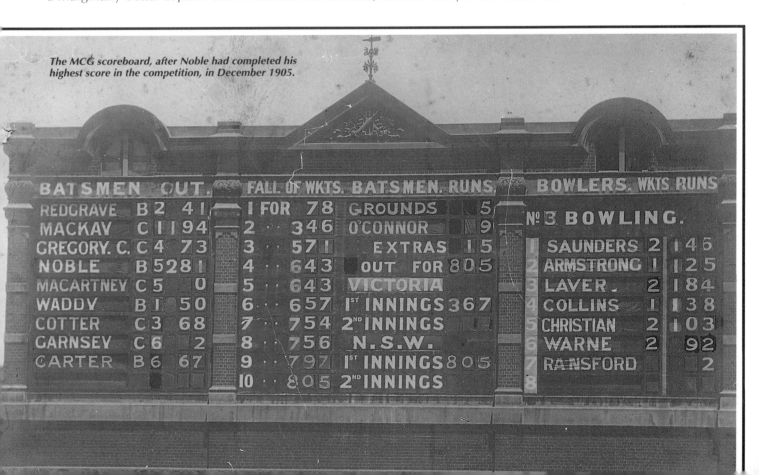

*The MCG scoreboard, after Noble had completed his highest score in the competition, in December 1905.*

South Australia:

"Fred Hack, one of the South Australian opening batsmen, was injured and called for a runner. The South Australian captain and great left-handed Test batsman, Clem Hill, came out to perform the function. Hill had been dismissed a little earlier.

'What are you doing back here, Clem?' Noble demanded

'I've come to run for Fred.'

'Listen, Clem. Go and get someone his own pace between the wickets or he won't have a runner at all.'

Hill left the ground and sent another batsman to run for Hack. Hack was slow between the wickets, owing to his huge feet. The new runner was faster than Hill, about Bradman's pace. Noble sent him back to Hill in the pavilion while the crowd waited for play to resume. 'Tell him to send out someone who is Hack's own pace,' Noble told the second runner. Hill came back on the field, crossed to Noble and said, 'I haven't got a runner who's as slow as Fred. Do you want me to put one in hobbles?'

'If you can't find the right runner, I will" said Noble. Eventually Hill found a batsman particularly slow between wickets and the game went on…"

Noble was one of three NSW selectors from 1899, and sole selector from the beginning of the 1901–02 season. His status in NSW cricket entitled him to the position, but being totally responsible for team selection was not a position he enjoyed, as cricketers and barrackers knew who to blame when things went wrong.

He remained a selector until the 1906 dispute with the NSWCA, but that conflict created animosities between Noble and administrators that took years to dispel. Noble was reappointed a delegate to the NSWCA for the Paddington club in July 1907, but could not find support in ballots for official positions with the NSWCA until after the first World War. He retired from big cricket after the 1909 tour of England, but in 1918 made a brief return to first-class cricket, as NSW captain. Noble acted as NSW coach for part of the 1927–28 season. In 1949, nine years after his death, the "New Members" grandstand at the northern end of the SCG was renamed the "M.A. Noble Stand"

Monty Noble was a man who commanded respect. Don Bradman wrote how a "fleeting glimpse of Noble, long after his best years had passed, left me with a feeling of admiration for him." Mailey called him: "The strongest personality I have met in cricket. Noble had a magnetism which made other people puppets in his company."

He was the dominant figure in NSW cricket in the tempestuous period up to the first Great War. His place in Shield cricket history is assured, and he is remembered long after the officials he argued with have been forgotten. The Sheffield Shield may have produced a leader the equal of M.A. Noble, but never a better one.

# 14

# GLORIOUS UNCERTAINTY

In January 1907, Victoria were bowled out for 31 in their second innings at the Sydney Cricket Ground, giving NSW victory by an innings and 266 runs. Eleven months later, also at the SCG, NSW, chasing 593 in the fourth innings of their match against South Australia, were finally all out for 572

They were two innings of total contrast, each the final innings of the match, each played on the same ground. And in the same year.

Victoria's debacle occurred on January 27 after heavy rain had reduced the pitch to a state where it was all but unplayable. The left-handed slow bowler Charlie Macartney opened the bowling and finished with 4 for 6. Co-destroyer was his captain, Monty Noble, who took 6 for 21. The Victorian total was their lowest against NSW since the first intercolonial contest of 1856, and remains their poorest return in one completed Sheffield Shield innings.

No Victorian batsman reached double figures. There were five ducks, and the innings lasted a miserable 77 minutes and 20.5 overs. The *Sydney Sportsman's* cricket writer was not impressed:

"Even admitting the wicket enabled the bowlers to make the ball cut almost any caper, it was not so bad as to account for the wretched performance of the batsmen. It did not kick or make the ball get up abruptly. A Worrall or a Darling or any aggressive batsman would have made better use of it. Noble and Macartney had a gala day."

In *The Referee*, J.C. Davis wrote: "M.A. Noble and C.G. Macartney on the bowler's wicket of Monday recalled Turner and Ferris in their invincible years of 1887–8–9. Macartney is the best left-hand bowler produced by Australia since J.J. Ferris was in his prime. On a bowler's wicket he is the most difficult Australian bowler since Turner's day."

This emphatic victory completed an undefeated interstate season for NSW. The Shield had been won for the sixth consecutive year, and the ninth time in all. At the end of January 1907, Victoria had won the trophy five times, and South Australia just once, back in 1893–94.

The next Shield season was an abbreviated one because of the complex itinerary of the A.O. Jones-captained English side. South Australia's home Shield matches were cancelled, the interstate series reduced to four matches, and decided in the final encounter when Victoria defeated NSW in Sydney in January 1908 by 211 runs.

NSW lost both their matches at the SCG in 1907–08, their first Shield setbacks at home since their one-wicket loss to Victoria in February 1901. The 1908 loss to Victoria was the most significant of the season, as it gave their fiercest rivals the Shield, but their defeat by South Australia a month earlier was far more memorable, as it came in a match the *Sydney Morning Herald* called "the finest contest in the history of cricket".

South Australia came into the match having lost their previous 13 games. The Englishmen had thrashed them for 8–660 in Adelaide in November, and Victoria ran up a massive 699 in their one clash of the season. In Sydney, on Friday, December 6, Clem Hill won the toss, and his side reached a respectable 349 (Hill 92 in 106 minutes, Edgar Mayne 91). A meagre attendance was blamed on the presence of the Englishmen: "There is very little interest in the interstate contests when the Englishmen are about," wrote the *Sportsman*. The first Test was due to start seven days later.

NSW replied with 276 (Noble 93), though at one stage they had been a commanding 4–211. South Australia took command with an impressive second innings of 519, with Hill scoring his second 90 of the match, Charlie Dolling reaching his maiden Shield century and Norrie Claxton getting 75.

The *Sportsman* could not understand why the once grand NSW batting line up had struggled in their first innings. In their previous match against England they had been bowled out for 101 and 96. The paper asked the question:

"Is old age creeping on, or is the sight becoming prematurely dim? Then why not, oh, my countrymen, imitate the example of the (English) visitors and put on spectacles. As matters are tending, some of our reputed cracks will be finding a pair without purchase. When the wheatfielders can make us put our backs to the wall it is time the new broom was brought into requisition, and fresh blood infused."

Victor Trumper and Reggie Duff started the NSW second innings with a stand of 89 in less than an hour, before the latter was bowled by Claxton. Duff, a small but powerful man with a reputation as a brave and forceful batsman, was already fighting personal difficulties with alcohol that would four years later claim his life. J.C. Davis described his brief second innings against South Australia this way:

"He made 37, and his batting was the best he has shown for New South Wales for some considerable time. Two or three of his square cuts were brilliant, one of them a cannon-shot stroke of a nature that will cling to one's memory. Under certain conditions I should say that Duff might easily and quickly come back into the most brilliant form, both as batsman and field. And these conditions depend wholly on himself."

Trumper had been scoring rapidly, but Noble went along even faster. The pair added 86 in an hour before Noble (51) was bowled trying to glance. Trumper was then 82. A few minutes and five strokes later he was 101, scored in 130 minutes, his third century against South Australia, but his first for nearly five years. Just before stumps Austin Diamond tried to put a slow full toss in the suburbs, but miscued to mid-off. His 8 would be the lowest score of the innings. At the close of day 4, NSW were 3–214, Trumper 111 not out.

Trumper added only 24 on the fifth morning, before lofting the spinner Wright to Chamberlain, running back at deepish mid-off. The nightwatchman, Frank Johnson, was bowled with the total on 260, and further wickets fell at 312 and 356 as the visiting bowlers laboured towards a precious victory.

NSW's Test all-rounder Bert Hopkins had been out of form, but this time he shaped well, and found a trusty ally in diminutive keeper Hanson Carter. Soon it was Carter who was dominating, and Hopkins slowed as the little man attacked. Early on the South Australians thought they had him caught behind, but the umpire said no, and Carter responded with a vigorous assault. The pair had added 118, and tea was fast approaching when Hopkins fatally sliced Claxton to Clem Hill in front of the track at deep third man.

Eighteen-year-old Charles Kelleway, in his debut Shield match, joined Carter, who was now thrashing at everything. One hundred and nineteen was still needed. The tiny crowd was very excited, and the struggling fieldsmen flagging noticeably, as propects of an impossible victory loomed. The young colt defended, while Carter raced into the 80s, and the innings total sped passed 500. Carter slowed as he reached the 90s, not so much from nerves as from exhaustion. As he tired the South Australians found their fifth wind, and the mood of the fielding side, defending 592, slowly changed from despair to growing optimism.

Carter claimed his hundred, and struggled to 125, before a weary heave lobbed a catch to Wright at wide mid-on. The ball bounced out, and away, from the fieldsman's desperate hands, but a full length dive re-secured it just as it threatened to hit the turf. Carter disputed the umpire's out decision, before trudging back to the pavilion. NSW would have to get the final 39 without him. J.C. Davis called his innings: "Quite the most brilliant of the match. His strokes square with the wicket on the offside were very fine indeed, and he made many runs by clean pulls and forcing shots to the on. It is quite the finest innings he has ever played."

It was some achievement to play the most brilliant innings of a match in which Clem Hill made 92 and 94 and Victor Trumper 135.

This was Wednesday, the fifth day of the match, and the Test was due to start on the coming Friday. Harry Whiddon, a leg spinner from Manly, came out to join Kelleway with stumps fast approaching. Immediately Whiddon was almost caught and bowled, but some brave (and lucky) shots were heartily cheered. Soon he, like all but one of his team-mates, was in double figures. There was conjecture that officials would demand the match be completed that night, and not one journalist at the game doubted that the New South Welshmen would get the runs if play was continued. But Hill made sure the umpires stuck to the rule book, and took the embattled visitors off, with Kellaway and Whiddon needing a frustrating 21 to win.

Years later the South Australian captain recalled those final minutes: "It has always been my custom to try and meet the wishes of the crowd when leading a side, but this was one fateful occasion when I could not possibly oblige them, and oh, what barracking we came in for. To the frantic yells of 'play on!', I led the South Australians from the field, knowing full well that bowlers and fieldsmen alike were done to a turn."

Two hundred spectators were present the next morning when Wright bowled the first over to Whiddon. They saw just three balls. Whiddon swung at the spinner, and sliced a chance to Chamberlain at extra cover. Diving forward, he grabbed the ball with both hands, before breaking his fall with his right hand and holding the ball triumphantly with his left. His team-mates raced towards him, and then, led by their excited captain, the South Australians scampered from the field.

Not all the heroes of interstate cricket find their names in the pages of sporting encyclopaedias. In an extraordinary match that featured three of Australia's greatest ever champions — Noble, Hill and Trumper — this final dismissal involved three obscure cricketers whose names are unknown to all but the keenest cricket historians. Such is the nature of the Sheffield Shield.

The batsman, Harry Whiddon, was a 29-year-old leg spin and googly bowler, who was making his Shield debut after an encouraging performance in a trial match involving what the NSW selectors judged to be the third and fourth best teams in the state. His three Shield matches and 16 wickets in 1907–08 were the total of his first-class cricket career.

The bowler, Albert Wright, was 32-years-old. A right-hand leg spinner of modest means, he had made his big cricket debut in Adelaide in December 1905, in a match NSW won decisively in less than three days. Wright, for his part, took 5–150 off 40.2 overs. He three times took six wickets in an innings against NSW, though in January 1907 at the SCG they cost him 209 runs, and once took 11 wickets in a Shield match. His farewell to the Shield was not until December 1920, when, aged 45, he took 3–164 off 36 overs in Sydney, bowling against Gregory, Andrews, Bardsley, Taylor, Hendry, Kelleway and the like. All up Albert Wright played 24 Shield games for his state, and took 95 wickets at 30.36, but his name is most prominent in record books as having scored a pair in each of his first three Shield appearances.

The extra cover fieldsman, William Chamberlain, was one of three brothers who played first-class

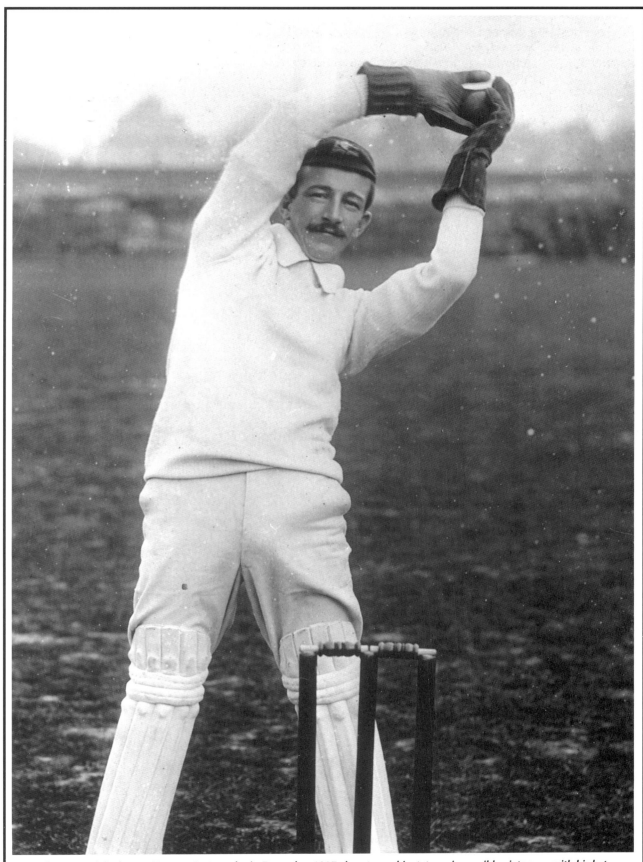

*The NSW wicketkeeper Hanson Carter, who in December 1907 almost won his state an impossible victory — with his bat.*

cricket in Australia, but the only one to play in the Sheffield Shield. He was 34 days short of his 19th birthday when he caught Harry Whiddon, and was playing in his third first-class match, having earlier in 1907 played against the Englishmen and Victoria. Chamberlain continued in Shield cricket until 1914, scoring 528 runs at 20.31 including one century.

Albert Wright took only two wickets in the NSW second innings, both of them caught by William Chamberlain. The second, the dismissal of Harry Whiddon, captured much of the attention, justifiably so, as it ended the historic match. But, perhaps the first Chamberlain catch — the type outfielders dislike, running away from the wicket to grasp a skier — was the more crucial, the one that prevented an unprecedented NSW triumph.

Victor Trumper was 135, set, and playing his way into top form. The gentle Vic was prone to throw away an innings if nothing depended on the outcome. But, like any champion, he craved challenges and was at his best when the best was needed. As Chamberlain held the ball tightly to his chest, and the great man walked off to the polite applause of the members, few would have realised that this was the moment South Australia really won this exciting and unique Sheffield Shield contest.

# 15

## ALGY GEHRS' AMAZING HUNDRED

Donald Raeburn Algernon "Algy" Gehrs was one of South Australia's best batsman in the years immediately before World War I. Born in 1880, he was an aggressive batsman in first-class cricket for nearly 18 years from 1902, accumulating 2,168 runs in 34 Shield matches (average 35.54). His record was sufficient to win him six Test caps, one against Warner's team of 1903–04, another in England in 1905, and the remainder against the first South African team to visit Australia, in 1910–11.

His Test record is not imposing — 221 runs at a little over 20, highest score 67 — figures that do not do his ability justice. He was a tall man, but powerfully built. Johnnie Moyes remembered him as "an attractive right-hander, whose hooking was his chief glory, for he could play it superbly against any type of bowler, and more than once thrashed Cotter unmercifully, bat exploding on the ball time and time again as Gehrs careered on to a century. He was a sheer delight to watch, for had he strokes, power (and) audacity."

Gehrs scored seven Shield hundreds, and topped the South Australian averages three times. In February, 1906, against Western Australia, he became the first man from his state to reach a century in each innings of a first-class match, scoring 148 not out, opening up, in the first innings, and 100 not out in the second. And yet, for all this, he is best remembered for one extraordinary Shield century — a blazing unbeaten 100 against Victoria at the Adelaide Oval on Melbourne Cup day, 1910.

It was a century scored in the fashion of Trumper, something only a Bradman, or a McCabe, or perhaps a Doug Walters could have emulated. And it ended with a Walters flourish — a mighty six into the Members' Pavilion with one run needed for victory, and six needed for the hitter's hundred.

The match was the opening fixture of the 1910–11 Shield season. South Australia were the reigning champions, captained by Clem Hill and containing Australia's then leading fast bowler, Bill Whitty, and the superb English all-rounder Jack Crawford. Victoria, winners in 1907–08 but victors in only two Shield matches since, were an inexperienced lot, a side reliant on the many skills of Warwick Armstrong, the courage of opening bat Tom Warne, the runs of the left-handed Vernon Ransford, and the medium-paced guile of the Test player, Gerry Hazlitt.

The match began in sensational fashion on Saturday, October 29, after the scheduled first day had been washed out. Clem Hill won a crucial toss, and sent the visitors in. Disaster struck the Victorians at once. Whitty's loosener spat over Warne's head, the second hit somewhere near the bat handle and spooned to Crawford in the slips cordon.

Batting was not possible, survival almost as difficult, especially against as dangerous a weapon as Bill

*The Australian team that toured England in 1905. Back row (left to right): A. Gehrs, W. Howell, W. Armstrong, A. Hopkins, A. Cotter, J. Kelly; Centre: V. Trumper, C. Hill, J. Darling (capt), M.A. Noble, C. McLeod, F. Laver; In front: R. Duff, P. Newland, S. Gregory.*

Whitty. Following a no ball, Ransford managed three to the vacant outfield, but was then absurdly run out, still looking for traction after his partner, Dave Smith, had called for a desperate single to short mid-off. Victoria 2–4, and Crawford had not bowled a ball.

There was no recovery until Armstrong and Hazlitt came together at 7–27. Armstrong had entered after the Ransford debacle, and struggled while his team-mates succumbed. Had Hazlitt been caught off either of the first two balls he faced, as he should have been, Armstrong's bruises would probably have been wasted, but the two fashioned a 51–run stand that was not broken until the first ball after lunch. The innings ended at a more than respectable 111, Crawford had five wickets, Whitty four.

Hill sought the heavy roller, and turned his batting order around, hoping to keep his best until after the Sunday rest day. The makeshift openers, keeper Gordon Campbell and all-rounder Bill Hewer, lasted half an hour, before the former popped up Laver to silly mid-on. Whitty, usually 10 or 11, batted at three, but grim defence was beyond him, and a desperate slog was caught in the outfield.

At a worrying 4–38 a defiant captain Clem came in himself, and changed the mood. After a watchful start he swung into Hazlitt, hitting him for 4–4–3, more runs than the Victorian had conceded in his open- ing ten overs. Yet the wicket was still stormy, and captain Peter McAlister called on his two experienced men, Armstrong and the crafty Frank Laver, to slow the tide. It was the right move, and two wickets fell for nought, including Hill to great celebration by the fieldsman, unluckily bowled by Armstrong via the inside edge and the back pad.

At stumps South Australia were 8–135, thanks to Hill's bravado and a stand of 51 between Crawford and William Chamberlain in the hour before stumps. The latter's dismissal was disappointing, stumped as the sun was setting, and then the suicide was compounded when Albert Wright was caught in the deep from what proved to be the day's final delivery. The meagre crowd lamented the fate of Crawford, all but stranded on 31. Much depended on he and Algy Gehrs.

Gehrs had not batted on the first afternoon because of influenza. In fact some had questioned whether he should have played at all. Still off colour but alert enough, he smashed 36 in even time when play resumed. On the Saturday night the Victorians had crowded the pitch, now they lined the boundary, and Gehrs and Crawford helped themselves to runs that were only dreams two days before. Crawford finished 79 not out, having been part of three crucial late-wicket stands. The South Australian lead was 109.

Jack Crawford had first come to Australia in 1907–08, with A.O. Jones touring English team, when he topped the Test bowling averages. Two years later, after a dispute with his county Surrey, he returned to Australia to take up a position at the St Peter's College in Adelaide. It was more than a co-incidence that in his first Shield season South Australia won the trophy for the first time since 1893–94.

He remained in Australia until 1914, taking wickets and scoring runs until he left for a coaching job in New Zealand. He was a tireless, attacking medium pacer, and when batting he struck the ball with murderous power. Perhaps his finest performance in Australia came in March 1913, when he scored 163 and took 8–66 in one match against Victoria. On a tour of New Zealand in 1914 Crawford and Victor Trumper added 298 in a remarkable nine minutes more than an hour, Crawford's contribution to the innings was an amazing 354, which included 14 sixes and 45 fours. His name is a significant one in the annals of Australian cricket, the first genuine and effective import in the history of the Sheffield Shield.

The Victorians bravely played their way back into the game on the Monday afternoon, and at stumps were well placed at 4–250. The recovery was largely due to a dynamic even-time 96 by the opener Smith and a patient 71 by an unwell Ransford. Smith had lost his century in controversial circumstances, the umpire responding to a token caught-behind appeal by Campbell behind the stumps. Smith didn't think it was out, and let everyone in the pavilion know. Ransford was also unlucky, bowled off his shoulder as he tried to avoid the last ball of the day, a bouncer from Crawford. The contrast in the wicket from the perils of Saturday was best reflected in Hill's decision to open the second innings with Whitty and the leg-spinner Wright.

In the press the next morning it was reported that the South Africans, who had arrived in Adelaide the previous week, had practiced enthusiastically at the Adelaide University. The most impressive net bowler had not been one of the tourists, but the remarkable 51-year-old George Giffen, who had perservered, without a break, for the entire two-hour session. On the third day of the Shield match, the South Australians played in the spirit of Giffen, firstly bowling the Victorians out for 305, and then racing to a spectacular victory.

The crowd on this third day was meagre, one of the smallest Shield crowds on record. Perhaps the Cup in Melbourne held more interest. Whatever, those fortunate few who did attend saw one of the Shield's most aggressive innings. Gehrs came to the crease at 3–50, after Armstrong had bowled both openers and Crawford. Clem Hill was cautious, looking in the main for singles, as the Victorians pressed, just one breakthrough away from a clear advantage.

Armstrong was at his most devious, bowling, as he had to Gehrs and Crawford in the first innings, with eight on the offside. But Gehrs was brutal from the start, and raced to 30 in even time. Hill was still wary, taking an hour to reach 30, and 95 minutes to get to 50, but once the South Australian total reached 100, the Victorians lost heart, and the once-even contest became a slaughter.

Gehrs had got within one of Hill's score in the thirties, but from that point he could not overtake his captain until he reached 69 to Clem's 68. In one over Gehrs took Laver for 14, to go to 77. The running between wickets was superb, a feature noted in all reports the next day. In fact Hill scored only three fours, but 28 singles, a cricket lesson for the few spectators watching. McAlister, having lost hope, gave Arthur Kenny an over, and Hill drove the first ball to Warne at mid-on, who dropped it. But the miss scarcely mattered, as Hill was bowled off stump swinging blithely in the same over.

Chamberlain came out with South Australia needing 20, and Gehrs on 78. The new batsman quickly scored three to his partner's two. The first four balls of Kenny's second over went scoreless, then Gehrs hit a four to the square leg boundary. To cheers from the outer, the last ball went way over Ransford at midwicket, and into the members' pavilion, the first six of the match. Gehrs was now 88. Chamberlain dutifully played out a maiden from Warne, setting up Gehrs to face Kenny, with South Australia just seven from victory.

The fairytale took only two balls. A mighty heave put Kenny's first ball to the rope at straight hit. It was almost six, and almost caught — by the leaping Smith, as the spectators held their collective breath and then madly cheered the four that levelled the scores.

The cricket correspondent for the Adelaide daily newspaper, *The Register* described what followed:

"'Hit another six,' piped the inevitable small boy. The cry became a chorus. 'I wonder whether Kenny will chuck him up one to have a go at?' asked an old stager, to whom the wish was father to the thought. He did not. The ball was short. Long or short made no difference to Gehrs. At that moment he was inspired. It was neck or nothing — six and a hundred against his wicket. Ajax defying the lightning was a mere circumstance to this young athlete defying the impossible. He lunged as far as he could, swung with all the strength he possessed for a shot to square leg for six."

The ball's landing created pandemonium among the members. The *Advertiser*, which in one column had estimated the crowd at just 100, in an editorial described the applause as "intense" and continued, "seldom has such an ovation been accorded a batsman." The *Register* thought the crowd more about 300, but wrote: "They made enough noise for 3000." It was all that Gehrs deserved. He had batted for just 93 minutes, and scored the game's only century.

Interestingly, and reflecting the excitement Gehrs generated, the papers the next day could not agree as to how the match ended. At least one writer clearly let the situation get the better of him. The *Advertiser* thought the match ended with two sixes in a row. Reports in the two Melbourne papers, the *Age* and the *Argus* were similarly confused. In Sydney, *The Referee* correctly agreed with the match finish described in the *Register:* Gehrs had hit two mighty sixes, but not off consecutive balls.

The South Africans unfortunately missed all the excitement, having gone to Melbourne to see the imported horse Comedy King edge out the favourite Trafalgar in the Cup. The following weekend they brought Gehrs back to reality in the opening first-class match of their tour. The wrong-uns and top spinners of Reggie Schwarz were implausible, and Gehrs struggled embarrassingly to make a single. But this was a minor hiccup in an otherwise successful season, and a defiant 60 in the second innings, and two more half-centuries in the Test series, redressed the balance.

Algy Gehrs played his last Sheffield Shield match in 1920, scoring 0 and 43 (batting three) against a Victorian attack led by Armstrong, Jack Ryder and Bert Ironmonger. He had captained his state in the 1919–20 season, but dropped out after that match against Victoria to provide an opportunity for a younger man. He was later an Australian selector. He died in 1953, little remembered by those who rely on Test match statistics, but a memorable figure in South Australian and Sheffield Shield history, if only for one remarkable afternoon of action in November, 1910.

# 16

## VICTOR TRUMPER

If Victor Trumper is judged purely on the number of runs he scored, he would be rated a fine batsman, a worthy contemporary of Hill, Noble, Armstrong, Duff, Macartney, Ransford and Mackay. Consider these Shield career averages:

| Batsman | Matches | Runs | Average |
| --- | --- | --- | --- |
| M.A. Noble | 51 | 4896 | 68.00 |
| J.R.M. Mackay | 9 | 727 | 55.92 |
| C. Hill | 68 | 6274 | 52.28 |
| W.W. Armstrong | 59 | 4997 | 50.47 |
| R.A. Duff | 26 | 2149 | 49.98 |
| V.T. Trumper | 46 | 3627 | 48.36 |
| C.G. Macartney | 43 | 2443 | 42.12 |
| V.S. Ransford | 49 | 3061 | 39.24 |

And yet, in the opinions of those who saw him, Trumper was the greatest batsman of his time. Perhaps of any time.

A.G. Moyes wrote of Trumper: "I was privileged to play against him in Sheffield Shield matches, to field on the fence or in the slips and be amazed at his artistry. It made one wonder whether he was playing with Esmeralda second and Oweenee third. Wren was close up. So far there are six boats which have scored points—Lina and Romp, 3 each; Rainbow and Esmeralda, 2 each; Florrie and Oweenee, 1 each. Mr. J. Fogg will give a trophy for the final race, which will be sailed March 21.

Lane Cove Club's 14-foot Championship was won by the Ariel from Effort. Marjorie and Nell also started. Ariel won by 4 1-2 minutes.

Sydney Canoe Club Class A Championship was won easily by Ernie, sailed by H. Messenger. The only other starter was Salonara, which was overdone with sail.

St. George Club 14-foot Championship was won by Maggie, with Euchre second and Edith third.

At Auckland last month the 36-rater Rainbow easily beat the 40-ton Volunteer, which won the Hundred Years Cup given by the New South Wales Government to mark the centenary of this State. The Rainbow has raced successfully in Sydney, but is probably not any more than a match for the Bona, our crack. It would be interesting to see a race between the champion Era and the Bona, good representatives of two distinct classes of racing yachts.

## Inter-State Cricket Match.

### NEW SOUTH WALES v. SOUTH AUSTRALIA.
#### BY SHORTSLIP.

The first of this season's Sheffield Shield matches was played in the middle of December, and was between New South Wales and South Australia at Adelaide. That contest was remarkable for an excellent partnership for the second wicket by Duff (94) and Noble (108), for Noble's 160 for once out, and Mackenzie's 77 amongst the New South Wales batsmen; 48 and 28 by Hack, and 40 by Reedman in the South Australian team. The bowlers who were prominent on that occasion were Kirkwood, Claxton, Jones, and Travers—the lastmentioned taking five for 54 in New South Wales's second venture—for the home team, and Howell, Noble, and Pye for the visitors. In that match New South Wales won at all points of the game.

The representatives of the mother State then travelled back to Melbourne, and there again New South Wales outplayed her opponents, this time by 136 runs. This was a peculiar contest, inasmuch as the wicket was said to be good although, yet success in the batting was limited.

V. TRUMPER AND R. A. DUFF.
Holders of the Australian First Wicket Record— 298 runs.

The world's record is 554, by J. T. Brown and J. Tunnicliffe, for Yorkshire v. Derbyshire, in 1898. The latter lost his wicket at 243, and his companion knocked his wicket down when he had obtained 300. The record for a first-class match in Australia is held by MacLaren and Hayward, for MacLaren's team v. New South Wales. The 298 by Trumper and Duff is, however, a record by Australian batsmen. The record in inter-state matches prior to Saturday was held by Darling and Lyons, 184, for South Australia v. Victoria.

There were three out for 130 of New South Wales, seven for 140, and all out for 198. R. A. Duff, who was the first man in with Trumper, was the last out. Duff followed up his 102 with 66, but the only other contribution in the second venture worth talking about was Noble's 60. The Victorians considered they were fortunate in getting the New South Wales side out for under 200, when there were 100 up without a wicket, but when they went in they found it just as difficult to get runs as the majority of the visitors had before them. They failed even to get the 100. In the 93 there were no more than three doubles. Graham 35,

Armstrong 22, and 10 from Noonan. The match closed on the second day at an interesting stage. Victoria had to get 318 to win, and they started with 57 for no wicket. Strange to say the South Australians had 57 up without loss when they had 375 to win, and they also lost. Both teams showed an improvement in their second innings, but Victoria had too much ground to make up, and was defeated, as before stated, by 136. Howell took nine wickets for 52 runs.

The third engagement of the series was the meeting of Victoria and South Australia at Melbourne on the first of the year, and this was sen-

sational for the last wicket record—211—in Australia by Ellis (118) and Hastings (106). Hill played a fine innings for 124, and with the assistance from the colts of the team the innings produced the fair total of 317, which was, however, too few by 155. In England South Australia would, perhaps, have followed on. In the Sheffield Shield matches the amount of arrears necessary to a follow-on is 200 runs. This heavy scoring was surprising after the small returns of the New South Wales-Victoria contest. There was, however, a falling-off in the second innings, the scores being—Victoria, 164; South Australia, 149. The best bowling performance for the whole match was Armstrong's four for 20 in the second effort of South Australia.

The play of the first half of the six engagements for the Sheffield Shield pointed strong'y in favour of New South Wales retaining possession of the shield for this season, though there is still plenty of time for Victoria to upset the calculations of the people this side of the Murray. Each State plays four matches. New South Wales have State plays four matches. New South Wales have won two to date, Victoria has won one and lost one, and South Australia has experienced two defeats.

The South Australian selectors have this season given their colts an excellent show. The retirement of Mackenzie from behind the wicket made way for Thamm and Newland, the latter being chosen for the eastern trip. The other colts are Claxton, Gehrs, Jennings, Waters, and Hewer, whilst Kirkwood, though he has been over here before, can scarcely be reckoned much more than a colt.

In the Melbourne match the young blood played up very well, but at Sydney they created a good deal of genuine surprise. Of the 412 which the first innings produced the colts accounted for 263, and there was not a great deal of encouragement in looking at the score on the board when the first of the batch, Claxton, took his place at the wicket.

The Submarine Yacht Club does not exist yet, but it will soon. An enterprising millionaire has placed an order with a firm of shipbuilders for a submarine yacht, and it is to be expected that other rich men will presently follow the example.

THE PLAY ON SATURDAY.
Duff and Trumper at the wickets; South Australians in the field. Trumper is seen making one of his favourite drives. This brilliant batsman made 178.

A. Gehrs.   R. Waters.   C. Jennings.   N. Claxton.   P. M. Newland.
NEW PLAYERS IN INTER-STATE MATCHES.

# INTER-STATE CRICKET : NEW SOUTH WALES v. SOUTH AUSTRALIA.
### SYDNEY CRICKET GROUND, JANUARY 10, 1903.

the same game or whether it was something he had made up for himself — some variation of cricket."

M.A. Noble recalled: "Every stroke he made seemed to be absolutely correct and he was always in the best position to make it. Even when he changed his mind, which he often did, he was invariably in position and the stroke seemed the only possible one to make."

Warwick Armstrong: "He could hit as quick as lightning all round the wicket, appearing to favour no particular hit, yet one could never place a man against him to stop his onslaught. Wherever the ball was pitched it was hit away for runs."

Clem Hill compared himself unfavourably to Trumper: "I wasn't fit to lick Vic's boots." Noble contended that Trumper changed cricket. In a famous essay in his book *The Game's the Thing* he argued that before Trumper cricket in Australia was being slowly suffocated by a passion for orthodoxy and safety first. Trumper changed all that through an approach to cricket that should have been foolhardy, but because of his genius, instead put him on a pedestal far above his team-mates.

"How Victor's wonderful demonstrations shocked old ideas and brought light out of semi-darkness is well known, particularly in Australia," Noble wrote. "With his coming the old order passed for ever."

Another Sydney grade cricketer of the time, Billy Fletcher, who later played first-class cricket for Queensland, recalled in 1935 the impact of Trumper:

"Everywhere you went, and in every club, young batsmen were standing up to the bowling and pelting it in glorious style, with the most brilliant strokes on either side of the wicket. Trumper exercised a wonderful influence on Sydney batting. In his period it became the most brilliant I have ever known."

Trumper was a free spirited opening batsman, who inevitably tried to hit the newest ball for four if the line or length deserved it. This attitude often brought glory, but sometimes a hasty demise and a subsequent demerit by the keeper of the batting averages. If his statistics are a relic of his style of cricket, so too is his status in cricket history.

As a child Trumper was a cricket fanatic. His early years were spent in the Sydney suburb of Surry Hills, just an off-drive from the SCG. His father, Charles, in an interview in 1913, recalled: "He would practice assiduously in our backyard for hours every day and when I saw to what extent he was taken up with the game I decided to encourage him in every possible way I could. Early every morning I would accompany him to Moore Park where I would assist him in his practice. We would remain there from 6 to 8am, and only knock off then on account of the fact that I had to prepare to go to my business and Victor to his school."

Victor Trumper made his Shield debut as a 17-year-old, in January 1895, scoring 11 and 0 against South Australia in Adelaide. Coincidentally, he scored 0 and 11 on his Test debut four and a half years later. He was relegated to 12th man for the next Shield game, the home match against Victoria, in which Monty Noble made his Shield debut, and was left out altogether for the final game of the season, the return match with South Australia.

He did not play Shield cricket again until January 1898, when he scored 48 and 13 in Adelaide. His first Shield fifty, a careful 68, came in the return game, and he finished the season with 163 runs from six innings. He scored another 68 against South Australia in NSW's first match in 1898–99, but failed to get past 23 in his remaining six Shield innings of that season. His last-minute selection in the Australian side to tour England at the end of the season owed much to a series of big scores in local club cricket, spectacular double centuries against Tasmania and a New Zealand XI, and also to the canny judgement of the Australian selectors, Joe Darling, Hugh Trumble and Syd Gregory.

The tour made Trumper (he scored over 1500 first-class runs, including a glorious 300 not out against Sussex), and he never had to worry about his Shield place again. In the summer of 1899–1900 he topped the first-class averages, and scored his first Shield century, 165 against George Giffen, who took 8–287 in NSW's only innings, and the other seven South Australian bowlers, who grabbed one wicket between them.

From January 1898 until January 1902 he did not miss a NSW Shield match. That run came to end when officials refused to delay the start of the opening day of the NSW-Victoria match in Sydney to allow the Test players to return from Adelaide, where the third Test had just been completed. This was the only NSW Shield match without Trumper until December 1904, when he refused to leave his newly opened sports store for the Christmas tour to the southern states. From 1898 to 1904 he played some famous innings, including a fighting 230 against Victoria in 1901, and successive centuries in 1903 against South Australia and Victoria — sharing in opening stands of 298 and 267 with his usual partner, the rugged and exciting Reggie Duff.

Trumper returned for NSW's home matches in 1904–5, and at the end of that season was selected for his third tour of England. He was clearly the megastar of cricket in Australia, a magnet and hero for crowds throughout the country, and the symbol of all that was good about this golden age of Australian cricket.

But what of Trumper the man. His team-mates seem united in their glorification of him. Clearly he was generous to a fault. Clarrie Grimmett remembered buying a cricket shirt at Trumper's sports store and Trumper refusing to accept payment. Noble claimed that Trumper would not go into the sporting goods business in competition with the NSW and Australian batsman Syd Gregory, fearing Gregory's profits may suffer. Only when Gregory took his career elsewhere, did Trumper establish his own store. He was a humble and remarkable sportsman, aware of his great ability, but aware too, of his fallibility and the unpredictable nature of the game he played.

Unfortunately, Trumper was as poor at business as he was superb with the bat. His sports stores failed, and when a testimonial was awarded to him in 1913, the funds were placed in a trust rather than presented to him, organisers fearful he might find a cause more worthy than himself. After leaving school, he had worked as a school teacher, then in the public service, before venturing into the sports goods trade. His major source of income were his cricket adventures in England. In a 1914 court hearing, over a dispute involving the organisation of his testimonial, it was stated that Trumper was "supposed to have made 2980 pounds out of his cricket tours."

Trumper's involvement with the formation of the NSW Rugby League in 1907 has been well documented. He was a much quoted spokesman, and the League's first treasurer. His motivation in this new venture appears to be twofold. A schoolboy footballer of some quality, he had a genuine compassion with working class footballers manacled by the strict amateur interpretations of the ruling Rugby Union. But also, Trumper, and his entrepreneurial associate, the NSWRL secretary (and former first-class cricket umpire) James Giltinan, saw in professional football a way of making big money out of an England tour in the way past cricket tours had generated huge sums. Almost before the NSWRL was formed, Giltinan and Trumper were talking of an English trip. Trumper, in 1899, 1902 and 1905 had seen how money could be made. If cricketers could bring in the bounty, why not footballers as well?

An Australian league team went to England in 1908, but the tour was a financial nightmare. In March 1909, Trumper lost his treasurer's job, sacked because of a secret fund he and Giltinan had been keeping. It appeared treasurer and secretary had decided exactly which was the best way of using the League's funds, and didn't want other committeemen hindering their strategy. This saga provides an insight into Trumper's character, as does a recollection of M.A. Noble's:

"Victor was a law unto himself. You could talk to him and coach him; he would listen carefully, respect your advice and opinions, and, leaving you, would forget all you had told him, play as he wanted to play, and thereby prove that, although you might be right, he knew a better method."

Because Trumper was never motivated by his own needs, always thinking and acting on behalf of the less gifted or the less fortunate, he found it impossible to accept the alternative views of people or administrations he saw as less charitable. Trumper was in constant dispute with the NSWCA from 1906 until 1910, clearly disapproving of attempts to take control of big cricket from the players. In February 1907 he was quoted in the *Australian Star*: "I revel in cricket, but it is too much to put up with the continued insults from a body (the NSWCA) which is largely influenced by men who represent nobody but themselves."

In 1940, Arthur Mailey gave an insight into the administrators' attitude towards the great batsman: "My advisers at the time told me that Victor Trumper was temperamental, obstinate and difficult to manage. I came into cricket when the glorious Victor was going out and only got a glimpse of his great character. He was one of the most generous and clean-thinking cricketers I ever met. He had a good word for everyone and was always silent when his so-called enemies were under discussion."

Philip Derriman, in his superb book *True to the Blue*, documents Trumper's apparent unwillingness to become involved in Shield cricket between 1904–05 and 1909–10. In these years he played only seven of NSW's 23 Shield matches, an extraordinary record for the country's finest batsman. Derriman suggests Shield cricket had lost the great man's interest, an attitude perhaps due to his bitter relationship with the NSWCA.

Following the retirement of Noble in 1909, Austin Diamond was appointed, in preference to Trumper, as NSW captain — a not illogical decision by the NSWCA considering Trumper's continued absences. Trumper responded by withdrawing from the side once again, and publicly denouncing Diamond's appointment in the press, complaining that had the players rather than the Association chosen the captain (as had always been the practice in the past) he would have been leader. South Australia won the Shield that year, with the Trumperless NSW winning only their two matches against the struggling Victoria. The following season the NSWCA relented. Trumper was given the skipper's job, and, after a difficult start, led NSW to their 11th Shield success. His appointment as leader was a watershed in his relationship with the NSWCA, and in July 1911, he appeared at the NSWCA annual meeting as a club delegate for the first time.

# Thrilling Batting Achievements.

TRUMPER CUTTING A BALL TO THE BOUNDARY.
The batsman was in brilliant form and scored 201 (not out), in 200 minutes.

WHEN 40, TRUMPER ON-DROVE CRAWFORD FOR A SINGLE,
REACHING 50 IN 58 MINUTES.
His century was obtained in two hours.

NEW SOUTH WALES CRICKET TEAM.

Back Row (Reading Left to Right) : H. L. Collins, R. J. A. Massie, S. Moore, J. B. Lane.
Sitting : C. G. Macartney, W. Bardsley, V. T. Trumper (Captain), C. Kelleway, R. B. Minnett.
On Ground : W. J. Stack, E. P. Barbour, D. Cullen.

SOUTH AUSTRALIAN CRICKET TEAM,

Back Row (Reading Left to Right) : G. C. Campbell, A. G. Moyes, N. F. Claxton (Manager), H.
  Bridgeman, E. R. Mayne.
Second Row : W. J. Whitty, D. R. A. Gehrs, C. Hill (Captain), J. N. Crawford, L. W.
  Chamberlain.
On ground : L. Waye, H. J. McKay, D. M. Steel.

MACARTNEY CUTTING GEHRS FOR A SINGLE IN THE FIRST INNINGS OF N.S.W., WHICH CLOSED FOR 513. THIS STROKE GAVE HIM HIS CENTURY IN 102 MINUTES.
HIS TOTAL SCORE WAS 125.

Trumper remained NSW captain until 1914. He was heavily involved in the infamous 1912 dispute with the Board of Control, which led to him, and five of his most celebrated colleagues, declining a tour to England. But this did not hinder his links with his state association, and he continued to attend NSWCA meetings until October 1914. His absence from this date was a result of a sudden, severe decline in his health.

Trumper had contracted scarlet faver in late 1908, an illness which at the time fuelled conjecture about the champion batsman's future in the game. He recovered to make the 1909 tour of England, but his friends believed the sickness permanently damaged his health. In November 1914, he developed the symptoms of the kidney disease that was to claim his life.

Trumper had been confirmed as the NSW captain for the 1914–15 season, but could not play, owing to his poor health. Even without their leader, NSW almost won the Shield, losing out narrowly on averages to Warwick Armstrong's rejuvenated Victorians. Trumper remained a selector, and was occasionally sighted at State practice, but he was too weak to play grade cricket and gradually slipped from the public eye.

Grave concerns were published in the Sydney press in early June 1915 as to his continued ill-health, but even so the announcement of his death on June 28 came as a great shock to a public conditioned by the tragedy of the War in Europe. His funeral attracted many of Sydney's prominent sporting and political figures, and his pall bearers were his Test cricketing colleagues, Bardsley, Cotter, Gregory, Hordern, Iredale, Kelleway, Macartney, O'Connor, Noble and Turner.

The tributes were many, and heartfelt. *Wisden* called him the best, most brilliant and most popular Australian cricketer. Hugh Trumble described him as, "the finest batsman that ever lived." In *The Referee* J.C Davis wrote:

"Boys such as Victor Trumper in cricket, Harry Searle in sculling, Barney Kieran in swimming, and SA Spragg in rugby union football, are little less than freaks, and it is wonderful that such a small nation, in the population sense, has turned out such prodigies. Alas, all have gone early, three at the zenith of their careers, and Trumper while still young and able enough to have represented Australia again if health and strength had been left to him. Those whom the gods love die young."

# BETWEEN
# THE
# WARS

# Introduction by Alan McGilvray

**B**ack in 1933, when I took my first tentative steps on to the Melbourne Cricket Ground, Sheffield Shield cricket was a wonderful thing to behold.

The Shield still plays a fundamentally important role in maintaining first-class standards and producing first-class cricketers.

But 100 years have knocked off some of the gilt in terms of public appeal and following, and that's a pity. Inevitable, perhaps, in a world that is offering more diversions all the time, but a pity nevertheless.

As I cast my mind back to my first experiences of Sheffield Shield cricket — and my first recollections would go back 70 years — it was a very different time, and a very different game.

A Shield tour was an event. There were long, overnight hauls in the old steam trains, and the games would attract crowds that these days are reserved for the very best of the international fare.

Of course there was not much else to command their attention. International tours were fairly rare, and the domestic competition was a centrepiece of the season's activity. All the great players were on hand, and the competition was as brisk as anything that is served up these days in the international sphere.

The atmosphere was competitive yet respectful. It was a very mature game in those days, with a rigid code of ethics that nobody dreamed of breaking. It was a game from which great friendships grew, and in which great men were seen to their very best advantage.

I suppose it is fair to say I had a dream debut. I went out to bat for the first time in a Shield match in Melbourne in company with Don Bradman. I stayed with him for the best part of a session, and left, bowled by Chuck Fleetwood-Smith, with 11 grand runs against my name. Bradman continued to 187 not out.

But to bat with him in front of 30,000 people well, that was really something. I bowled to Bill Woodfull and Bill Ponsford in my first over, and though I was fairly shaking with nerves, I almost had both of them. I finished with 0–65, but it didn't seem to matter, for I was pleased enough just to be on the same ground.

Perhaps memories grow fonder with time, but when I look back on those days my most vivid memories, apart from the sheer class of the players through that golden period, was the attitude that prevailed.

I can remember, as I continually played and missed at the Victorian opening bowler Hans Ebeling, kind words from their skipper Bill Woodfull, who offered advice as to where I should place my feet, and how I should settle.

There was a great camaraderie between the teams.

On one occasion I was bowling in Adelaide to "Slinger" Nitschke, a big hitter who played a couple of Tests, and was renowned for his ability to take an attack apart. Vic Richardson was at the other end.

As Slinger cautiously played back the first couple of balls, Vic admonished him.

"Hey Slinger, this bloke can't bowl," he said disparagingly. Slinger proceeded to thrash the next four deliveries for six.

"You're right Yorkie, he came back. He can't bowl."

A modern player, it seems to me, might react to that sort of banter with some volatility. Vic Richardson became one of my finest friends, and I used to visit Slinger in Adelaide on many of my visits there, a long time after our own cricket was a fading memory.

But that was the way it was. Hard, competitive, fair and full of respect for team-mate and opponent alike. It was a grand era in which to play.

The quality of the players, of course, was something special in the era between the wars, there was a purity to the game which decreed that strokeplay was essential.

It seems strange, I suppose, to applaud the fact that players in those days made hitting the ball their first priority, rather than some of the defensive nudging we too often see today. Spinners were very much more predominant than they are today, and were prepared to take a few risks to "buy" their wickets. It made for a brand of cricket that produced lots of runs, and lots of action.

Spinners were of a quality unsurpassed, I am convinced, in all the years since. Clarrie Grimmett, who still hauled in vast numbers of wickets for South Australia beyond his 50th birthday, and the great Bill O'Reilly were paramount.

Together they were a lethal pairing, and they bowled their overs sufficiently quickly to make the 90-overs a day considered fair in modern Test matches absolutely laughable.

O'Reilly also was an example in courage for any bowler. His competitive streak would have him bowling for interminable stretches in search of wickets, even when his feet were bruised and blistered and his socks soaked with blood.

The batsmen were wonderful artists. Stan McCabe had a fluency that could be breathtaking at times, and the inimitable Bradman almost defies description.

There was surely something unique in the Bradman anatomy that allowed eyes, hands, feet and mind to co-ordinate with such blinding speed and awesome power.

In many years since those days, in my role as broadcaster, I have seen some mighty cricket in Sheffield Shield competition.

The Sheffield Shield has been a wonderful servant of Australian cricket, producing players of a consistently high standard, tuned to the needs of the innings building and working for wickets that is the preserve of the first-class scene. Our Test cricket has thrived because of it, and will continue to do so.

But of all the Shield days that I have experienced, my fondest memories remain those of my own involvement, when I was privileged to play under the immaculate Alan Kippax, and later to captain a New South Wales team of rare skill.

I always felt a little unworthy to share a field with some of the great men of that day. But I was very glad to have the friendship of so many of them, and to have been involved in a competition which ultimately shaped my life.

*The doyen of Australian cricket broadcasters, and a former NSW captain, Alan McGilvray.*

# 17

# END OF THE SHIELD?

It had been decided soon after the First World War concluded that it would be inappropriate for the Sheffield Shield to be played for in 1918–19, as many of Australia's finest cricketers would still be overseas. Interstate matches would resume in 1918–19, as organised by the individual state associations, and it was presumed the Shield competition would recommence in 1919–20.

Plans for 1918–19 were still in the embryonic stage when a Board of Control meeting was held in Sydney on December 6, 1918. The following evening, delegates from NSW, Victoria and South Australia met to discuss the future of interstate cricket.

Reports of that meeting were brief, but the ramifications hit the cricket world like a bombshell. *The Sydney Morning Herald"*, wrote:

"...It was also decided to recommend to the associations that commencing with 1919–20 the Sheffield Shield should be played for for three years, and that the state with the best record for that period should become the sole possessor of the trophy. It was further recommended that no Sheffield Shield medals should be awarded in the future."

The recommendation, which amounted to a decision to end the Sheffield Shield competition, was not popular, especially with former players and established cricket writers.

J.C. Davis of the *Sydney Referee* was appalled. "Apparently the idea is to get rid of the Shield at any price," he fumed. "The competition for the Sheffield Shield has done a tremendous lot of good for Australian cricket, for at the time the 100 guineas donation was made by the late Lord Sheffield interstate cricket was at a very low ebb in public opinion...I hold that the Sheffield Shield should be perpetuated; but if it must go, a better method of determining how it shall be won should be devised...South Australian cricket has been benefitted by the Sheffield Shield competition. Prior to its origination, New South Wales and South Australia had played only three interstate matches, but from 1892 on — save in two cases — these states have played home-and-home matches unbrokenly. If there had been no Sheffield Shield, this record, I believe, would have been somewhat different. And if the shield be passed out, it may be different in the future, whenever a little lukewarmness is shown or a matter of finance obtrudes. The Associations concerned ought to reject the proposal with a view to hitting upon a better one or abandoning the idea."

The decision not to resume Shield competition in 1918–19 disappointed the South Australians, despite the fact that no A-Grade cricket had been played in Adelaide during the war. As debate raged during the next few months over the decision to terminate the Shield, it was clear the South Australians placed a much higher value on the competition than their counterparts in the eastern states.

Criticism of the move to end the Shield mounted. It should be pointed out that the decision was no more than a recommendation for the delegates to take back to their respective state associations. It required the concurrence of all three state associations for the Shield competition to end, a crucial factor as things turned out. In the Christmas edition of *The Referee* one former NSW cricketer was quoted as saying: "They evidently forget what we old chaps did against those tough fighters in flannels Victoria had in our day. They were a very hard side to beat. They fought to the death, and it took a darned fine side to beat them."

Another veteran commented: "There can't be much sentiment among the delegates now. Why, cricketers should never lose sight of what the Sheffield Shield stands for in Australian cricket — the renaissance of Australian cricket."

Why then did the delegates recommend that the Shield be discontinued?

At a VCA meeting on January 13, 1919, Ernest Bean, one of the Victorian delegates at the Sydney meeting which recommended that the Shield be terminated, told those assembled: "The other states were tired of it (the Shield), and when it was disposed of some other trophy, or different scheme, might be substituted."

Bean's statement that "the other states were tired of it" seemed a rather paltry and nonsensical reason for the decision made. After all, no Shield match had been played since early 1915. The real motivation appears hidden in the politics of cricket administration of that time. The fact that the shield was an initiative of the old, maligned Australasian Cricket Council may have been a motivator. Did the Board of

Control have visions of a grand new trophy bearing its stamp? Perhaps the NSW and Victorian associations did not like the concept of being obliged to play the South Australians twice every season, especially the requirement of making a usually less than profitable trip to Adelaide. (In fact some interstate matches, including the scheduled South Australia-Victoria match in Adelaide, were cancelled in 1918–19, but not owing to finances, but because of a Spanish Influenza outbreak which had reached Australia at this time.)

Jack Worrall, the *Australasian's* cricket columnist since the death of Tom Horan, was mystified. "As one who has played in many stirring contests under Sheffield Shield conditions," he wrote, "it is difficult for me to gauge the underlying reason why the competition for the honour of holding the shield and its accompanying medals should cease...It seems to me that the reasons publically given for dispensing with the shield are inadequate, especially in view of the fact that it is the intention of substituting some other trophy or scheme. Privately I have been told the chief reason actuating the various associations is that the trophy is considered too valuable for any association to take the risk in holding it for any given period. That reason alone does not justify the stand taken by the associations, as all of them will be willing to hold it permanently if finally won on the cricket field."

Worrall wrote of the "great deal of sentiment among the players who have had many a prolonged and strenous battle for the honours and the prizes," and finished his remarks with a stinging postscript for the cricket officials of the day: "I can't help reflecting that if many of our cricket legislators had participated in those contests, the Sheffield Shield competition would remain an honoured institution."

The December recommendation to end the competition was not relayed to the South Australian Cricket Association until a meeting held on February 18. It was here that the Shield won its reprieve. It was revealed that the recommendation to present the Shield to the state with the best record over the following three seasons had been a NSW initiative. The Victorians also wanted the shield killed off, but preferred that the trophy be won by the first state to win the Shield twice from 1919–20. South Australia's delegates wanted the competition to continue as it had, and that is the way the SACA voted.

The matter lulled over the off-season. In October 1919 a meeting took place in Melbourne between delegates from the three states to discuss the future of the Shield competition. The Victorian and NSW representatives came ready to bid the trophy goodbye. But the South Australians could not be swayed and, as the rules required unaminous support for any change, effectively determined that Shield matches would continue as before.

Mr B.V. Scrymgour, one of the South Australian delegates later commented on the meeting: "A pleasing feature was the decision to keep the Sheffield Shield contests going between New South Wales, Victoria and South Australia. The trophy incurs a certain amount of expense and unnecessary worry in assuring the safety of it, which they (the NSW and Victorian delegates) do not feel inclined to undertake, consequently they prefer the games to go on without any trophy being attached to them. This view is held by practically all the states, and though turned down by the cricket committee of the SA Association last season, it is almost certain to be adopted when brought forward again."

The matter was not brought forward again, perhaps fortunately for the future of the Sheffield Shield. It appears the South Australians had seen a hidden agenda in the NSW and Victorian efforts to end the Shield competition, but, if Mr Scrymgour is to be believed, were in late 1919, finally prepared to accept what seems, decades later, to be a quite ridiculous argument — that the trophy was too elaborate to be maintained.

The meeting subsequently ruled that the awarding of Shield medals to players would become a matter for the individual associations. The Victorians quickly announced they would continue to award medals to their players if they won the competition. Ironically the South Australians did not, deciding such awards were too expensive.

An interesting sidelight to the dispute over the future of the Shield, was a coincidental debate between Sydney and Melbourne over the starting times of interstate matches, and the matter of matches being played out to a finish. In 1919–20, matches began at 11am in Sydney, and midday in Melbourne and Adelaide.

In Melbourne, Jack Worrall thought the limiting of matches as being "un-Australian", and felt that starting games before noon was too taxing on players. "In extremely hot weather," he wrote, "the hours of 11 to 6 on consecutive days are too severe a test on the endurance of the players."

J.C. Davis did not agree. "First-class cricket in this country is not meant for physical weaklings," he wrote, suggesting that if a cricketer could not handle starting before 12 o'clock he was not fit enough. On the matter of playing matches to a finish he wrote on October 29, 1919:

"The play-to-a-finish rule in this country will eventually give way to curtailed matches, of either three or four days, with an earlier start each day. I have watched match after match in which the spirit of players has been dominated by the feeling that time was no object. The Associations of Australia interested in the Sheffield Shield, sooner or later, will have to make a definite restriction of a period for a match."

Davis was ahead of his time. In fact Sheffield Shield cricket was heading towards an era of huge individual and team totals. Time limits were still eight years away. The rungetting records of Giffen, Hill, Noble and company were about to be blown from the pages by exciting new champions such as Ponsford, Kippax and Bradman. All the Shield needed was a clean and polish that the administrators seemed reluctant to provide, and it would be ready for one of the great eras of Australian cricket.

# 18

# THE FIRST DRAW

Between the first Sheffield Shield match in December 1892 and the start of the 1920–21 season, 139 Shield matches were played, every one of them ending in an outright result. The first draw did not occur until the third match of 1920–21, and came about in controversial and acrimonious circumstances, with South Australian officials, players, former players and followers making it very clear they had little time for the treatment they had received from the officials of the NSW Cricket Association.

The South Australian team of the time were not a competitive side. After their 86-run defeat of Victoria in the final Shield match of the 1913–14 season, they did not win another match until January 1925, an exhausting, frustrating sequence of 27 matches.

Season 1920–21 was particularly dismal. In the first Shield match, Victoria piled up 639 runs in their only innings, Dr Roy Park and Jack Ryder flogging centuries and Vernon Ransford belting 93. A week later the touring Englishmen scored 5 (declared) for 512 in their one innings, and then in Melbourne, Victoria scored (only) 310 and then 724 in the match made famous by Warwick Armstrong's 157 not out and 245. In all, the South Australian bowlers conceded 4,688 runs in 1920–21, in just six matches, at an embarrassing average of 62.5 runs per wicket.

The worst of the carnage was in Sydney, where the scorebook told of NSW reaching 802 in their first (and only) innings. Warren Bardsley scored 235, captain Charlie Kelleway 168, and the dashing Sydney University opening bat, James Bogle, 103. For South Australia it was the ultimate in cricket futility. The Sheffield Shield, for a short period, had lost its sense of challenge.

The South Australians had fielded in a state of near exhaustion. Having dived for days at Armstrong's mighty drives, they were obliged to jump on the Sydney train, race from the station to the hotel to the SCG, and then, having inevitably lost the toss, bowl their blunted arrows at a lineup that included illustrious names such as Bardsley, Andrews, Taylor, Gregory, Kelleway, and "Stork" Hendry.

When it was clear in Melbourne that Armstrong's massive scoring would take the Victoria-South Australia match into a fifth day, Wednesday, December 1, the South Australian manager, Mr Eddie McCarron, had cabled the NSW Cricket Association, suggesting that the scheduled Friday start of the NSW-South Australia match be put back to Saturday. It was not possible, Mr McCarron had said, for his team to be in Sydney much before midday on the Friday, making play for that day illogical.

The NSWCA having received this cable, left a message at Albury station informing McCarron and his weary team that the Association would do no more than put the starting time back from 11.30 to 2 o'clock. For the NSW officials a better solution would have been for the last day of the Melbourne match to have had an earlier start, so that the South Australians could have jumped on an earlier train.

When the battle-weary South Australians finally arrived in Sydney, they again sought a 24-hour delay, but were again denied. Some of the visiting men made it clear they did not want to play, but their captain Donald Steele decided to keep faith with the few spectators at the ground. As it was, the game did not begin until 2.45pm, and by stumps NSW, having struggled early, were securely placed at 3 for 224. There were times late in the day when the South Australians were a pitiful sight, the bowling no more than a charade, and the fieldsmen wasting no opportunity to lie down and get some rest.

At around 8pm, McCarron received the following letter from the NSWCA secretary, Frank Iredale:

*I am directed to write and ask if you will kindly give me an explanation of the delay of your team in not arriving in time to commence the match between South Australia and New South Wales at the Sydney Cricket Ground at 2pm, the advertised time of starting. My committee is meeting tomorrow at the Sydney*

*Two leading figures in NSW cricket in the years after the first World War: Below: The intimidating all-rounder Jack Gregory. Right: The superb left-handed opening batsman, Warren Bardsley.*

*Cricket Ground, and I shall be glad to have your reply, so I may place your letter before them.*

McCarron's reply read:

*In reply to your inquiry as to the reasons of my team's delayed arrival at the Sydney Cricket Ground yesterday afternoon, I have to state that owing to our late arrival in Sydney we were unable to reach our hotel before 12.15. As you are aware, we had some trouble with our luggage, and as the team was more or less jaded and in need of baths and changes of linen, it took a little more time than usual in preparing for lunch. This, coupled with the time occupied in travelling to the ground per tram car, will account for the interval that elapsed between the time of our arrival in the city and taking the field at 2.45. Your committee timed the beginning of the match at 2 o'clock on the understanding that my team would arrive by the limited express, which reached Sydney an hour earlier than the train we travelled by. You will therefore see that the team were at least a quarter of an hour earlier, not withstanding the difficulties they were under.*

*I very much regret that your committee did not see the way clear to postpone the start of the match until Saturday, as requested by me by wire on Wednesday and Thursday, and thus obviate the necessity of your letter and this explanation.*

*I finally add that I am amazed at your letter, and very strongly protest against the treatment meted out to my players by your association.*

McCarron made sure both letters were seen by as many press representatives as possible. When asked by a *Sydney Morning Herald* writer what the players thought of the situation, he replied: "Think of it? Disgusted! To a man they will be glad when they change trains at Albury."

On the Saturday, NSW slaughtered the South Australian bowlers, and finished the day at 7–675. All reports commented on the vitality of the visitor's outcricket, but admitted that the bowling was hopelessly outgunned. The South Australian keeper, Legh Winser, was forced from the field with badly bruised hands in the afternoon, and the redoubtable Victor Richardson took over behind the stumps.

Winser was an extraordinary figure. Born in Cheshire in England, he was an exceptionally talented all-round sportsman, who not only kept wickets for South Australia in five Shield matches between 1913 and 1920, but was also a skilful enough golfer to win eight South Australian Amateur titles, and the Australia Amateur Championship in 1921. Jack Worrall thought Winser was a better keeper than Bert Oldfield in 1920, and the former NSW player, and later coach, George Garnsey, rated him "a wicketkeeper of Test-match calibre". Later Winser was private secretary to six successive South Australian governors. For a period before he died in 1983, aged 99, he was the oldest living Shield cricketer.

Sunday was the rest day, eagerly sought by the bowlers. Further respite came from a hefty thunderstorm, which flooded the square, making play on the Monday impossible. From Adelaide came a telegram from the SACA President, Mr Mostyn Evan, denouncing the NSWCA. In the Sydney papers, the stance of the NSWCA was deplored, one writer to the *Herald* trusting "that Mr McCarron and his team will not judge the whole of the local people by the poor sporting spirit of the association". Another correspondent wrote:

"By its lack of consideration the NSWCA has disgusted our South Australian friends and every lover of fair play; and infinitely worse, it has weakened the war forged bonds of a strong Australian sentiment. Mr Kelleway would have redeemed an unfortunate situation had he adopted the heroic expedient of sending the tired SA XI in to bat."

Play resumed on the Tuesday, and NSW reached 802, thanks to a brisk last wicket stand of 77 between Hendry and Arthur Mailey. For the leg-spinner Mailey this was just the beginning, and he confirmed his spot in the soon-to-be-announced Australian side during the afternoon by taking eight wickets, three of them stumped by another Test candidate, Oldfield. The batting, after a confident opening stand of 55 between "Nip" Pellew and Vic Richardson, lacked spirit, and Mailey had a field day as the batsman gave themselves away.

At stumps, the South Australians, following on, were 0–6. This is where the game ended. Persistent rain washed out the next two days play, and a request from Steele, acting for McCarron who was ill, on the Thursday that the game be abandoned was acceded to. It seemed some of the South Australians could not stay in Sydney beyond Saturday because of work commitments, and the weather had made it unlikely that a NSW victory would be achieved by then.

Therefore the match was drawn. There was much conjecture as to whether NSW should be awarded the match, and in some reports NSW were incorrectly declared the winners, it being suggested the South Australians had "retired' from the contest. Any controversy was avoided when NSW won their other three 1920–21 Shield matches, to take the competition without the need to go to averages or to debate on the ramifications of unfinished matches.

The South Australians returned to Adelaide to a warm and appreciative reception. McCarron told the greeting throng of the "miserable" action of the NSWCA, and claimed: "They invited me to dine with them at the Oval, but I replied that I preferred to lunch with my team." It seems the manager had won the respect of his players, if not the admiration of the NSWCA, by his actions in Sydney. One of the South Australian players called the NSWCA officals "narks", and it was revealed that the team had presented McCarron with a set of pipes to thank him for his attempts at standing up to the NSWCA administration.

There the matter ended. The game remained the only drawn Shield match until 1927–28, when matches were reduced to four full days (plus one extra session if necessary) and points awarded for first innings victories. Looking at the match 70 years later, it is difficult to find anything positive to write about the uncompromising stance taken by the NSWCA. It was patently unnecessary to give their team a head start, but it does not appear that that was their motive. Rather it seems the NSW hierarchy were exercising an opportunity to put the South Australians in their place. The NSW Cricket Association ran cricket in NSW, and no situation, person, or body was going to alter that fact.

# 19

# THE MURDER OF CLAUDE TOZER

In the first week of December 1920, the touring M.C.C. team played a three-day match against an Australian XI in Brisbane. The Australian side was a strong one, captained by Warwick Armstrong and including Herbert Collins, Alan Kippax, Charles Macartney and Hanson Carter. With those stars was a 30-year-old NSW batsman, Claude Tozer, who scored 51 stylish runs in the first innings, and 53 in the second.

Within 15 days, Tozer was dead, shot by a jealous lover after he had told her of his intentions to marry another woman. It was a scandal that shocked the Australian public, and rocked the sporting community. Tozer died while England and Australia were fighting for the Ashes on the Sydney Cricket Ground. On the third day Tozer was watching the Test from the seats near the sightboard at the northern end, in the company of Alan Kippax's father. Two days later the Australian players were wearing black armbands in honour of his memory.

Claude Tozer was a right-hand batsman, originally from the Sydney University club, who had made his debut for NSW in the 1910–11 season, against South Africa. That season he topped the batting aggregate in the Sydney grade competition, scoring 794 runs at 72.18. He again topped the grade figures in 1913–14, with 842 runs at 76.55, but a representative career was severely restricted by his concentration on medical studies.

In fact his first appearance in the Shield did not come until January 1920, when he was unluckily run out after shaping well for 37, batting three against the South Australians. Tozer had gained a University Blue in cricket, and also excelled at lawn tennis. On the outbreak of the First World War he had enlisted, risen to the rank of major, and been awarded a D.S.O. for his bravery in France. He arrived home from the battlefields of Europe wounded and diseased. The coroner would later tell of a piece of shrapnel found embedded at the base of Tozer's skull.

By 1919, Dr Tozer was fully recovered, and a candidate for the NSW team. However the NSW batting order was nearly as strong as the potential Test line-up, and his appearances in first-class cricket were limited to the South Australia match, and a game in Brisbane where he scored 51 and 103.

J.C. Davis wrote of Tozer: "Scarcely a greater batsmen has been turned out by the University, his rungetting during his association with the club having been great and constant. He was tall, possessed a splendid defence, and had good strokes on both sides of the wicket, especially on the drives."

Tozer made a sensational start to the 1920–21 season in Sydney grade cricket. Now playing with Gordon (only undergraduates could play with the University), his first four scores were 110, 211, 131 and 39. Critics pondered whether he would emulate Trumper, Mackay, Bardsley and James Bogle, the only men to that time to score 1000 runs in a Sydney grade season.

Despite his brilliant run, Tozer was only 12th man for NSW's match against the M.C.C., though many at the Gordon club felt he should have been preferred to Bardsley. The Australian selectors showed their high rating of him by inviting him to Brisbane for the Australian XI match. He had declared himself unavailable for the Christmas trip to Adelaide and Melbourne, but had been chosen as captain of the NSW second XI that was to play Queensland while the Shield team was away.

Tozer was a genuine contender for a place in the Australian team to tour England at the end of the 1920–21 season. Ten NSW players were eventually selected, and another, Charles Kelleway, was chosen but could not go. Tozer needed no more than a continuation of his impressive early-season form to be in with a chance.

It was never to be. Tozer's death was reported on December 22. The previous day his body had been discovered at the home of Mrs Dorothy Mort, a Sydney north shore socialite. He had been shot twice, through the head and heart. Mrs Mort had also been shot, and poisoned, but was alive.

On December 23, *The Sydney Morning Herald* reported that Tozer's death was not a mystery to the police, but that the authorities would not confirm the circumstances behind his shooting. It was later revealed Mrs Mort had confessed to the killing, and to a secret relationship with Dr Tozer that had existed for a number of months.

The subsequent committal hearing and murder trial created bizarre headlines. Tozer had first met Mrs Mort six months before his death, after her husband had sought a doctor to treat her for depression. An affair developed that did not end until Tozer informed her he was leaving to marry another woman. At the trial it was claimed Mrs Mort decided that if she could not have Dr Tozer then no-one would, so shot him…and then attempted to kill herself.

The jury subsequently found her not guilty, on the grounds of insanity.

At the time of his murder, Tozer was three months past his 30th birthday. NSW colleagues Macartney, Bardsley, Collins and Kelleway were all older, and many, including the NSW selectors and the Sydney sporting press, saw the well-educated Tozer as a future NSW captain. There is litle doubt Tozer would have had an impact on the NSW and perhaps Australian teams but for his dalliance with Dorothy Mort.

# 20

# COLOSSUS OF MELBOURNE

In all its years the Shield has never had a more controversial figure than Warwick Windridge Armstrong. Born in 1879, and a Test cricketer for 20 years, his achievements stand imposingly to today as arguably the finest all-round records set up by a Victorian in first-class cricket. And yet he is remembered as much for the controversies he caused, or was involved in, as for the enormity of his performances on the field of play.

Warwick Armstrong stood 188 cm (6ft 3in) in his massive size 14 boots. When he first appeared in Shield cricket, in 1899 against South Australia in Adelaide, he was a tall, awkward figure. By 1921 when he was the Victorian and Australian captain, and a huge man, weighing the wrong side of 125 kg, but still nimble enough to get to the pitch of the loftiest leg break.

M.A. Noble, in the *Sydney Mail* in 1920, said of Armstrong: "He always was a 'lump of a fellow', but bulk does not necessarily imply great reserves of strength such as he is blessed with. He has a splendid defence, and can on occasions fling doggedness to the winds and show himself a fast scoring, punishing batsman."

Armstrong was at times very much a lone figure at the head of Victoria's Shield battles. Never a cavalier like Trumper or Macartney, he was the ultimate cricket realist, and saw winning as the primary reason for entering the cricket field. Dr Leslie Poidevin, once a Shield cricketer, and then a Board of Control representative, in *The Sydney Morning Herald* in December, 1920, wrote:

*The "Big Ship" of Victorian and Australian cricket, Warwick Armstrong.*

"With the bat Armstrong is never a stylist, the great merit of his batting lies in its results. He may not be as attractive to watch as many of his great Australian predecessors, but he wields the broadest of broad blades, and there is behind his patient, painstaking exterior an obstinate and deliberate soundness that in opponents, at all events, commands respect and anxiety, and best of all — it wins matches. It is much the same with his leg break bowling — laboured in style, perservering in method and highly successful in performance.

At the bowling crease, Armstrong was rarely aggressive, and often saw his role as no more than plugging up an end. Jack Worrall wrote of his bowling: "He runs up to the wicket with a leg break delivery and action, rarely turning the ball. It is rather disconcerting when one expects the ball to turn to find it coming through quicker than expected. That is why Armstrong gets so many LBW decisions. Occasionally a ball turns, which adds to the uncertainty. In cricket language, Armstrong bowls a straight leg-break. But it is the marvellous length he maintains that stops scoring."

"Don't let big Warwick Armstrong drive you back," Clem Hill always told his South Australian side. "Keep out to him, or he'll be through."

In 1915 in Sydney, Armstrong, with nine fieldsmen on the leg side (including the wicketkeeper Carkeek, who took up position a metre wide of the leg stump), bowled consistently wide of Warren Bardsley's leg stump, while the left-arm spinner Bert Ironmonger bowled Victoria to a narrow victory from the other end. The local critics panned the strategy as being bad for the sport, but Armstrong pointed to the scorebook, which told of only the second Victorian victory in Sydney in 14 seasons.

In 1920–21, Armstrong completed an extraordinary feat against South Australia, scoring 157 not out and 245 — becoming the first Australian to score 400 in a first-class match. The South Australian bowling was very weak, and Armstrong used his bat as if it were a feather, disdainfully flaying the bowling to all parts of the ground. As he stood at the crease, unconquerable, the bowlers seemed like tiny archers, shooting arrows at a battleship.

One pictures Armstrong as a Gulliver of his time. Certainly he viewed the cricket administration as being beneath him, an attitude which brought him into situations of conflict, especially with the much-maligned secretary of the VCA, and Victorian and Australian selector, Ernest Bean.

Bean was one of the major Board of Control figures in the dispute of 1911–12 that saw Armstrong and five others refuse to tour England with the Australian side. A decade later, Bean was one of three Victorian selectors (Mat Ellis and Peter McAlister were the others) who dropped Armstrong, the then Australian captain, from the state XI to play England in early February, 1921 — an apparent disciplinary measure after Armstrong had, at the last minute, dropped out of the Shield match against NSW in Sydney the week before. That game was the 100th betwen the two great states, and a victory for Victoria would have been enough to win them the trophy. But Armstrong, it had been reported, left himself out of the side and ventured instead to the nearby Victoria Park races.

The selectors acted against the big man without seeking an explanation from him. When it was revealed that Armstrong had in fact been ruled out by the team's unofficial doctor, teammate and qualified surgeon Roy Park, and only after consultation with vice-captain Edgar Mayne — owing to severe bruising suffered during the captain's second innings century in the Third Test — the Melbourne cricket community was outraged. A protest meeting was scheduled for the Saturday of the Victoria-England match, February 5, to be held right outside the MCG.

When asked why Armstrong had been dropped, Bean answered: "It is not customary for a selection committee to make any statement regarding composition of any team which may be selected, and the present committee sees no reason to depart from the usual practice."

Armstrong had been given no reason for his axing, though he, like almost everyone else, had the same theory. On his arrival back in Melbourne after the train journey from Sydney, he was asked if he knew anything about his omission. "I know nothing whatever about it," he told reporters. "I'm sorry to hear of what has been done." He added that no-one in the VCA executive had sought an explanation for his late withdrawal in Sydney.

Letters to the Melbourne newspapers were indignant. "My advice to the team is that they refuse to play," wrote one *Age* reader. "There will be such a demonstartion that will make the obnoxious clique hide their heads in shame," fumed another. "I may state that the matter has caused me a good deal of annoyance and worry, and if it occurs again I shall be quite unfit for work of any sort, and will have to join the public service," sneered a third, making a sarcastic jibe at the working lives of the three selectors.

The arguments about Armstrong's omission quickly developed into a "them against us" debate. The ruling class against the working class. The Australia captain was soon a martyr, perceived as a one-man band, gallantly battling against the elite, arrogant establishment.

"If this sort of thing continues it will kill cricket in Australia," warned Clem Hill from Adelaide. "It is the old trouble cropping up again, and the sooner the men responsible for it get out of the game the better it will be for all concerned." Hill had never forgotten the players battles with the Board of Control before the war. Neither it appeared had Ernest Bean.

The Saturday protest meeting drew a large crowd, estimated at 8,000. The VCA had decided that no pass-outs would be given, which kept most of the paying patrons in the ground, but a flood of members left the pavilion, and were joined outside the ground by many who had decided to ignore the tour match completely. A number of women were in attendance, as, for a brief period, were some members of the England team. Among the organisers on the podium were federal and state politicians. As the *Age* put it: "All classes were represented."

The meeting became a public tribute to Armstrong and a villification of the cricket administration. The selectors had been invited, but declined, wisely in view of the mood of the gathering, to attend. Speaker after speaker outlined Armstrong's virtues and the officialdom's vices. Armstrong's sacking was described as "the most infamous act perpetrated in the history of cricket." Bean was described as "the most bitter of men." The selectors had been "taunting and flounting the public for twenty years," roared one speaker. "Now it was the turn of the public to taunt. They would leave no stone unturned to deliver justice."

One man, a Mr Cotter, a local member of parliament, exclaimed: "Billy Hughes (the then conservative prime minister) in his worst moments has never done anything as bad." Mr McKenzie from the Returned Sailor and Soldiers League appealed to the eight members of the Australian XI who were Diggers to "frustrate this attempt to put out of cricket one of the best of men." He went on, suggesting, "the cricketing authorities could not expect men like (Herbert) Collins, (Jack) Gregory and the rest of the Digger element to submit to such a position." McKenzie called on every Digger to stand up for "clean sport, clean politics, clean citizenship and clean selections." A motion was carried with much enthusiasm condemning the treatment of Armstrong. A second motion called for the resignation of the three selectors. It too was carried amid great cheering.

At a meeting on the Monday evening, the VCA closed their doors to the press — a decision *The Age* called "the star chamber policy". The press ban was in retaliation to what a majority of VCA committeemen felt was unfair coverage, but the ban did nothing to improve the Association's image. After a motion suggesting the selectors had lost the confidence of the meeting was defeated 17–10, a statement was prepared which stated:

"That this association, having heard Messrs Armstrong and Mayne and Dr Park, consider that Mr Armstrong was justified in not playing in Sydney, but regrets that the manager of the team was not informed earlier of the likelihood of Armstrong not being able to play. If this had been done the present trouble would not have arisen."

There, as far as the VCA was concerned, the matter ended. The next day Armstrong confirmed he would tour England with the 1921 Australian side, having received an assurance he had sought from Board officials that he would be captain. This, despite Australia's impeccable record in the Test series, had not been certain. Armstrong had only got the captaincy at the beginning of the series by a single vote.

The Armstrong Protest Committee held further, well-attended, meetings on February 9, 10 and 15, but could not budge the Victorian selectors. But by this stage Armstrong's stature with the Victorian cricketing public was akin to that of a god. When he went into bat with Australia struggling in its first innings on the second day of the fourth Test, at the MCG, he was given an extraordinary reception. Jack Worrall recalled the moment for the *Australasian*.

"As the figure of Armstrong emerged from the pavilion, bat in hand, there was a demonstration the like of which had never been seen before on the famous old ground, even outrivalling the ovation accorded Clem Hill at the time of the old trouble, which is also the new. There was cheering and counter-cheering by over 30,000, which the champion courteously acknowledged."

Armstrong went on to score a crucial 123, 79 of them on the third day, when he was clearly unwell suffering from a recurrence of malaria. Australia's subsequent victory was the fourth of eight straight Armstrong would superintend in 1920 and 1921, a record unique in Australian Test history. He was inevitably the hero of the day.

After the tour of England, an adventure that aroused more than its fair share of ill-feeling and controversy, Armstrong played only one more Shield match, against South Australia in Melbourne over the 1922 new year. He died in 1947, aged 68, remembered as much for his build and his battles, as for the wonderful record he put together on the cricket field. He regretted nothing, and was remembered fondly by the public, to whom he was such a pivotal figure.

Ernest Bean remained VCA secretary until 1925. For many years he was the Victorian cricketing public's enemy number one, which was perhaps unfair, though it seems public relations was not his strong suit. He came out of the Armstrong sacking controversy very badly, having let the acrimony of the pre-war disputes get the better of him. But it should not be forgotten that Bean was a hard-working administrator who devoted himself to the sport for little financial return. And he was always prepared to shoulder criticism (and occasionally trouble) in the fight to improve the game he loved. Especially the Victorian game.

Neither Bean nor Armstrong were men for sitting on the fence. When they jumped they never landed on the same side, and always seemed to land with a bang that was meant to overpower the other. Their battles have entered cricket folklore. They remain the two most significant figures in the first 20 years of 20th-century Victorian cricket.

# 21

# THE RUN MACHINE

There are two schools of thought concerning the celebrated run accumulator of the mid-1920s, Bill Ponsford. The more negative view is that Ponsford was fortunate to be at his best during a period in which pitches were at their most perfect and bowling at its most mediocre. Basically that line of thought is that he was overrated, a product of his time rather than a champion of all time.

His records suggest otherwise — that he was very definitely in champion class, an inexhaustible gatherer of runs and statistics who dominated bowlers in a manner only Bradman managed to surpass. Consider the following, just some of the many feats that had the record books reeling:

• Ponsford is the only man to twice pass 400 in an individual first-class innings.
• He was the first man to score a century on his Sheffield Shield and Test match debut.
• He was the first man to score centuries in each of his first two Tests.
• He was, between February 1923 and January 1930 the holder of the record first-class score. That score, 429 v Tasmania, came in only his fourth first-class innings. In December 1927, he broke his own record when he reached 437 against Queensland.
• Of those who have scored more than 10,000 first-class runs, only Bradman and the Indian, Vijay Merchant, have averaged more than his 65.18.
• He scored centuries in each of his first four matches against Australian states.
• He was the first man to score 1,000 runs in a single Shield season.
• Between January 23, 1925 and January 3, 1928 his Shield scores were: 79, 138, 214, 54, 151, 352, 108, 84, 12, 116, 133, 437, 202, 38 and 336. A breathtaking 2454 runs at 163.60.
• That innings of 214 was scored out of a team total of 315, an extraordinary 67.9% of his team's total.
• In 1926–27, he scored at least a century in each of the six first-class matches he played.
• Between January 1926 and January 1928 he played in 12 first-class matches in Australia, and scored at least a century in all of them.

Ponsford, born on October 19, 1900, was one of those who suffered from the Victorian selectors predilection for experience in the years immediately following the first great war. Despite excellent and consistent form in Victorian pennant cricket, his first Shield match did not come until 1922–23, after he had scored that first quadruple century in a non-Shield game.

The next year he scored a century in each innings against NSW and another century against South Australia. At the start of 1924–25 he was in everyone's Test side and, two centuries later, had ended his first Test series with 468 runs. However not all were impressed. The great English opener Jack Hobbs was one who questioned his reputation.

"I thought little of Ponsford, judged by international standards," said Hobbs. "He had been so highly praised I expected to see a really fine bat. He has some glaring weaknesses in his stance, and the way he

The great Victorian and Australian opening pair, Bill Woodfull (left) and Bill Ponsford. (Inset) Ponsford stepping out to drive in the first innings against NSW at the SCG in January 1926. He scored 79. The NSW keeper is Bert Oldfield, the slip fieldsman Jack Gregory.

meets the ball."

Ponsford was the youngest player involved in the Test series, and his run-getting in the next few seasons suggests that he had either developed rapidly after his initial Test series, or that the bowling in interstate cricket was less than international standard. Over the next few seasons he became the most feared batsman in Australia, the man least likely to be dismissed, most certain to score hundreds.

His philosophy was simple: "I don't think I had the intention of big scores at the start of an innings, but when runs did come along I guess I thought to myself that this same opportunity might not happen again and that I would do well to make the most of it."

"If you saw a batsman crouching slightly, cap on the side of his head, gathering runs with a remorseless certainty," wrote Johnnie Moyes, "you would know that it was Ponsford." Always in the right position, with a broad bat offering no encouragement to a generation of weary bowlers, Ponsford is most famous in the Sheffield Shield story for two massive innings. One, the superb 352 on which Victoria's record 1107 against NSW was built in December 1926, is perhaps best remembered for his alleged "Cripes, I am unlucky!" reaction when finally bowled off his pads. His other great innings was in Melbourne in December 1927, the world record 437 against Queensland.

The Queenslanders had performed reasonably well in 1926–27, their debut Shield season. In fact their defeat of Victoria in that season's final game had sent the Shield to South Australia. Reality arrived in their sophomore year, but not until after they had had the better of a draw with NSW in their opening match, in Brisbane.

The Queenslanders first mistake in Melbourne was to win the toss — and then to send the Victorians in. The weather was hot, a northerly blow made conditions oppressive and the pitch was baked hard after a series of sweltering days. The visitors were without Ron Oxenham and Percy Hornibrook, arguably their two best bowlers. The decision was inexplicable. At stumps the home side, scarcely believing their luck, were 2–400, with Bill Ponsford 234 not out. The northerners reticent captain, Leo O'Connor, tried to justify his crazy decision, by saying: "If we had got rid of two of their best batsmen, Ponsford for preference, cheaply in the morning all would have been well."

Ponsford and Hendry (129) had added 314 in 221 minutes for the second wicket, the third time (in three matches) the duo had been involved in a 200-plus partnership against Queensland in a Shield match. On the second day Ponsford went on, and on, sharing a century stand with Jack Ryder, and dominating half-century partnerships for the 4th, 6th, 7th and 8th wickets. All that concerned the 10,977 crowd on the second day were the records that were there to be broken.

One milestone had come the previous afternoon, when at 205, Ponsford reached 1,000 runs for the season in club and first-class cricket. At 300 he became the second man (after W.G. Grace) to reach that figure three times in first-class cricket. At lunch he was 315, and after the break he came out to race towards Clem Hill's Shield record of 365.

By this stage the Queenslanders had given up hope and reverted to blatant leg theory. *The Age* match report makes this strategy sound very much like a similar tactic adopted by an English captain named Douglas Jardine five seasons later:

"Later in the day the Queenslanders apparently despaired of dismissing him and planned to make it as difficult as possible for him to score. The bowlers persisted in fast leg theory with the majority of fieldsmen clustered around the wicket on the on side. Thompson, in his anxiety to keep the ball away from the champion's bat, bowled five wides. In order to defeat these tactics, Ponsford would take block far outside the leg stump and frequently would force the ball away to the off, where there were many gaps in the field. On one occasion, a ball which pitched a foot outside the leg stump was actually cut for three! The bowlers did not employ these tactics against any of the other batsmen, which was a great compliment to Ponsford."

The leg theory continued from soon after lunch until when Ponsford was finally dismissed, just before stumps. Hill's landmark was passed, to great applause, then Charlie Gregory's record first-class score against Queensland (383 for NSW in 1906–07) was broken. His 400 was reached with a powerful drive as Ponsford closed in on his own world record, most of his runs coming from cuts and prods to the vacant off-side field. The record came with a flourish, a powerful drive that flashed through the Queenslanders to the fence. "The cheering was renewed again and again," wrote *The Age*, "and then thousands of people left the ground." The world records clearly attracted the crowd. A slaughter did not.

Not that a thrashing eventuated. Soon afterwards, Ponsford's mighty innings ended with a weary push back to a grateful bowler. The final two Victorian wickets fell for a single, and the innings was completed at 793, just before stumps — a record total by Victoria against Queensland.

The Queenslanders were finally defeated by an innings and 197 runs, despite a gutsy fightback on the final day, when they reached 407 in the second innings. Ponsford was lauded for his rungetting. "It is likely that no other batsman will ever repeat such things as he has done, with possibly more to come, " wrote J.C. Davis. "We thought some years ago the limit had been reached when Trumper, Hill and Mackay and others achieved things prodigious; but apparently there is nothing ever achieved in cricket that is unlikely to be eclipsed sooner or later."

But how good was the bowling? Certainly the pitches were more placid than at any other time in Australian cricket history. A year earlier, Warwick Armstrong had said: "We have not in Australia at the present even a decent second-class bowler. This explains the phenomenal scoring this year. We cannot tell whether our batsmen are stars or not until they are tested by good bowlers." Armstrong was being hard on Grimmett, but probably no-one else. It was not until the emergence of Bill O'Reilly in the early 1930s that Australia once again had a bowler of the highest quality.

That the bowling standards of this time were less than other eras is unarguable, but that was hardly Ponsford's fault. Ponsford was a master of slow bowling, always in the right place to stifle the spin, in an era in the Sheffield Shield when perfect batting pitches limited the impact of the fast men, and googly merchants and left arm finger spinners were encouraged at the expense of the less-positive medium pacers and off breakers. Bill Ponsford could do no more than take advantage of the bowlers he faced and the conditions he batted in. But for Bradman, many of his records would remain today, and he, with Trumper, Chappell, Border and company, would be fighting for the tag of having been the very best.

# 22

# THE BRIEF CAREER OF DR HARRY ROCK

Of all the cricketers who have taken part in the Sheffield Shield has there been anyone as unlucky as Dr Harold Owen Rock? The only man to score centuries on debut against both Victoria and South Australia, and one of only three cricketers to take a century Shield batting average into retirement, Harry Rock played just four Sheffield Shield matches — and was twice dropped after scoring hundreds in his previous appearance at the batting crease for NSW.

Rock was a prolific-scoring Sydney University opening batsmen, who had the misfortune to play his cricket in the mid-1920s, a time when candidates for the NSW batting spots included Charlie Macartney, Herbert Collins, Johnny Taylor, Warren Bardsley, Tommy Andrews and Alan Kippax, plus the allrounders Jack Gregory, Charles Kelleway and Otto Nothling. For four consecutive years from 1920–21, Harry Rock scored over 500 runs in a grade season, but never once was called up for Sheffield Shield action.

Competition was fierce, opportunity rare. A chance finally came for Harry Rock in late November 1924 when, with Collins, Bardsley, Kelleway and Macartney unavailable (Taylor later dropped out as well), he was selected in the NSW side to play South Australia at the SCG. Rock's debut was a confident one. He scored 127 and 27 not out as NSW won by nine wickets. It was the sixth time a NSW player had scored a century in his debut innings in Shield cricket.

J.C. Davis in *The Referee* was clearly impressed: "Rock's 127 in 2 hrs 20 mins (fourteen 4s) was choice cricket, uncommonly entertaining to the spectators and classy for one making his first appearance against South Australia. The bowling was made to look very easy by the manner in which he met it. His defence was very sound and the square cut so crisp and well timed that many of the strokes were real gems and as classic as anything seen this summer from any of the international batsmen."

A bright future was naturally forecast, and a place in the Australian tour to England in 1926 mentioned, but with all but Macartney available for the Christmas Shield match in Melbourne and Glebe's high-scoring Gordon Morgan preferred as 12th man, Rock was unluckily relegated to the captaincy of the NSW Second XI.

Rock did get a late call-up to the NSW side for the Victoria match, in rather bizarre circumstances. The

**Victoria's Sheffield Shield Team Taking the Field Against N.S.W. in Sydney.**
The players (reading from Left to Right) are: Liddicutt, Woodfull, Mayne (captain, with the ball), Wallace, Hendry, Tarrant, Blackie, Willis, Hartkopf (behind Willis), Schneider, and Ellis.

the gods will smile more favourably on his efforts, and that he will achieve the distinction his ability and his hard work in the field entitle him to look for. He is a grand batsman, a very correct player, with any amount of strokes, and he does what many first-class batsmen of to-day fail to do—that is, always places himself naturally in the correct position to make his strokes. When watching him at the wickets one is seized with the possibilities that should accrue to his methods and the forcing character of his play, and one wonders why it is that he does not achieve more. I regard him as one of the finest batsmen in the world; but his batting averages are not a proper reflex of his ability. Yet, however great may be one's confidence in his batsmanship, and however one may look to him to do great things, there is always a lurking doubt in one's mind as to whether he will do them. It is a psychological influence, I suppose; but there it is. Freeman again proved himself a splendid man at a pinch. He helped Hendren to put on 41 for the last wicket, of which his own contribution was only six. That was a fine effort. He showed pluck and resourcefulness in diverting the strike to his partner and in keeping up his own end at a most critical time for his side. To my mind, Freeman is a much better batsman than he is generally supposed to be.

ENGLAND finished up with a total of 365, or 124 behind Australia. In view of the two gruelling days they had in the field when Australia was batting, and the unfortunate accidents which robbed them of the assistance of their three main bowlers, it was a fine fighting effort. In the old days we would have looked upon 365 in a first innings as almost a match-winning score, or at least as one giving us a very big leg-in. Now, apparently, we cannot say that any total whatever is likely to carry a side through. Look at the Melbourne Test, for instance. In the first innings Australia, with 600 on the board, should have been absolutely safe for victory; yet we only won eventually on the seventh day because of the sudden collapse of the Englishmen when they needed less than 100 runs and had four wickets in hand. To me the changed perspective seems to have been brought about almost wholly by a falling away in the ability of the bowlers. Certainly, without in any way attempting to belittle the efforts of Mailey, Gregory, and Co., I do not think we have a bowler in the Australian team to-day about whom one could truthfully say that he is likely to get a side out on any kind of wicket. Our need is for medium-paced trundlers who could keep pegging away all day, with men of the Gregory-Mailey type to act as fast and bosie "shock" bowlers. We would thus get variety into the attack that would keep down runs, prevent the batsmen digging in, and probably shorten the matches. For confirmation of this opinion one has only to look at the bowling analyses and compare the figures with those established by the star bowlers of old.

**MORGAN PULLING HARTKOPF TO LEG.**
In New South Wales's first innings he played splendidly all round the wicket, and, with Rock, put on 202 runs for the opening partnership.

I HAVE always claimed that the winning of the toss is worth 100 runs. Add to that the 124-run lead Australia had secured, and you will see that her position looked well-nigh impregnable when she started her second innings. She had only a few hours to bat, but by the time stumps were drawn she had made 211 for three wickets, with Ryder (the double-century man of the first innings) 86 not out, and Ponsford (who has been so prolific a run-maker in these tests) not out 40. The hypothetical position thus was 435 runs in hand and seven wickets to fall. The game looked as good as over; but once again Fate took a hand, and for the first time during these Tests rain began to fall on the fifth morning. It was heavy enough to necessitate the postponement of the opening for three-quarters of an hour. This was England's opportunity, Kilner and Woolley, the two left-handers, being put on to bowl; and the way they went through the batsmen was a treat to see, the whole seven wickets falling for an addition of 39 runs. The side was thus out for 250. This was the third sensational collapse since the match started, and it immediately altered the whole complexion of the game. It was bad luck for Ryder that he was not able to reach another century, but the rain-damaged wicket was too much for him and he fell an early victim to Woolley. Ponsford also succumbed early, to Kilner, after adding but two to his overnight total. Kelleway, seasoned batsman that he is, was the only one to make a stand, and he carried his bat for 22. There was lamentation in the camp at such an unexpected turn of fortune's wheel. Still, such conditions have always been associated with cricket, and always will be. One has to get used to them and to learn to master the difficulties they present.

THERE is nothing like a bad wicket to bring out the qualities of great batsmen; that was the standard by which the giants of the past were judged. The necessity for getting right back on top of the wicket to play the good ball, and jumping into and judiciously hitting hard and often between the fielders placed in the country, has to be realised, and it is only by practice

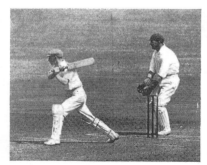

**ROCK HITTING OUT TO WALLACE.**
His great score in the first innings against Victoria was one of the most memorable in the annals of Sheffield Shield cricket. He made 235.

on this kind of wicket that the batsman is able to educate himself up to that state of proficiency. Nothing is finer or is more appreciated by the great cricket-loving public than to see a batsman overcoming the adverse conditions of a gluepot and giving an exhibition of masterly play when his comrades are falling around him. Such a display shows ability, cleverness, and sometimes genius. These three attributes are more associated with batting of this character than with knocking up runs on a perfect wicket. Yet perhaps it is not wise to compare the batting in this regard to-day with that of old-time champions, because pre-

sent-day cricketers do not get the opportunity to develop themselves on wickets of this character. It is not that they lack the ability to make good on bad wickets, but that the opportunity is denied them owing to the custom of covering the wickets in our State matches. It is regrettable that this practice was ever introduced, for it is certainly tending to reduce cricket generally to the commonplace rather than adding to the charm of its uncertainty. The suppression of individual effort and personal initiative such as is necessary to overcome the difficulties of a wet wicket encourages purely automatic play, which is not in the interest of the game.

HOBBS and Sutcliffe again opened the innings—the last of the match—for England. The responsibility of opening is always great, but on this occasion it was doubly so, because of the colossal nature of the task ahead, 375 runs being required to win. A good start for a side placed in such a position is vital, because it not only brings confidence to the batsmen in their big enterprise, but it stimulates those who have to follow, and gives them confidence. On this occasion, unfortunately, we were not to see what we had come to look upon as the regular settling-down process of this great partnership, for Hobbs, swinging briskly at a short one from A. Richardson, pulled it very hard and low to Collins at square-leg, and the Australian captain took a really brilliant catch. The first wicket was thus down for 63, of which Hobbs's share was

**KIPPAX CUTS HENDRY TO THE BOUNDARY.**
The Waverley batsman, although slow in starting, played a great innings of 212 not out.

27. It was a valuable contribution, however, when we consider that, just previously, Australia had lost seven wickets for 39. The batting of Hobbs and Sutcliffe had afforded a fine contrast to that of the home side. These two are truly wonderful performers under such conditions, for both are masters of the bat on bad wickets. When playing back they watch the ball right on to their bat; they are quick on their feet, and they get down the pitch with alacrity to anything that looks dangerous, thus preventing its breaking, as it is probably intended to. The longer they could remain in, even scoring at a very slow rate, the better would it be for their side, as the wicket was drying fast, and those to come later would be able to bat under better conditions. As it was, there were too paces and two heights in it—conditions usually associated with a recovering wicket—and this was the cause shortly afterwards of Hendren being out lbw to Kelleway, when he had scored only four, the ball skidding off the pitch faster than he anticipated and hitting his pads before he had time to get his bat to it. One naturally looks for this sort of thing in a two-paced wicket. The majority of the balls come along at an even pace. You play them easily; then you shape for the next one in the same way, and it skids through and leaves you standing, with disastrous result. This early dismissal of two of her mainstays was a big loss to England. Meantime Sutcliffe was pegging away cautiously and with fine tenacity of purpose. Good as he is, however, he is not quite in the same street (Continued on Page 32.)

M. A. Noble was a keen spectator of the Sheffield Shield match between New South Wales and Victoria at the Sydney Cricket Ground. He was out looking for talent among the younger cricketers, whose interest he always has very much at heart. That he found it goes without saying, for the game was one of the best seen for a long time. In next week's issue he will give his impressions of the play and the players.

First Test against Gilligan's Englishmen continued for seven days, eventually not finishing until December 27, and it was clear after four days that the NSW and Victorian players in the Test would not be able to play in the Shield match as well. Rock was one of five players promoted from the NSW Second XI, but the trip to Melbourne was a fruitless one, as rain washed out the first two days, and with the second Test scheduled to start on New Year's Day, officials decide to postpone the State game until later in the season.

Another drawn-out Test match led to Rock being selected at the last minute for the Shield game in Adelaide starting on January 9. Rock this time declined the trip, but another chance came in late January. The Test players were unable to get back from Adelaide after the third Test for the NSW-Victoria match in Sydney, and Rock opened the NSW batting and scored 235 and 51.

At stumps on Day One, NSW were 2–393, Rock, 188, and Alan Kippax unbeaten on 93. Again Davis compared him favourably with the Test men, and continued: "H.O. Rock is a veritable stoic at the wickets. He takes his stand with ease, and has no semblance of movement or mannerism until he moves the bat to meet the ball. Then everything is done with mechanical accuracy that makes batting look an easy, effortless thing. He stands up straight, inclines the bat to his body, and times the ball choicely on the square cuts, drives and glances."

Davis also had an interesting opinion on the 42-year-old Victorian slow bowler, Don Blackie, who was making his first-class cricket debut: "Blackie once or twice was flighty, but he is a trifle too old to come into Sheffield Shield cricket and though a trier is not a smart field." Four years later, Don Blackie was in the Australian Test side.

The Victoria match was Rock's last first-class opportunity of the season. In a ludicrous situation, the postponed NSW-Victoria Shield match in Melbourne began the day after the NSW-Victoria Shield match in Sydney finished. Consequently, none of the players in Sydney were available for the Melbourne game, which did not harm NSW, who were able to include their seven Test men, but meant Victoria had to field a virtual second XI, who did extremely well to get within three wickets of the powerful NSW side. Harry Rock had to be content with scoring a stylish 60 for Sydney University while the Shield match was being concluded in Melbourne.

University exams kept Rock out of the second NSW-England match in late February. One must assume that, had he been available, he had done enough to keep his place in the side. He finished the season atop the Sydney grade aggregates, with 656 runs at 54.68, and the NSW averages, with 440 runs at nearly 147.

Season 1925–26, with the England tour at the end of it, could have been a significant one in the cricket career of Harry Rock. He started perfectly. Although missing from the early grade rounds, he was chosen for NSW's first match of the season, against Western Australia in Sydney, and scored 151. He was named in "The Rest" side that played an Australian XI in Sydney, a virtual selection trial for England, but made only 12 and 35. Much mention was made of the superb delivery from Jack Gregory which bowled him in the first innings. Rock had tried to drive the good length ball wide of mid-on, but at the last it dipped away and smashed the off bail.

Rock was a member of the NSW side that travelled to Adelaide in December, but on the morning of the match was made 12th man. In Sydney there was much criticism of his omission, but the NSW batting order was Collins, Bardsley, Macartney, Taylor, Andrews, Kippax, Kelleway, Gregory, Oldfield, Mailey and Everett. Who else, the selectors might have cried, could they have left out?

J.C. Davis thought just about anyone, Macartney, Bardsley and Collins included. He called Rock's sacking: "The most extraordinary case of the omission of a player from the New South Wales team for over thirty years. On the fast true wickets of Australia, I consider that no NSW batsmen is superior to Rock. The omission of Rock from NSW is as inexplicable as that of Ponsford would be from the Victorian Eleven. Rock is easily the finest cover driver in Australian cricket today."

From Adelaide the team travelled to Melbourne, where Rock, batting seven, replaced the injured Everett. He scored 81, and was unluckily out, LBW off the inside edge. NSW scored 705 in their only innings in this match. Of the 10 batsmen dismissed, Kippax's 29 was the lowest score. Rock was third highest, centuries coming from Kelleway and Oldfield, who added 226 for the ninth wicket.

Rock, obliged to sit for a crucial final exam at the University, was unavailable for the match against South Australia in Sydney, but was back in the side for the return fixture with Victoria two weeks later. That match against the South Australians was a remarkable one, won by NSW by 541 runs, after a record-breaking 1929 runs were accumulated by both teams over six days. Collins, Bardsley and Kelleway scored centuries, and Andrews 98, in the NSW first innings of 642, while in the second innings, Macartney reached three figures, and five half-centuries were scored in a total of 593.

In an extraordinary season of high scoring, eleven different batsmen scored centuries for NSW in first-class matches in 1925–26. Two who didn't, Andrews (highest 98) and Taylor (highest 95) were selected in the team to tour England. The worst Shield first innings by NSW that season was 554.

Against Victoria, NSW's final match of the season, Rock scored a run-a-minute 39 after coming in at 5 for 465. And that, remarkably, was the end of Harry Rock's Shield career. He missed selection in the team for England and, having passed his medical exams, gave up big cricket and travelled 160 kilometres up the NSW coast to Newcastle, to begin a doctor's life.

His Shield career statistics are extraordinary: an aggregate of 560, for five times out, average 112. His first-class career average is just less than 95. He could quite easily have become a key figure in NSW cricket had he continued in the game, especially as so many of NSW's senior players did not come back to the Shield after the 1926 tour. But it was not to be. He remains a remarkable figure in the annals of the Shield, more by the games he was left out of than by his runs. He was, because of his misfortune, perhaps the best example of the batting strength of the NSW side in the years between 1920 and 1926.

# 23

# STORMY DAYS IN VICTORIAN CRICKET

Despite the extreme pressures of the Warwick Armstrong affair of 1921, the Victorian selectors of that time, Ernest Bean, Mathew Ellis and Peter McAlister, continued in the job until the completion of the 1925–26 season.

Victoria won the Shield in 1921–22, 1923–24 and 1924–25, but these successes did little to spare the reputations of the three men, who were constantly villified in the press, and given little credit when victories occurred. The general feeling in the sporting pages was that the selectors were hampering the development of Victorian cricket by a continued reliance on experience and reputations, and that the strength of Victorian pennant cricket was such that had younger players been given their opportunity the results of the Shield side would not have suffered.

At the start of the 1924–25 season, Bean, Ellis and McAlister controversially resurrected the first-class career of 43-year-old Frank Tarrant, the Melbourne-born all-rounder who had enjoyed much success at Middlesex in London before the First World War. Tarrant had not played for Victoria since scoring 79 and 206 and taking three wickets against NSW in Sydney in January 1908.

One critic summed it up for most when he labelled Tarrant's inclusion: "One of the worst blots in the history of team selection in Victoria."

Tarrant became a significant figure in Victoria's push to the Shield that year, taking key wickets in a season dominated by centuries. Despite the successes, the criticism of selection policy continued. Wrote one correspondent in December 1925: "Victorian cricket is being tossed unwittingly on the stubborn waves of absurdity by the three selectors, and it will suffer the pangs that accompany senile decay within the next few years unless a more reasonable and sensible attitude be immediately adopted."

The average age of the Victorian team for the first match of 1925–26, against South Australia, was fractionally less than 34 and a half. Don Blackie, Edgar Mayne and Bert Ironmonger were all in their 44th year. Only Bill Ponsford (25) and Bill Woodfull (28) were less than 30. Five of their opponents were younger than 25.

The selectors had more problems in the first week of 1926. With the home match against South Australia due to begin on Friday, January 1, they had somewhat foolishly left it until the afternoon of New Year's Eve to announce their team. Admittedly they had been forced into a corner by the late withdrawals of four players, Mayne, Tarrant, Liddicut and Hartkopf, who had announced they would not play for Victoria again at the MCG after receiving a fearful barracking from the crowd during the just completed loss to NSW. Mayne commented: "I would not play if I got 500 pounds." The home supporters had not been impressed by the fielding display of some of the Victorian elder statesmen. Wrote Jack Worrall in

*The big-hitting Jack Ryder, Victoria's captain through the tribulations of the 1925–26 season.*

*The Australasian*: "I am not making any excuses for the crowd's anger and conduct, but the selectors kept asking for it year after year, and they got it, and it was bound to come in the long run."

Late on the Thursday night some players were still unaware they had been called up to the State team. The next morning it was revealed that a further three players, Ponsford, Jack Ellis and Fred Baring, were unavailable. Ellis was injured, while Baring and Ponsford were not in a position to get leave from their respective employers. A reserve player, Alan Thomson had not sought permission from his employer for leave but now that he was in a position to make his Shield debut, decided to play regardless. The other two late replacements, Karl Schneider and Carl Willis could not at first be located. Then it was ascertained Schneider was in the country, and Willis at work. When contacted, Willis explained he had business engagements the following week that could not be broken, and could not play. The veteran left-hander Vernon Ransford was next choice, and was found at Flemington racecourse, showing some visiting British friends around Melbourne. He reluctantly agreed to play, rather than leave the VCA in the lurch. The last spot eventually went to the exciting 19-year-old Richmond footballer and Hawthorn-East Melbourne all-rounder Keith Millar.

That final vacancy was not filled until sometime after lunch, a ludicrous situation that would have been exacerbated had Ryder not won the toss. Much comment was made at Ponsford's withdrawal. He had told the VCA secretary, Mr Brereton, on the Thursday that, with the tour of England fast approaching, he was not in a position to ask his employer, the State Savings Bank, for any more leave. He had taken 87 days leave owing to cricket in 1925. That message had been passed on to the selectors, who had decided to ignore it and pick Ponsford anyway.

When Ponsford insisted he was unavailable, the VCA executive were incensed. Chairman Ernest Bean said: "Ponsford's refusal to play is viewed with extreme disapproval by members of the executive, and it is possible some action will be taken against him." Later Bean suggested it was possible the VCA may stand Ponsford down from big cricket — a poorly veiled threat to leave him out of the English tour.

This incident highlighted a trend among players at this time to question the time and money that Shield cricket was taking from their working lives. An earlier example had involved the NSW Test all-rounder Charles Kelleway who, in December 1924, had told the NSWCA he could not afford to play Shield cricket for the small allowance the Association paid him. Many felt Kelleway's stand cost him a place in the 1926 Ashes touring team.

The selections fiasco prior to the 1926 Victoria-South Australia game, and Bean's subsequent remarks concerning Ponsford's unavailability caused a storm in Victorian cricket circles. Pressmen wrote of the political atmosphere of Victorian cricket, and painted a deplorable picture of various interest groups plotting the downfall of each other. A cluster of senior officials were apparently heard gloating in the members' bar over the failure of the teenager Millar. Once again a campaign was launched seeking the resignation of the three selectors, and, just as had occurred in 1921, arrangements were made for an indignation meeting to be held.

The senior delegate from the Northcote club, Mr E.C. Yeomans announced he would be moving a motion at the next VCA meeting, scheduled for January 11:

*That the selectors have lost the confidence of this Association and that they be asked to resign.*

Almost immediately, the other Northcote delegate, Mr W.S. Stott, said he would be proposing the following amendment:

*That all the words after "that" in the first line be omitted and that the following substituted: In view of the success of the Victorian players in winning the Sheffield Shield in three out of the past four seasons and 14 Sheffield Shield matches out of 16 in that period, a feat unparalleled in the history of Victorian cricket, this association expresses its regret at the unfair attacks made in a section of the press on the selectors and certain members of the team.*

One wonders whether the two men from Northcote had discussed the motion and amendment at their own club's committee meeting! In the event, neither motion nor amendment were put to the vote. After a lively debate, the experienced Melbourne Cricket Club delegate, Dr Ramsey Mailer, suggested the matter should be allowed to stand over indefinitely. Mr Yeomans, in reluctantly withdrawing his motion, claimed: "Many of us do not know what is being done in the association."

Once again these three controversial yet indefatigable selectors had survived, but for Bean and Ellis, this was their last season on the committee. Both retired following Victoria's disappointing season, to be replaced by Bill Woodfull and Dr Roy Minnett. In many ways this was the end of an era. After the 1926 England tour many of Australia's senior players departed from the first-class cricket scene. In NSW, almost an entire eleven retired in one breath.

An unlikely sequel to this affair came in 1930, following the controversial axing of the Australian captain, Jack Ryder from the side chosen to tour England. Ryder's sacking aroused great emotions in his home town Melbourne — most of the city suggesting he had been the victim of a sordid Sydney-based conspiracy. An indignation meeting was held at the Collingwood Town Hall, at which a motion was moved calling for changes in the method of selecting Australian teams. The man who moved that motion was Ernest Bean.

# 24

## QUEENSLAND MAKES THE GRADE

In *The Brisbane Courier* of May 8, 1926, appeared the announcement all cricket followers in Queensland had been waiting for.

"QUEENSLAND ADMITTED. UNANIMOUS DECISION." was the headline, and below were the historic details of the Board of Control's expansion of the interstate cricket competition, the first such innovation since the Shield had begun in December 1892.

Queensland had been involved in interstate cricket since 1864, when, in Brisbane, NSW had decisively beaten the 22 best locals available. The Queenslanders initial first-class match did not occur until April 1893, a rather bizarre affair at the Exhibition Ground in Brisbane against a weakened NSW XI and which was concluded in less than the two days, in Queensland's favour.

Their next victory did not come until 15 years later, again against NSW, this the first win at the Brisbane Cricket Ground (known affectionately as the 'Gabba). This win was over another below-strength NSW side. Suggestions were made that Queensland should be involved in the Sheffield Shield, although it was difficult to assess the true worth of the Queensland cricketers, who were rarely opposed to the best of the southern states. The failure of the rival state associations to send their best players frustrated the Queenslanders, as Mr F. McCaffery, a QCA offical explained in Sydney in 1913:

"It has helped us considerably by (the NSWCA) sending teams to Brisbane, but, if I may make a suggestion, if it were to always send its best team north, it would do even more yet for us. Brisbanites would gladly flock to see Trumper, Macartney and Bardsley pulverising our trundlers and we might thus augment our funds sufficiently to develop facilities for local cricket."

In December 1921, a Queensland side spearheaded by the left-handed medium-pacer Percy Hornibrook, defeated a NSW second XI comfortably at the 'Gabba — a triumph that strengthened Queensland's push for admission to the Shield. The next year NSW sent a much stronger side, including Collins, Macartney, Hendry, Oldfield and Mailey, but could do no better than struggle to a finely-balanced draw. Soon afterwards an application was made by the QCA to the three major cricket associations for a spot in the Shield competition, but only the NSWCA supported the bid. The tyranny and cost of distance, plus doubts as to the quality of the Brisbane turf pitches thwarted the approach.

In September 1923 another Board of Control conference was held to discuss the Queensland matter, but again the northerners were rejected. However these frustrations strengthened rather than demoralised the administration's resolve. The QCA decided to shift many of their important matches back from the 'Gabba to the Exhibition Ground, a ground the Board of Control preferred. Soil was imported from Melbourne to improve pitches throughout Brisbane, and especially at the major grounds. And money was spent on tours for the state's best players to the southern states.

The efforts were finally rewarded on May 7, 1926. At a smoke concert being conducted by the QCA, three cheers were given for the officials, for the Shield, and for Queensland. Much praise was given to Jack Hutcheon, the former Queensland captain and then Chairman of the QCA Executive, who had led the campaign for Queensland's admission.

From 1926–27 Queensland would be playing home and away matches with NSW and Victoria, and one match a season with South Australia, the venue of that match to alternate each year. With not all states playing the same amount of matches, the Shield would be won by the state winning the largest percentage of matches, and in the event of a tie, bowling and batting averages would come into play as before. At the same meeting it was ruled that matches would continue to be played to a finish.

Queensland's first season in the Shield was a thriller, the destiny of the trophy not decided until the final game. Their first match, the opening Shield fixture of the season, set the mood, an absorbing five-day contest with a young NSW side featuring six new caps, and led by Alan Kippax. Most members of the Australian touring team had been back in the country for less than three weeks, and were not available. Nor were Harry Rock and Charlie Kelleway.

The match ended with Queensland, chasing exactly 400, all out just nine runs away from a historic victory. The honour of the first Shield century by a Queenslander went to Cecil Thompson, who had made his first-class debut for Queensland back in 1912. In their second innings, the captain, wicketkeeper Leo O'Connor, faced the first ball of the fourth day (at 1–13, the opening stand having been broken the previous evening) and batted all day, for 191 not out, sharing a 135 alliance for the fourth wicket with Ron Oxenham, and an unbroken ninth wicket stand of 41 with Alex Mayes. At stumps on that fourth day, Queensland were 8–378.

The next morning, Mayes was out at 381, popping up a timid shot to mid-on. Kippax's strategy was simply to keep O'Connor from the strike. Singles came slowly until O'Connor, finally at the batting end late in an over, tried to sneak one to mid-off to keep the bowling — only to be run out by inches when his number 11, Harold "Bill" Noyes, sent him back.

Despite the loss, the match did much for Queensland morale. It proved they were competitive, and also allayed doubts over the standard of the Exhibition Ground pitch. "Queensland is a much better team than they are generally accreditted," said Kippax. "I would not be surprised if they gave some of the states a shaking up before the series is completed."

First to be shaken up was NSW. Revenge was quickly sought by Queensland, and won, when NSW, despite the return of Macartney and Tommy Andrews, were beaten comfortably by five wickets. O'Connor, who scored a hundred in each innings, and Oxenham, who made an unbeaten 134 batting eight with a runner, were the stars. Significantly the match drew a record attendance for a NSW-Queensland match in Sydney. The quality and resilience of Queensland cricket had been accepted and recognised by the Sydney public, as had the rungetting of Alan Kippax and the precocity of Archie Jackson.

In Melbourne, the Queenslanders had the same problem everyone else in Australia was having. They couldn't get Ponsford out. In Adelaide they were thrashed by a South Australian side who were proving impossible to counter at home. These losses ruined any pretensions to the title, but did not stifle ambition.

*The Queensland side that played NSW in Brisbane in November 1926, the state's first appearance in the Shield. Back row (left to right) : H. Noyes, E. Bensted, N. Beeston; Centre: F. Gough, F. Brew, R. Higgins, R. Oxenham; Front row: W. Rowe, C. Thompson, L. O'Connor, A. Mayes, L. Oxenham.*

*Alec Hurwood (left) and Percy Hornibrook, who in 1930 became the first Queensland Shield players to be selected for an Australian tour of England.*

By the time the Victorians came to the Exhibition Ground for the final Shield match of the season, the destiny of the trophy rested with the Queenslanders. Victoria needed to win, otherwise the Shield was destined for Adelaide.

Ponsford, who had missed Victoria's thrashing by NSW the week before, came north to revitalise the batting. O'Connor won the toss and batted, and with Oxenham (104) steered his side to 4–261 by stumps. The next day the innings ended at 399, after which the Victorians — Ponsford, Hendry and all — were bowled out for 86. Oxenham, bowling medium-paced spinners, had 4–18, a memorable double. The last nine wickets fell for 53. The pitch was placid, Hornibrook devastating, the batting poor.

O'Connor did not enforce the follow-on, and eventually set Victoria 753 to win the Shield. Ponsford and

Hendry started with a 225 stand, but only Keith Millar and Fred Baring showed much resolve from that point on, and they fell 235 short. The Shield went to South Australia for the fourth time, and many laurels were showered on the gritty Queenslanders, who for the third time in five matches had shown their battling worth.

Queensland's first season in the Sheffield Shield provided an opportunity for the men from the northern state that had not been available to their predecessors. More than that it gave Australian cricket a chance to appreciate the abilities and character of the cricketers from the north, and to appreciate the advantages of promoting the game in that state, and into the future, in Western Australia and Tasmania.

In September 1927, the Board of Control, much to the consternation of the press and public in Sydney, awarded Brisbane a Test match, the first of the 1928–29 Ashes series. In that series three members of the Queensland Shield team, Otto Nothling, Oxenham and Hornibrook, were selected in the Test XI. The previous men to be chosen for Australia as a representative of Queensland cricket were C.B. Jennings and J.W McLaren, who toured England with the weakened Australian team of 1912. It was also decided that each state in the Shield would meet each other twice.

In his detailed book on Queensland Cricket *A History of Queensland Cricket*, published in 1947, the former Queensland player and selector, E.H. Hutcheon, looked back on that historic and vital season for Queensland and Australian cricket.

"It must be considered a particular honour to have been in the Queensland XI in that season," Hutcheon wrote. "The successful entry of Queensland into Sheffield Shield cricket was acclaimed throughout the country. It brought pleasure to many ex-Queenslanders overseas, and to all those friends of the state, who saw in the Queensland successes something that might eventually bring strength to Australian cricket. It was this aspect of the matter that appealed to hosts of Australians in every state."

# 25

# LONG LIVE VICTORIA!

In season 1925–26 NSW won both their matches against Victoria by an innings, reaching a team total of over 700 runs on both occasions. The Victorians' revenge the following season was brutally decisive, albeit shortlived.

On December 28, 1926, Victoria demoralised the NSW bowling, reaching an unprecedented (in firstclass cricket) score of 1107. Bill Ponsford scored 352, captain Jack Ryder 295, Bill Woodfull 133 and Stork Hendry 100. The great legspinner, Arthur Mailey, finished with 4–362, a record for the most runs conceded in one first-class innings — and one that will probably last forever.

One month later, the Victorians were all out in the first innings in Sydney for 35! Ponsford, Ryder and Woodfull were all unavailable, and this time the NSW bowlers had a damp pitch to aim at. Even so, the contrast is totally unbelievable. Two first innings against the same state in the same season...and a difference of 1072 runs.

NSW arrived in Melbourne for the Christmas match with an inexperienced side, only four of the team having played at the MCG before. Of the nine New South Welshmen who had toured England in 1926 only Tommy Andrews and Mailey were available, but the young tyros approached the match with some confidence. Just two days earlier they had won in Adelaide after scoring 6 for 446 in the fourth innings.

They were led by Alan Kippax, the controversial omission from the 1926 tour. In 1925–26 Kippax had scored 271 against Victoria in Sydney. In the first two games of the 1926–27 season he had scored three more big hundreds. Also in the side was the promising Archie Jackson, just turned 17, but already the scorer of a Shield century.

The home side was at full strength, and in imposing form. Ponsford had scored his remarkable 214, out of 315, in their first innings against South Australia in the first week of December. Hendry had belted 177 in the second. The pair then smashed centuries against the inexperienced Queenslanders two weeks later. Woodfull was back from topping the averages on the English tour.

Kippax won the toss, batted on a perfect wicket, and saw his team crumble for 221. His young batsmen could not cope with the accuracy of Arthur Liddicutt, the fast-medium opening bowler, and Don Blackie, the veteran off spinner. Opener Norbert Phillips made 52, Andrews 42 and 20-year-old Jim Hogg was left 40 not out.

Victoria's reply began first thing the next morning. At stumps they were 1 for 574. Ponsford was uncon-

*Below: Arthur Mailey, one of the Shield's great characters, and, despite his bowling figures against Victoria at the MCG in 1926-27 (4-362), one of its greatest spin bowlers. Right: Hunter "Stork" Hendry, who smashed an even hundred as Victoria reached 1,107.*

quered on 334, he and Woodfull having created a new opening-wicket Shield partnership record of 375. Hendry was 86 not out.

It might have been different had Woodfull been run out in the third over, as he should have been. Ponsford had lofted a no-ball straight to Kippax at mid-on. Woodfull's illogical call for a single was ignored, but the NSW captain's high throw to the bowler, Ray McNamee, was fumbled, with Woodfull stranded in mid-pitch.

At lunch Ponsford was 75, at tea 228, with Frank Tarrant's record score for a Victorian against NSW of 206 superceded. The Victorian opening partnership record against NSW was passed at 155, and the Trumper-Duff best for NSW in these matches went soon after tea, at 268.

The scoring rate was phenomenal. The NSW total was passed in 143 minutes. The 100 runs between 150 and 250 took just 41 minutes. Ponsford might have survived a stumping chance in this time, though few were sure that Andy Ratcliffe, the NSW keeper, had a chance to get at the ball. Woodfull, when 117, was dropped by Andrews, a difficult caught and bowled chance. As Andrews lay on the pitch, some of the fieldsmen must have wondered if a wicket would ever fall, but soon Woodfull was out, held by the keeper off the same bowler. The run chase continued unabated, Ponsford racing past 250, breaking Armstrong's Victorian record Shield score.

Hendry was missed by poor Ratcliffe when only six, and then slaughtered the tired bowling. Ponsford reached 300 in 285 minutes, and then marched past Billy Murdoch's record 321 for Victoria-NSW matches. At stumps Mailey had 0-148 off 28 overs. Ponsford went to bed with his sights set firmly on the records he had not already broken.

The new day saw a mini-collapse, but only after the Victorian second-wicket partnership record was beaten. Hendry rushed to his hundred, and then sliced Mailey to slip. Ponsford was strangely subdued, and added only 18 in 40 minutes, before playing Gordon Morgan into the ground, from where the ball spun back into the stumps. "Cripes, I am unlucky!" he is reputed to have said.

Ryder had entered after Hendry was dismissed, and immediately flayed the bowling. "Hammy" Love, later a Test wicketkeeper but playing here as a batsman, was stumped off Mailey for 6 at 614, and 20-year-old Stuart King (7) went the same way at 657. Ryder then found another ally in Bert Hartkopf. Scoring at 75 runs-per-hour, Ryder smashed his way past 150. Hartkopf was out for 61 with the score at 834. Liddicut came out and did more than hold up an end, as Ryder set sail for 200. When the 900 came up, the captain was 195.

He then went berserk, smashing the bowlers everywhere. Ryder was swinging so consistently, he seemed like a man determined to throw his wicket away. Yet his dismissal seemed so unlikely, with his hitting so pure, and the gaps in the outfield seemingly enormous. Liddicut was bowled at 915, three runs and one hit before the Shield record of 918 was broken.

Soon after, a Jack Ellis single brought up the thousand. Ellis, the Victorian's keeper who had toured England as Bert Oldfield's deputy, celebrated by dancing wildly and chanting: "Long live Victoria!" This for many was as good as winning a Test match.

Stumps still seemed a long way away. Late in the day it seemed as though Victoria would bat forever. Years later, Mailey remembered his captain coming up to him and sarcastically saying: "How about getting someone out?" Later Kippax commented: "Maybe we'll still be here for the Melbourne Cup."

"I looked Kippie straight in the eye," Mailey recalled, "and said if that chap in the brown derby at the back of the grandstand had held his chances I'd have had them out days ago."

Ryder, not caring for his 300, hit Andrews for 4,6,4,6 before holing out to Kippax at mid-on. Frank Morton was then run out for a duck (fancy scoring a duck in an innings total of 1107), but the exhausted New South Welshmen's misery continued as Ellis and Blackie added 61. During this frantic, sadistic last-wicket stand the world record first-class innings total of 1059 was passed, and just as when the 1000 was reached Ellis celebrated in patriotic fashion. Then the Australian record for any cricket, the 1094 scored by Melbourne University in 1897–98, disappeared.

Ellis was finally run out trying to keep the bowling, and the NSW agony ended. Mailey, the pragmatist, could still smile, despite his bowling figures. It was a pity the innings had ended, he said, as he was just finding his length.

The next day NSW batted again, needing a mere 886 to make Victoria bat once more. They failed by 656, Jackson unbeaten on 59; the team crawled away to the train station, little knowing what was in store in less than a month's time.

For the return match Victoria were without Love and Hartkopf, as well as their three chief rungetters of Melbourne. NSW welcomed back Macartney, Oldfield and Johnny Taylor. For Macartney, who took over as NSW captain, and Taylor, this was to be their Shield farewell.

Whereas at the MCG, NSW had struggled on the opening day after winning the toss, here they took command and at stumps were 8–424. The highlight was Kippax's glorious, undefeated 187 and the batting of Jackson, who made just 42, but made them in style. J.C. Davis, in *The Referee*, used the Trumper analogy to celebrate the skill of the teenager: "Jackson is the first very young batsman for some years to recall Trumper in his scoring shots. He drives with the same crispness of power and places the ball in those off shots with something akin to that of the master."

Play on the second day started late and finished early. NSW went to 469 (Kippax 217 not out) and Victoria started badly, losing Fred Baring and Hendry for 15 before the rains came back to end the day. On the third day, play started 45 minutes late on a damp pitch, and Victoria promptly lost 6 for 3.

McNamee, who had taken 0–124 off 24 overs in Melbourne, now ran through the innings, taking 5 for 0 in a superb opening and finishing with 7–21. Macartney, recalling his best bowling days of before the war, grabbed the other three wickets and barely conceded a run.

One correspondent wrote: The uncommon smallness of the total was a reflection on the quality and enterprise of the batting…no-one showed the skill and daring of the old Victorian champions."

The same writer said of McNamee: "An improving bowler — and cricketer — this summer's experience has been of material value in enhancing his knowledge of the finer points of bowling."

One can only wonder how much McNamee learnt when being belted by Ryder and company to all parts of the Melbourne Cricket Ground.

The wicket was better, but still not perfect when Victoria followed on. Liddicut managed 55, McNamee 3–49, and the innings ended at 181. NSW had won by an innings and 253 runs — an astonishing reversal of the humiliation in Melbourne.

Victoria's first innings was not their worst against NSW — they had made only 28 in the first intercolonial match in 1856, and 31 in 1907 (when Macartney took 4–6) — but stood in dazzling relief so close to the 1107!

The contrast, even one so extreme, in many ways typifies cricket, especially cricket played in the days before wickets had to be covered. If the pitches stayed hard and true, then the rungetters were remorseless, the boundary fieldsmen busy, the bowlers weary. But things could change swiftly, and occasionally the game was only as predictable as the next day's weather forecast.

# 26

# THE COMING OF BRADMAN AND JACKSON

Until the 1928–29 season, the careers of Archie Jackson and Don Bradman had run along similar paths. Two sensational teenagers, emerging just as the last traces of Armstrong's all-conquering 1921 Australian side disappeared into their cricketing sunset, they arrived as the sporting community in Australia started questioning the quality of cricket they were watching.

Bradman was born at Cootamundra in country NSW on August 27, 1908, Jackson in Scotland one year and eight days later. In August 1913, little Archie arrived in Sydney with his family, to be raised in the inner-city Sydney suburb of Balmain, and to achieve early cricket successes with the local grade club. Don Bradman grew up in Bowral, 160 kilometres south west of Sydney, where he practised assiduously and in his teenage years earned an enviable local reputation as a prolific rungetter.

By the time Bradman made his debut in Sydney grade cricket in late November 1926, travelling by train from Bowral to score a century for St George against Petersham (*The Referee* wrote after this innings: "Though not a stylist, he possesses a good variety of shots."), Jackson was a NSW player, having made his debut in the first Shield match of 1926–27. Immediately the scribes recognised the style of past champions in his cricket. The young man from Bowral's first Shield appearance occurred a little more than 12 months later. Both were instantly successful, Jackson scoring 86 (run out) in the second innings of his first match, and Bradman starting with a century in Adelaide, against Clarrie Grimmett and company. Bradman's Test debut came in the first match of the 1928–29 Ashes series, less than two months before Jackson made a triumphant start to his international career, in the 4th Test in Adelaide.

By this 1928–29 season the pair had cast their reputations. Bradman was the remorseless rungetter, the name inevitably at the top of the averages. Jackson was the stylist who played the way everyone wished they could play, the throwback to the Golden Age. Bradman was the man for the people, Jackson was one of the people. Together they were the two most popular cricketers of the late 1920s, the young sportsmen who would lead Australian cricket back after the loss of the Ashes in 1926, when Herbert Collins' elderly Australian team had been conquered at The Oval after six glorious years at the forefront.

When Jackson was just 16, Arthur Mailey had walked him into the office of Sydney sporting journalist Claude Corbett and said: "Claude, I want to introduce you to Archie Jackson, who will be playing against England in a couple of years time." Soon afterwards Jackson started in the big-time.

He scored a second-innings century in his second Shield match, and unbeaten second-innings fifties in matches three and four (the first to guide NSW to a gallant victory, chasing 446 in Adelaide; the second as NSW batted after Victoria had bludgeoned their historic, Ponsford-dominated 1107). For a while he carried the sobriquet "Second Innings Jackson", especially after he scored an unbeaten 104 against South Australia in the final innings of NSW's next match. J.C. Davis likened his driving in that game to "the fearless and vigorous type common in the days of Trumper". He finished the year with a stylish first-innings 42 against Victoria.

In April, Davis used the Trumper analogy once more to describe the 17-year-old Jackson: "In footwork, style and strokes he is more like the champions of the Trumper, Duff, Mackay period than those of later days, when so many batsmen have cultivated the push-to-leg shots to the detriment of beautiful off-side punches and full-armed drives."

Jackson also scored five first-grade centuries in 1926–27. Bradman managed just the one, though the young St George colt did return to the Southern Districts of NSW late in the year to score a highly publicised 320 for Bowral at Moss Vale in the final of the local competition. This was the second year in a row he had taken 300 runs off the hapless Moss Vale bowlers.

Jackson started season 1927–28 with a century against New Zealand at the SCG, but failed against Queensland, and then in Adelaide had to drop out owing to a spiteful boil above the knee. That ailment gave the intended 12th man, Bradman, the opportunity to score a century on his first-class debut — 118, batting seven, but in at 4–250 after Kippax had to retire because of heat exhaustion.

Jackson was back in the side for the Melbourne match, batting five, one place ahead of Bradman. Neither succeeded, Jackson scoring 6 and 16, and Bradman 31 and 5 as Victoria ground out a comfortable win by 222 runs. The immovable Ponsford scored 202 and 38, to take his Shield aggregate for the month of December 1927 to 810. Before the end of the month he would add another 336 against South Australia. As a remorseless run gatherer, Ponsford was at the height of his powers. Also in this match, Bill Woodfull scored 99 and 191 not out.

Back in Sydney, both Bradman and Jackson struggled again in the home match against Queensland. This was a marvellous match in which NSW batted first for 639 (Kippax 315 not out, Jackson 19, Bradman 0), Queensland replied with 276 and (following on) 590, and NSW stumbled to 8–100 (Bradman 13, Jackson 9) on a dampened wicket, as the northerners almost found an impossible victory.

The NSW-South Australia match in Sydney began the day after the Queensland match concluded. The demands on Shield player's time had expanded still further with the inclusion of Queensland, and four of the NSW team could not make themselves available for both matches. Archie Jackson was one who could, and took two superb centuries off the South Australian bowlers, the youngest man to score a hundred in each innings of a Shield match. Don Bradman scored a breezy 73 in the second NSW innings, his most promising outing since Adelaide, although *The Referee* report suggested there was still some of the naive teenager in his batting style:

"Bradman's batting was really the brightest of the match," suggested the report. "But he is inclined to draw away from his wicket and leave it wide open, even to slow bowlers; and second, he must run on the correct side of the wicket. Then he will not bump into his partner."

Bradman had also established a reputation as a world class fieldsman, epitomised by his run out of the veteran South Australian fast bowler and tailender Jack Scott. At 8–246, chasing 291 for first innings points, Scott responded to a call from his partner Doug McKay, who had driven a ball to Bradman at deep mid-off. Bradman darted for the ball, and instead of lobbing the ball to the nearby bowler's end, threw for all he was worth for the far end. The ball sped past the lumbering Scott and scattered the stumps, the startled batsman still more than a metre from safety. Soon after McKay was bowled and NSW had the lead.

*Archie Jackson (below) and Don Bradman, the two young batting stars of NSW cricket in the late-1920s.*

Another young cricketer to impress in this match was the 22-year-old South Australian left-handed batsman, Karl Schneider, who scored 54 in the second innings. One paper called him a Lilliputian who played like a Giant. Just 162 cms tall (5ft 2in) and originally from Victoria, Schneider was a pocket dynamo for his adopted state in 1927–28. He scored three centuries, averaged 52 in ten innings, and finished higher in the Shield averages than either Jackson or Bradman. A clever player, surprisingly powerful, and an outstanding fieldsman, his brief story is one of the saddest in the history of the Shield. In mid-February 1928, Karl Schneider was selected in an Australian representative team that toured New Zealand, where he showed the first indications of a condition, leukaemia, that would, just six months later, claim his life. He died on September 5, 1928, Archie Jackson's 19th birthday.

Jackson also won a place in that Australian team, but Bradman did not, despite scoring an unbeaten 134 in the second innings of NSW's final match, against Victoria. His was one of eight centuries scored in the match, a new Australian record, but Jackson could do no better than 11 and 44.

Before the 1928–29 season, Bradman moved from Bowral to live in Sydney to obviate the stresses of travelling from Bowral for Sydney grade matches. This was the season Don Bradman first showed his unprecedented ability to produce consistently high scores. Ponsford's records began to disappear before the ink had dried on the record books. In all first-class matches Bradman finished with 1690 runs at 93.88, a record aggregate for an Australian first-class season. In the Sheffield Shield he had a remarkable run — 131, 133 not out, 1, 71 not out, 5, 2, 340 not out, 35, 175 — ending up with 928 runs at 154.67. His unbeaten triple century against Victoria at the SCG set a new record for the ground, and was made despite a groin strain which later prevented him fielding.

His only double failure was in Adelaide, where he opened the batting with Archie Jackson and scored 5 and 2. Jackson in the same match was superb, scoring 162 and 90 to force his way into the Test side. At this stage, despite Bradman having a Test century under his belt, many felt Jackson to be the finer prospect. A week later, Bradman broke the SCG record to make Jackson supporters think again, but then the Balmain teenager scored that immortal 164 on his Test debut. Arguably it is still the greatest debut innings played by an Australian in Test cricket.

In his 1949 autobiography *Farewell to Cricket*, Bradman wrote of this innings: "The score did not matter so much. It was the manner in which he scored his runs."

By season's end their reputations were established. Jackson perhaps the more gifted, Bradman the more prolific. In *The Referee* J.C. Davis celebrated the return of Australia's youth, writing fervently not only of the two Test men, Bradman and Jackson, but also of Stan McCabe, Alex Marks, Len Darling and Jack Fingleton.

In the week before Jackson's Test debut, Davis had written: "Jackson has many years of big cricket in front of him. If he develops on the lines nature intended, he should become one of the most attractive international batsmen seen since Victor Trumper was in his prime."

Cricket history records this was not to be. While Bradman went on to a rungetting career unique in the sport, Jackson's career gradually fell away. In 1929–30, while Bradman was scoring 894 runs at 111.75, Jackson played in just three of NSW six Shield matches, scoring 195 runs at 39. The other three matches were missed through illness, the first signs of the tuberculosis that would ultimately claim his life. His cruelly premature death in February 1933 was mourned, especially by all who had yearned for the return of the glory of Trumper. His rightful place in the list of all-time great batsman can only be speculated upon, but many who saw him put him up with the best there have been.

One who bowled at him was Mailey, who in the 1960s picked Jackson in his best-ever Australian team, batting five in a line-up that began with Trumper, Ponsford, Macartney and Bradman and also included the allrounders Noble, Keith Miller and Jack Gregory. Most who rate the greats put Bradman first and the remainder well behind. Yet if one looks at the early career of Bradman and Jackson in the Sheffield Shield, and then ponders on the Bradman records and the glory, it is difficult not to think of Archie Jackson...and what might have been.

# 27

# THE KIPPAX-HOOKER LAST WICKET MIRACLE

Alan Kippax, the NSW leader and prolific runscorer, walked onto the Melbourne Cricket Ground, a captain under pressure. In eight previous matches at the MCG he had never scored a century. His four Test innings of the season had brought just 50 runs. Already the cynics, reaching for alibis to explain Australia's feeble form, were saying Kippax lacked the temperament for the Test match battleground. Any more failures and his Test spot, the position he had fought so hard to confirm, might be gone.

His partner was John Edward Halford ("Hal") Hooker, a man whose previous innings in Shield cricket had brought the unremarkable total of 11 runs — 4, 7 not out and 0. Hooker was a fine bowler, a right-arm medium fast man of swing, skill and stamina. He was a batsman of perhaps more ability than the usual number 11…but not much more. His only pretension to batting talent was in the practice nets, facing the schoolboys and the opening batsmen.

The partnership began on Christmas Day 1928 — the first time in Melbourne first-class cricket had been played on December 25. Not all agreed with the decision to play, but the VCA's options had been narrowed by a Test-dominated itinerary. NSW had crashed to 9–113, chasing 377 for first innings points. Kippax was 22, having survived while Andrews, Bradman, Kelleway and company had disintegrated. He had taken 45 minutes for his first two runs. At one stage, just before stumps on Christmas Eve, five wickets had fallen for four miserly runs. The exuberant Victorian bowlers included the young paceman, Ted a'Beckett, the former Queensland left-arm veteran spinner, Bert Ironmonger and Hunter Hendry, all bowlers in the Test series, and the young opening bowler Hans Ebeling, who would tour England successfully in 1934.

Kippax may have been tempted for one last slog, but resisted. With Andrews and Bradman having failed, and Ponsford out injured, his Test place was safe, at least in the short term, and he knew Hooker was an intelligent cricketer who would do what was required to keep the innings afloat. But for how long? The pitch was perfect, betraying the inadequate batting of those who had fallen. Hooker started comfortably, and Kippax went looking for runs wherever they could be found.

Many began commenting how Hooker resembled Hendry, in stature if not in batting style. The 10th wicket stand was a little cameo, a minor delay causing amusement rather than concern. But Jack Ryder was not amused. He knew how good Kippax was, and how good the pitch was. His rival was a man of experience and ability, who had been toughened by his controversial omission from the 1926 English tour. A man who had scored 14 Shield centuries, one of them a 315 not out slaughter of Queensland, four others double centuries including three against Victoria.

Slowly at first, then slightly faster, then at a some speed the scoreboard started to roll. A look at the scorebook showed the 150 up, a look at the middle showed Hooker entrenched, reliant on a straight bat and the encouragement of his captain. The partnership was suddenly established, as last-wicket stands are prone to do. The bothersome little hold-up was now a serious concern. Valuable time was being wasted. What was once an innings victory was now anyone's guess. Ryder rang the changes, and the fieldsmen crowded Hooker, like detectives seeking a confession.

For the first time in living memory the crowd cheered the New South Welshmen, especially after the interval when many arrived following Christmas lunch. Last-wicket miracles transcend state boundaries. Kippax had reached 60 by the first break. Hooker was 18, NSW 9–170.

In the first 25 minutes after lunch only ten were added. Hooker scored only four in half an hour. Ryder gave Ebeling and a'Beckett three overs each, then switched to Hendry and Ironmonger. But still Hooker could not be ruffled, and Kippax opened his shoulders, hitting straight down the ground. At no stage did the Victorian fieldsmen leave Hooker's pocket, and at no stage did he give them any reason to stay. Kippax reached 90, his highest score at the MCG, with a neat glance to the fence. Then the 100 stand came up, the fifth time the NSW last wicket had put on a hundred in a Shield match.

Almost immediately Kippax had Hendry through the cover field for his century, scored in just over three hours. His control of the strike was masterly, and he made sure Hooker faced only as many balls as could not be avoided. Ryder tried his net bowlers, without luck, and Kippax rode his fortune, once or twice miscuing drives to where Victorians might have been. At tea it was 9–270, Kippax 145, Hooker 32.

*Alan Kippax, a stylish and prolific run-getter for NSW between the wars. On Christmas Day, 1928, he and the unheralded Hal Hooker established a world last-wicket partnership record that will, in all likelihood, never be beaten.*

Hooker was asked later if he felt disillusioned going to the wicket with nearly 300 still needed.

"Not a bit of it," he said. "At first I made up my mind to keep an end up if possible so that Alan might get some good practice for the Test match — until he had made 70 perhaps. Then I set out to keep my end going until he might reach the century. He was going brilliantly. Shortly afterwards, Alan said to me: 'We want only about 150 runs. I think we can get them."

The NSW record for the last wicket (169 by Dr Roy Minnett and Cecil McKew against Victoria in 1911–12) was passed straight after tea. Hooker, to the surprise of the crowd and his opponents, cover drove Reg Ellis, the seventh bowler tried, to the fence. A NSW win was now a talking point, the follow-on long forgotten. The 200 stand came up, Hooker's contribution being 40. Ryder tried the same changes again, but by now most were asking only whether the runs would be scored that night. With Hooker on strike, a'Beckett moved ever closer at short leg, while John Scaife never moved from silly point. But Hooker was unperturbed. The Sheffield Shield record, Ellis and Hastings' famous 211 of 1902–03, was passed, then Kippax reached 200 to generous applause. He had been batting 309 minutes. Soon after, Hooker reached 50 to the greatest ovation of the day. Perhaps only Trumper, of all NSW batsmen, has ever brought louder cheers. Or so it seemed.

The next landmark to fall was the world first-class record of 235, previously set by the Kent pair of Woolley and Fielder in 1909. It disappeared in the final hour, a period when it always appeared touch and go whether the first innings points would be won before stumps. Baring and Ironmonger quietened Kippax until 10 minutes from time, when, breaking from his temporary shell, the NSW captain lofted the left-armer to the unguarded long-on fence. Twelve to win. The fieldsmen moved in closer at Hooker, but the bowling was tired and impregnable defence was now a habit. At stumps Kippax and Hooker needed 10 to win. Nobody at the MCG had spent a Christmas Day like it.

It took Kippax only ten minutes the next morning to get his side in front, Hooker needing only to face two deliveries. Hooker lost concentration after the Victorian score was passed, and might have been out once or twice until Kippax quietened him down. At 290, the Australian 10th wicket record at any level, previously set in an Adelaide club game in 1901–02, was passed. After that there were no more records to be broken, only unclimable barriers to be built. Kippax reached 250, and then the 300 stand came up. The score reached 420, the partnership 307, when Hooker, on 62, finally swung rashly, to be caught comfortably by Ryder at mid-off. It was the first chance of the partnership.

Kippax finished 260 not out, scored in 387 minutes and including 30 fours. Hooker had somehow managed three fours, one the flashing cover drive of the day before, another a lusty swing at a Hendry full toss that brought up his fifty. The other no-one could recall. The partnership had lasted four minutes more than five hours.

Hooker had this to say of his role, and the batting of his captain: "I used the good old straight bat in defence, and he played a glorious innings. You had to be at the other end to see it. His drives, hooks, cuts, and forcing strokes to the on-side were amazingly brilliant."

One of the most curious feature of this most extraordinary game happened after the NSW innings ended. The Victorians went in for the second innings, on the same MCG pitch where Halford Hooker had batted more than five hours, and collapsed to 4 for 45. Alan Fairfax at one point had 3–3. A recovery was led by Hendry and a'Beckett, and Victoria were finally able to make a token declaration of the final day. The match ended in a draw.

A cricket enthusiast, W. Walker of South Melbourne, had a letter published in *The Age* the next day, in which he listed the team he would have selected to represent Australia in the third Test. Kippax was omitted, while three of the bowlers he had embarrassed, a'Beckett, Hendry and Ebeling, were in the side. W. Walker probably wrote his letter before the Kippax-Hooker miracle, but one wonders how much he appreciated having his opinion published just a couple of columns from a story headlined "INTERSTATE CRICKET. NEW SOUTH WALES TENTH WICKET PARTNERSHIP. INCREASED TO 307 RUNS. KIPPAX 260 NOT OUT." Being a cricket selector is never easy.

For Alan Kippax, the tenth wicket miracle was a turning point. The next week he walked out onto the MCG to score his first Test century, a confident, superb even-hundred that ridiculed those who had doubted his ability or nerve. He would later go on two England tours, in 1930 and 1934, and set a Shield run-scoring record for NSW (6096 runs from 61 matches) that still stands.

Halford Hooker had further Shield glory just a month later. In the return match with Victoria, after Bradman had pummelled a chanceless unbeaten 340, Hooker completed a hat-trick to end the Victorian first innings. First Ebeling had been bowled off his pads, then Bert Gamble missed a straight one, and Ironmonger's feeble prod was caught in the follow through. Tommy Andrews enforced the follow-on,

Charlie Nicholls bowled the first over, and then Hooker scattered Ernest Austen stumps first ball, completing a sequence of wickets unique in Australian cricket.

Australian cricket was crying out for bowling talent, and in no time, Hooker had become one of the hopes for the future. Perhaps unluckily, he never got closer to a green cap than a Test trial, but continued in first-class cricket until 1932. Later he became a cricket commentator on the ABC.

After the Christmas Day match in Melbourne, the VCA organised a tribute to Kippax and Hooker. The last two balls used during the remarkable partnership were mounted and presented to the batsmen. One interesting talking point to come out of that game involved the unprecedented decision of the VCA to play on Christmas Day. The Melbourne Cricket Club authorities had made it clear they did not agree, and only reluctantly opened their ground. The crowd was good, more than 14,000.

But had play started a day earlier, and Christmas Day been a rest day, the Test men — Ryder, Hendry and Kippax — could not have played, as the second Test did not conclude until the Thursday before the Shield game began. On such administrative decisions are built some of cricket's great moments. Without Alan Kippax there would have been no record tenth-wicket stand, and Halford Hooker would have had to rely on his unique four wickets in four balls to keep his name in Sheffield Shield folklore.

# 28

## CLARRIE GRIMMETT

The table of leading wicket takers in the long history of the Sheffield Shield competition is the most telling relic of Clarrie Grimmett's remarkable cricket career. Grimmett was a leg-spinner, a little man of unequivocal spirit, who spun his trade without flourish, but with resounding effect, for most of the seasons between the two Great Wars.

Thirty three men have taken 200 or more Shield wickets. Seven have taken more than 300 wickets, the second highest Geoff Lawson with 367. But the greatest wicket taker remains the right-hand leg spinner, Grimmett, with his colossal tally of 513. The magnitude of that figure amplifies when you consider that Clarrie Grimmett played his cricket before Western Australia and Tasmania entered the Sheffield Shield, and that his Shield career took in nine matches before the advent of a fourth team, Queensland, in the competition. All up, he averaged almost six and a half wickets per Shield match; on 48 occasions he took five wickets in an innings (the next best is 25); 13 times he finished with ten or more wickets in a match.

Only three times (out of 79) did he fail to take a wicket in a Shield match. Once in 1925–26, again in 1934–35 (when he bowled just a single maiden over in a match against Victoria, due to gastritis), and in 1938–39, when he did not bowl in the second innings against Victoria due to a strained leg muscle.

Like another sporting hero of his time, the legendary racehorse Phar Lap, Grimmett was New Zealand-born. He was a Christmas Day baby, born in 1891, and he played first-class cricket in New Zealand before his 20th birthday. In 1914 he visited Sydney for a holiday, but stayed after finding a job as a signwriter plus a spot in Herbert Collins' Sydney club. In 1917, he moved to Melbourne to be closer to the girl he would later marry. There he played for the South Melbourne and Prahran clubs, and was chosen five times for Victoria.

Only one of those five appearances was in the Sheffield Shield. His Victorian debut came against NSW in 1918–19, the season immediately after the First World War when the Shield was not up for competition. His next first-class match was the infamous game against Douglas' English tourists that was overwhelmed by that extraordinary Armstrong indignation meeting. Clarrie Grimmett copped a hiding from the great Englishman Patsy Hendren, and retreated back to pennant cricket, not to reappear until February 1922 at which time he opened the bowling for the Victorian second XI against Tasmania in Launceston.

Grimmett was chosen just once in 1922–23. By February 1924 he had almost finalised negotiations to move to South Australia when the controversial selection panel of Bean, Ellis and McAlister, responding to criticisms in the local papers, resurrected him for the final Shield match of the season — against South

Australia. Given only three overs in the first innings, Grimmett took eight wickets in the second, a record that still stands for the best innings figures on Shield debut. Then, despite last-minute efforts from red-faced Victorian officials to make him change his mind, he packed his bags for Adelaide.

He was transferring to a state that had not won a Shield match since February 1914. His debut for South Australia was against his former teammates, but there was no fairytale result for Grimmett, although he did take 5–97 to give his new state a substantial first-innings lead. Victoria had to make 409 in the fourth innings to win. But despite bowling 50 overs on the final two days, Grimmett could not gain his side that elusive victory.

*Two of the great figures of South Australian cricket. Below: The gallant and persistent leg-spinner Clarrie Grimmett, the greatest wicket-taker in the history of the Shield. Right: Victor York Richardson, an inspiration to a generation of South Australian sportsmen with his brave batting, superb fielding and shrewd captaincy.*

Jack Worrall spoke for many Victorians when he wrote after this match: "There is no possible shadow of doubt but that he (Grimmett) was an underrated man in Melbourne. He is a gritty little fellow; punishment never disheartens him."

In one match, Grimmett had won the respect of his teammates, and established himself as the mainstay of South Australia's bowling attack. He gave his adopted team a weapon, after years of having little more than a brave spirit, and prayers for a sticky wicket.

To the South Australian captain, Vic Richardson, Grimmett was a godsend. In his 1967 autobiography, *The Vic Richardson Story*, he wrote: "I often wonder how much older than my 72 years I would feel had not Clarrie come from New Zealand, via Victoria, to help make life bearable for South Australian fieldsmen. Before he joined us, we thought nothing of spending two days in the field dismissing New South Wales and Victoria, and it is fair to say he reduced that time by about half."

Grimmett was a leg-spinner who bowled with an economy derived from seasons of rejection. He was a small, balding man, who stooped a little to flick the ball out from behind his back with an accuracy that stifled the logic that wrist spinners could never land the ball on the same spot. Jack Worrall called him a "three-quarter arm bowler", a reference to his round-arm action. His precision was derived from years of practice — aided by the dedication of a fox terrier which acted as retriever while his master bowled for hours in the nets at a solitary stump.

He bowled more than just the conventional leg break and wrong 'un, relying more than most on the top spinner. Later he developed a "flipper", a ball squeezed out by the thumb that sped through faster than the usual top or leg break and aimed at bowling batsmen who were late on a pull shot. He was easier to pick than Mailey but less charitable. And he operated in an era when true, hard wickets meant well-set run-scorers had to be thought out more often than spun out. Perhaps his greatest asset was his confidence. Never has a batsman existed that could not be mastered, even if the scoreboard would sometimes suggest otherwise. If Vic Richardson would suggest a spell, Grimmett would reply: "I may as well keep bowling as chasing the ball for the other fellows."

There was little of cricket he did not learn. One has the picture of a studious, unpretentious campaigner, his cunning almost hidden by the baggy cap that never left his head. Most cricket teams in the local park have their sage, the cricketer short of pomp and ceremony who, by merely getting on with it, gets the job done. From 1924 until 1941, as he bowled over after over after relentless over, he was that man for South Australia. His final career figures are a tribute to his skill, stamina and persistence, and a betrayal of the lack of firepower at the other end. Only the rapid Tim Wall, and later the legspinning Frank Ward, gave Grimmett continued assistance. Too often he was left to battle alone. Grimmett bowled nearly 6,000 more deliveries than any one else in Shield history, and conceded more than 4,000 more runs. Clarrie Grimmett took so many Shield wickets because he bowled so many overs. He bowled so many overs because he was, by a very long way and for a very long time, the best bowler in his side.

He had his unsuccessful days, though given the prolific nature of his success it seems almost churlish to mention them. In December 1925 he finished with 0–174 from 39 overs sent down against the renowned NSW batsmen. Later that season he captured ten wickets in the match in Sydney, but conceded the most number of runs (394) and bowled the most number of balls (848) in a first-class match in Australia to get them, as NSW piled up 642 and 593. In a 33-day period in December-January 1926–27, he conceded at least a 100 runs in seven of the eight Shield innings he bowled in.

But these less fruitful days were overwhelmed by the wicket-taking dividends of his cricketing labours. In 1927–28 he took 42 Shield wickets, the best this century until "Chuck" Fleetwood-Smith took 60 in 1934–35. In that year of Fleetwood-Smith's great success, Grimmett took 49 wickets, despite bowling no more than a solitary over in South Australia's match in Melbourne. In 1939–40, just short of his 50th birthday, he took 49 wickets again, including 11 against NSW in Sydney and 10 against Queensland at the Adelaide Oval.

He had many battles in the Shield against some of Australia's finest batsmen. One of the best came at the Adelaide Oval in December 1929, in the same year as Archie Jackson's wonderful Test debut, and less than a month before Don Bradman's world record 452 not out against Queensland at the SCG. This is how the Adelaide *Advertiser* described the action:

*The triangular duel between Jackson, Bradman and Grimmett when New South Wales started their second innings was one of the cleverest exhibitions of cricket finesse seen at the Oval for years. Richardson realised early that the wicket offered little assistance to Wall, and he relied on Whitfield and Palmer to keep an end going while Grimmett tossed up enticements from the other crease. Jackson and Bradman viewed every ball of Grimmett's with the deepest suspicion. Mostly they played back, watching* the ball right onto the bat. Now and again the tactics became wearisome and they stepped out with intent to drive and smother. Almost invariably they changed their minds and leaped back to their crease, like rabbits to their burrows. The mounds shouted with laughter at the performance, but they did not forget to cheer the colts when they picked loose ones from any bowler to send to the pickets. Jackson was an artist with his feet, and brilliantly turned full-length deliveries to either side of the wicket. Except for the ones Grimmett deliberately intended them to hit, they were never completely the masters of the slow bowler and on numerous occasions the play was delayed for a few seconds while they went into close caucus about it in the the middle of the pitch.

Both batsmen reached the eighties, but in the end Grimmett snared the pair of them. Bradman was LBW to the top-spinner, trying to pull to mid-wicket and Jackson was caught from the leading edge, as he tried to push for a single what seemed a slow, overpitched leg break.

South Australia won that match by five wickets. The victory came on Christmas Eve, and the day after-wards another Shield match, against Queensland, began. Grimmett in this game became a hero of another kind, seeing out the final overs with number 11 Tom Carlton, to prevent a Queensland victory.

A year later South Australia thrashed Queensland by an innings, with Grimmett taking 4–23 and 5–31. During this harvest he took his tally of Shield wickets to 212, breaking Ernie Jones' record. Two of his first innings wickets came when batsmen were bowled not offering at wide-pitched deliveries. Cecil Thompson fell victim to a leg break, Vic Goodwin was embarrassed by a wrong 'un.

The seasons went on and on. In 1934 Grimmett took 16 wickets for 289 against Queensland in Adelaide, equalling Giffen's record for most wickets in a Shield contest. In this match the first four South Australian batsmen, Vic Richardson, "Slinger" Nitschke, Bert Lonergan and "Jack" Badcock, all scored centuries in a first innings total of 7 (declared) for 664. At one stage the score reached 2 for 561. South Australia won easily, by eight wickets.

In 1936, Grimmett was controversially left out of the Test side, never to return. For his state he sol-diered on. In his first match after the selectors' decision was announced, Grimmett took 6–64 and 2–81 against NSW. The *Advertiser* described his first innings effort as "a wonderful bowling performance".

But for the War, Grimmett would have been happily taking Shield wickets long after the census takers had recorded his half century. He rarely captained South Australia, instead taking his wickets for two of the state's finest leaders, Richardson and Bradman. He remains one of the most celebrated figures in the history of the Shield, a bowler some have matched in skill but none in brave persistance. The expression "a heart as big as Phar Lap" is one of the most over-worked cliches used in Australian sport. Never though could it be more appropriately applied in Australian cricket than in the case of Clarrie Grimmett.

# 29

# "THEY CAN'T BE ALL OUT, I'M ONE OF THEM!"

In 1931–32 Victoria had a powerful batting side, spearheaded by the prolific Ponsford and Woodfull. To follow were the recently Test capped Keith Rigg, the soon to be Test batsmen Len Darling, Leo O'Brien and Ernie Bromley, and the evergreen Jack Ryder, in his penultimate Shield season.

The bowling attack was led by the robust, erratic fast man, Harry Houston "Bull" Alexander. He was short of stature for a fast bowler, and relied on a broad chest and rapid arm action to generate his pace. Best remembered in Test cricket for a quick bouncer that caught Jardine during the Bodyline series, Alexander was one of Victorian cricket's characters, a boisterous product of the working class and, inevitably, a popular figure with the MCG outer.

Strangely he did not make his Shield debut until after his December 1929 selection in a "Woodfull XI" v "Ryder XI" selection trial for the 1930 tour of England. He was not chosen for Victoria's next game after the trial, but finally made his Shield debut against NSW in Melbourne in the annual Christmas match.

From there he was a regular choice until 1933–34, when the Victorian selectors preferred the future internationals Ernie McCormick and Hans Ebeling. He later toured India in an unofficial tour led by the old Victorian allrounder Frank Tarrant.

Alexander was at his best in 1931–32, and approached the Christmas match with NSW in Melbourne in peak form. This was a game that evolved into an exciting tussle, won by three wickets by the home side, despite a first innings Victorian collapse that had given NSW a lead of 173.

NSW had lost the toss, been sent in, and were bowled out just before stumps on the first day for 276. Alexander had two wickets, for 71. In the time remaining before stumps, Victoria lost two wickets for 6, Woodfull, LBW to Bill O'Reilly for 2, and the nightwatchman Stanley Smith, bowled by O'Reilly for a duck.

The next morning the much-vaunted Victorians crumbled for just 103, O'Reilly taking three more wickets, of the seven that fell. It was only seven because the last batsman, "Bull" Alexander, was not at the ground when it was his turn to bat, and he went into the scorebook as "Absent Out". The story behind Bull's absence is one of the most unlikely to come from the Sheffield Shield.

The punters in the Victorian side had been told of a special in the first at Caulfield. With the regular SP bookie, the chief members'-stand barman, not at work, Alexander was given the responsibility of getting the money on. He sought out his captain, Bill Woodfull, before play began, to get permission to leave the ground. Woodfull, like Bull and almost everyone at the MCG, did not think the number 11 would be required in the immediate future. He wanted his fast bowler back before the completion of the lunch break.

Ninety minutes later, Bull jumped aboard a tram at the corner of Spencer and Flinders Streets in the heart of Melbourne, ready for his return to the cricket.

"What's the score?" he asked the tram conductor. Bull was well aware that tram conductors knew just about all that happened or was about to happen in the city.

"They're all out," replied the conductor.

"I'm talking about the Shield match at the MCG," countered Bull.

"They're all out," repeated the conductor.

"They can't be all out. I'm one of them!" Bull is reputed to have said.

This match was also a significant one for perhaps the greatest of all the great Australian bowlers. NSW's new medium-paced leg spinner, Bill O'Reilly. O'Reilly had learned before the match that he had been dropped for NSW's encounter with Queensland in Sydney, scheduled to begin three days after the completion of the Melbourne game.

O'Reilly had disappointed in Adelaide in the first match of NSW's southern tour. Vic Richardson, the South Australian captain who had scored a century in that game, later recalled wondering what the NSW selectors saw in him. However in Melbourne, O'Reilly was superb in the first innings, though strangely ineffective in the second as Woodfull and Darling scored centuries to achieve an unlikely victory.

Despite the disappointments of Adelaide and the fourth innings in Melbourne, O'Reilly had impressed many people on the tour, including Dr Reg Bettington, the NSW captain. Back in Sydney, Bettington dropped out of the NSW side, specifically to make room for O'Reilly.

O'Reilly took 2–19 and 0–37 against Queensland. Against Victoria in the return match he took 3–52 and 1–73, and with that was in the Test team, for the fourth match of the series against the South Africans. Exactly why O'Reilly was chosen is a mystery, though in the years that followed he vindicated the selectors' judgement time and time again. One must assume he had made a huge impact on Bill Woodfull, the Australian captain, in the first innings of the Shield match in Melbourne — a match that is most fondly remembered for a wicket Bill O'Reilly did not take. That of Bull Alexander.

# 30

# FAST EDDIE GILBERT

Thirty years after the sad ending of Jack Marsh's brief Shield career, another notable aboriginal fast bowler came into top-line Australian cricket. Eddie Gilbert, a fascinating cricketing character from the Queensland country settlement of Barambah, arrived on the Shield scene in 1930–31. A season later, in one dramatic and thrilling over, he bowled the fastest sequence of deliveries the Shield had seen. In a succession of five short, searing balls, the great Bradman was forced into a desperate sidestep, struck a painful blow to the body, and then caught by a wicketkeeper standing as far back as any keeper has ever had to go.

Gilbert, like Marsh, was an unusual bowler, with a swift, jerky arm-action which propelled the ball towards the batsman at a sometimes frightening speed. He too ran into problems with opponents, critics and umpires who questioned the legality of his action. And when he disappeared from the cricket fields, his life degenerated into one of poverty and distressing misfortune.

He was born in August 1905. At his peak Gilbert weighed less than 63kg, and stood not much more than 170cm. He possessed unusually long arms and when he first appeared on the cricket scene, bowled fast from a distracting, short approach to the wicket, more a walk of only four or five steps than a run-up. His pace came almost solely from his shoulder and bowling arm, assisted by a pronounced body turn.

He first came to prominence in Queensland through a series of forays on Barambah's concrete pitches. From country representative teams he found a place first in a Country Colts XI, then the Queensland Colts and finally the Queensland Shield side, for the first match of the 1930 season. That match was against South Australia in Brisbane, and was won by Queensland by seven wickets, after the visitors were caught on a wet second-day pitch and bowled out for 72. Gilbert bowled the first over of that innings, and finished with 2–22.

Gilbert's next match was against NSW at the Exhibition Ground, the last Shield match to be played at that location. NSW, batting first, made 566 (Wendell Bill 153, Alan Kippax 158, Stan McCabe 161, Gilbert 4–118), but lost first-innings points when the locals reached 687. Cecil Thompson, playing the innings of his life, ground out 275 from 10-and-a-half hours at the crease, and captain Frank Gough took over five hours for his 137. The NSW leg-spinner Hugh Chilvers finished with 2–219.

Gough was a controversial figure that season, and had a prominent role in a dispute that evolved between the QCA and the Queensland players. In earlier seasons the responsibility for the selection of the final Queensland XI while on tour rested with a panel made up of the captain and two other players. In 1930–31, the regular QCA panel opted to do the job themselves, and advised Gough as to what the team would be. Gough had not wanted Gilbert in the touring party, and had even suggested he would resign rather than captain a side with Gilbert in it. Gough was alleged to have claimed that: "Gilbert will interfere with the social side of the team."

When the tour finished, after a draw in Sydney and two embarrassing losses, the QCA held a series of inquiries which revealed: that Gough had wanted Gilbert made 12th man in Sydney, against the wishes of the selectors; that the eleven that played in Sydney and Melbourne had not been the one chosen by the selectors; that all the touring players had, in Melbourne, formed a "Players' Defence League", and taken up the responsibility of selection themselves; and that Gough and a number of the Queensland players and officials felt that Gilbert was a chucker.

After a series of meetings behind closed doors, the QCA announced that, unless the players they identified as the trouble makers apologised they would be suspended. Only Ron Oxenham did so and five players were suspended, and two others were threatened with suspension. The others, including Gilbert, were said to have been "dragged into the trouble".

Only four of the southern tourists were in the side selected for Queensland's final Shield match of the season, against Victoria in Brisbane. Three of the four subsequently announced they were not available, including Gilbert who claimed to have a sore shoulder. Oxenham intended to play, but fell ill and probably would not have played if the game had gone ahead. The match was eventually washed out without a ball being bowled. The dispute finally fizzled out, after the Queensland Chief Justice, Sir James Blair, acted as a mediator betwen the players and the QCA. All references to the players' suspensions were expunged from the records.

Gilbert finished his first Shield season with 15 wickets, and a reputation as a likely prospect. The NSWCA Yearbook singled him out as Queensland's most promising youngster. However the controversy concerning Gilbert's action was gaining momentum. It was revealed that NSW players had questioned his action after their first meeting in Brisbane. These rumours had reached the Queensland selectors, who obtained a slow motion film of Gilbert bowling before sending him on that stormy southern tour. There he was passed by some of Australia's best scrutineers, including the respected South Australian Test umpire, George Hele.

At the start of 1931–32 Gilbert was banned for a short period from his local competition, because officials feared for the safety of batsmen facing him on concrete pitches. The first Shield match of the new season was the visit of NSW to Brisbane, and the first chance for Eddie Gilbert to bowl at Don Bradman.

Their clash was delayed just slightly, as Queensland batted first, but made only a meagre 109. The wicket was lively, as quick a Gabba pitch as had been seen in years. When NSW went in, "Pud" Thurlow bowled the first over, a maiden into a stiff breeze to Jack Fingleton. Then Gilbert started. His first ball, from that ridiculous casual run, was a flier, and Wendell Bill could do no more than save his life, and cock a catch to wicketkeeper, Len Waterman, playing in his first Shield match.

Gilbert had wanted to get at Bradman, and now, with the ball still new and hard, the legend of that famous England tour was in. His teammates had told of Bradman's 452 not out, of how the Englishman Larwood had been no more than a medium pacer to the Bradman blade. For the battling aboriginal fast man from outback Queensland, this was his moment. In times such as these the body can react in wonderful ways. Never again would Eddie Gilbert send them down as rapidly as he did this over.

Bradman, right back on his stumps, parried the first ball down at his feet. The next was a vicious flier, and Bradman overbalanced as the ball flew high to the keeper. The third delivery shot though as well, and Bradman could do no more than dive for cover. The 4,000 crowd watched agog — stunned, excited and

*Left: Eddie Gilbert, bowling for Queensland in Sydney in 1930. Note the suspiciously bent elbow. Below: Prior to the 1931–32 Shield season, Alan Kippax took this side, made up of past-and-present NSW Shield players, to the NSW country for a series of matches. Back row (left to right): W. Ives, H. Love, W. Hunt, W. Bill, A. Fairfax; Seated: R. Gostelow, S. Hird, E.L. Waddy, A. Kippax, A. Jackson; At front: D. Bradman, S. McCabe.*

apprehensive. If something was better than a Bradman century this might just be it.

The fourth ball was at the body, too quick to avoid, and Bradman took a blow as angry as any he would ever receive. After a delay he resumed, but the next ball was on the same line, and Bradman, fashioning a deflection, snicked it through to the keeper. NSW 2–0, Gilbert 2–0, the crowd in uproar.

Bradman walked off with a wry smile on his face. "The luckiest duck I ever scored" he called it later. Some politely applauded him in. Others, more boisterous, cheered for a new hero, the little aboriginal fast man. But Gilbert, in the space of seven balls, had bowled himself out, the nerves and adrenalin were gone, and he lasted just two more overs. Before stumps he came back for two more, but his pace had departed, and Fingleton and later Stan McCabe handled him comfortably. He did manage to get through Alan Fairfax with a good one that swung in from the off and took the middle and leg stumps. Fairfax was caught unprepared, it was one of the few balls in Gilbert's five overs that pitched in the batsmen's half of the wicket.

The other incident of this eventful final session was the injury to Kippax, who was struck a dreadful blow to the face after Thurlow came on downwind. The NSW captain had been hit in a friendly game at Parkes in western NSW a few weeks earlier, when a ball had caught a spike hidden beneath a matting wicket. This second blow broke his nose, badly, and — it has been suggested — his confidence against fast bowling. Never again would Kippax bravely hook the bouncers to the boundaries. Before the match the ailing Archie Jackson had been forced to hospital with what was reported as severe influenza. Now Kippax was in the adjoining bed.

The next day McCabe scored one of the greatest of his many great Shield centuries. Gilbert was ponderous and ineffective, scarcely resembling the fiery tyrant of the night before. McCabe went on to an unconquered, glorious 229, and won NSW a lead of 323. Certainly the wicket was much calmer, as was the bowling, but this was an innings in the spirit of McCabe's most glorious Test efforts. Fingleton finished with 93.

The match ended in a massive innings victory for the visitors. The third day was washed out entirely, and when Queensland batted they knew little of how to counter the NSW attack on a wet pitch, and fell for a miserable 85. Bill Hunt, the clever left–hand spinner, at one stage had 4–3, and finished with 4–25.

Following the match word leaked out that most of the NSW players felt Gilbert's bowling action was unfair. To a man they contended that the over to Bradman was little short of cheating. "If Gilbert bowled fairly he is one of the cricket finds of the century," commented one un-named player. The NSW manager, Mr A.L. Rose suggested that most of Gilbert's deliveries on the first afternoon were illegal, and that he threw every ball delivered to Bradman. Rose was supported by the former Queensland captain, Leo O'Connor, who said: "Whenever Gilbert tried to get extra pace into the ball he invariably bent his arm, and I would say definitely that he threw."

Bradman too had no doubts. In his 1949 autobiography, *Farewell to Cricket*, Bradman called the over: "The fastest 'bowling' I can remember. I say 'bowling' because, without wishing to castigate the umpires, the players all thought his action decidly suspect."

Gilbert was unrepentant. He was quite prepared to abide by the opinion of the Queensland selectors, and was not worried what the NSW manager thought. He did consider that Mr Rose's comments were a decided slur on the Queensland umpires. Mr J.S. Hutcheon, the QCA President supported his opening bowler, saying: "Every umpire whose business it was to decide the question passed him, and while the umpires are unanimous on the point the (NSW) manager's opinion can scarcely be permitted to overrule them."

However one of the umpires in the Brisbane match, Mr J.A. Scott, made a startling admission following the match: "I could not say whether he was guilty of throwing in his first over to Bradman. I was the umpire at the bowling end when Gilbert was bowling on Friday, but after watching his approach to the wicket I concentrated on his feet." He continued: "I have watched him from square leg position and have frequently doubted his delivery. However in view of what happened last year, when Gilbert's action was passed by a moving picture test, and by southern umpires, I have been prepared to give him the benefit of the doubt."

Scott had been at square leg for most of Gilbert's overs on the second day. The other umpire, Mr J. Bartlett, stated he could not find anything illegal with Gilbert's action.

Gilbert went south for Queensland's southern tour, but immediately ran into trouble in Melbourne, where Umpire Andy Barlow no-balled him 13 times in his only three overs. When the Queenslanders reached Adelaide they asked George Hele to watch Gilbert in a special trial before the Shield match there. Hele passed him without question. Gilbert bowled 27 overs in the South Australia match, without a murmur from the umpires, and took three wickets.

Following that match in Adelaide, Gilbert did not play another first-class match away from Brisbane until December 1935, when he took 1–128 at the MCG. He was restricted by a chronic shoulder injury, which kept him out for the entire 1933–34 season, but did play eight matches at the Gabba in that period, always passing the scrutiny of the local umpires, and occasionally terrorising the visiting batsmen.

A week after that Melbourne match in 1935, Gilbert went to Adelaide for the first time since Hele had passed him in 1931. Leading the South Australian team was Don Bradman, who had waited four years for a second opportunity to face Gilbert. Revenge was swift and decisive. Bradman finished with 233, scored in little more than three hours. In the two hours between lunch and tea on the first day he raced from 43 to 200, the fifty between 150 and 200 taking just 14 dynamic minutes. This was his third consecutive double century against Queensland. Gilbert finished with 2–121.

Eddie Gilbert disappeared from big cricket after the 1935–36 season. He left the Sheffield Shield with 73 wickets, at that time the third greatest wicket-taker for Queensland in the competition, behind Ron Oxenham and Pud Thurlow.

He died in the Wolston Park Hospital, near Brisbane, in 1978, having spent the last years of his life sick and penniless, institutionalised in the Queensland country. He is recalled by some, unfairly, as no more than the man who threw at Bradman. There seems little doubt he did throw his quickest ball, but most of the time he was probably no more than extremely loose limbed, and a fine and unique fast bowler. But for one over at the mighty Bradman, he might have been remembered just as that.

# 31

## TIM WALL GETS THE LOT

I n the Sheffield Shield match between South Australia and New South Wales at the Sydney Cricket Ground yesterday, Wall, the South Australian fast bowler, took 10 New South Wales wickets for 36 runs. After lunch he took nine wickets for five runs in five overs, four wickets falling in one over. The side was dismissed for 113 runs.

Dramatic incidents did not end there. South Australian batsmen made as poor a showing, the visitors at the end of the day's play having a first innings lead of only one run. Howell was the most successful New South Wales bowler. He took five wickets for 31. O'Reilly's figures were one for 34.

Twenty wickets fell during the day for the meagre total of 237 runs. The remarkable bowling performances were not due to the wicket. It was a run-getting wicket — easy and even paced.

So began *The Sydney Morning Herald's* report of one of the most incredible of Sheffield Shield days. Thomas Welbourn "Tim" Wall, in clearly the greatest performance of his career, ran through the renowned NSW batting line-up, Bradman and all, to take all ten wickets. This was the first time such a feat had been performed in the Shield (only George Giffen, in 1884, had taken ten wickets in one first-class innings in Australia) and remains today the best return won by a bowler in a big-time cricket match in Australia.

At the time Tim Wall was the best opening bowler in Australia. He bowled his overs in an era dominated by huge scores, flat wickets, high bowling averages and persistent spin bowlers. He made his debut for South Australia in the first Shield match of 1924–25, the same game in which Clarrie Grimmett first wore the South Australian cap. Wall played in all four of his state's Shield games that season, though in Sydney he bowled just a single over before retiring with a leg strain. He did not reappear in the competition until the final week of 1927, but from then until retirement at the conclusion of South Australia's successful 1935–36 season, he was a mainstay of the South Australian attack.

His record Shield haul at the SCG came in the middle of the angry, tumultuous bodyline season. Wall played in all but the fifth Test of that series — Australia's only pace reponse to the dangers of Larwood and Voce. He laboured gallantly, just short of genuine speed, and had his best moments in Melbourne, where with O'Reilly and Ironmonger, he bowled Australia to its only victory of the summer.

Johnnie Moyes described him this way: "Taking a long run, in the Australian tradition, he had a good

*Opposite page: This Sydney Mail cover in 1914 featured the most popular cricketer in the city at that time — Victor Trumper.*

112

Registered at the General Post Office, Sydney, for transmission by Post as a Newspaper.

No. 96: Vol. IV (New Series).—No. 2629: Vol. XCIII. (Old Series).

# THE Sydney Mail

Wednesday]     [Jan. 28, 1914.

**3**D.     Special Article on Cricket of the Past and Present.     **3**D.

# The Australasian
## PICTORIAL

approach, and as he reached the bowling crease kicked his feet about like a frisky colt as he brought his arm right over and bowled at a quick speed. He could move the ball freely, and sometimes disconcertingly, had splendid stamina, (and) was a magnificent trier."

His 10 for 36 came in the first week of February, between the third and fourth Test matches. "Hammy" Love, acting NSW captain for the unavailable Alan Kippax, had won the toss, batted, and watched Fingleton and Bradman guide NSW to 1–82 at lunch. Half an hour had been lost due to a brief shower, and the ineffective covers may have left some water in the pitch, but there was no inkling of the drama which was to unfold after the break. Wall had troubled Bradman at times, after dismissing Bill Brown with a sharp bouncer that was deflected by keeper Charlie Walker, for first slip Dick Whitington to grab the catch. But Fingleton had been solid, and Bradman sometimes brilliant. Late in the session the champion took Wall for 13 in a single over. Wall's bowling figures at lunch were 1–31.

Clem Hill was the South Australian team manager, and of the after-lunch play he said: "I have never seen anything like this day of the bat's failure on a good wicket." Wall, who before lunch had relied on the outswinger and the occasional fast bouncer, now attacked the stumps with a series of inswingers, and crashed through Fingleton, who played back when he should have played forward, and lost his off-stump.

Stan McCabe's previous match at the SCG had been the first Test, in which he had scored a historic, brave 187 not out against Larwood and company. Wall's first ball to him swung down the leg-side, and McCabe helped it on its way, but too fine, and Walker, running across, took a stunning catch. The young left-hander, Ray Rowe, sparred unsuccessfully at the hat-trick ball, pushed nervously at the next, a no-ball, and then was horribly bowled, hardly jabbing at an away-swinging fast one. Frank Cummins, a nephew of the great Macartney, played at the last ball, and was given out, caught by Walker, though some thought the ball had flicked no more than the pad.

Bradman was 40 not out. He and Love added 11 priceless runs, all but one to Bradman, and all but one off Grimmett. Then Wall conned Love with a slower yorker. Bradman went to his fifty, but then lost the young, grandly-named all-rounder, Clement Hill, bowled trying to cut a broad inswinger. Next man Bill Howell, the son of the former great bowler, kept out two slower balls, and was then bowled, standing defenceless, by the quicker one. This was the rampant Wall's 100th wicket in the Sheffield Shield, the sixth duck of the innings, and Howell the fifth man to have his wicket shattered.

Since lunch Bradman had scored 18 of the 24 runs. Then his time came. Wall tried another bumper, and Bradman hooked at it, miscuing towards the leg side. Alf Ryan, fielding near the square leg umpire, dashed in and grabbed the ball before it reached the turf.

Grimmett had been trying for all his might to get his name among the wickets. Now, bowling to number 11 Gordon Stewart, he aimed well wide of the off stump to give Wall his ten-wicket chance. The last pair added seven, amid great tension and nervous applause, before Wall finally got through to O'Reilly's stumps.

The crowd cheered Wall all the way back to the pavilion. Nearing the gate, some spectators rushed the field and chaired him from the ground. "I've bowled better than that and taking 0–100," he is reputed to have said. Such is the way of cricket, although there is little doubt this was an inspired effort, the greatest day in the life of a very good bowler.

His after-lunch figures were 5.4 overs, 2 maidens, 5 runs and 9 wickets.

The former NSW player, Dr. Eric Barbour, writing in the *Herald*, thought Wall had found a yard of pace since the first Test. "Let us not detract from the glamour of a grand performance," he wrote, "and, instead of distributing lemons among the batsmen, let us hand to the great-hearted Tim Wall the laurel wreath for the finest piece of bowling seen for many a day." In a reference to the touring Englishmen's bodyline stategy, Barbour continued: "He never looked dangerous to the batsmen's person, but he was dangerous to their wickets, and it is a sheer nonsense to say that he could not make a success of the much-debated leg theory."

In the NSW second innings Tim Wall could manage no better than 2–91 from 22 overs. Bradman was dismissed for 97, the highest score less than a hundred he ever made in the Shield. NSW finally won the match by 98 runs, to clinch the Sheffield Shield for the 20th time.

Tim Wall never enjoyed another day like that one in all his years of playing cricket in Australia. His next best bowling performance in a Sheffield Shield innings was 5–82 against Queensland in December 1928, the only other time he took five wickets in a Shield innings. In fact he managed to take five or more wickets in an innings as often in Test cricket in Australia, as he did in Sheffield Shield matches. His 10–36 and 2–91 in Sydney in February 1933 was the only time he took more than ten wickets in a first-class match in Australia. His was one of the grandest once-in-a-lifetime performances in all the years of the Sheffield Shield.

---

*Opposite page: Tim Wall of South Australia, who at the SCG in February 1933 had the cricket day of his life. He took all ten wickets in the NSW first innings, including Bradman, McCabe, Brown and Fingleton, for 36 runs.*          115

# 32

# BRADMAN

Some critics over the years have attempted to construct flaws in Don Bradman's astonishing record — suggesting he was less than supreme on rain-affected wickets, that he lacked courage against the fastest bowlers, that Trumper was a better player, that Ponsford was a more difficult batsman to dismiss...and on and surprisingly on.

Such criticism is nonsense. Victor Trumper may have been a more *stylish* batsman — but then that could also be said of Charlie Bannerman, Alan Kippax, Archie Jackson, Greg Chappell and Mark Waugh. But to suggest any of these superb players were in the same class as Bradman is to suggest that cricket matches are won in the same manner as gymnastics or diving. Batting is about runs, and Don Bradman averaged substantially more of them per first-class innings than any other cricketer in the game's history.

In Shield cricket his average was an amazing 110.19, in a career that ran from December 1927 until March 1949. He scored 36 centuries and 20 half centuries in 96 innings, 15 of those 96 being uncompleted. The next closest to him in terms of Shield hundreds achieved is Greg Chappell, who scored 27. Significantly, 60 batsman have been dismissed between 50 and 99 in Shield matches more often than Bradman, a telling tale of his appetite and ability.

Johnnie Moyes wrote in 1954: "Don Bradman is of average height, slimly built yet very wiry. Otherwise he would not have been able to stand the strain of long days in the sun, a strain which caught up with him later on. His stance at the wicket was easy and comfortable, with no exaggeration such as we sometimes see in these days, and he was able to watch the approaching bowler clearly with both eyes. His footwork was fast and clever, for he could move to the ball, or step back inside his own ground to hook it viciously, or force it away, after making it the length he required for his purpose. His aim was always to place the ball on one side or other of the fielder, and he developed this art to the limit."

Bradman's first great performance in Shield cricket came in the opening match of 1928–29, when he scored centuries in both innings against Queensland in Brisbane. This was the tenth time such a feat had been performed in the Shield but, significantly, and certainly reflecting this era of runs and placid wickets, the sixth occasion since 1923–24. Another big double, 87 and 132 not out against Chapman's M.C.C. team, had Bradman in the Test XI, but it was not until late January 1929 that Bradman went past 134 in a Shield match.

Against Victoria at the SCG, Bradman scored an unbeaten 340 out of 6 (declared) for 713 in NSW's first innings. This was the highest innings against Victoria on record, and the highest scored by a cricketer under 21. J.C. Davis wrote that Bradman played the ball "with the accuracy of a Walter Lindrum at billiards", but also suggested that two 18-year-old NSW colts, Stan McCabe (who scored 60) and the left-handed Alec Marks (56), "were really more enterprising and entertaining than he (Bradman) was, and scored faster".

Bradman's innings was chanceless, bar for two or three mishaps running between wickets. Once he found himself at the bowler's end with his partner, Alan Fairfax, but managed to beat a slow inaccurate return from mid-off to the wicketkeeper. And late in the innings he called Jack Fingleton, making his Shield debut, for a single, was stranded when Fingleton did not respond, but was saved by a dreadful mix-up between three Victorians trying to complete the run out at the bowler's end. Davis implored all the young NSW batsman to read the chapter on running between wickets in Warwick Armstrong's just released instructional book, *The Art of Cricket.*

The following Shield season was, one innings apart, a relatively disappointing one for Bradman. Victoria won the Shield and Bradman scored just the one century. But that hundred is perhaps his most famous away from the Test arena, still the record score by an Australian in first-class cricket, 452 not out against Queensland at the SCG.

What is perhaps not as well-known is that the record score came in the second innings, after Bradman, opening up, had been caught behind in the second over of the match. NSW, dismissed for 235 in their first innings, narrowly won first-innings points only because of a stirring bowling performance by Stan McCabe. The Queensland first innings ended eight runs short soon after lunch on the second day, Saturday, January 4, and by stumps Bradman was 205, and NSW had a lead of 376 runs with Monday and Tuesday to come.

Bradman reverted to his customary number three spot for the second innings, but was at the wicket at 1–22. The Queensland attack was led by Hugh "Pud" Thurlow and Alec Hurwood, both destined to open the bowling in a Test match. At 33, a second NSW wicket fell. Alan Kippax came in, and he and Bradman changed the game. The hundred was reached in an hour and a quarter, the second 50 taking just 20 breath-taking minutes. When Bradman reached his hundred, Kippax was 68. J.C. Davis had seen little like it:

"He (Bradman) had run clean away from Kippax, though the latter was playing very fine cricket of a less punishing variety. Bradman's batting had all the verve and joyousness of a boy in his teens and Kippax the elegance, skill and dare of an Aramis of the sword. The timing of both men was very precise, that of Bradman remarkable."

Kippax reached his century in 137 minutes, but Bradman had outscored him two to one. Kippax was

*Don Bradman is carried from the SCG by his weary Queensland opponents after scoring an unbeaten 452 in January 1930, to break Bill Ponsford's Shield record.*

out for 115, with the total at 305. "His had been the innings of an artist," wrote Davis. "It lacked the whirl-wind aggressiveness of his young comrade, but it had its own special charm of grace and brilliancy."

Soon after Bradman got to 250, the Queenslanders tried leg theory in a effort to slow him down. In 20 minutes he scored only six, but just as the bowlers waited for the weary stroke of an exhausted man, he exploded into action again and reached his 300 close to lunch. At the interval he was 310. After lunch he passed his previous highest score of 340, in 326 minutes, and then was almost dropped by the keeper, who leapt high and wide to just miss a miscued drive.

The only maiden over of the innings was bowled by the brave Hurwood when the score was 624. Hurwood was to finish the innings with 6–179 from 34 heartbreaking eight-ball overs, a performance that won him a place in the 1930 team for England. NSW by this stage were five wickets down, and before Bradman reached 400 they lost two more wickets. He was now outscoring his teammates at an extraordinary rate, and reached his fourth century with a rapidly-run three, one ball after an all-run four. Perhaps he was looking tired...but there were still mountains to climb. Bradman admitted later he had Ponsford's record score of 437 in his sights for most of the innings, and as he closed he became ever more cautious, forsaking the boundary for the quickly run single.

Ponsford's score of 429 against Tasmania was equalled with a prod to square leg. His total crept along to 434. Two checked drives were stopped in the covers, but then Thurlow bowled a short one, and Bradman, ever grateful, hooked it to the fence.

The crowd cheered all aroung the ground. The Queenslanders came to the wicket and gave the new record holder three cheers. Then sections of the crowd, one following the other, did the same. Bradman took it all in with a boyish grin. Davis called him "the imp of the wickets".

With the SCG clock showing 4pm, and the total at 756, Kippax declared. Some critics felt he could have batted longer, though his closure was amply rewarded, the battle-fatigued Queenslanders losing 7 for 70 that evening. Following the declaration, Bradman, who had batted in total for 415 minutes, was chaired from the field by his beaten opponents, but only after a burly patron from the outer had raced out and tried to do the job on his own. Both Bradman and Bradman fan finished flat on their backs.

This innings remains today as the highest in first-class cricket on a turf pitch. For Bradman it was the forerunner to one of the greatest years of his fantastic run-scoring life. He came back from the 1930 tour of England the most remarkable batsman in the world, having scored 974 runs in a five-Test series, and almost 3,000 runs on tour. In 1930–31, he played in only the Shield matches against South Australia and Victoria, and scored three centuries, including two double centuries.

The next year he played just three Shield games, and strangely scored more ducks than centuries. First Eddie Gilbert was too rapid for him in a famous match in Brisbane, and 18 weeks later, South Australia's Tim Wall got through in the second innings of the season's final Shield match, in Sydney. In between Bradman past three figures for the fourth time against Victoria.

And so his career went on. Bradman rose to heights that his immediate run-getting predecessors, Kippax and Ponsford, could only have dreamed of. And he did it in a hurry. As only Trumper before him had done, Don Bradman changed the public's perception and appreciation of Australian cricket. His skill attracted crowds in a manner no other cricketer has been able to match, at a time in Australian history when people had to be careful with the money they spent. And he was fortunate to begin his fabulous career just as Australian families were installing the latest wonder, the radio, in their homes. Bradman's exploits were broadcast to a vastly wider audience than just those who turned to the newspaper sporting pages.

In the way that people invested their money on Phar Lap knowing they were going to collect, spectators went to the cricket to see Bradman score a hundred. Bradman was never better than even money to score at least a century. And when he finally retired he took with him many of his fans, who could do no more than ruefully compare the best of the post-Bradman era with what had gone before.

In 1933–34 Bradman scored four Shield centuries in five matches, the highlight being a brutal double-century against Queensland in Sydney. He shared a 363 third-wicket partnership with Kippax that took eight minutes less than three hours, and twice scored a century in a session. In the previous match against Victoria he had scored 187 not out and 77 not out. When he finally threw his wicket away against Queensland, after hitting the first four first-class sixes of his career, he had scored 517 successive runs in Shield cricket without being dismissed.

The final Shield match of that season, between NSW and Victoria in Sydney, amounted to a virtual Shield final. Victoria needed to avoid outright defeat to claim the trophy. Kippax won the toss and NSW batted, and Fingleton, Bill Brown and Bradman added 340 for the first wicket, Fingleton having retired hurt at 148 with an attack of cramps. Brown went on to 205, and Bradman to a quickfire 128, the last 118 coming in less than an hour and mostly from the bowling of Fleetwood-Smith.

Fingleton came back at 4–486 and was involved in an unusual incident. He sliced Ironmonger, playing his last first-class match and at 51 years 298 days the oldest ever Shield cricketer, to Hans Ebeling at slip, who dropped the chance. Ebeling lobbed the ball back to keeper Ben Barnett, who seeing Fingleton out patting down the pitch took off a bail and appealed to umpire George Borwick at square leg. Borwick gave Fingleton out. The Hill was not amused, but Bill Woodfull withdrew the appeal and called the rueful Fingleton back.

Kippax declared at 8 for 672, but the Victorians managed to bat for more than two days to claim the Shield by a single point. On the final day, all but keeper Oldfield bowled for NSW, Bradman bowling three unsuccessful overs of leg breaks for 19 runs.

In 1934 Bradman transferred to Adelaide after receiving a job offer with a stock broking firm owned by Harry Hodgetts, a South Australian representative on the Board of Control. He had yearned for a career disassociated from his sporting life, but in Sydney could find nothing that did not rely on his famous name. A severe illness suffered on the 1934 Ashes tour cost Bradman the entire 1934–35 cricket season, and the opportunity to tour South Africa in 1935–36. It was not until April 1935 that he commenced working for Hodgetts' firm.

With the long-serving South Australian captain Victor Richardson leading the Australian team in South Africa, Bradman was given his adopted state's captaincy for the 1935–36 season, and with the aid of fellow imports Jack Badcock (from Tasmania) and Frank Ward (from NSW) led South Australia to the Sheffield Shield.

Clem Hill wrote after Bradman's first match as South Australia's Sheffield Shield captain: "With his wonderful cricket brain he has imparted a tremendous amount of confidence to the players." His leadership, as well as his run-getting feats, received much praise in 1935–36.

Bradman's scores in his first Shield season for South Australia were: 117 (one less than his debut innings for NSW in the competition), 233, 357, 31, 0 and 1. The duck came about after a shrewd piece of strategy by NSW captain Alan McGilvray, who placed a short fine leg for his left-handed opening bowler Bob Hynes and successfully took advantage of Bradman's penchant for a push to the square leg umpire for his opening single. An edge from the eighth ball was gleefully caught by the specially placed man, Ray Little. The final failure, against Victoria, mattered little, as Badcock scored 325 and Ward spun out nine wickets, as South Australia cruised to a massive innings victory.

With Alan Kippax's retirement as NSW captain after the 1934 tour, Bradman could quite easily have expected to be that state's leader had he remained in Sydney. Bert Oldfield led NSW in 1934–35. By moving to Adelaide, Bradman probably did his chances of leading Australia little good, with Vic Richardson entrenched as South Australian captain. Bradman's lingering illness meant that he did not play under Richardson in 1934–35.

Suggestions were made by SACA committee members to Richardson, who was 42, that he retire following the South African tour (where Australia won four Tests to nil but Richardson managed only 84 runs in five Test innings). However he opted to continue, leaving the choice of South Australian captain in the hands of the SACA committee. This was a difficult decision, as Richardson was highly regarded by the players and all sportsmen in the state. But Bradman, the Australian vice-captain in 1934, was the obvious choice as Australian captain for the 1936–37 Ashes series, having proved in 1935–36 that he was a shrewd, incisive and successful Sheffield Shield captain.

The SACA went for Bradman, a decision that upset some senior players, especially Grimmett, but not the newspaper writers, who expressed no surprise or disappointment at Bradman's appointment. In 1936–37, Bradman played in four of South Australia's six Shield matches (Richardson, who followed the Test series as a reporter, played in two) and scored two centuries, but the Shield went to Victoria, who won three matches outright and three on the first innings.

The drawing power generated by Bradman was quite remarkable. The crucial NSW-Victoria match at the SCG in January 1934, attracted more than 64,000 people, including 32,587 on the first day. The corresponding fixture in 1934–35 drew less than 34,000; in January 1935, the match crowd figure was 18,370; and in 1936–37 the *Daily Telegraph's* Jim Mathers was able to count the crowd on the third day — 27 on the Hill, 26 on the benches in front of the Hill, 63 in the "Bob" stand, and 37 on the "Paddo" hill at the northern end.

With Bradman playing for South Australia, the NSW v South Australia match in Sydney became a bigger earner for the NSWCA than the traditional battles against Victoria. In 1934–35, with Bradman absent, the crowd for the SA game, which lasted just over three days, was 11,264. The same match in 1935–36, because of rain and then the death of King George V, involved play on only two days — but attracted a healthy 18,716. In 1936–37 the game drew more than 32,000 for the four days, and in 1937–38, the match attracted 37,486 including more than 20,000 who went on the first day when Bradman faced Bill O'Reilly.

Bradman's clashes with O'Reilly in the years before World War II inevitably brought larger-than-usual crowds. In Sydney in January 1939, in temperatures that reached a devastating 113.6 degrees farenheit (45 degrees celsius), nearly 8,000 went to the SCG, and saw Bradman keep wicket. Regular keeper Charlie Walker had damaged a finger in Brisbane the week before, and Bradman gave himself the substitute's role. Wearing a sombrero to keep the sun at bay, he did the job with what J.C. Davis called "ardor and skill".

Days two and three were lost to rain, after the heatwave had broken on the Sunday. This was a disaster for the NSWCA treasurer, still smarting over his Association's inability to keep Bradman in Sydney after 1933–34. On the final day, with the result a foregone conclusion, 4464 chanced the threatening weather to watch Bradman score his fifth straight Shield hundred, and his record-equalling sixth in a row in first-class cricket. Six weeks later, nearly 18,000 were at the Adelaide Oval on a cold, grey day to see Bradman try for an unprecedented seventh consecutive century, but when only five he turned a innocuous ball from Frank Thorn to Fleetwood-Smith close up at square leg, to end the sequence.

In the New Year's match in Melbourne in 1939–40 a Shield record 77,022 went to the MCG to see Bradman take on Victoria. He scored 267, batting late on the second day and most of the third. Two weeks later in Sydney nearly 76,000 watched the action, including more than 11,000 on the final day, a Wednesday, when South Australia resumed on 3–74 (Bradman not out 35) chasing 371, but lasted just over an hour. Bradman scored only five more, before miscueing a Cec Pepper leg break.

One unlucky Bradman fan bemoaned that final collapse. "I had settled down at the cricket with a few chicken sandwiches and two cold bottles of lager, ready to see Bradman go on to hundreds," he explained. "But when he went out, I went home, had lunch, and then got to Ascot (racecourse) half an hour before the first race. If the cricket had lasted I wouldn't have bet a shilling, but at Ascot the favourites went down like South Australian wickets, and I lost 450 pounds."

In the *Daily Telegraph*, Arthur Mailey wrote of the vanquished: "It seems as far as South Australia is concerned, everything depends on Bradman. If he fails, South Australia loses. If he scores his usual double century, his team wins."

Up to the second World War Don Bradman was involved in five Shield championship wins, three with NSW (1928–29, 1931–32, 1932–33) and two with South Australia (1935–36, 1938–39). In that time he scored a great many runs, including an unprecedented number of big centuries, at an unbelievable average. But despite the enormity of such statistics, Bradman was about very much more than runs and victories. He was the most effective magnet for cricket crowds the game has ever seen. He took away some of the mystery and uncertainty that has been part of the game since the days before the Shield, and lured to the cricket people who had previously looked elsewhere for their leisure and entertainment. Fans who paid to see Bradman knew what they were getting and usually got it. He was the greatest player of his time, and of any time.

# 33

# THE GENIUS OF FLEETWOOD-SMITH

In the Sheffield Shield season of 1896–97, Tom McKibbin, a slow off-spinner from the NSW country town of Bathurst, took a competition-record 44 wickets in NSW's four matches. McKibbin was a fascinating figure in late-19th century Australian cricket. He made his debut for NSW in November 1894 against Stoddart's touring team, travelling ten hours from Bathurst, and then walking to the SCG from the city. He toured England with moderate success in 1896, but doubts about his bowling action curtailed his representative career. In his great Shield season, his bowling figures in eight innings were: 7–51, 8–74; 5–47, 3–80; 4–62, 4–101; 8–111 and 5–129.

Those 44 wickets stood as a Shield season's record until 1934–35, when, in one summer, three bowlers raced past McKibbin's total. First there was the Victorian left-hand wrist spinner, Leslie "Chuck" Fleetwood Smith, whose 15 wickets against NSW in January took him to 52, snared in five matches. Three weeks later, the NSW leg breaker Hugh Chilvers bagged ten wickets in Brisbane, to finish with 46 wickets for the season. And on the same day, Clarrie Grimmett was spinning South Australia to a 107 run victory over Victoria at the Adelaide Oval, and taking his wicket-taking aggregate for the season to 49.

All three were superb practicioners of the spinner's art. The remarkable story of Clarrie Grimmett is told in a separate chapter in this book. Hugh Chilvers was a valued member of the NSW Shield side between 1929 and 1936, more than once spoken of as a potential Test player. In 1930 some suggested he be taken to England instead of the proven Grimmett. With the emergence of Bill O'Reilly, Chilvers was pushed somewhat into the background, but when the great leg-spinner was unavailable for much of 1934–35 Chilvers relished another chance at a leading role.

The third member of this triumvirate was Fleetwood-Smith, originally from Stawell in Victoria, and an eccentric and unusual sportsman. It was reported many times that he was a natural right-hander who only developed his left-hand bowling while his right arm was broken. In his excellent 1991 biography of Fleetwood-Smith, *A Wayward Genius*, Greg Growden confirms this was a fallacy the bowler never bothered to challenge. Fleetwood-Smith in fact was ambidextrous, and realised as a child that he seemed a better bowler with his left hand than his right.

At his best, Fleetwood-Smith was as difficult a spinner as the game has created. He could turn the ball both ways quite viciously, and was all but impossible to pick when he got the wrong 'un working. As with all bowlers who really spin the ball, when it came out right the flight was awkward and unpredictable. Too often, especially early in his career, his length was erratic, his concentration lacking, his commitment poor. It was nothing for him to interrupt the tension of a vital game with a bird call from the outfield. But when the conditions suited, and the mood was in him, few batsmen could plan a lengthy stay.

His Shield debut came in March 1932, against South Australia in Melbourne. He had already taken 22 first-class wickets in three matches that season, and in his first Shield game tricked and turned out 11 South Australians, for 120. The next year he took 50 wickets in the first-class season, 30 of them in the Shield — but in two crucial matches Bradman and the Englishman Wally Hammond gave him scant respect, and he was never a serious contender for the Test side.

The next year he again passed 50 wickets, but once again Bradman was too good for him, blasting a century in each of the three matches they were both involved in. Despite the final hundred, scored in just 87 minutes, and including three huge sixes from Fleetwood-Smith, who finished with 2–178, the left-hander was included in the 1934 England tour, thought of as a luxury — but too skilful to leave behind.

He went away as the third-choice spinner behind Grimmett and O'Reilly and never played a Test, as the famous duo took advantage of Bradman, McCabe and Ponsford's runs to spin the Ashes back to Australia. But the tour made Fleetwood-Smith as a bowler, and he came back a more precise, more devious and more intelligent tactician.

Before he had a chance to show off his improved bowling repertoire in the Shield, he displayed some unknown batting talents. On the second morning of Victoria's opening Shield match of 1934–35, Fleetwood-Smith joined his fellow "rabbit" Ernie McCormick with the first innings score 9–276. McCormick's previous highest Shield score, in nine matches, was 16, but here he was 50 not out and going well.

The week before Fleetwood-Smith had been an interested spectator at a women's cricket match at the MCG between Victoria and England. There he admitted to Jack Worrall that he had not taken batting seriously, but intended to in the future. "If I can make a dozen or so," he explained, "the chances are that the other man will also be helping himself, and what an advantage to the side. A man could be, in all probability, set when I get in."

Little did he realise that that man would be McCormick. "If Ernie can make them, then so can I," he told his stunned teammates. The pair added 98, Fleetwood-Smith dominating, in 57 crazy minutes. They were aided by the deplorable fielding of the Queenslanders, so bad few correspondents at the game agreed as to the final dropped catches tally. It was somewhere around a dozen, at least seven off poor Ron Oxenham. Fleetwood-Smith hit nine fours and a six, was missed at least twice, and finally caught near the boundary for 63, attempting another towering hit.

It was the highest score of his life, and more than he had scored on the entire England tour. But it was not a sign of things to come. Except for a powerful straight drive back past a startled Eddie Gilbert in the return match in Brisbane, this would be Fleetwood-Smith's only batting glory for the summer.

With the ball he was a magician. In this first match he took nine wickets, and with McCormick and the new captain, Hans Ebeling, bowled his side to an innings victory. Wrote an impressed Worrall: "He commenced doing damage at once, sending down many wrong 'uns and turning and flighting the ball splendidly, short ones being few and far between. The trip (to England) has improved his command out of sight."

A week later, the old enemy NSW were in Melbourne. Fleetwood-Smith grabbed eleven wickets in a thorough nine-wicket triumph, revelling in Ebeling's forthright leadership. The NSW lefthander Gordon Horsfield was bowled by a vicious bosey he made no attempt to play. The veteran Kippax was LBW to what Worrall called "the King ball", the one that spun back sharply from the off. The last NSW second-innings wicket to fall was Fleetwood-Smith's 100th Shield victim. Little more than half an hour later, the match ended, in pouring rain, NSW captain Bert Oldfield refusing to use the weather as an excuse to save the game.

Fleetwood-Smith took six wickets in the ten-wicket defeat of South Australia in the New Year's match in Melbourne, and then grabbed 11 wickets in Brisbane at the start of Victoria's northern tour. A week later in Sydney he produced his greatest perfomance of the summer, 15 wickets for 226, dominating the match after the Victorian batsmen scored 420 in the game's opening innings.

McCabe, who top-scored in both innings, and O'Reilly were back for NSW — their first Shield games of the season — and Chilvers was effective, especially in the second innings when he spun his team back into the game. But the star was Fleetwood-Smith, the catalyst for Victoria's Shield-clinching fifth straight outright win. In the second innings he came on after four overs, and bowled unchanged, mostly with his captain keeping the other end virtually runless, and took 8–113 off 17.6 overs.

On the second afternoon McCabe scored 92, and thrashed Fleetwood-Smith for a period. At one stage McCabe took him for three fours in a row, but Ebeling knew his bowler and left him on. The slow man took it all in his stride, always coming back for more, and finally netted his man, caught in the slips half-driving at a well-flighted googly.

Kippax's demise in the final innings was extraordinary. After McCabe had hit successive fours and then been dropped in the outfield, Kippax received a very wide, very short, apparently harmless off-break. Fleetwood-Smith, still smarting from the missed catch, turned to walk back to his mark as the ball pitched. Kippax, the cagey campaigner, recognised four runs when he saw them, and leant back to thrash the ball through the off-side. But the ball, however badly pitched, was loaded with off and top spin and jumped back at Kippax, who could do little but try and frantically readjust. The result was a dreadful jab and a lobbed catch back towards the bowler. Fleetwood-Smith had his back to this chaos, but alerted by the shouts of his colleagues, turned to see the chance falling away from him. All he had time for was to stick out his left hand. The ball stuck, a dismissal none could recall the like of in all their years of watching or playing the game.

Much was made of Fleetwood-Smith's performance. J.C. Davis called him the most dangerous bowler in the country, more lethal even than O'Reilly because of his greater spin. Davis also had kind words for the Victorian captain: "Ebeling's leadership in this match is the best one has seen from an Australian for many years. His grip of the game, and of tactics, is similar to that of the successful pre-war leaders, G.H.S. Trott, M.A. Noble, and H. Trumble — and W.W. Armstrong. His methods in handling the field are quite different from those of W.M. Woodfull. His are aggressive; Woodfull's defensive, in the main."

An outright win in Adelaide would have made Ebeling's team the first to gain maximum points from all matches since the hours of play were restricted in 1927. However South Australia won comfortably, perhaps because Fleetwood-Smith had his only poor day of the season, being taken for 186 runs in the home team's second innings. Their innings total of 415 was only the second time the Victorian bowlers had conceded more than 300 runs in a single Shield innings all season. The three wickets Fleetwood-Smith bought, however expensive, took his tally to 60 for the season, a record figure that still stands.

He continued taking wickets all the way to the second World War, but his great days were between 1934 and 1938. He missed the 1935–36 Shield season, touring South Africa with Vic Richardson's Australian team, but made a triumphant return to Shield cricket in December 1936, taking 7–17 and 8–79 against Queensland in Melbourne. It was his second 15-wicket haul in three Shield games. No-one has taken 15 wickets in a Shield match since.

In the New Year's game in 1937–38 he dismissed all but Bradman in South Australia's first innings, for 135, becoming second Victorian to take nine wickets in a Shield match. His old batting partner McCormick had taken 9–40 against South Australia in Adelaide the year before. He made his second English tour in 1938, but when he came back some of the magic was gone, and productive days with the ball became less frequent. His final first-class match was the last Shield match before the war which ruined the competition for five depressing seasons.

After the War Fleetwood Smith sadly swapped the life of a Test cricketer for the life of a derelict. Late in his life he faced the ignominy of a court appearance to answer a vagrancy charge. Never far from skid row, he was managing a brave fightback when he died, aged 62 in March 1971.

He is remembered by cricket lovers as the closest thing to a natural bowling genius the game in Australia has produced. Had he the tenacity and work ethic of Grimmett or O'Reilly he would have been the greatest bowler of all-time. The wickets counterpart to Bradman's runs. But that could not have been Fleetwood-Smith's style — a big part of the package was the free and easy spirit. He was a one of a kind, the most colourful joker in the pack.

# 34

# THE TIGER

Bill O'Reilly first appeared in Sheffield Shield cricket in 1927, failing to take a wicket in 13 overs against Queensland at the Exhibition Ground in Brisbane. This was his only Shield experience until late in 1931, when, apart from the first innings of the wonderful match in Melbourne made notorious by Bull Alexander's unfortunate exit on a punting mission, he had little success on NSW's southern tour.

Back in Sydney, O'Reilly bowled without luck in the Shield, until the final match of the season, against South Australia. In his autobiography, Vic Richardson remembered this game:

"It was not until I batted against Bill in Sydney that I realised Australia had found a champion. In this game he took 5–68 and 5–59, thanks mainly to his quickly dropping wrong 'un and viciously turning, faster leg break."

J.C. Davis was another impressed observer. Following the South Australian first innings he wrote: "If anyone has any doubt as to the class of W.J. O'Reilly as a bowler his form on Saturday must have convinced him that Australia's recent experimenting has brought forth something. O'Reilly's length was very precise; his direction was good. He made pace off the pitch."

*The Australian Cricketer* wrote that his performance "gladdened the hearts of the critics in the stand." Here was the first potential Australian champion bowler to appear for many years. By the end of the following season, O'Reilly was clearly the leading bowler in the country. In the Tests he often had little support as he gallantly toiled against the powerful Englishmen. In the Shield he took 31 wickets in five matches, including nine (for 66) in Brisbane and seven (for 102) in Adelaide.

O'Reilly's bowling return in the opening Shield match of the 1933–34 season — 13 for 111, in Brisbane — remains the best match figures ever gained in a Shield game at the Gabba. In Melbourne over Christmas, he took 12 for 142, including 9–50 from 35 superb overs in the second innings. Only keeper Ben Barnett, bowled by Shield debutant Alan McGilvray, failed to go in the O'Reilly bag. At season's end he left for England where, in tandem with Grimmett, he took the wickets that helped Bill Woodfull's side regain the Ashes.

Owing to work commitments, and the 1935–36 South African tour, O'Reilly played just one Shield match in the two seasons following the England tour. In 1936–37, Test commitments kept him away from all but two matches, NSW's thrilling one wicket win in Brisbane and a rain-ruined contest with South Australia in Sydney. In the Sydney match, O'Reilly stunned an 18,000 Saturday crowd by trapping Bradman LBW for 24 after a short, exhilarating duel.

Lindsay Hassett wrote of O'Reilly: "No bowler could have been more abundantly blessed physically. The 'Tiger' stood 186cms (6ft 3in) tall, had the well co-ordinated body of an athlete and possessed long arms and unusually large hands. Added to this he had a searching curiosity which probed into a batsman's methods and a well-above-average intellect which took little time to arrive at the best method of attack.

"His thinking was always positive and the only way he knew to play the game was with an almost savage aggression. His attitude is probably best illustrated by an incident when, after completely beating a batsman with a vicious wrong 'un, he lifted the heavens with his appeal for the LBW decision. The umpire declined with the explanation that the ball had just touched the edge of the bat. O'Reilly's reaction was:

*The fearsome "Tiger" – Bill O'Reilly.*

'I knew he hit it — that's where the bloody rule's wrong'."

As did many champion NSW cricketers, O'Reilly came from the country. He was born in the far-west of the state, at White Cliffs, and raised at Wingello, not far from where Bradman discovered the game. He bowled off a lengthy run for a spinner, but appropriate for a spinner of his pace, and delivered the ball only after his bowling arm had completed a full circle. He had an unusual grip for a leg breaker, and despite a tall bouncy approach, stooped slightly to send the ball on its way. It was rare and awkward for a man of his speed to turn and control the leg break, and almost unfair that he could also disguise a spinning, bouncing googly.

In South Africa, Richardson gave O'Reilly a squadron of short legs for the first time, and they became a feature of his bowling from that tour onwards. For NSW, Jack Fingleton and Arthur Chipperfield spent much time in close, waiting for inappropriate responses to the substantial bounce. From 1937 until 1940, O'Reilly was the key to his side's fortunes, the strike bowler who had to be countered before NSW could be beaten.

In Adelaide in December 1937, O'Reilly produced perhaps his ultimate Shield performance. Batting first, NSW made 337, captain Stan McCabe (106) playing what Vic Richardson thought to be his finest hand on the Adelaide Oval. When South Australia batted on the Saturday they were devastated by the champion spin bowler. The *Advertiser* headline told the story: "SA CRICKETERS ROUTED BY O'REILLY: SLOW BOWLER TAKES FIVE WICKETS FOR ONE RUN IN SIX OVERS"

At tea, South Australia were 1–109, Jack Badcock having been dismissed in the opening over. Bradman was in excellent form, and the South Australian century had arrived in just under two hours, the last fifty in 44 hectic minutes. There was no hint of what was to come. After tea, McCabe made a crucial change, switching O'Reilly to the northern end, into the breeze. His first five overs after tea brought just six runs, but no wickets. At this stage of the game, the scoreboard showed O'Reilly's figures as 16 overs; six maidens; 15 runs; no wickets.

Over his next six (eight ball) overs his figures changed as follows:

17 overs; 7 maidens; 15 runs; 2 wickets
18 overs; 7 maidens; 16 runs; 2 wickets
19 overs; 8 maidens; 16 runs; 2 wickets
20 overs; 9 maidens; 16 runs; 3 wickets
21 overs; 10 maidens; 16 runs; 4 wickets
22 overs; 11 maidens; 16 runs; 5 wickets

He used the full leg trap for all but Bradman, who had to worry only about Fingleton at short leg. The first wicket to fall in this inspired spell was Dick Whitington. The opening bat had defended for more than three hours for 54 before prodding a catch to the leg trap. In the same over Ray Robinson was bowled, playing all around a well flighted wrong'un.

Next to fall was Bradman, out for 91 miscueing an attack on a slower ball. His journey from 50 to 91 had been a difficult one, taking 109 minutes. In this cautious time he had managed just one four. The *Advertiser* wrote: "Throughout his innings Bradman was pinned to the crease by O'Reilly, and it was a magnificent tribute to the NSW bowler that the greatest batsman in the world, eager for opportunities to score, was restricted to desperate defence. Bradman was unable to show sustained aggression until White and Cheetham took over the attack."

Mervyn Waite was caught behind by Bert Oldfield, swinging across the line, then Charlie Walker was bowled by a quicker leg break. Rarely has a first-class match on a comfortable wicket been turned around in this manner. Ron Hamence spent the final 50 minutes struggling to 5 not out. At stumps, South Australia were 6–163, O'Reilly, who bowled unchanged from tea to stumps, had 5–18, from 23 overs.

Of O'Reilly's fabulous performance, Vic Richardson wrote: "One of the finest performances I have ever seen, and the batsmen cannot be blamed for having gone down before this almost superhuman effort. There are many people who consider that under these circumstances O'Reilly should be attacked, but they are always sitting in the pavilion."

The third day, the Monday, was O'Reilly's 32nd birthday. He took his figures to 9–41, from 33.6 overs, still the best return by a NSW bowler in Shield cricket. When NSW batted again they disintegrated to 9–70, before reaching 104. Grimmett had 4–30 from 14 overs, but the last pair ruined his figures to some extent. A feature was an astonishing catch that dismissed McCabe. Badcock, running back towards the crowd at square-leg, dived at the boundary as the ball fell to earth, and held a dramatic one-handed catch less than a metre from the fence.

With 45 minutes left before stumps Bradman changed his batting order, sending his tailenders in with Badcock. The strategy was a disaster, and at the close South Australia were 3–34, Badcock 19, Bradman 2. The next day, these two batted through to lunch, scoring most of their runs when McCabe gave O'Reilly a breather, although in one O'Reilly over just prior to lunch Badcock slammed three fours in a row. For most of the morning O'Reilly attacked, with McCabe joining Fingleton and Chipperfield close to the bat.

Four runs after lunch, and still in the first over, O'Reilly spun one past Badcock to kill the partnership. In O'Reilly's next over, Bradman was caught at silly mid-on, to end the contest. The innings was over at 191, Ray Robinson the only remaining batsman to show any fight. O'Reilly finished with 5–57.

Between 1936 and 1940, O'Reilly versus Bradman was an entrepreneur's dream. In January 1940, just a fortnight after O'Reilly had taken the remarkable match figures of 14 for 45 against Queensland in Sydney, 24,317 went to the SCG to see the two champions opposed. In his second over of the day O'Reilly beat Bradman with a superb googly. The peerless batsman was clearly LBW, and appeared almost to walk as soon as the ball was through. O'Reilly finished with 6–77 this day. By 1939–40's end he had 52 wickets, his best haul ever in a Shield season.

Bradman had his lucrative days against O'Reilly, and with Lindsay Hassett was the only batsman to now and then dominate the great bowler. In Adelaide in late 1939, Bradman had his best match against his native state, when he scored unbeaten innings of 251 and 90. O'Reilly took five wickets in the first innings, but conceded 108 runs, most of them from Bradman, from 22.1 overs, a most un-O'Reilly rate of benevolence. Bradman considered this his greatest Shield performance. In all, he scored three Shield centuries against O'Reilly, but on four occasions champion bowler triumphed over legendary batsman.

Bradman thought him the best he ever played with or against. In 1953, Johnnie Moyes rated him, with the "demon" Spofforth, as the greatest bowler Australia had produced. In 1940, J.C. Davis wrote: "O'Reilly has become the modern "Demon", if not in pace, then in deed. There can surely have never been a better bowler than O'Reilly." Nearly 50 years later, Alan McGilvray had this to say: "O'Reilly to my way of thinking was the best spinner ever to wrap his fingers around a ball."

Perhaps the most telling plaudit for O'Reilly's skill is a Sheffield Shield statistic. At the beginning of the 1992–93 season, 33 bowlers had taken 200 Shield wickets, including most of the legends of 20th century Australian cricket — Jones, Grimmett, Fleetwood-Smith, Lindwall, Benaud, Davidson, Lillee, Thomson and so on. Only one of that elite group has a Shield career bowling average of less than 21. That man is Bill O'Reilly, whose 203 wickets cost just 17.10 runs each. He stands above his fellow bowlers as clearly as Bradman dominates the batting averages. He was the greatest of them all.

# 35

# FROM BUNDABERG TO THE BIG-TIME

Time has a nasty habit of embarrassing cricket selectors, although the men who pick the teams make inspired choices often enough. For every success story there's a clanger — and few decisions look worse in cricket history than the one made by the Australian selectors in 1938, to leave Don Tallon in Queensland rather than take him to England. Within 12 months the brilliant young wicketkeeper had completed an unprecedented 34 Sheffield Shield dismissals, including 12 in one match, and seven in another single innings.

Tallon had been playing Shield cricket since December 1933 when, at 17, he kept wicket against Victoria. A native of Bundaberg on the Queensland coast, he had kept for a Queensland Country XI against Jardine's Englishmen a year earlier, and had the distinction of stumping the superb opening bat, Herbert Sutcliffe. He took nearly a season to establish his place in the state team, and for a period had to be content with playing purely as a batsman.

From January 1935, when he was 18, he was the Queensland keeper, and in the next two and a half seasons established a reputation as the country's most promising keeper/batsman. His first Shield century came in February 1936, an impressive three-hour second-innings 193 against Victoria at the Gabba, which saved a game most thought lost. Earlier he had completed four catches and a stumping in the only completed Victorian innings.

Tallon scored his second Shield century in the opening match of the next season. It came again in the second innings, after NSW had won a lead of 190. When dismissed, the crowd politely applauded him off, thinking he had unluckily missed his hundred by four runs. However Bert Oldfield later suggested that a ball that went for four byes had actually glanced Tallon's bat. At the end of the day the umpires decided the runs should go to the batsman, which suited both Tallon and the veteran NSW custodian, who consequently kept a clean sheet for the entire match.

That match ended in an exciting one wicket victory for NSW, won in the final over, in gathering gloom. With six to get "Bob" Hynes had been bowled and Oldfield run out after a mix-up with Bill O'Reilly. But a snick through slips and two desperate singles gained a thrilling victory. In the dressing rooms the decision of NSW captain Alan McGilvray to go to the umpires during the tea interval and claim four overthrows that his batsmen had declined to accept was talked about in varied tones. There was conjecture as to whether Tallon had been interfered with as he dived for a wild return.

By 1938, Tallon was on most people's shortlists for the England tour. But he missed out, apparently the victim of the bargaining and compromising arbitrators love to do. It has been suggested that when the three selectors sat down to finalise the squad he was in each of their teams. One wanted Tallon and Oldfield, another Tallon and Victoria's Ben Barnett, the third Tallon and Charlie Walker of South Australia. Somehow Barnett and Walker were the names that were read out. While Oldfield retired, the unlucky Queenslander was left to wait for the following summer, and the chance to prove the selectors wrong.

Tallon was tall for a keeper, but remarkably agile, and as the bowler approached he crouched as low as any gloveman had done before him. His catching was so sure it should have come with a warranty, and he was superlative at reaching the all-but out of reach. He was also a marvellous stumper, one of the few

*Left: Don Tallon, who in January 1939 dismissed 12 NSW batsmen in one Shield match. Centre: Bill Brown, the first Queensland Shield player to captain Australia in a Test match. Right: Bert Oldfield, NSW and Australian keeper from 1920 to 1937.*

who actually could get the bails off in less than a flash. He was a batsman who loved to drive, and loved to hit fours, though in the years after the war he attacked less often, and became a man of ones and twos.

Queensland's first match in 1938–39 was the customary opener against NSW in Brisbane. After the locals made 501, NSW collapsed for 171. The left-arm spinner Charlie Christ took 5–47, but the star was Tallon, who had three catches and three stumpings, one off his brother Bill, who was making his Shield debut. NSW held on for a fortunate draw, thanks to a fighting century by Sid Barnes.

In Melbourne in December, Tallon had a quiet match, completing just two catches, but in the eyes of most analysts more than outshining the Test keeper Barnett. In Adelaide he was one of Clarrie Grimmett's six victims on the first day, and sat behind the stumps as Bradman made his only double century of the summer. In the second Queensland innings captain Bill Brown batted right through, fighting a losing cause, finishing with 174 out of 311.

The Queenslanders caught the train back to Sydney, for a match over the New Year period — and what proved to be their first outright win of the season. The hero was their wicketkeeper, who equalled the world first-class record for most dismissals in a match and most catches in a match by a keeper. Only Edward Pooley, the champion Surrey gloveman of the 1860s and '70s, had previously made 12 dismissals, until Tallon caught four and stumped two New South Welshmen in the first innings, and caught five and stumped one in the second. The previous Shield record had been nine. Only the great English batsman and close fielder Wally Hammond had taken more catches in a first-class match.

The NSW batting, lacking the unavailable McCabe, Fingleton and Arthur Chipperfield, was poor, as was the bumpy pitch, but the bowling was persistent and the fielding superb. Tallon rose above the cranky wicket, inspired his colleagues, and impressed the critics, including Charlie Macartney, who wrote: "Tallon's wicketkeeping could hardly have been surpassed. His sureness and swift movement were astonishing."

Eight of his nine catches were held standing back to the faster bowlers, and he had to play a part in the demise of five of the last six batsmen to equal the record. His 12th dismissal was the NSW keeper Frank Easton, caught off the fast bowler John Ellis. That was the 19th NSW wicket to fall, and the statisticians in the crowd pondered the odds of a new benchmark. Once he removed the bails, but the stumping was not to be. Soon after Ron James swung at Bill Tallon, and was caught at square leg.

After the match, Don Tallon was interviewed by the *Daily Telegraph*. "I don't feel I am keeping wickets any better than in recent seasons," he said. "I was just fortunate enough to get more opportunities than usual in the present game. I was quite satisfied with six dismissals in the first inings, but didn't give myself a chance of obtaining another six."

One of the first into the Queensland dressing room to congratulate Tallon was Oldfield, who had always looked upon the northerner as a kind of protege, and the pair were photographed together for the morning papers: the old champion with the new. Had an Australian XI been chosen at that moment, Tallon would surely have been in it.

Queensland, chasing 279 on a wearing pitch, ultimately won the match by eight wickets, thanks to Brown who scored a masterly 168 to go with his 95 from the first innings. After the retirement of Ponsford and Woodfull, Brown was Australia's leading opening batsman until the emergence of Arthur Morris. A tough and gritty right-hander, who could bat attractively when the circumstances allowed, he would eventually finish the season just ten short of a thousand Shield runs, a feat only Ponsford had achieved to that point. Brown had been playing for Queensland since the 1936–37 season, when the QCA engaged him as a player/coach, after first playing for NSW in late 1932. In 1946, in New Zealand, he became the first Queensland Sheffield Shield player to captain Australia.

A week after his achievements in Sydney, Tallon scored a superb first-day hundred against South Australia in Brisbane. On the second day he caught the only visiting wicket to fall, Dick Whitington for 125, but then injured a thumb and took no further part in the game, missing the chance to witness close-up Bradman's fifth straight first-class hundred. Fortunately the Shield calender gave the injury almost four weeks to heal, and Tallon was fit for the home match with Victoria, beginning on February 4.

On the first day he completed five dismissals, three stumpings and two catches. The highlight was a wonderful catch off the opener Ian Lee, held centimetres from the ground only after a full length dive in front of the slip cordon. The next day he snared two more, one stumped, one caught, to secure another Australian record, and equal the world record for most wicketkeeping dismissals in one first-class innings.

He finished the season with 21 catches and 13 stumpings — 18 more dismissals than Walker, his closest rival, and 28 more than Barnett.

Throughout his first-class career, which extended to season 1953–54, Tallon averaged more than one stumping for every three catches he held. He was as fast to a bail as perhaps any man who ever lived. Yet in the 1938–39 season, it was his catching standing back that caught most attention. In *The Referee*, J.C. Davis wrote: "His agility and certainty in getting to and judging catches wide on either side against fast bowling have been of rare merit."

Tallon was one of the first to go back away from the stumps for more than just the fastest bowlers. This did not impress everyone, including the former great keeper, Hanson Carter, who, when asked about the Queensland keeper's style, commented: "Wicketkeepers now go back to short stop to take the bowling of men to whom we stood up to the wickets in our time." In the same interview, Carter did confess to being a great, if somewhat grudging, admirer of Tallon.

After the war Tallon developed a reputation that perhaps no Australian keeper has ever matched. Most who saw Oldfield, Tallon and Rod Marsh, put the Queenslander in front, and the few who plump for Marsh on the basis of his batting skills probably never consider Tallon's pre-war run-scoring exploits. When he retired he had made more runs for Queensland than anyone except Bill Brown. He was Queensland's first home-grown champion, a cricketer who built his reputation in the Test matches immediately beyond the Second World War, but who was perhaps at his peak in that remarkable Shield season which followed his omission from the 1938 Ashes tour of England.

# 36

# A POCKET EDITION HERO

One of the most celebrated of all cricket innings is Stan McCabe's 232, scored saving a lost cause in the first Test at Nottingham in 1938. Such was McCabe's skill and daring that the Australian captain Don Bradman later called his display: "What I firmly believe to be the greatest innings ever played."

Five and a half years earlier, during the 1932–33 Bodyline series in Australia, McCabe had played another famous innings — for one brief, heady episode, taming the bullets of Larwood and Voce as he blasted an undefeated 187 on the SCG. Some who saw both great innings, including Bill O'Reilly and the Englishman R.E.S. Wyatt, claimed this hundred was marginally the finer of the two.

During the 1939–40 Shield season, the NSW opening bowler, J.G. "Ginty" Lush, was a regular contributor to the sports pages of the Sydney *Daily Telegraph* and *Sunday Telegraph*. On the back page of the Sunday paper of January 28, 1940, following the second day of the NSW v Victoria Shield match at the SCG, Lush wrote the following:

*The pressure is on with a vengeance in this New South Wales v Victoria game. Both teams must go for an outright win to snatch the Shield from the clutches of South Australia.*

*Victoria needed only a first innings win for supremecy…and what a fight they put up.*

*Lindsay Hassett was a pocket-edition hero.*

*I saw Stan McCabe flay Jardine's bodyline at the Sydney Cricket Ground for 187 not out. In England last year (sic) I saw him make his double century at Trent Bridge. These were the greatest innings I had ever seen.*

*But Stan takes a back seat in my memory now, and Lindsay Hassett's effort occupies first place…*

Rarely has an individual Sheffield Shield innings been given a grander recommendation. Hassett's feat was to score 122 against a NSW attack led by an in-form and hostile Bill O'Reilly. The champion leg spinner was on the rampage, having, soon after Hassett had taken guard, dismissed three of the Victorians — Keith Miller, Ian Johnson and Percy Beames, in the space of 11 balls. From 6–118 Hassett took his side to within 11 of NSW's first innings score of 309, taming the O'Reilly fire in an unprecedented manner.

Hassett was one of the smallest men to take a bat into first-class cricket. Before the war he was a player who loved to attack and won most laurels by the artistry of his strokeplay. Things changed later in his career when, responding to the bridle of the Australian captaincy, he became a more dour, more dependable but less exciting cricketer. He played the late cut as well as anyone after Alan Kippax, and his footwork was nigh on perfect, always an advantage against the spinners. Many thought him the best player of

O'Reilly to have played the game.

In Sydney in 1940, Hassett was the fledgling bantamweight, O'Reilly the heavyweight champion of the cricket world. The first job was to negotiate O'Reilly at the height of his successful spell. Once this sparring was over, Hassett proceeded along in a masterly, aggressive style, often lofting the great spin bowler towards the sightscreen and long-on boundary. Never once did he look confused or beaten by the bosey, nor was he ever inclined to think or act defensively. But, ever wary, he never forgot the knockout punch the great bowler could bowl. Against the other NSW bowlers he was superb in technique and faultless in delivery — driving, cutting and pulling, always along the grass, and always with great effect.

The seventh wicket fell at 185 (Des Fothergill for 32), the eighth at 241 (Doug Ring for 29). With number 10, fast bowler Barry Scott, at the wicket, Hassett became involved in a game of wits with O'Reilly and McCabe, the NSW captain. It was a battle he enjoyed, and all-but won, adding 52 with Scott, who scored only nine. Hassett could not be kept from the strike and had stroked Victoria within sight of the all-important first innings points, when he pulled O'Reilly hard to square leg to be caught cleverly by the diving Cec Pepper — a catch that, as things turned out, went a long way to winning NSW the Shield.

When Hassett had reached three figures, all at the ground rose to acclaim him, even O'Reilly. "I saw for the first time since I have been watching cricket Bill O'Reilly applauding an opponent." wrote Arthur Mailey. Later O'Reilly remembered meeting Hassett in midwicket after being lofted for another four.

"And the little bastard isn't even good looking," snarled the angry bowler, turning sharply on his heel.

Centuries by McCabe and Sid Barnes and a fine 71 by Ron Saggers put NSW within sight of the Shield. With a day remaining Victoria needed 415 to win outright points and the trophy. They had eight wickets in hand. NSW had to have the outright points. A draw — and the Shield would go the SACA offices in Adelaide. Hassett, in at first wicket, was 23 not out. Before the last day of the season began, Arthur Mailey wrote: "I think NSW has it in the bag, but I'll be more certain about it when Lindsay Hassett is back in the pavilion."

And so it proved. In his second superb innings of the match, Hassett went on to a second 122, again proving the master of O'Reilly, but not masterful enough to prevent a NSW victory. Hassett thought nothing of the draw, instead playing the shots needed to win the match and the competition. The O'Reilly death squad of short legs was quickly dismantled. More than once the great bowler was forced out of attack, as McCabe sought an alternative means of keeping the Victorian quiet. And then the field was slowly spreadeagled as Hassett found gaps in whatever McCabe planned.

He had his century well before lunch, but soon after the break fell to a sensational diving catch by Arthur Chipperfield, alone in the slips, off the bowling of Lush. McCabe then brought O'Reilly back, and he cleaned up the tail, improving his bowling fiigures from 0–73 to 3–79. NSW won the match by 177 runs, and the Shield by two precious points.

This was the final Shield match before the War. Interstate matches were played in 1940–41, but for "patriotic purposes" rather than for the Shield.

Lindsay Hassett's Shield career had begun in his 20th year, in the 1932–33 season, for Victoria against South Australia in the last Shield match of that season, a game that coincided with the fourth bodyline Test. He scored 4 and 9 in a game finally won by Chuck Fleetwood-Smith's eight wickets. Hassett did not reappear in the competition until December 1935, when he scored 12 and 4 against Alan McGilvray's NSW side, was dropped to 12th man for the next match against South Australia — then recalled for the return match in Sydney, where scored his initial Shield half-century in the second innings.

It was not until the following season, after he scored 82 and 71 not out against NSW in Melbourne and then 93 and 56 in Brisbane that he was assured of his place. That 93 should really have been his maiden Shield century. Hassett had been 93 at stumps the evening before. The first ball of the day, from Ron Oxenham, was off line, down the leg side. Hassett glanced it with most of the face, but Tallon, at the stumps, had anticipated the stroke and caught it brilliantly before it ran towards the fine leg fence. Oxenham, the Queensland captain, later called Tallon's effort "the best catch at the wicket I've ever seen."

When Hassett was chosen in the 1938 England tour, he was still without his elusive maiden Shield century. It finally came in his first match back — 104 against Queensland in Melbourne. From that moment until his retirement in 1953 he was one of the most prolific scorers of centuries in Australian cricket, finishing with 59 in his first-class career, 18 of them in the Sheffield Shield.

When he retired no-one had scored more Shield runs for Victoria. But perhaps his greatest achievement was to score a century in each innings of a match in which William Joseph O'Reilly was leading the opposition bowlers. No-one else in the history of cricket was able to do that.

*Opposite page: The fabulous Stan McCabe, a Test hero against the bodyline attack in 1932–33. A year earlier in Brisbane he had played a similarly brave and extraordinary innings for NSW against the pace of Eddie Gilbert. On page 132: "The Don" — the Shield's greatest batsman.*

# The Australasian

## TEST MATCH SUPPLEMENT

# The Australasian
## PICTORIAL

# TOWARDS
# THE
# TELEVISION
# AGE

# Introduction by Richie Benaud

Although to play for your country at Test or limited-overs international level is the ultimate for any youngster, I can assure you that playing Sheffield Shield for NSW often felt like being in a Test match. The makeup of the NSW teams through the 1950s and early 1960s was such that to make it into the twelve was an achievement. Being in the eleven was wonderful! There were cases where the century maker or hero one week could next week be 12th man, down four places in the batting order, or out of the side. In 1961–62 the selectors used only 12 players the whole summer, Grahame Thomas was 12th man in the first two games and Ray Flockton the other eight.

I was lucky enough to come into the NSW team in the 1948-49 season when Ray Lindwall, Keith Miller and Arthur Morris were the three outstanding players. Another eight were Jack Moroney, Jim Burke, Bill Donaldson, Jim de Courcy, Ron James, Alan Walker, Ron Saggers and Fred Johnston. All the matches were played in fierce competitive spirit, particularly those between NSW and Victoria which sometimes were more competitive than a Test. In those days there was a saying, "when NSW and Victorian cricket is strong, Australian cricket is strong." I suspect it was born in administrative conceit and quickly seized on to promote the cause of players in the eyes of the national selectors.

Whatever the reason there was no doubt that in the 16 summers from 1948–1949 to 1963–1964, the Sheffield Shield produced cricket of the highest quality, in the same way as it did in the 28 years after 1964 and in the long period prior to 1948. This was one of the reasons Australian cricket was strong in that time, the players came through the toughest of schools where they were continually provided with the most searching examinations with bat, ball and of their character. Just as importantly, their careers benefited from discussions in the dressing-room during and after the game.

I was taught nearly as much by Miller, Morris and Lindwall after the day's play as during it. If things had gone well they would be congratulatory and suggest how we might have played better. If things hadn't gone well, they would be helpful, but realistic, and their advice would be sound for next time. It was the same in dressing-rooms around the country with captains like Lindsay Hassett, `Pancho'

Ridings, Les Favell, Ken Meuleman, Barry Shepherd, Ken Archer, Ken Mackay and others. They made certain your education didn't stop the moment you walked off the field.

It is quite true crowds these days are very low at Shield matches but that certainly doesn't mean a lack of interest in the competition itself, but rather that potential spectators, as we approach the turn of the century have more to do with their time and money than watch a competition that is below international status, one in which they may not see a result on the day they attend.

However, there is no doubt, should the Sheffield Shield disappear, Australia's international cricket fortunes and the skills of the players would instantly deteriorate. For this reason it is vital that limited-overs internationals and sponsorship should continue to finance this competition.

When Lord Sheffield, in 1892-93, paid W.G. Grace what these days would be the equivalent of a million dollars to tour Australia, he would have had little idea he was about to be the instigator of the strongest domestic cricket competition in the world!

One of the best things about Australian domestic cricket lies in the variety of pitches to be found on all the Sheffield Shield arenas. At Brisbane's `Gabba there is bounce and movement off the seam on the first day and then it generally settles down, although there have been times where an excess of zeal in watering before the match makes winning the toss something akin to a lottery. The Sydney Cricket Ground has always allowed the spin bowlers full rein and the first game I saw there was in 1939–40 between NSW and South Australia; Bradman played, so too McCabe, who led NSW, and I was one of 30,400 spectators on the first day, a Saturday, having travelled with my father from Parramatta, first on a steam train, and then a toast rack tram from Eddy Avenue.

Grimmett (11), O'Reilly (10), Pepper (6), Ward (4) and Klose (3) took 34 of the 40 wickets to fall and, aged nine, I was up at the crack of dawn the following day trying to bowl leg breaks like Grimmett. A few years later, Colin McCool, Ian Johnson and Jack Iverson were among spinners who had rich pickings. There was only one proviso. Although the ball has always turned in the past 50 years, you needed skill as well. It has never been just a matter of rolling the ball out of your fingers, as many have found to their cost!

Melbourne's pitch, traditionally made of a very hard black Merri Creek clay which shrinks and leaves wide cracks towards the end of the match, might now have a new lease of life with different techniques being used in preparation. Adelaide Oval has always been a ground of immense beauty with an excellent surface for batting and for bowlers who are prepared to bend their backs; there they have the advantage of a very good curator, Les Burdett. Tasmania's main ground at Bellerive seems to have something for everyone. The WACA pitch in Perth varies these days but, at its best, it is a fast, bouncy surface where the back foot player has a real chance and bowlers of all kinds are in the game because of the bounce and spin available, as well as the influence of the prevailing wind, the 'Fremantle Doctor', which still affects the ball, even though the pitch angle has been changed.

Although the tendency is to bemoan the lack of crowds and reminisce about the good old days when crowds of 25,000—30,000 would watch a day's play of Sheffield Shield, I'm afraid it simply isn't true. The 30,400 mentioned above is, in fact, still the biggest crowd for a day's play and, when Shield cricket resumed after the Second World War, crowds were normal and then began to fall away with the extended use of the motor car and advent of the jet plane. People lived different lives.

For those who continually point out to me that the period in which I played is so vividly memorable for spectators pouring through turnstiles, the unfortunate fact is that from 1948 when I started, to 1964 when I finished, there were more than 1,000 days of Sheffield Shield cricket and only 55 of them drew more than 10,000 spectators.

The only one in excess of 20,000 was a day between Victoria and NSW at the MCG on December 28, 1953.

A clear head is needed then to balance the immense value of the Sheffield Shield and, at the same time, understand that, as loss makers go, it is in the very highest bracket. Also that, no matter how we might dream, nothing in the olden cricketing days was necessarily any better than it is in the modern era. A NSW team at the height of its powers captained by Miller or Morris might well have been something to behold, but so were the teams captained in recent times by Geoff Lawson and others before him. The same applies to other States and Australia's cricket has been strengthened in the past 20 years by the presence of Western Australia.

WA won the Sheffield Shield again in the 1991–92 season and the quality of the play they produced was outstanding. When Dennis Lillee played for WA and Jeff Thomson for Queensland, where Allan Border is now based, the quality was visible. When players of that calibre are on Test duty or touring there are many fine young cricketers able to press for higher honours. That was how I achieved permanency in the NSW team and I hope the structure of the Sheffield Shield in future seasons never wavers. It remains the best and most important domestic cricket competition in the world.

# 37

## THE BRILLIANCE OF KEITH MILLER

The first ball of Victoria's first Sheffield Shield match after the second World War was bowled by the left-handed Bill Johnston to the South Australian Reg Craig. It was driven for four, right through the hands and feet of Keith Miller, fielding in the covers. It was a bad mistake by the fieldsman, but a rare one, for Miller was usually a superb man in the field. In the months that followed he was all but faultless in everything he did for his Victorian team.

The match began on November 15, 1946. Miller was a likely, but not quite certain selection in the Australian XI for that season's Ashes Test series. An outrageously gifted all-rounder who had batted for Victoria before the war and made his reputation with the Australian Services team in 1945, Miller was seen by most enthusiasts as a vital member of the national side, a jewel too valuable to be ignored. He was the man who could provide strike power with the ball and flair with the bat. His best form, combined with the hoped-for renaissance of Bradman, was essential if Australia was to overcome the challenge of Wally Hammond and his Englishmen.

In *Australian Cricket: A History*, Johnnie Moyes wrote of the Miller he saw playing for the Services' team in 1945–46: "During this series Australians saw Miller bowling for the first time in big cricket and they liked what they saw. It was perfectly obvious that another Test player had been developed by a Services' team, a batsman of quality and a fast bowler with real speed and clever skill as well."

After that fielding fumble of the opening delivery of the 1946 Shield, Miller the bowler was relatively quiet in the South Australian first innings, sending down just 11 overs. This game, and for most of the Shield season, it would be the Miller blade that would win the headlines. Bradman, in his first Shield match since 1940, but favouring a leg he had strained while scoring a century against Hammond's team in Melbourne the week before, scored 43. Ron Hamence, later a teammate of Miller's on the 1948 England tour, was out in controversial circumstances, lbw to George Tribe for two, off the 10th ball of an over. The umpire had simply lost count of the number of balls bowled.

Tribe finished with 7–85. A left arm wrist spinner of the Fleetwood-Smith style, he was a lethal mixture of turn and deceit in interstate matches. In 1946–47 he finished with 33 Shield wickets, from four matches, but could find just two wickets from 95 overs in that season's Tests, and after missing selection in the '48 team for England, packed his bags and headed to a lucrative career in English league and county cricket.

South Australia batted for all of the opening day for 270, and by stumps on day two, Saturday, Victoria had first-innings points, having reached 3–285. Miller was 56 not out, and with Lindsay Hassett, unbeaten on 43, had provided the most exciting cricket of the match. On Monday, the pair went on to centuries, Miller 188 and Hassett 114. The 1948 *Wisden* described Miller's effort as "one of the finest batting displays ever seen at Adelaide."

Harry Kneebone, in the *Advertiser*, reflecting the thoughts of most critics, wrote: "If Miller was not a certainty before his century against South Australia that innings must have convinced the selectors that the ex-Services star has regained his top form."

Miller was superb, but not explosive, and batted in all for 345 minutes, as if he had heard from others that his Test place was not secure. But he was never pedestrian, and was particularly severe on the leg-spinner Bruce Dooland, who at one stage had 2–220 and finished with 4–229. Victoria finally won the match outright, by nine wickets, despite Bradman and Hamence scoring second-innings centuries. On the final afternoon, South Australia lost their last six wickets for 36, to give their opponents 35 minutes to score 79. Hassett and Miller opened the batting, and in a torrent of fours and quick singles, the target was achieved with two minutes to spare. Miller was out in what proved to be the final over, when four were needed and five minutes remained.

Keith Miller the batsman was an entertainment package. His many shots and many hundreds were worth the journey to the ground purely for the manner in which they were made. Moyes, in 1954, described him this way: "He always looks the complete batsman when he takes up his stance, and often plays that way, for his cover drive came out of the pages of the best text-book, his hits for six leave no doubt as to where the ball will go, while his forcing shots between mid-on and mid-wicket is a sight to make old men young."

In January 1947 he produced further evidence of his skill and daring, a powerful second-innings double century in Sydney. This match featured many of the finest cricketers from this most fruitful era in Australian cricket history. Hassett scored a rapid 190 on the opening day. Ray Lindwall had a successful match with the bat, scoring 46 and 62, but was less productive with the ball. George Thatcher, in the *Sunday Telegraph,* wrote of Lindwall's "Macartney-like hooks". Neil Harvey scored a first-innings duck, but batted brightly for 49 in the second. Arthur Morris was magnificent late on the first day when he and fellow opener Keith Carmody scored 63 in half an hour. George Tribe finished the match with 12 wickets, and his spin support, the off-spinner Ian Johnson and the leg-spinner Doug Ring, was effective.

Miller bowled just 16 overs, for the wicket of "Ginty" Lush. With the bat he was devastating, the game's undoubted star, producing an innings featuring some of the biggest hits ever seen on the Sydney ground. Victoria batted most of the first day for 356. On the second NSW fell 27 short, and at stumps Victoria were 0–33. Miller came in at 2–114, after just over 100 minutes of cricket on the day, and by stumps was unconquered on 206, having hit 15 fours and three sixes in 232 minutes of glorious sport.

His sixes were phenomenal. The first was a mighty swing off the leg-spinner Fred Johnston that finished on the roof of the old Members' stand. The second was off the part-time bowling of Arthur Morris, and went exactly straight, about three metres above the sightboard at the Paddington end. The third was a powerful heave off Toshack that ended in the depths of the Ladies' stand beyond square leg.

At times Toshack had three men on the fence in the arc from long-on to long-off, so frightening were Miller's drives. Old-time members could not recall seeing a cover field so far away from the wicket yet still preventing singles. One bullet struck the pickets on the full and rebounded almost back to the bowler Morris. Lindwall was reduced to operating with an outfield and a single slip. It is unlikely a cricket ball has ever been struck with such power on the Sydney Cricket Ground.

The next day Tribe and Johnson bowled Victoria to victory, to seal the Shield. An unsung hero was keeper Ted Baker, who like Miller was a VFL footballer. In 1931 Baker had captained Geelong to the premiership. In the NSW second innings he completed three dismissals to give him nine for the match, including five stumpings in the first innings. Earlier in the season Baker had gloved nine victims in the match against NSW in Melbourne (six catches in the first innings, three in the second). Before 1946, no Victorian keeper had completed six dismissals in one Shield innings, or nine in one Shield match.

Prior to the start of the 1947–48 season Miller transferred his employment to Sydney, a move that would have excited no group more than the NSW fieldsmen, who no longer had to dive at those brutal drives. He would become the most popular Victorian to ever play in Sydney, a glamorous figure who would provide many more remarkable innings at the SCG, and would continue too to strike sixes that aroused memories of the longest hits everyone had ever seen.

After the 1946–47 Shield and Test matches, Miller was on the threshold of a dazzling career, an established Test batsman and Test bowler, as distinct from a batsman or bowler who could also bowl or bat a bit. He lacked only the focussed ambition necessary to climb to the very top of every facet of the game. He was happy to be no more than an involved and key member of every team he was a part of. Perhaps Sid Barnes summed up Keith Miller the cricketer as precisely as any critic has when he wrote: "If Keith had had the same outlook as Bradman or Ponsford he would have made colossal scores. He could, if he desired, have become the statisticians' greatest customer."

# 38

## SLAMMIN' SAM

Many of the Sheffield Shield's finest players have also excelled in the various codes of football. In 1911 the future NSW and Australian cricket captain Herbert Collins was a member of Eastern Suburbs competition-winning Sydney rugby league first grade team. In 1946 Ray Lindwall missed a last-minute kick at goal from the sideline that would have won St George the league premiership. Test cricketers Johnny Taylor and Otto Nothling were good enough rugby union players to win selection in NSW sides of the 1920s. Alan Walker, a NSW fast bowler between 1948 and 1953, also scored one of the most renowned of all Australian rugby union tries, after a spectacular kick-and-chase against England at Twickenham in 1948.

And for every first-class cricketer who has succeeded in league or union, there are countless more who have made the top grade in Australian football, a game originally devised to keep cricketers fit during winter. Some of the best-known names of Australian cricket have reached the highest level in Victorian football, including Jack Blackham, Jack Worrall, Harry Graham, Warwick Armstrong, Ted McDonald, Keith Miller, George Tribe, Gil Langley, Max Walker and Simon O'Donnell. In Adelaide, such men as George Giffen, Clem Hill, Ernie Jones, Jack Reedman, Vic Richardson, Neil Hawke and Eric Freeman played senior first grade football. Western Australians to excel at both cricket and football included Keith Slater, Ian Brayshaw and Mick Malone.

In the Victorian Shield side that played Queensland in Melbourne in December 1946 were two of the VFL's most prominent players. Batting four was Des Fothergill, who in 1940 as a Collingwood rover, had finished level with South Melbourne's Herbie Matthews at the top of the Brownlow Medal counting. At number five was Sam Loxton, who in the previous five winters had dominated the forward line at St Kilda.

Loxton was making his Shield debut. Fothergill had played for Victoria prior to the war, with limited success. Neither had played in Victoria's opening Shield match of the 1946–47 season in Adelaide, but now, with Lindsay Hassett, Keith Miller, Ken Meuleman, Ian Johnson and George Tribe in Sydney for the second Ashes Test, they had their chance. The Queenslanders had travelled to Melbourne in a style no previous Shield side had tried — by air. They were without two Test men, the leg-spinning Colin McCool and their superb gloveman, Don Tallon. The new keeper was 19-year-old Wally Grout. He and another colt, the 21-year-old southpaw batsman Ken Mackay, were making their Shield debuts.

At stumps on day one, Victoria were 5 for 377. Loxton was 159 not out, after nearly three-and-a-half hours of aggressive, belligerent batting. From soon after the time he joined Fothergill at 3–73, Victoria were in command. Fothergill eventually fell for 60 at 178, after an 82-minute partnership, and Loxton and Doug Ring then dominated, adding 189 in the 100 minutes between 4.20pm and stumps.

*The Age* report of the Shield encounter was ridiculously brief, as all its cricket writers were in Sydney for the Test. Of Loxton's batting the paper said no more than: "Loxton has given a fine display of powerful driving, hooking and pulling for 159 not out, made in just under three hours and a half. His quick judgement, nimble footwork and clever placing made the Queensland bowling look easier than it actually was."

The fifty between 100 and 150 had taken Loxton just 48 minutes. The next day he went on to 232 (22 fours, one six), still unbeaten when the final Victorian wicket fell at 543. At 183 he had given himself a frightful whack on the head with his own bat, swinging too exuberantly at a hook shot. He was shaken, but too much in-form to retire. He and Ring took their fifth wicket stand to 289, a new Shield partnership record for the sixth wicket. The stand took just 160 minutes, Ring's share 145, his maiden Shield century.

Loxton's score remains the highest made by a batsman in his debut Sheffield Shield innings. Such was the competition for places in the Victorian side that his retention for the following match was no certainty, though the *Argus* correspondent commented the next day: "For 334 minutes he gave a splendid exhibition, and although he gave two fairly easy chances yesterday morning his display should guarantee him a place in Victoria's team against New South Wales."

Loxton bowled the second over of the Queensland innings, and almost immediately had Rex Rogers caught, pulling timidly at a fast riser. From there the two spinners, Alan Jinks, bowling his off breaks into the wind and Ring, with the breeze over his shoulder, went through some feeble batting. The only positive note for Queensland was the gutsy defence of Mackay who, when the innings ended just before stumps for a paltry 155, had batted more than two hours for 30 not out.

The second Queensland innings was little better. After Jinks broke an opening stand of 67, the pace-men, Loxton and the left-hander Bill Johnston went through the batting order. Loxton had the number three Aub Carrigan caught in slips, and Ken Archer bowled soon after. At stumps the visitors were 8–237, and they made just 21 more the following day. Mackay stood defiant once more, this time on 63. He had batted for more than three hours in the second innings, and hit just two fours. In the course of the two Queensland innings he had seen 13 wickets go, without falling himself.

In the seasons that followed Mackay developed a reputation that belied his ironical nickname of "Slasher". Loxton could not have been more different — a swashbuckling cricketer who was always brave, never subtle. Johnnie Moyes wrote that "he was born to attack". Neil Harvey said of him: "Sam was one of those cricketers who give all whether batting, bowling or fielding."

He bowled right-arm fast medium, not quite fast enough to be daunting, not quite tall enough to be awkward. But always right at you. He was a batsman who struck the ball hard and often, and loved to loft the ball to and over the fence. But perhaps his greatest strength was his fielding. Rarely has a cricketer thrown the ball with greater power, or surer aim.

In the match following Victoria's trouncing of Queensland, Loxton bowled only six overs at the power-ful New South Welshmen, but took three wickets. With the bat he scored a typically aggressive 73, after Miller and Mervyn Harvey had scored centuries. Then in Brisbane he scored 87, adding 172 runs in 100 minutes with Hassett, who scored an even 200.

It was not until the return match with NSW in Sydney that Loxton (37) failed to score at least a half-cen-tury in a Shield match. The season's final fixture, South Australia's visit to Melbourne, was destroyed by rain, and Loxton did not get a chance to add to his season aggregate of 429, at 143. He needed all of that average to finish at the top of the averages. Hassett amassed 567 runs at 141.75, and Miller scored 667 at 133.40. Loxton was also at the head of the bowling averages, his seven wickets costing just 98 runs.

Following his successful cricket season, Loxton retired from big-time football. Before the end of 1947–48, he was in the Australian side, scoring 80 on debut in the final Test against the outgunned but enthusiastic Indians. He was one of Bradman's "Invincibles" in 1948, a prominent figure in the last three Tests of that tour, especially at Manchester where he smashed a quickfire 93. Later he toured South Africa and played the first three Tests against Freddie Brown's England team in 1950–51.

He continued in the Shield, always on the attack, until 1957–58, scoring six more centuries, the high-est 169 against NSW in Melbourne in late 1952. Before his Shield career was over he was a conservative member of the Victorian parliament, elected as the representative for Prahran in 1955. He remained a politician for more than 20 years. One day at the SCG he had a terrible time trying to get bat on ball, as Keith Miller was having one of his best bowling days. The torment continued until a wag on the Hill sug-gested he have a look in Hansard, and see if he could find the ball in there.

Perhaps his approach to the game is best summed up in a single incident from the Victoria-Western Australia match in Perth in 1947. The local team, in only their second Shield match, had drawn level with the Victorians on the first innings, and still had six wickets in hand. Loxton, with bowling figures of none-for-plenty, was charging in at Les Bandy as if the next delivery would decide the fate of the Shield. He appealed gallantly and loudly for an lbw, and then waved his arms and argued with the umpire when the shout was turned down. When the ball was tossed back to him he snatched at it, and then kicked it away. Later his captain, Merv Harvey, would explain apologetically: "Loxton is a great trier and gets wrapped up in the game."

The assault continued, the bowler fervently chasing the 6–0 needed to save the day, but soon after, to the jubilation of the local patrons, Bandy hit the winning run. Of all the people in the WACA Ground who joined in the applause, none clapped louder than ex-footballer Sam Loxton.

# 39

# THE FIFTH STATE

In 1947 the Western Australian Cricket Association appointed as their state cricket coach the NSW and former Services opening batsman Keith Carmody. It would be his job to lead WA into their debut season in the Sheffield Shield. This was an inspired choice. Carmody was a brilliant student of the game, an innovative and inspiring leader, and would prove to be as significant a figure in the history of cricket in the western state as notable later captains such as Tony Lock, John Inverarity and Rod Marsh.

Carmody had first played Shield cricket in 1939, starting with a duck and 30 for NSW in Brisbane. This was his only appearance in the competition until 1946–47, when he played consistently in all six of NSW's matches, without a century. During the war he was a fighter pilot with the RAAF until shot down off the coast of Holland and incarcerated in a prisoner-of-war camp in Berlin. Liberated by the Soviets, he later joined the American advance on the German capital. Back in London he was appointed vice-captain to Lindsay Hassett in the Services' team.

Carmody was the man responsible for the "umbrella" field, a strategy where almost all the fieldsmen were placed in a ring from gully to leg gully, waiting for snicks and glances from the edges of batsmen facing a new ball and fired-up opening bowlers. In 1956 Keith Miller wrote that the umbrella field was the most revolutionary idea introduced into cricket in his lifetime.

It began over drinks in a pub in London in 1945. Miller, Carmody and some other members of the Services' side were talking cricket, and discussion turned to the number of snicks that did not go to hand. Carmody's solution was to bring as many men up into a ring, to concentrate on possible wickets rather than guard against possible boundaries, and he brought the strategy with him to Perth. He was a leader confident enough to try innovations such as this, and had an eye for weaknesses in batsmen few could match. And he believed passionately in the value of high-quality fielding as a means to an outright win.

Western Australia's first day in Sheffield Shield cricket was on Friday, November 14, 1947, against South Australia at the WACA Ground in Perth. The Western Australians had been admitted to the competition on a two-year trial and had guaranteed to meet the cost of flying opposition teams to Perth. In their debut season they were scheduled to play only four matches, two at home, against South Australia and Victoria, and one each in Sydney and Brisbane. West Australia's points from these four matches would then be converted to a percentage, and the Shield winners determined by comparing the figure to that of the states playing seven matches. Carmody was confirmed as captain only after the other states had raised no objection to his appointment. The normal residential qualification was three months for a player without previous first-class experience but 12 months for those who had played for another state. Keith Miller, who had moved to Sydney, received a similar exemption.

The Western Australian side was a mixture of Carmody's experience and captaincy skill, some untried talent and a passion and spirit the skipper would need to take full advantage of. Opening the bowling was Charlie Puckett, a fast-medium and off-spin bowler who had played once for WA in 1940. His support came from the opening bowler Ken Cumming and the spinners Tom O'Dwyer and Morgan Herbert. O'Dwyer was a left-arm wrist spinner and Herbert a leg breaking all-rounder, perhaps the best regarded bowler in the state. Such was Herbert's form in the game against the touring Indians in late October, that the Australian selectors called him up for the Australian XI match against India in Sydney, and he was obliged to miss WA's Shield debut.

Carmody's batting support was led by the opener Alan Edwards, the medical student George Robinson, the aggressive Dave Watt, the youngster Fred Buttsworth and the all-rounder Wally Langdon. Edwards was highly rated in the eastern states, an outsider for the trip to England at the end of the season. Watt had scored 85 and 157 against Hammond's English team in 1946 and would, before 1947–48 was out, blast the fastest century of the first-class season. Buttsworth was the son of Fred, a former WA opening bowler and would, like his brother Wally, later play VFL football for Essendon as well as first-class cricket for Western Australia. Behind the stumps was Gwilyn "Glyn" Kessey, a capable gloveman, and the focus of Western Australia's superb and highly-drilled fielding.

The South Australians approached the Perth match with some confidence. One week before the game, they had beaten Victoria outright in Adelaide. In that fixture, Don Bradman had scored his 99th first-class century and Phil Ridings had a notable double of 151 and 17 with the bat and 4–66 with the ball. Now, however, they were without Bradman, Ron Hamence and Bruce Dooland, all in Sydney for the Australian XI game. In 18 previous clashes, Western Australia had won only once, in 1906, the same season Ernest Parker scored the sole WA hundred in these matches. Never before had Western Australia scored more than 293 in an innings against South Australia.

The match started at 11.30am, and by 6 o'clock, the locals were jubilant. The primitive WACA scoreboard showed Western Australia were 5–375. Carmody was 166 not out, reward for five-and-a-half hours of discipline and judgement. He was lucky early on, dropped by the keeper after a too-fine leg glance when only two. With the bespectacled Robinson he added 159 for the second wicket. Watt made a quickfire 43, and Langdon, who was bowled by the third new ball (a new ball could be taken every 40 eight-ball overs), a steady 21. Buttsworth was bowled around his legs for a duck. The only negative for the day was the attendance figure. The local administration had made arrangements for many more than the 2,260 people who walked through the turnstiles.

Carmody's score was a record for a Western Australian and his first Shield century. From Sydney came a telegram from Stan McCabe, which read: "Congratulations on your great effort. Keep your nose on the pitch." Another telegram came from a fellow ex-inmate from the German POW camp. The next day, while Bradman was scoring his 100th first-class hundred in Sydney, Carmody went on to 198, scored in 390 minutes. His team's total ended at 444, the highest ever by Western Australia in first-class cricket.

On the Saturday afternoon, South Australia in a paltry reply, were bowled out for just 109. Wrote the *West Australian* correspondent: "Delighted as the West Australians were at having batted and bowled themselves into such a commanding position, the whole thing was so easily achieved as to be almost beyond belief."

The key to the collapse was the bowling of O'Dwyer, who confused and defeated the leaden-footed batsmen with flight and turn. Puckett bowled, both fast and slow, all but four-and-a-half overs from the southern end. And the last two wickets fell to Watt, who rarely bowled in pennant cricket, but took his wickets anyway — with a grin spread all about his face. The bowling was full of effort, and the captaincy aggressive, though Carmody was allowed to keep a close field by the especially timid batting.

Western Australia completed their first Shield win on the third day, when in the last scheduled over of the final session, Puckett held an easy catch in the outfield. South Australia had been dismissed a second time, for 211. There was much celebration in the Western Australian dressing room, players clasping stumps and bails, and Puckett showing, but not releasing, the ball that completed the victory. The South Australians were generous in defeat, though some muttered about the pitch which had deteriorated as the game went on. More than one of the vanquished had fallen to balls that had done little more than shoot along the ground. "I feel sure you will do a good job against Victoria," said a sporting captain Ridings at a post-match function, referring to WA's next match. "There are some fine players in WA and I wish them every success."

Congratulatory telegrams were received from Herbert, who had bowled and batted with limited success in Sydney, and from the Federal Labor parliamentarians Tom Burke and Kim Beazley. A day later Herbert was back in Perth, and at the airport he commented: "Everyone I met, with the possible exception of Bradman (the regular South Australian captain), was delighted with Western Australia's victory". Herbert caused much comment when he suggested Edwards was a better batsman than the teenage Victorian left-hander Neil Harvey, who had scored 32 and 56 not out in Sydney.

The Victorian team that came to Perth in the first week of December included Harvey, and his brothers Mervyn (who was captain) and Ray, but was minus the Test players Lindsay Hassett, Ian Johnson and Bill Johnston. Herbert came back into the local eleven, in place of the unlucky Buttsworth. Western Australia had defeated Victoria just once before the game, in 1910 in the second of two matches between the states that season. In the first 1910 match WA had scored a then-record 424 in the second innings, Ernest Parker scoring 101 of the first 110 of that score.

For the Victoria match, the WACA had improved their ground's scoreboard. Now all fieldsmen's names were featured, and it was promised that, unlike the opening match, all the names would be legible to everyone seated inside the ground. The first message displayed was that Victoria had won the toss and would be batting. And for most of the day it was the surname "Harvey" that dominated the board.

Merv scored 141, and shared a 173 third-wicket partnership with Neil, who was outstanding. The local papers compared the younger brother to the former West Australian left-hander Ernie Bromley, who had batted in the bodyline series and toured England in 1934. Until Neil Harvey fell, caught off a careless stroke when 94, the bat was in complete control, but four more wickets fell before stumps to bring the locals back into the game.

The next day Western Australia took command. At stumps they were 2–307, chasing 370. Robinson was undefeated on 121 and Watt was 54. Earlier Edwards had become the first locally-born player to score a Shield century for his state. The crowd on day two was 7,000, the best attendance for one day thus far, a tribute to the quality of the cricket the home team was producing. The next day the Victorian total was passed four down, and the innings went on to 429. The match ended without an outright result, after Carmody called off a last-session run chase following the fall of the fifth wicket.

After the match there were celebrations in both dressing rooms. The first innings points put Western Australia on top of the Shield table, while news had reached the Victorian dressing room that Neil Harvey had been added to the Australian squad for the second Test.

Before Western Australia's eastern tour a WACA representative on the Board of Control told the press he had been unofficially informed that his state had earned the right to regard itself as certain of its place in the Sheffield Shield. The two victories in Perth had proved the quality of WA cricket, and affirmed the claims for full Shield status. In fact the anonymous official was a trifle presumptuous — WA were not given permanent status until after the 1954–55 season, and it was not until 1956–57 that each state played the West Australians both at home and away in the same season.

In January Keith Miller was a late addition, with Ernie Toshack, to the NSW team for the Western Australia match. The Test players had originally been left out as it was thought the Shield match would clash with the fourth Test in Adelaide, but the Test finished early, and when Tom Brooks and Vince Collins dropped out of the NSW side, Miller and Toshack were co-opted into the eleven. This late change was devastating for the visitors as Miller scored a superb 170 in three hours and then bowled well as NSW won outright with 20 minutes to spare. Two of Miller's sixes were among the biggest seen, the first landing on the roof of the Ladies' stand, the second sailing through the gap between the old members' and new members' (now M.A. Noble) stands. Later WA's Charlie Puckett got one back by slogging leg-spinner Fred Johnston deep into the Sheridan stand.

This result was a hiccup, but other results meant that an outright win over Queensland would have the Shield in Perth. Queensland were without their Test men, Don Tallon, Len Johnson and Bill Brown, and the injured Colin McCool. The game aroused great interest in Western Australia, and three Perth radio stations decided to broadcast half-hourly updates of the match in Brisbane. These reports were always encouraging, and at 3.37pm on the fourth afternoon the final Queensland wicket fell, giving WA a decisive 183-run win.

The hero on the final afternoon was Puckett. Before the day's play began he told his colleagues: "I'll bowl 'til my arms drop off." And he all but did, bowling fast and slow to take 6–48 off 23 eight-ball overs. In his last six overs he took 5–9 as Queensland crumbled to 130 all out. Earlier Watt had scored a scintillating hundred, blasted in just 83 minutes, and O'Dwyer had taken seven wickets in the Queensland first innings.

After the victory Carmody looked back on this triumphant season. "Western Australia's success in the Sheffield Shield was not in any way due to luck," he claimed. "In fact luck was against the side most of the time. The team spirit was exceptionally good among the Western Australian players and was largely responsible for the win. The high standard of running between wickets and fielding earned praise in both NSW and Queensland." The team manager Dick Bryant commented: "We made runs quickly and our men became known as 'strong-armers' as fieldsmen."

There is no doubt the Shield program in 1947–48 clearly favoured Western Australia and only the most optimistic in Perth suggested that their Shield success would be repeated in 1948–49, especially after Robinson announced he was leaving for England for 12 months to further his medical studies. But in 1947–48 there was nothing more the Western Australians could have done. Their spirit and verve on the field was a tribute to their preparation and their captain. Of all the imports, from other countries and from other parts of Australia, that the various states have brought in to try to improve their Sheffield Shield performances, few have had the impact of Keith Carmody. His efforts with Western Australia in their inaugural Shield season rank high on the list of captaincy achievements in the history of the competition.

# 40

## FAREWELL TO THE DON

Don Bradman played in only three Sheffield Shield matches after the second World War, an extraordinary statistic considering that in the same period he played in 15 Test matches. His performances after the war were as follows:

> 1946–47: 43 and 119 against Victoria in Adelaide.
> 1947–48: 100 against Victoria in Adelaide.
> 1948–49: 30 against Victoria in Adelaide.

In the first two of these matches he went into the scorebook as he had throughout his long career, D.G. Bradman. For the final match he was Sir Donald Bradman — the one and only time a knight has put on the pads in a Sheffield Shield match.

The knighthood had been announced on New Year's Day, 1949. He called it: "A tribute to a wonderful sport." At that stage he had played in just one first-class match since returning from a triumphant tour of England in 1948 — a testimonial match staged in his honour in Melbourne in the first week of December. That match ended in a sensational tie, after Bradman had scored a first-innings 123 in front of more than 53,000 people. In the last day's final hour, Don Tallon smashed 91 of the last 100 runs scored, to bring his side within one run of victory.

Sir Donald did not play again until late-February, when he agreed to support the Alan Kippax-Bert Oldfield testimonial match in Sydney. He scored 53 in his only innings, and attracted more than 41,000 to watch his SCG "farewell". He came through that match sore but able, a relief to those organising the Arthur Richardson testimonial match in Adelaide, in which Sir Donald had agreed to play. The promoters were relying on the final appearance of the champion to bring the patrons through the gate. The SACA had permitted the Shield match with Victoria to be a testimonial to Richardson, a former South Australian and Australian player of the '20s, and the state coach.

The Australian team to tour South Africa was announced two days before the start of the Shield match. The side caused great consternation in cricket circles, the omission of Miller being severely questioned. In Adelaide there was dismay that only the fast-medium opening bowler Geff Noblet had been chosen from the state side, the first time since 1921 that only one South Australian would be a member of the Australian squad.

The South Australian captain was Phil Ridings, who had grown up in the same Adelaide suburb as Noblet and first played the game in a side-street, with Noblet as the opposition and a lamp-post the wicket. Despite Bradman being in the side, Ridings kept the leader's role; it was the only time Bradman played in but did not captain the South Australian team. The Victorians were led by Ian Johnson, as the soon-to-be-announced successor to Sir Donald as Australia's captain, Lindsay Hassett, was kept in Melbourne by business.

Johnson won the toss and batted, a manoeuvre that delighted the benefit organisers as it made it more likely that Bradman would bat on the Saturday. However the South Australian paceman Kevin O'Neil changed things with a devastating spell before tea that reduced the visitors to 9–174. O'Neil took 5–7 off 18 deliveries. Last man Bill Johnston ambled in, began poorly as an incompetent number 11 should, and then slogged his way to 38 in 33 minutes. One hit ended in a hedge in the gardens outside the ground.

Bradman came to the wicket with more than half-an-hour to bat on the Friday evening, and with testimonial officials' hearts in their mouths and all eyes on all timepieces. He batted slowly, inevitably concious of the significance of his survival, but had to withstand a typically forceful effort from Sam Loxton before stumps were drawn.

Twenty-year-old opening batsman Colin McDonald, making his first Shield appearance of the season, put down a sharp chance from Bradman just before stumps, to the disgust of Loxton. Wrote Harry Kneebone of the *Advertiser*: "Apparently Loxton considered the fact that his father, who is with the Victorian party, had made a contribution to the benefit fund gave him carte blanche to wreck the match." Later Loxton had a flamboyant but unsuccessful shy at the stumps after Bradman had pushed a delivery back towards the bowler's end.

At stumps Bradman was 18, Ridings 3, South Australia 3–57. The next day the crowd was disappointing, just below 10,000, although some may have changed plans to venture to the cricket after Bradman was bowled, off the inside edge, after adding just 12 runs to his overnight score. In the same Bill Johnston over an excited yell for a catch behind had been turned down by the umpire. Bradman threw his head back after his dismissal, and hit the ball away from his feet towards fine leg in disgust. Eight South Australians would reach double figures, but only Bradman more than 17, and the innings ended at 154.

Later, when South Australia were fielding, Bradman stepped on the edge of the grass-filled hollow of a sunken sprinkler, was unbalanced, and stepped on the ball he was attempting to field. The result was a twisted ankle and he had to be assisted from the field. Ken Meuleman, the Victorian 12th man, came on to field for Bradman, as the South Australian substitute, Len Michael, was fielding for Keith Gogler, the local opening batsman, who had strained a thigh.

Sir Donald took no further part in the match, which was won comfortably by Victoria by 271 runs. On the third day he announced he would not be batting again. "I would like to have a second knock," he said. "But the doctor has ruled it out. Anyway you can see for yourself that it is out of the question." The diagnosis was a badly sprained ankle and an order to keep off the damaged leg as much as possible. The new knight was left to ponder his remarkable career, and to talk cricket with the wartime British foreign secretary and later prime minister, Mr Anthony Eden, who visited the Adelaide Oval during the third day.

So ended the career of the world's greatest cricketer. His involvement in the game continued well after his playing career had ended, as an administrator, journalist, selector, author and elder statesman. His records, his runs, and his consistency are beyond belief. To a cricketer at any level, from the local park to the turf of Sydney, Melbourne or Lord's, the precision and certainty he brought to the batting crease made, and still makes, a mockery of the difficulties and intricacies that batting involves.

Bradman dominated cricket for 20 years the way Kieren Perkins dominated the Olympic 1500-metre freestyle at Barcelona in 1992. He was the Fraser, the Elliott, the Lindrum, the Phar Lap, the Griffo, the Laver, the Mackay of his sport. And he was that little bit more. He was more than just a sportsman; he was a giant of Australia's *history* generally. He will, by his runs and his feats, and the manner in which he made them, remain the single most important figure in the story of Australian cricket for as long as the game is played.

*The South Australian side Don Bradman captained to the Shield in 1935–36. Back row (left to right): F. Collins, F. Ward, T. Wall, G. Williams, T. O'Connell, R. Moyle, A. Richter; Seated: R. Parker, C. Walker, D. Bradman, A. Ryan, M. Waite; In front: R. Hamence, C. Badcock.*

# 41

# A TENSE AFTERNOON AT THE GABBA

In 1951–52 five batsmen scored over 500 runs in the Shield season. They were the two young Victorians, Colin McDonald and George Thoms — who opened the Australian batting that season in the fifth Test against John Goddard's West Indians — the NSW captain Arthur Morris, and two South Australians, Phil Ridings and Neil Dansie.

Ridings first played Shield cricket in the last two days of 1938, scoring 33 against Victoria from the number nine position in the batting order and taking two wickets. In those days he was an opening bowler, seen by some as a likely successor to Tim Wall. After the war he slowed his pace, concentrated on runs, and became a key member of the South Australian batting line-up. He was always a superb fieldsman, reckoned by some the best cover field of his day. Johnny Moyes wrote of him: "Lacking real style, Ridings had tremendous courage and could hit the ball very hard on both sides of the wicket, while he could defend stubbornly if the need arose. No situation could daunt him, and his value to South Australian cricket was inestimable."

In 1946–47 he scored 166 against NSW in Adelaide, his first Shield hundred in his first match as SA captain — and the following year reached the century mark three times, including an undefeated 186 in Melbourne. Ridings finished with the leading Shield batting aggregate that season, and was considered at least slightly unfortunate to miss the last chosen batting position in the Australian side of 1948; it went instead to his state colleague Ron Hamence.

Eight years later Ridings was still without an Australia cap, but spoken of yet again as a possible England tourist. In the fierce debate that took place in the Sydney and Melbourne press over the choice between Keith Miller (the NSW captain) and Ian Johnson (the incumbent Australian and Victorian leader) as the 1956 Australian captain, some suggested Ridings, the South Australian skipper, as a compromise candidate. History records that Johnson was given the job, and Ridings remained in the Shield, where he played one more season before retiring, after 76 matches, 11 seasons as captain, nine centuries, 4,501 runs, and a Shield championship in 1952–53.

Neil Dansie's Shield career began in the last match of Ridings' fourth year as South Australian captain. The following season he was a regular, a robust, aggressive member of the batting order. Early in his Shield career he opened the innings, but later transferred to the middle order and began snaring wickets with leg breaks. He scored 17 Shield centuries for South Australia, including three in 1958–59, and was the first cricketer from his state, and the second man ever, to play 100 Shield matches. When he retired, after the final game of the 1966–67 season, no-one had played more Shield games than Dansie's 107.

Dansie scored two Shield centuries in 1951–52, both against Queensland. The first, in Adelaide in the second week of the new year, was a swashbuckling even-hundred, most of the runs coming during a 170-run partnership in two hours with the Test man, Graeme Hole. A month later Dansie scored another second-innings century, the best batting exhibition of what turned into the most exciting match of that season.

The match began on February 9, 1952, three days after the death of King George VI. Before the match the national anthem was played over the public address, and players and umpires wearing black armbands stood to attention in front of the members' pavilion. After Ridings lost the toss, the Queenslanders dominated, and South Australia collapsed before the fast-medium pace of the Shield debutant Ron Archer and the leg breaks and googlies of Colin McCool, who each grabbed five wickets, Four of McCool's victims fell to keeper Wally Grout, three of them stumped.

The following day Ron Archer's elder brother Ken top-scored with 76 as Queensland won a 100-run first innings lead. Before stumps, two South Australians were out for 47. Dansie remained, having totally ignored his natural instincts and stonewalled to stumps; he was six not out.

The next day he ground out an uncharacteristically slow 110, scored in exactly five hours, providing the backbone of a South Australian fightback, and by stumps the visitors were 225 ahead, with one wicket still to fall. The key partnership of the day was between Dansie and his captain, Ridings, a stand of 96 in 90 minutes that turned the mood of the game. Ridings' contribution was crucial, and later stands involving Colin Pinch, the 19-year-old colt Dean Trowse and Jack Manning gave the South Australians the chance of an outright win.

The final day's fare built into a cliffhanger. The target for Queensland was 237, in five minutes more than five hours. Their initial response was appalling, Leyland Sanders and Ern Toovey falling for ducks and Keith Jack for six. Ken Archer dominated a recovery partnership with Grout, but after Archer was caught behind off Geoff Noblet for 60, at 76, and Aub Carrigan was bowled in the same over, the game looked lost. Much depended on the Test experience of McCool, and he and Grout became involved in the second worthwhile stand of the afternoon.

McCool had been struggling with the bat for much of the season, but soon he found his timing as Ridings reverted to a deep field. Grout stayed with him while 98 were added, many of them singles to the well-protected boundaries. McCool was a naturally aggressive batsman, strong on the hook and cut, and good enough to score a century against England. Grout was also a fine hooker of fast bowling, and before his long career was over he would open the batting for his state.

Ridings had only himself and Dansie to complement his four front-line bowlers, who had worked themselves to the limit in the hot Brisbane sun. Through his field settings, he worked McCool and Grout into a situation where the clock became a bigger enemy than the bowlers, and at 174, the Queensland keeper, after reaching a gallant 61, drove a a simple catch back to the bowler Bruce Bowley. Within seven runs Ken Mackay was run out after a misunderstanding. McCool steadied, and with "Mick" Raymer, pushed Queensland within 26 of victory, as time ran down.

Raymer was one of the competition's characters. Slightly deaf following war service in Asia, he slaughtered NSW paceman Tom Brooks one day while everyone else was struggling on a greentop. Brooks had a peculiar habit of grunting when he bowled, and Raymer mistook the grunts for the umpire shouting "no-ball". All he could do was laugh when his teammates congratulated him after that knock.

On the late afternoon of February 12, 1952, Raymer concentrated on defence and the loud calls of his senior partner as the scoreboard inched towards 237 and the clock raced towards stumps at 5.30pm. Into the last half hour, Raymer was bowled by the spinner, Manning, leaving Ron Archer to try and accompany McCool home.

Ridings kept Manning on, as McCool and Archer relied on singles as much as they could. Archer would never play in a more thrilling Shield match than his first, and actually outscored McCool as the clock and the target converged. McCool had reached 77, the innings' total 230, and one ball remained in Manning's 17th over, with the clock all but showing time, when his luck ran out. Making room, he lost his middle stump, to groans from the crowd. Archer would have to get the final seven runs on his own.

Ridings opted for Bowley to bowl the final over. Queensland number eleven was Laurie Chapman, a fine fast-medium bowler, but an ordinary batsman. Archer's instructions were apparently to keep Chapman out of danger, away from Bowley's final eight balls, and he made no more than a token effort to win Queensland the game. The fear of losing first-innings points already won outweighed the possibility of an outright win. Two runs came from the fourth ball, but singles were ignored, and the game ended in a draw, just four runs and one wicket separating the two sides.

Gabba veterans could not recall a more tense afternoon. As the spectators and critics fell back into their seats, most praise was for Ridings, who had won as much from the afternoon as any captain could. He had attacked only as much as he was able, and used his bowlers and his strategies to conjure a thrilling photo finish. He was a great Shield captain for South Australia, a worthy member of a distinguished club that includes Joe Darling, Clem Hill, Vic Richardson, Don Bradman, Les Favell, Ian Chappell and David Hookes.

# 42

## CUP DAY

Some memorable and crazy events in Sheffield Shield history have occured on the occasion of the annual November event, Melbourne Cup day. It was Cup Day, 1910, when Algy Gehrs scored his sensational century for South Australia, an innings described in chapter 15. A year later, the South Australian Harold Webster kept wickets as if his concentration was more focussed on the Cup sweep than the cricket, conceding 24 byes and being struck on the body a number of times while standing back to the fast left-arm of Bill Whitty.

In 1924, while the crock Stand By was achieving a Cup miracle by running Backwood to a head in a stirring finish, Clarrie Grimmett was completing his first five-wicket haul for South Australia. Nine years later, as the champion colt Hall Mark set about winning the final leg of the AJC Derby-Victoria Derby-Melbourne Cup trifecta, the South Australian batsmen were gambling and losing against the eccentric spin of Chuck Fleetwood-Smith. In 1936, NSW edged out Queensland by one wicket in the final over of the match, only hours after Wotan had shocked the nation by winning the Cup at 100–1.

In some states, play would be delayed while the Cup was broadcast over the public address. In his autobiography, *Slasher Opens Up*, Ken Mackay told a sad story of the despair such a broadcast once caused. Mackay was playing for Queensland against NSW in Brisbane in 1955, and was having a dreadful match. He had already spilt a simple catch from the all-rounder Pat Crawford while fielding on the fence in front of the patrons on the Gabba Hill (one of nine catches missed in the innings), and been bowled by a screamer by Alan Davidson in the first innings for a duck.

"I was approaching the wicket for my second 'dig' in this disastrous match," recalled Mackay, "when someone realised it was two minutes to Cup time. So play was halted for the yearly ritual. There were three things on my mind; the dropped catches, my first innings 'blob', and the fact that I had drawn the Cup favourite, Rising Fast, in a sweep organised among the teams.

"The race start was delayed for four minutes, further time for agonised thought. Then the odds began to stack up against me. Rising Fast was beaten. I shuddered at the omen, and nine minutes after walking onto the ground I took my stance against, of all people, Pat Crawford. Almost fearfully I watched Pat run in and bowl the ball that was to complete my degradation. It pitched, apparently well outside the off stump and swung at the last moment, a split second quicker than my jabbing bat. There I stood, castled for the second time in the match. That nine minute wait for one ball and a 'pair' must be a record."

What Ken Mackay never mentioned in his book was that a year earlier he had batted through most of Cup Day for an unbeaten century against NSW. On that day, when Rising Fast became the first horse to complete the Caulfield Cup, Cox Plate, and Melbourne Cup treble, Mackay was at the bowler's end when NSW leg spinner Jack Treanor completed a hat-trick of another kind, spinning out Ken Archer, Leyland Sanders and Peter Burge in consecutive balls.

One of the greatest Shield performances on Cup Day came in 1950, the year the Jim Cummings-trained Comic Court trounced a hot field to win at 25–1. Don Tallon, the Queensland captain, had declared his second innings closed as the horses were cantering down towards the start at Flemington, leaving NSW the daunting equation of 131 minutes to score 225 runs. Ken Mackay later claimed that Tallon only declared because the Cup was not broadcast over the public address in Sydney, and the great wicketkeeper wanted to hear the race. Mackay also suggested that the prompting of one Keith Miller, a keen punter, may have had something to do with the unlikely declaration.

It was apparent to all at the ground that the players were bent on getting to hear the race broadcast. Queensland batsman Mick Harvey had crawled through the eighties and early nineties, while NSW fieldsmen glanced anxiously at the Members' Stand clock. With the time fast approaching 3.00pm, the advertised Cup starting time, Miller came on to bowl — and sent down a series of full tosses, which Harvey swept away for his hundred. Before the final boundary had reached the fence, the players were sprinting for the dressing room…just in time for the Cup start.

After the race was won, and jockey Pat Glennon had brought the latest Cup hero back to scale, NSW skipper Arthur Morris took the irrepressible Miller out with him to chase the runs. And they chased them in grand style. Through a mixture of sheer power and daring singles, the first 50 was reached in 27 minutes, the 100 stand in 54. By this time it was clear that the Queensland captain was to be the unluckiest punter of the day. Miller struck 16 fours, and one huge six off the medium pacer Aub Carrigan, in scoring an undefeated 138. In comparison, Morris was subdued, but never less than aggressive in making 78, and the target was achieved with 11 minutes to spare. Melbourne Cup Day has never seen a better exhibition than this one put on by two thoroughbreds of the game.

*Below: Ken "Slasher" Mackay, a cricketer who saw the best and worst of Melbourne Cup day. Left: Arthur Morris, one of the great left-handers in the Shield's history, who combined with Keith Miller for a famous victory in Sydney on Cup Day, 1950.*

# 43

## SOUTH AUSTRALIA ALL OUT 27

Australian sport had had nothing to rival the golden age of the 1950s, when for a brief, exciting period this country was one of the world's leading sporting nations. There were the athletes, Jackson, Landy, Strickland and Elliott, and the swimmers Fraser, Crapp, Rose, Devitt and Henricks, and there were all the rest...Peter Thomson and Kel Nagle, Frank Sedgman, Clive Churchill, Ted Whitten and Ron Barassi, Stuart Mackenzie, George Moore, Tulloch, Todman and Rising Fast, and so many more.

On November 20, 1955 sports fans in Sydney had a remarkable smorgasbord of local talent to admire. At White City, Lew Hoad defeated Ken Rosewall in four sets to win the NSW singles crown. On the Parramatta river, former Olympic Gold medallist Merv Wood won the single sculls at the Sydney Regatta. At Randwick, winning jockeys included George Mulley, Billy Cook, Ray Selkrig, Arthur Ward and Jack Thompson. Missing was Neville Sellwood, still in Melbourne appealing over a two-month suspension imposed after his winning Melbourne Cup ride on the Tommy Smith-trained Toporoa. At the Sydney Sports Ground, Marlene Matthews had to shatter the NSW 220 yards record to beat Betty Cuthbert in an inter-club event.

Right next door to the track and field was the greatest single attraction of the day. At the SCG, Keith Miller was bowling at the absolute peak of his form, reducing South Australia to the lowest innings total in the history of the Sheffield Shield.

Early on the Friday morning before the commencement of the Shield game, Miller's wife gave birth to their fourth child, a baby boy. From the hospital, Miller went straight to the middle to win the toss and elect to bat. Less than six hours later he had become the first Shield captain to declare an innings closed on the first day. At 4.47pm, despite a darkening sky, Miller called a halt with NSW's score on 8–215.

He hoped for at least half an hour at the South Australians, but was given only 12 balls, before the umpires, following their third conference, offered a way to the dressing room for the grateful opening batsmen. The NSW captain was not amused, and as he strode from the field suggested to his teammates that the visiting batsmen may yet regret his declaration, however foolish it looked right at that moment.

Most of the great captains succeeded because they were prepared to gamble and had, in themselves or in their team, the ability, the confidence and the good fortune to justify their adventures. One hundred and sixty six points of rain fell in Sydney as Miller celebrated the birth of his new son, and the next morning play was delayed by 17 minutes as the groundstaff mopped up after the excesses of the night before.

The NSW and later Australian batsman, Brian Booth, in his autobiography *Booth to Bat*, told the story of Miller's appearance at the ground that morning: "Our captain had not arrived and the team was lined up at the door ready to follow the umpires. Keith came through the open dressing room door like a rocket, carrying coat and tie, his shirt unbuttoned to the waist. Coolly he called: 'I won't be a minute.' His shirt was off as he disappeared into the dressing room. The next moment he appeared dressed in flannels, shirt and boots. He just kept on walking through the door saying: 'Come on, you fellows, we have a game of cricket on. We don't want to be late.'"

South Australia had scored two runs in the gloom of Friday afternoon. Now Miller was at them, not bowling at full steam, but controlling his pace and swing as few had seen before. Newspaper reports suggest there was nothing in the wicket to justify the carnage that followed. Tom Goodman in the *Sun Herald* thought the pitch was "good". Phil Tresidder, in the *Sunday Telegraph*, described the surface as "pacy but true". Bill O'Reilly could scarcely believe it: "Not a drop of the overnight rain had come through the covers. No ball bounced unusually high and not one shooter was served up throughout the day."

Even the South Australian captain, Phil Ridings, described the pitch as "perfect".

Miller bowled from the northern, M.A. Noble stand end, with a genuine breeze blowing in from over the Hill at the southern end. Immediately he had his inswinger right on line, and in his second over bowled Les Favell off the inside edge. From the Randwick end, his new-ball partner Pat Crawford bowled with greater speed, and scarcely less control, and had David Harris dropped by Richie Benaud at third slip. Next over Harris overestimated the inswing and sliced Miller to Crawford in the umbrella field. Dean Trowse survived the first ball, but not the second, which swung back late from outside the off-stump line, and upended the middle stump.

Miller had 3 for 0 from 3 overs, the innings score was 3–4. Ridings, when one, was dropped by Peter Philpott at second slip off Crawford, and with Colin Pinch scrambled the total to double figures. Pinch was unlucky. Having pushed Crawford to leg for an all-run four, he was bowled off the inside edge, to give Miller's accomplice his first wicket. The partnership of six was to be the highest of the innings, the all-run four one of only two such scoring shots in the entire debacle.

Graeme Hole was completely beaten and bowled by a beauty from Miller. 5 for 15. Then Ridings, having somehow got to eight, played inside a fast one from Crawford and it was 6 for 17. One of the bails finished down near the third man boundary, 50 metres from its normal resting spot. John Drennan was bowled by Crawford, and then Langley, after getting Miller to the square leg fence, was deceived and ruined by the inswinging reprisal. The final two wickets fell to Miller, to give him 7–12 from 59 deliveries. Crawford, from eight overs, had 3–14. South Australia were all out for 27.

The plaudits heaped on Miller were rich and varied. Here are a few:

Bill O'Reilly: "It was heady bowling by an artisan who knows just how to make full use of a head-on wind."

Johnny Taylor: "Few batsmen could have withstood him today. What a debt post-war cricket owes him."

Phil Ridings: "Keith swung the ball in almost unplayable fashion."

Arthur Mailey: "I did not see the South Australian innings. I was fixing my buttonhole."

In the *Sun Herald* the next day, Miller wrote: "Bowling into the crosswind helped me to exploit swing. I was able to dip the ball into the batsmen. What's more, the ball sometimes skidded back off the pitch." In the dressing room after the innings, he pondered what Alec Bedser, the famous English medium-pacer, would have done in the conditions. At least part of Miller's bowling return that day could be credited to the experience he had gained during the previous decade.

The 10 wickets had fallen in an hour and a quarter. Richie Benaud, in his superb book *On Reflection*, tells the story of two South Australian supporters arriving at the ground just before lunch, and seeing the scoreboard showing Favell on 5, Harris 7, the score 0–12. Said one to the other: "Well, I suppose it's pretty slow…but the first-innings points are what matter. They'll push it along a bit more after lunch." It was, of course, the second innings!

Miller bowled just two more overs during the day. At stumps, the visitors were 4–184. The major casualty of the afternoon was the NSW keeper Ossie Lambert, who stopped a mis-directed flier from Alan Davidson with his face as he stumbled down the leg–side. Bob Simpson took over, and later in the day held a clever catch to dismiss Favell, who drove at a Benaud leg break. Later in the day Lambert returned, to stump Harris off Philpott. The game ended on the Monday in a comfortable nine–wicket victory for the home team. Benaud finished the South Australian second innings with six wickets, Miller bowled just four more overs, without taking a wicket.

Keith Miller had been NSW captain since 1953–54, the season in which NSW began a run of nine consecutive Shield titles. He was a leader who tried to entertain, and who sometimes won results through unorthodox means. In his first match, after losing the toss on a sweltering day, he introduced the leg spin of Benaud after five overs of the opening day, a move which almost had Queensland out before the luncheon break, Benaud at one stage having 5–17. Later in that season, Miller won five–wicket innings hauls from two unheralded leg-spinners. Bob Roxby, from Newcastle, took 5–84 against South Australia, and later in Perth, in a match attended by the touring Duke of Edinburgh, 17-year-old Bobby Simpson finished with 5–37 in the Western Australian second innings.

In December 1955, Miller chose to keep his side out in the field at St Kilda Oval, despite steady rain falling. His opposing captain, Ian Johnson, could scarcely have denied a request for NSW to come in, but Miller did not want to disappoint the 10,625 people who had come to the ground. Tom Goodman, in the 1957 *Wisden*, called Miller's decision: "One of the most remarkable gestures to a sporting crowd made in Australia." Eventually the match was abandoned after the final two days were lost completely.

He was never a reckless captain, rather a sensible man who was prepared to gamble if the odds or situation demanded it, and he would never let a game become mundane, for his team's sake as much as the crowd's. When he retired, following the 1956 tour of England, his captaincy ideas were apparent in the approach taken by Ian Craig and Benaud, who followed him to the helm of the all–conquering NSW side. Miller remains one of the greatest entertainers and greatest players to be a part of the Sheffield Shield, and cricket's most formidable contribution to Australia's golden era of sport.

# 44

# THE RETURN OF BODYLINE

There was a sensation shortly after the resumption of play in the Queensland — WA Sheffield Shield match at the WACA Ground yesterday when the WA fast bowler Ron Gaunt was warned for bodyline bowling.

*He was warned by WA's leading and most experienced umpire O. Cooley under the law of cricket relating to fair and unfair play.*

*After speaking to Gaunt about his frequent bumpers with a cordon of four leg-side fieldsmen close to the wicket, Cooley stopped play while he told Ken Meuleman, the WA captain to discontinue these tactics.*

*Meuleman, who was fielding at silly leg, then moved to the off-side of the wicket, the remaining fieldsmen in the leg trap spread out, and play was resumed.*

This was how the *West Australian* newspaper led their front page story of the final day of the most controversial Shield match of the 1956–57 season. Gaunt was cautioned after the Queensland batsman, Jack McLaughlin, was struck on the body. On the other side of the country, the headline on the main story in the sports page of the Brisbane *Courier-Mail* was "WEST AUST. USED FIRST BODYLINE ATTACK SINCE '32". It was an ugly story that reflected the bitter feeling that developed between the two sides, as a combination of a placid pitch, a tiresome drawn match, and a demanding Shield schedule created a dismal and acrimonious day's cricket.

Queensland were in the middle of their best season since joining the Shield in 1926. An outright win in Perth would have put them in an excellent position to win the Shield title for the first time. They were led by the champion former NSW paceman Ray Lindwall, and included names such as Wally Grout, Ken Mackay and Peter Burge. In their previous match they had won a decisive outright victory against Neil Harvey and company in Melbourne, a triumph set up by Lindwall's superb 5–60 on the opening day.

The "bodyline" match in Perth was played from December 15 to 19. This was Western Australia's first season as a fully fledged member of the competition and they were struggling from the impact of a tiring program, which required them to play their first six matches in seven weeks, a difficult ask for players not accustomed to the stresses of constant first-class cricket. Their batting was highly dependent on two imports, the gifted young colt from Sydney, Bobby Simpson, and the experienced former Victorian Ken Meuleman, who had come to Perth in 1954, and taken over the captaincy from Keith Carmody at the beginning of the 1956–57 season.

Meuleman was no certainty to play in the match against Queensland, having been hit by influenza in the days before the game. However on the morning of the match he confirmed he was strong enough to start, but lost the toss to Lindwall and was obliged to field. Early on the WA captain had his problems. His new opening bowler Hubert Bevan was hostile but could not get his run-up right and was no-balled nine times. After this disruptive start things improved, and Queensland struggled to 7–242 at stumps.

Gaunt was outstanding, especially in the middle session when he ripped apart the top order after Mackay and the opener Ray Reynolds had taken Queensland to 1–115. Reynolds was bowled by an inswinging yorker, Mackay caught by Alan Preen at leg slip, and Peter Burge caught sensationally by Lawrie Sawle running in from the fine leg fence. When Meuleman had Des Bull caught behind, Queensland were 5–170, and they plodded from there until the close.

Gaunt was a strong, stocky fast man in his second season of first-class cricket. In his debut Shield match, against Queensland at the WACA Ground in December 1955, Lindwall and Ron Archer were criticised in some quarters for bowling too many bouncers, a strategy Gaunt absorbed. He captured 11 wickets from three matches in that first season, and in 1956–57 finished with 24, and impressed sufficiently to be chosen as a replacement for the Australian team's trip to South Africa under Ian Craig. Later he would transfer to Victoria, and tour England with the Australians in 1961.

Queensland were bowled out for 290 on the second morning. Apart from Simpson, who scored 96, the home side's batting was below standard, the discipline poor. The WA innings finished 20 minutes before stumps, for 175 — a dismal return, especially considering Lindwall could not work up full pace because of a stomach disorder. Even so the Queensland captain bowled eleven overs for just eleven runs,

*Right: Ray Lindwall, who led the NSW attack for eight seasons before moving north to Queensland in 1955.*

*Below: Western Australia in 1956–57. Back row: M. Vernon, B. Shepherd, D. Hoare, K. Slater, R. Gaunt, A. Preen; Front row: R. Strauss, B. Rigg, K. Meuleman (capt), A. Edwards, L. Sawle, B. Buggins.*

and the wicket of Meuleman, caught behind by the excellent Grout. In the *West Australian,* Alan Newman wrote: "Even if he is a spent force as a Test cricketer, Lindwall showed he could be of value to Queensland for several years to come."

Lindwall's sickness was a prelude to a problem that would strike at a number of the Queensland team. Following the third day's play, when the visitors batted tediously through to stumps for an overall lead of 402, with six second innings wickets still standing, a pale Lindwall told pressmen that five of his players were suffering from the stomach virus. "I'm hopeful these players who have been ill will recover sufficiently to make an all out effort towards an outright win," Lindwall said.

Grout, Bull, McLaughlin and the all-rounder Jim Bratchford were all suffering, as was Simpson, who had apparently batted under some duress. The next morning these five were all able to play, but Lindwall, under doctor's orders, was confined to his hotel bed. Vice-captain Mackay took over the captaincy.

It was apparently Mackay's decision to continue batting on the final morning. He argued that with five of his team less than 100 per cent it was impossible for Queensland to achieve an outright victory. To the locals the strategy seemed heartless, akin to hitting the exhausted bowlers over the head with a bat, and they reacted as they did.

Preen aimed his spinners well wide of the wicket with eight men on the leg side, and then Gaunt adopted his bodyline attack. The wicket was docile, and Gaunt's bowling was more display than intimidatory. The few spectators cheered the bouncers and barracked the defensive shots, and after 25 minutes and 14 runs Mackay mercifully called a halt.

The remainder of the match was a benefit for Simpson, who scored his first Shield century for Western Australia, an undefeated 112. Sawle made a dour 66 and W.A finished on 3–255. After the match the WA players suggested Gaunt was "just messing about" when he bowled to his bodyline field and claimed that the umpire had overreacted. The WA Cricket Association left the matter on the field, choosing not to penalise or even question any of the players involved.

So the affair ended. What remains the most contentious aspect of the drama was the tactics adopted by Mackay. A target of 402 in a single day's play (330 minutes) was clearly much more than a difficult one, even considering the docile pitch and the health problems of some of the Queensland bowlers. Western Australia had no chance in the Shield while Queensland were up with the front-runners. Keith Carmody said later that had he been in the Queenslanders' position he would have declared at 5 o'clock on the third afternoon, and set a target of around a run-a-minute. It seems the Queenslanders were fearful of losing the first-innings points they had already won. By dithering Mackay not only created an unpleasant and ugly scene on the fourth morning, he also cost his state any chance of outright points.

Six weeks later the full significance of the decision to bat on became apparent. Queensland missed the Shield championship by a solitary point. A more aggressive approach in Perth may not have won that point.

But then, it might have.

# 45

## THE FIRST TIE

When it was all over, and the crowd was finally able to lean back in their chairs for a breather, a gentleman in a loud, blue jacket and a gleaming white panama turned to his exhausted colleague and said: "Pretty close, wasn't it?"

It was close alright — the first tie in Sheffield Shield history, a result that came about when NSW's last pair, one batting with a broken finger, the other sickened by a stomach virus, could score only 12 of the 13 runs they needed to win NSW an outright result against Victoria. It was a game to rank with any played in the Shield, the ending a spectacular finale to a day of sometimes slow, but nonetheless intensely exciting first-class cricket.

*Three significant figures in the Shield's first tie. Below: The Victorian captain Neil Harvey. Below right: Richie Benaud, who took over as NSW skipper after Ian Craig fell ill, and then hit a defiant 70 on the last day to all-but win the match. Right: Jim Burke, who broke a finger early in the NSW second innings, but came back to get his side within one of victory.*

The match began just two weeks after the completion of the Melbourne Olympics in 1956. Sporting headlines were dominated by events in Adelaide, where Harry Hopman, Ken Rosewall and Lew Hoad were preparing to defend the Davis Cup against another American challenge. New South Wales, the Shield champions, were captained by Ian Craig; Victoria, struggling after successive losses to Queensland and Western Australia, by Neil Harvey. The venue was the St Kilda Cricket Ground, as the MCG was still suffering the effects of Olympic fever.

The young Victorian batsmen could not cope with the spin of Richie Benaud on the first day and were bowled out for 244. Colin McDonald managed a solid fifty, Harvey batted grandly for 44, and fast bowler Ian Meckiff slogged a crucial half-century late in the afternoon. The next day Meckiff was impressive again, threatening all but Jim Burke and Norm O'Neill with his left-arm speed as NSW crept to 281. Burke batted through the innings, undefeated on 132, while 19-year-old O'Neill drove powerfully in the middle order. The rest of the batting was mediocre, Alan Davidson the third top score with 22.

The injuries (and later illnesses) that were to punctuate the game began to appear on the second day. Firstly, Harvey cracked the third finger on his left hand trying to catch nightwatchman Jack Treanor in the slip cordon. Doctors told him he was finished for the match, but Harvey announced he would be batting in the Victorian second innings. Late in the day, John Shaw, batting three where Harvey would normally have been, was struck a fearful blow when he ducked into a riser from Davidson, and had to retire.

The next day Shaw came back to make a fighting half-century, and Harvey batted under difficulty to reach 22. Much of the afternoon was played out in constant drizzle, NSW acting captain Benaud opting to stay out in the rain in the hope the moisture would quieten the deteriorating wicket. Benaud was in charge because Craig had been confined to his hotel bed by tonsilitis. The gamble appeared to pay off. None of the Victorians attacked the sodden ball and the Vics could muster only 197. At stumps NSW had all 10 wickets in hand and required just 161 for outright victory.

Both sides had needed further assistance from the medical staff. The Victorians lost opening bowler John Salmon because of strained rib muscles. NSW paceman Alan Wyatt had bowled only four overs in the Victorian second innings because of a stomach disorder. The next morning, after play had been delayed due to the state of the ground, Meckiff smashed Burke's little finger on the right hand, when a ball spat up at the bat handle. Earlier in the over the batsman had been struck a stinging blow on the shoulder. This incident set the mood for a sensational collapse, as Meckiff and the left arm spin of Lindsay Kline reduced NSW to an unbelievable 7–70.

Surveying the carnage from the bowler's end was Benaud. The batting had been slow and timid, and now he was joined by his ailing captain, who had struggled from his hotel bed when told that wickets were falling. Craig gave himself the defensive role, while Benaud counter-attacked and gradually turned the game around once more. Against the assault of Benaud, Kline wilted. The batsman was down the pitch at him, then back on his stumps to pull the short one to the fence. With Meckiff tired and Salmon off the ground, the bowling lost its bite, and at tea 38 were needed with three wickets still in hand.

Straight after tea Benaud would have been run out if Sam Loxton had not fumbled at the bowler's wicket. The partnership had NSW within 16 of victory, when Benaud finally gambled once too often. He swung at Kline but miscued, and the ball fell into the hands of the backpeddling Shaw at slip. Back to the middle came Jimmy Burke, broken finger strapped up tightly, to help his captain eke out the win. But the below-par Craig had been happier in the supporting role, and now, obliged to take up the reins, he could do no more than spoon a weak drive to Bill Lawry at cover.

The last pair needed 13 to win. Alan Wyatt managed a single, then Kline spun one through both Burke and keeper Len Maddocks for two byes. Wyatt, still unwell, was batting under difficulties, but managed to keep out Meckiff, who was back for one last effort. Burke pounced on a dreadful full toss from Kline to reduce the target to six, but could not get the single to keep Wyatt away from Meckiff.

Still Meckiff could not get through. Then Kline bowled to Burke who shaped to drive, but was beaten in flight, and could do no more than jam down on the ball and ground as it pitched in the blockhole. The jar on his shattered finger was terrible, and after a delay he could do no more than gently prod away the rest of the over.

Wyatt forced Meckiff away to fine leg for a precious single. NSW needed five to win. Only now did the frantic Victorian supporters think in terms of the tie. Burke nudged another single, through the gully, to keep the bowling, and then late cut the spinner past the despairing Shaw at slip for two to narrow the gap to one. The field was brought in to stop the vital single, but Burke chanced a push into the covers for the shortest of runs, and Wyatt made it home. The scores were now tied.

Kline had one ball at Wyatt, but the number 11 kept it out. The stand had been alive for 27 minutes.

Now it was Meckiff at Burke, a battle that had been ongoing since that angry blow on the shoulder so much earlier in the day. The crowd watched in a hush, as if awaiting the winning kick in a football grand final. They had not long to wait. Meckiff's first ball was short, too short, and veering further away. Burke jabbed at it, got the faintest touch, and the jubilant Maddocks snared it, throwing the ball high in the air as his teammates screamed their appeals.

Of the dramatic cricket after tea, the former Victorian and Australian captain Ian Johnson wrote in *The Argus*: "It was a magnificent fightback by Victoria, but it was too, a grand display of courage by three unfit New South Wales players."

Percy Beames in *The Age* wrote of the "much needed boost" the result would give to first-class cricket. In many ways this game was the beginning of the turn around in the fortunes of Shield cricket, which for a number of seasons had been pushed into the backblocks by the demands of Test cricket. The Shield was about to be inhabited by a bold new generation, featuring the younger players from the immediate past, such as Harvey, Benaud, Davidson and Wally Grout, and the budding champions, O'Neill, Meckiff, Peter Burge and Bob Simpson. The historic St Kilda tie can be seen as a prelude to a golden era of the Sheffield Shield.

# 46

## PROVING A POINT

When the 1956 Australian team returned from their eight-month tour of England, India and Pakistan, the NSW selectors surprised by naming Ian Craig as their new captain, replacing the retired Keith Miller. Richie Benaud, who had led the side in Miller's absence in 1955–56, was the anticipated choice, but at the highest administrative levels neither Benaud nor the new Victorian captain, Neil Harvey, were thought of as future Test captains — and Board of Control officials intimated to their NSW counterparts that they would like to see Craig given the job.

Craig was just 21 years old, but already a veteran of two tours of England. In February 1952 he had scored 91 on debut, against South Australia, when just 16. No younger cricketer has played in the Sheffield Shield. In 1952–53 he scored 213 for NSW against South Africa, and later that season played in the 5th Test, at 17 years 239 days becoming the youngest Australian Test cricketer. As captain of NSW he began with a first-innings win in Brisbane and followed with outright defeats of Western Australia (twice) and South Australia. Then came the historic tied match in Melbourne, followed by a setback — a first-innings loss to the powerful Queensland side at the SCG.

In January 1957, to the surprise of few in Sydney and most in Melbourne, Craig was appointed Australian captain for a non-Test tour of New Zealand — the first time a NSW-based player had been made captain of a top-class touring Australian side since Herbert Collins had led the 1926 side that lost the Ashes in England.

Neil Harvey was appointed Australian vice-captain for that New Zealand tour, but only because the Queensland all-rounder Ron Archer was unavailable owing to a knee injury. It was assumed in most circles that if Archer was fit, he, and not Harvey or Benaud, would be Craig's deputy for the tour of South Africa scheduled for 1957–58.

In Melbourne, the local press denounced the passing over of Harvey, who had been Victoria's, and Australia's, leading batsman since 1949. Harvey was a left-hander of the highest quality, the best Victorian player of spin bowling since the great Bill Ponsford. A small, but brave batsman, with the skill to get out to drive and the courage to hook the fastest bouncer, Harvey was a highly popular figure, especially in his home town. He admitted later to his regret at missing the Australian captaincy. In his autobiography, *My World of Cricket*, he wrote: "I must confess I was very disappointed. I felt I had earned the captaincy, and to know that I had been overlooked hurt me deep down inside. But it made me all the more determined to do well against New South Wales."

*NSW's Ian Craig (right) and Neil Harvey of Victoria, the two leading contenders for the Australian captaincy in 1956–57. Craig was given the national job, and Harvey responded with the best Shield innings of his life.*

Craig's appointment was announced on January 24. NSW were to meet Victoria in Sydney two days later. Harvey went into the match in the peak of form, having already scored three Shield centuries in the season, and six in his previous eight Shield matches. Conjecture over the captaincy had been deflected to some extent by the excited interest being placed on the performances of a 19-year-old NSW batsman, Norman O'Neill, who had scored a superb century against South Australia a week earlier.

A late-season surge by the Queenslanders had brought them level with NSW at the top of the Shield ladder, and technically in front because of their superior average. As a point was awarded to teams which lost on the first innings, NSW needed to do no more than avoid outright defeat to retain the Shield, and deny the northerners their inaugural competition success. On the morning of the match Harvey announced that young opening batsman, Bill Lawry, would be 12th man. The wicketkeeper, Len Maddocks, would be the stopgap at the top of the order.

Harvey and Craig met for the first time after the captaincy announcement when they went out to toss before the Shield match. "Bad luck, Nin. I thought you might have got it," was Craig's opening remark. Harvey called incorrectly, but surprisingly the new Australian captain sent the Victorians into bat.

Harvey returned to the visitors' dressing room to the news that his one regular opener, Colin McDonald, had broken his nose in the practice nets while the toss was being completed. It was too late to revise the starting eleven, and all Harvey could do was grab the pads and head out to the wicket himself. He later recalled his mood:

"Having lost the Australian captaincy, the toss against NSW and my best opening bat as well, I don't suppose I could have been blamed for thinking the fates were loaded against me. So with no-one else to do the job, I went in with Maddocks to open the innings. I feared the worst, but as things turned out we fared very well indeed."

At stumps Victoria were 3 for 375. Harvey had been dismissed just before the close for 209, having played an innings of style and glory. Craig, Australian captain-elect for just two days, was slammed by the Sydney press for his decision to give his rival first use of the wicket. "Craig's decison defied imagination," thundered Jim Mathers in the Sydney *Truth*. "A colossal blunder," wrote George Thatcher in the *Sun Herald*. The NSW captain could do little more than point to previous games at the SCG in 1956–57, when the pitch had been at its most lively on the first day.

Harvey had set the mood in the match's opening over, when he struck Alan Davidson for three fours. Thirty came from Davidson's first three overs, and the 50 partnership was reached in 33 minutes. Captains who send in the opposition expect breakthroughs not boundaries. Maddocks fell at 69, having done his job, and John Shaw came in to play a straight bat while Harvey played the Shield innings of his life.

A feature was a wonderful duel between Harvey and Benaud soon after lunch. The leg-spinner bowled superbly, always on line, but Harvey used his feet to stifle the turn and keep control of the game. If the spinner was fractionally short, Harvey was on him like a hawk, pulling and cutting to the fence. Benaud spent all day fighting back, but the great left-hander on this day was his master. Benaud finished with 0–73 from 20 overs, having seldom bowled better.

In the *Sunday Telegraph*, R.S. Whitington compared Harvey's batting to an innings of the Englishman Len Hutton at the SCG in 1946–47 — that knock one of the most revered of all the superb performances by opening batsmen at the SCG. Harvey's hundred came in 159 minutes and most agreed it was his finest hand on the Sydney ground. Shaw fell at 253, after a patient support role. In Ian Huntington the Victorian captain found a third determined ally, and added another 107 for the third wicket, before he finally departed, falling to a tired, unsuccessful drive at the long-suffering Davidson. He had batted for 308 minutes and struck 21 fours.

The next day, after Victoria had stumbled to 444, NSW collapsed meekly to 149, and officials in Brisbane started moving furniture in the QCA offices to make room for the Shield. The NSW batting was terrible, the Victorian bowling, led by Sam Loxton and Ian Meckiff, outstanding. Benaud and Davidson fell in successive balls. O'Neill was dismissed in ludicrous fashion, run out by Harvey at short leg after the batting hero of the previous day had put down a hot chance, but regained the ball and thrown the stumps down with the inexperienced colt loitering two or three metres down the wicket. Only Craig batted with conviction, staying close to two hours for 45. Harvey enforced the follow-on, and before stumps, NSW opener Billy Watson was dismissed once more.

On the third day the NSW batsmen battled back, scoring at a funereal pace. Nightwatchman Ossie Lambert batted for nearly an hour for 15, and Jim Burke stonewalled for 102 minutes for 24. Craig and Sid Carroll came together at 12.31pm and continued until stumps, neglecting all but the safest shots and taking NSW within 94 of making Victoria bat again. Carroll batted throughout with a badly cut and bruised right hand. After lunch, Maddocks had to leave the field after a deflected ball caught him on the chin. McDonald, broken nose and all, was the substitute keeper. The pitch had now become the proverbial batsman's paradise, and little hope was held for an outright result, especially as the Victorians' key bowler, Meckiff, was out of the game with a damaged thigh and Loxton was also in trouble, with a weary shoulder.

After Craig and Carroll took their stand to 166 in 259 minutes, a clever spell from the left-arm spinner Lindsay Kline almost turned the game in the middle session of the final day. In eight overs, Kline took 3–10, to reduce NSW to 7–280. O'Neill failed for the second time, cutting at a ball that turned back at him and deflecting a catch to the keeper. Davidson and Johnny Martin added a crucial 52 for the 8th wicket to steady the floundering ship. Martin was the ninth wicket to fall, at 356, and his departure gave the Victorians one last chance, but they could not break the last-wicket pair of Alan Wyatt and Jack Treanor.

The plucky Treanor was batting with a broken thumb, but kept his end up until almost full-time, when Wyatt was stumped swinging at Alan Dick. Victoria needed the impossible ask of 109 in a single over, and Craig used the opportunity to give Lambert his one over in first-class cricket.

For Queenslanders this match would rank with the finals of 1985 and 1986, when they came within late-wicket partnerships of the trophy, as the closest the northern state came to winning the Sheffield Shield. For Neil Harvey, despite the disappointment of the final two days, it was probably his most treasured interstate contest. In 1958–59 he transferred to NSW, and, playing under the captaincy of Benaud, scored a century in his first innings for his adopted state — against Queensland. He continued scoring runs for NSW and Australia until 1962–63, and went out on a magnificently appropriate note, scoring his highest first-class score, 231, in his farewell Sheffield Shield match.

# 47

# ANOTHER BRADMAN?

The front page of *The Sun-Herald* of January 26, 1958, screamed its message: "O'NEILL! HAILED AS A NEW BRADMAN". In the paper's sport section, respected cricket writer Tom Goodman enthused as he had rarely done before over the prodigious gifts of NSW's latest batting star:

*It was back to the Bradman days at the Cricket Ground yesterday.*

*Norman O'Neill, 20, in his farewell match for NSW, played a magnificent innings of 233 runs in 244 minutes (38 fours) against Victoria in the vital Sheffield Shield match. His innings brought him a Bradman ovation as he walked back to the dressing room.*

*It was an innings that, with its pulversing power and its rich variety of stroke play, was worthy of Bradman himself in the hectic days when the champion's name was the greatest word in cricket. Not since Bradman have I heard a Sydney crowd react in such a frenzied way as yesterday's 8,310 did as O'Neill thrashed his way to his first century.*

*NSW hit up 411 runs with the loss of only four wickets in 332 minutes. On this memorable day:*

*• O'Neill made his first double century in first-class cricket; his fourth century in his last five Shield matches.*

*• He became the first batsman since the record breakers, Bradman and Ponsford, to reach an aggregate of 1000 runs in a Shield series.*

*• He and Brian Booth, who is 107 not out, created a new record for the fourth wicket in any Shield match when they put on 325 runs in 233 minutes. The old record has stood for 50 years, 315 by M.A. Noble and S.E. Gregory for NSW against Victoria at the SCG in 1907–08.*

*O'Neill and Booth had put on 190 runs for the same wicket against Victoria in Melbourne at Christmas time. The competent Booth, a self-effacing fellow and great team man, had to play second fiddle to his dynamic partner throughout their four hours together yesterday. But the crowd, after O'Neill's dismissal 13 minutes before "stumps", stayed to applaud Booth's first century in a Shield match.*

*Below: Norman O'Neill, who won comparisons with Bradman after a sensational double century for NSW against Victoria in early 1958.*
*Right: O'Neill's batting partner for most that innings, the dependable, elegant Brian Booth.*

*I count myself fortunate to have seen Norman O'Neill play two double-century innings within eight days. I had seen him make a majestic 201 not out for St George club at Waitara the previous Saturday. Yesterday's innings carried even more power. The Victorian bowling, especially that of medium pacer John Edwards, had looked highly respectable in the hour and three quarters before lunch, during which NSW made only 59 runs and lost three wickets. But as soon as O'Neill cut loose after lunch the bowling deteriorated.*

*The fielding remained keen throughout. There were many great saves — 12th man Mick Aylett on the leg boundary superb. But there were sore hands all round the field long before O'Neill had got to 200.*

*There were fierce hooks, some of them daringly from outside the off stump; there were flowing drives through the covers. There was one straight drive, unforgettable because the ball was sent bullet-like through a narrow gap between the bowler and mid-on. There were sweep shots that were hit harder than by any other player since Bradman.*

*Bradman again! One cannot escape the mention, because O'Neill, like Bradman, is a "power" player, and a great one.*

*The real highlight for the crowd came when Victoria's seasoned skipper, Sam Loxton, decided upon an over of "bumpers" to O'Neill. O'Neill hooked three successive balls, each one delivered a little further to the offside, to the boundary. The crowd roared. Then the young batsman tried to cut another short one and the ball was sliced, luckily, over slips. Another four.*

*That made O'Neill 99. The crowd gasped as he mistimed the next ball to the onside. But it fell safe, short of square leg, and the single came. O'Neill made his first hundred in 123 minutes, and his second in 95 minutes...*

In an accompanying article, Bill O'Reilly wrote: "O'Neill is another Bradman — a blind man can see it."

Norm O'Neill was not the first young cricketer to be given the "Second Bradman" tag...and would not be the last. Ian Craig had worn the label for a period after his promising debut as a 16-year-old in 1952. Later Doug Walters was likened to "The Don" after scoring hundreds in each of his first two Test matches. In an earlier time cricketers such as Archie Jackson, the South Australian colts Colin Alexander and Jack Rymill, and before them Alan Kippax had won comparisons with the legend of Victor Trumper. Before Trumper, young Australians had been likened to George Giffen, Billy Murdoch and Charlie Bannerman. It is cricket's way...

O'Neill had been compared to Bradman in 1956–57, when he scored a powerful century against South Australia in Sydney. These plaudits subsided briefly, but were revived during the 1957–58 season, as O'Neill scored century after century in Shield matches. Not only would O'Neill finish at the head of that Shield season's batting statistics, with an average of 83.75, but his leg breaks topped the bowling averages, with 26 wickets at 20.42.

Australia's best cricketers were in South Africa in 1957–58, providing O'Neill with his opportunities. Early in the season he had decided he was no certainty to retain his Shield place when the Test players returned, and, as Bob Simpson had done two years earlier, negotiated for a position interstate where he felt he could better push his claims for a Test cap. Before the Shield match of the Australia Day long weekend he confirmed he was transferring to Adelaide, where a job had been found for him. Fortunately for NSW, he later changed his mind, and stayed on to score many more Shield runs.

The comparisons with Bradman did little for his future. Only one man in cricket history could consistently set his sights on centuries, and O'Neill found himself in a position where his best performances were rarely in keeping with the unrealistic expectations established by one superb season. His Test career batting average of 45 and Shield average of 50 are more than most of his critics would believe. Later in his career he became a very nervous starter at the crease, but remained, in full flow, an inspiring and sometime brutal batsman. No Australian cricketer since O'Neill has played the cut stroke with more telling effect.

He retired following the 1966–67 season, when he again topped the Shield batting averages — his retirement forced by recurring knee trouble. Of the comparisons with Bradman, O'Neill wrote in his 1964 autobiography, *Ins and Outs*: "I have never considered myself worthy of such praise and I don't think anyone has or ever will be. It is almost a 'kiss of death' to be given such a label, and I am sure any young batsman of special talent is better off without a comparison that is embarrassing to try to fulfil."

# 48

## SIMPSON v THE REST

To tell the story of Bob Simpson's 1959–60 Shield season is to list a series of remarkable batting feats. Simpson, the Western Australian vice-captain, in five matches scored 902 runs, at the freakish batting average of 300.66. He began his spree with 98 at the WACA Ground against Victoria, scored 236 not out against his former state, NSW; an unbeaten 230 against Queensland in Perth; 79 at the Adelaide Oval and 98 and 161 not out against NSW, in Sydney.

Simpson, born in Sydney in February, 1936, made his Shield debut in January 1953, and quickly won a reputation as a promising batsman and superb slip fieldsman. Obliged to compete with the many outstanding cricketers in NSW at this time for a chance in the Sheffield Shield, Simpson was never assured of his place, and in 1956 moved to Perth, where he perceived he had more chance of catching the notice of the Test selectors. His 527 runs in his first season in Perth were sufficient to win him selection in Ian Craig's team to South Africa, but a disappointing season in 1958–59, when he began opening the WA batting, cost him a place on the Australian tour of Pakistan and India in the first half of the 1959–60 season.

The courageous NSW and Australian opening batsman, Jim Burke, had retired following the 1958–59 season, and this provided an opportunity for Simpson to win back his Test place. A season in the Lancashire League, which ended with 11 consecutive half-centuries, tightened his technique — and his sacking from the Australian team toughened his resolve. The hook shot was jettisoned, and he became a much more "side-on" player, perhaps more cautious, clearly more appreciative of the value of big scores. In the somewhat brittle Western Australian batting order he was a linchpin.

He had decided that only runs and more runs would get him the place in the Australian side, and he resolved to bat for as long as he could. So dominant was Simpson in 1959-60 that the former NSW and Australian batsman Sid Barnes suggested Western Australia should have been playing under the name of "Simpson". His unconquered 236 against NSW in Perth was the highest score achieved by a West Australian in Shield cricket, passing the mark set by his captain Ken Meuleman. In fact Meuleman delayed his declaration so that his record could be broken. It was Simpson's second century for WA, and with Meuleman, who scored his ninth century for his adopted state, he added an undefeated 301 for the fifth wicket — the first time a pair from the western state had added more than 300 in the Shield.

In that game NSW were slaughtered by an innings, Simpson taking 5–45 on the final day, including a sequence of three wickets — Brian Booth, NSW captain Ian Craig and Neil Marks — in five balls, as NSW collapsed from 1–81 to 8–117. Bruce Buggins, the WA keeper, completed five dismissals in this second innings, three of them stumpings off Simpson. Later in the season, after Bill O'Reilly criticised the absence of a right-hand wrist spinner in the second XI team for New Zealand, the side's captain, Ian Craig would describe Simpson as "Australia's second best (after Richie Benaud) leg spinner".

Simpson had been on the field for every ball bowled in the defeat of NSW, and in the following match against Queensland was on the field throughout once more. After the visitors disintegrated for just 117, WA reached 9 (declared) for 399. Simpson took his aggregate for the season to 564 for once out. He had batted in Shield matches for more than 1000 minutes since last being dismissed, a remarkable statistic, and become the third man, after Bill Ponsford and Don Bradman (who achieved the feat three times), to score successive double centuries in the Sheffield Shield.

Against South Australia in Adelaide, Simpson batted for 185 minutes, to complete a run of 1269 minutes (21 hours nine minutes) without being dismissed. The following week WA was in Sydney, to face a NSW side bolstered by the return of their international stars, Richie Benaud, Alan Davidson, Norm O'Neill and Neil Harvey.

On the opening day the central figure was O'Neill, who slammed an impressive, undefeated 161 in four hours, after Harvey had fallen to a brilliant left-handed slip catch by Simpson off Ron Gaunt. O'Neill was at his powerful best, and one drive struck the wrist of cover fieldsman Barry Shepherd so hard that the burly Shepherd had to leave the field. With Booth (80), O'Neill added 131 for the third wicket, and late in the day he dominated an exciting partnership with Davidson. Unusually for a day's cricket that included an O'Neill century, the shot of the day did not come from O'Neill but from Brian Booth, who sweetly hooked a no-ball from Des Hoare onto the roof of the "Bob" stand beyond square leg.

*NSW captain Richie Benaud (left) congratulates W.A.'s Bob Simpson, after Simpson had taken his 1959–60 Shield season batting average to 300.66, by scoring 98 and 161 not out at the SCG.*

The next day Benaud closed NSW's innings at 9–470. O'Neill had added just 14 before being run out, slipping after Davidson had rejected his call for a single to Hoare at square leg. The West Australian fight-back was inevitably led by Simpson, who at stumps was 67, WA 1–129. His duel with Benaud was an absorbing one, and more than one leg break spun past the outside edge. Despite these hiccups, Simpson enjoyed the challenge, and gained confidence as the afternoon wore on. He was more at home against the left-arm wrist spin of his former Petersham club-mate in Sydney, Johnny Martin. The contest took place before a crowd of 10,000 people, to that time the largest single day's attendance to watch a Western Australian Shield team.

By stumps on the third day Simpson was 88 not out in his side's second innings, after having been dismissed in the first just two runs short of his third century of the summer. In the first innings he batted for all but the final 23 minutes, sixth out after snicking an off-break from Martin into his leg stump; in the second he batted for 208 minutes as WA reached 3–158 at the close — still 109 runs away from avoiding an innings defeat.

On the final day he batted throughout the remainder of the innings — in all 415 minutes of resolute defiance — which almost prevented the expected NSW victory. No West Australian opener had previously carried his bat through a completed Shield innings. Benaud finished with 12 wickets for the match (6–74 in each innings). The game ended in unusual circumstances, Meuleman declining the opportunity to appeal against the rain, lightning and gloom as Booth, Craig and O'Neill swatted the 28 runs needed for victory. Less than five minutes after Booth had lofted the winning boundary, the constant drizzle became a downpour. The WA captain had considered it inappropriate for NSW to be denied the victory they had all but won.

"I have no doubt that we would have been successful in any appeal," he said. "But we did not feel it was the right thing to do."

That final innings of Simpson's Shield season was his finest. Tom Goodman wrote that on the final day Benaud "at times spun the ball like a top", but gave high praise to the batsman's judgement in picking the ball to hit, his ability to discover gaps in the field and his technique in stifling the spin. Phil Tresidder in the *Daily Telegraph* wrote of Simpson's "Hutton-like defensive technique to smother Benaud's probing leg spinners".

Western Australia batted for 2644 minutes during the five matches in which Bobby Simpson played during the 1959–60 season. Simpson was at the crease for 2170 of those minutes. In two matches he was on the field, either compiling a double century, spinning leg breaks, or grabbing slip catches, for the entire match. In a third match, he was involved for all but 23 minutes of that game's 20 hours.

After returning from New Zealand, Simpson played just one more summer in Perth before returning to Sydney, his place in the Australian side now assured. In the seasons that followed he developed a reputation for sustained rungetting few modern batsmen have matched, best typified by a colossal effort of concentration described in chapter 50. He retired in 1968 to focus on a business career, but returned for six Shield matches in 1977–78, the season in which he became Australian captain once more in response to the emergence of World Series Cricket. There have been few more significant figures in post-war Australian cricket than Bob Simpson, few players more able to achieve what they originally set out to do.

# 49

# RICHIE BENAUD

The seasons immediately following the retirement of Sir Donald Bradman saw a not altogether surprising slump in the fortunes and popularity of the Sheffield Shield. Despite the qualities of leading players such as Miller, Harvey, Hassett, Tallon, Lindwall and Arthur Morris, the Shield lost some ground in the post-Bradman years.

Above: The NSW team, featuring the
young Richie Benaud, that played
Queensland in Brisbane in 1951–52.
At back: J. Burke; Standing (left to right):
R. Madden, R. Flockton, K. Miller,
R. Benaud, G. Trueman, R. Kissell;
Seated: S. Barnes, A. Morris (capt),
G. Barter (manager), J. de Courcy,
A. Walker; Inset: R. Lindwall.

Right: Benaud bowling in the nets —
sustained aggression.

There were a number of reasons for the slide. In 1949–50, the Shield was without not just Bradman, but also the best 15 Australian cricketers, who were touring South Africa under Lindsay Hassett. The following year the Shield played no more than a supporting role to the tour of Freddie Brown's M.C.C. tourists. Then came the first Test series in Australia featuring the West Indies, followed by the third tour of Australia by a South African side. The significance of the Shield had always been based on the quality of the cricket played and on the participation of Australia's greatest players. For four straight seasons the Shield was pushed into the background by the demands of the Test arena.

The final ignominy for the Sheffield Shield came in 1954–55, the summer dominated by Len Hutton's M.C.C. tourists. That season cricket authorities opted to reduce the competition to just nine matches. The draw was a ludicrous one: NSW did not play South Australia or Western Australia. Western Australia played only two matches, home and away against South Australia, and would have won the Shield on averages had they taken their "final" match in Perth. In this lacklustre season the Shield sunk to its lowest ebb since 1919.

The competition desperately needed a revival. Some fine cricket was played in 1955–56 and 1956–57, highlighted by the thrilling tie in Melbourne in the latter year, and the batting all that season of Neil Harvey. In 1957–58, the Test side was in South Africa, but the Shield was kept buoyant by the talents of Norman O'Neill, and a shrewd administrative decision to allow teams to win points in matches where they led on the first innings but lost outright. It was thought this would reduce the likelihood of teams which led on the first innings closing up a game rather than aiming for an outright win. And so it proved, no more so than in Sydney where NSW captain Sid Carroll offered South Australia the chance to score 237 in 225 final-day minutes. The small crowd was treated to a day of cavalier batting — 420 runs all told — as the visitors won by six wickets with 18 minutes in hand.

The home side may have lost that match, but they kept their first-innings points, and, as things turned out, did not hinder their chances of winning the competition. More significantly, the small crowd had been entertained, and in all likelihood had spread the word to absent friends of the quality of the cricket they had missed.

The following season Richie Benaud was appointed NSW captain, in a tight decision over the Australian vice-captain, Neil Harvey. Australia's incumbent captain, Ian Craig, had been struck down by hepatitis, and Benaud stepped into that breach too. At the time the NSW team was at the height of its powers, and the Australian side on the up after a successful South African tour.

History proved him exactly the right man for the occasion. Benaud brought to the two captaincy positions the skill, panache and daring the posts required. He was a captain who recognised the value of a timely declaration or a calculated gamble, both to his side and to the patron who had handed out his money at the gate. Keith Miller had taught him the importance of keeping a match interesting — and in the years ahead Benaud led a revival in Australian interstate cricket that peaked in 1961–62, when, in a summer devoted to domestic cricket, Shield crowds climbed to levels unprecedented since the days of Bradman.

When Richie Benaud first came into Sheffield Shield cricket, the matches were tough, often bruising affairs. Interstate rivalry was at its height, perhaps best illustrated by a situation that developed while the Australian team practised during the 1950–51 Ashes series. Victorian and Australian "mystery" spinner Jack Iverson, who spun veiled off and leg breaks with a weird and unique grip, was bowling in the nets, when the NSW opener Morris went in for a hit. Seeing Iverson bowling at Morris, then NSW captain, was too much for the Victorian and Australian captain Lindsay Hassett, who ordered Iverson to spin his tricks at a Victorian colleague in an adjoining net. Morris was not amused. Miller told of being moved from his usual slip position when Iverson bowled during the series, lest he get a better look at the spinner's methods.

In his book *On Reflection*, Benaud told of two incidents that occured in Shield cricket in the '50s — incidents which reflected the fierceness of the competition. On one occasion he and Ray Lindwall, who was bowling for Queensland, had a short, angry on-field exchange after a catch at square leg off Lindwall's bowling had been denied. At another time, South Australian captain Phil Ridings, made it very clear to NSW fast bowler Alan Walker that if he persisted in bowling bouncers at Ridings' injured team-mate Bruce Bowley, Walker had a better than even chance of having Ridings' bat wrapped around his ears. Shield was as tough then as it ever had, or has been since.

Into this environment Benaud brought qualities of flair and intuition that the Shield needed. Never at any stage did he sacrifice his main intention — to win. And he had the major advantage of being in charge of the finest of the Shield sides. When he was handed the NSW captaincy the state was in the middle of its greatest run — nine successive Shield titles — but he added style to these victories, and conviction to his belief that victory could be won by more exciting methods than those explained in the cricket textbooks.

He had first played Shield cricket in the first week of 1949, scoring two and not getting a bowl against Queensland in Sydney. In the next four seasons he rarely starred, but showed sufficient promise to win his first Test cap in January 1952 and selection on the 1953 England tour. Back in Australia the following season, he flourished, scoring three aggressive Shield centuries. Against Queensland in Brisbane he took five wickets in the opening session, and then belted an emphatic 158 after NSW had crumbled to 4–85. However it was not until after the 1956 England tour, when Benaud was asked to bowl the key overs, rather than contribute after others had failed, that his bowling consistently impressed. With the retirement of Miller and Ian Johnson, the decline of Lindwall and Pat Crawford, and injury to Ron Archer, Benaud and the fast-medium left-hander, Alan Davidson, became the key attacking weapons in Australian cricket.

Benaud was a leg spinner more in the style of Grimmett than Arthur Mailey, though never as methodically miserly as the South Australian veteran. Like Grimmett, he developed a "flipper", the leg break squeezed out by the thumb to spurt along the pitch. He was taller than most of his leg-spinning predecessors, which explained his ability to get the ball to bounce at the batsmen and his teasing flight. His wrong 'un and top spinner were clever and disguised, but rarely turned excessively. His greatest advantage was his appreciation of the game, which won many a battle, and his courage, which often regained matches considered lost.

In reviewing the 1961–62 season in *Wisden*, Tom Goodman wrote: "Increased attendances were recorded at all centres and spectators were highly appreciative of many days of enterprising cricket. Altogether, it was a fitting season to follow upon the animated summer when the West Indies toured. Other captains followed the lead of the imaginative New South Wales leader, Richie Benaud; there were sporting declarations, influenced by the incentive of four points to the team which led on the first innings as well as by the attempt to keep the last day 'alive'. Several exciting struggles resulted."

The season was also boosted by the displays of three of the most exciting of the fabulous West Indians. Wes Hall, bowling fast for Queensland, took the most wickets (43) in the competition, to that time the greatest season's haul ever captured by a Queensland bowler in the Shield. Rohan Kanhai played some scintillating innings for Western Australia, including two centuries. Gary Sobers was highly popular in Adelaide, and scored an amazing second-innings 251 that won South Australia a gripping match against the Shield champions, NSW.

However the season's star was Benaud and the season's best cricket played by the New South Welshmen. After their first match against Western Australia had been all-but ruined by rain, Benaud conjured an exciting finish out of the clash with Queensland in Brisbane. Before the final day, Benaud closed his second innings, leaving his opponents all day (five-and-a-half-hours) to score 274. They fell 49 runs short. At first glance Benaud's declaration seemed brave, even arrogant, but he knew his bowlers and the conditions, and that few sides can score 270 on anything but the most placid of final day pitches.

In Melbourne, NSW won by 174 runs. On the opening day they scored 398 runs, after the first six wickets had fallen for 141 runs. Grahame Thomas and, inevitably, Benaud added 255 in three hours for the seventh wicket, an extraordinary fightback. The captain's contribution was 140, including two sixes and 17 fours, before he was caught on the boundary. The 13,000 crowd gave him a huge ovation as he strode from the field.

Thomas remained 119 not out when Benaud declared overnight. Victoria struggled, and their stolid batting, contrasted with Benaud's display. Bill Lawry stonewalled for 65 in the first innings and 113 in the second, his approach reflecting the mediocrity of his team's batting, just as Benaud's flair expressed the talent and confidence of his team.

Against Queensland in Sydney, the two captains, Benaud and Ken Mackay, created a fabulous final afternoon, after Benaud declared at lunch with his side 273 ahead. Mackay accepted the challenge, threw off his defensive cloak, and led his side on a thrilling assault. Had he not been run out for 96, after batting for just 89 minutes, Queensland would surely have won, but they fell 31 runs short of victory. The last seven wickets had collapsed for just 14 runs in 22 minutes, and NSW prevailed with 20 minutes to spare. The match provided record Shield takings for the NSWCA.

When South Australia came to Sydney, NSW won decisively, but again in exciting style. The final margin was six wickets, four batsmen being dismissed in a hectic chase for 37 runs on the final afternoon as a thunderstorm grumbled in the background. The match was in fact won by the NSW batting in the first innings, their total of 443 being achieved in 81.3 overs, Booth making 109, Davidson 68, O'Neill 62, Craig 61 and Benaud 54. This aggressive approach proved crucial when the entire third day was lost to rain.

The return match against Victoria in Sydney was won easily, and highlighted by a magnificent innings by Davidson, the majority of which was thrashed during a stunning last-wicket partnership with keeper

Doug Ford. Davidson scored 106, his first century at the SCG, and made 58 of the last 59 runs flayed in the innings, the other being a leg bye. Ford remained unbeaten on nought. The partnership ran for just 25 minutes. Neil Harvey wrote later of Davidson's batting: "There was no recklessness about it, just the sweet combination of power and strength."

Ford was the NSW keeper for seven successive seasons from 1957-58. In that time he played 56 consecutive Shield matches, and completed 160 dismissals, without ever threatening Wally Grout and Barry Jarman for a Test cap. In 1961–62, Davidson was in the middle of his second-last season in Shield cricket. Both he and Benaud had began the season with 189 Shield wickets, both thus were within sight of Bill O'Reilly's NSW Shield record of 203. By season's end Davidson had 227 Shield dismissals, Benaud 228.

NSW travelled to Perth with the Shield all-but won for a ninth consecutive year. The season's triumph was sealed by a dramatic victory, courtesy of a superb all-round performance by Davidson, who belted the innings of the season — 108 out of 218 after NSW had been 6–38 on the first day — and then took 7–31 in the West Australian second innings as the home side crumbled for 106. The locals had started the fourth morning at 4–84, chasing 174 for outright points. Again much credit was given to the NSW approach, Benaud rarely failing to attack despite the often desperate position his side found itself in.

The Shield champions' final match, in Adelaide, was dominated by Gary Sobers, who took 6–72 to bowl NSW out for 270 on the final day to go with a brilliant double century he had scored. South Australia won the match by 130 runs. Sobers' great seasons with South Australia were still to come. The following year he took 701 runs and grabbed 46 wickets, and in 1963–64, when South Australia won their first championship since 1952–53, he topped the competition's batting and bowling aggregates.

The total attendance for NSW's match in Adelaide was a post-war record for the Shield at the Adelaide Oval. The public's imagination had been caught by the quality of the cricket played, and by the knowledge that captains were considering the patrons more so than the possibility of avoiding defeat.

The credit for the revival in the Shield's fortunes goes very much to Benaud. He continued in Shield cricket until 1963–64, always aggressive — and in his final season scored centuries in his last two Shield matches. In his farewell appearance, in Adelaide, he scored 120 not out in NSW's second innings, in a thrilling match that NSW won by just six runs with two minutes left on the members' stand clock. It seems somehow appropriate Benaud remained not out in his final Shield innings. He, like any other player, had lost matches, series, and competitions. But as a captain and cricketer the great Richie Benaud was never really beaten.

# 50

## WHEN 613 WAS NOT ENOUGH

Twice in the history of the Shield Queensland have scored more than 600 runs in an innings. In 1930–31, in reply to NSW's 566, the northerners reached 687 for a brave and memorable victory. Thirty three years later in Brisbane, Queensland were not so lucky. Batting first, they amassed 613 against NSW, but had nothing to show for it, as NSW reached 661 in reply. Never before or since has a Shield side scored so many runs in its first innings, and not won first-innings points.

A season earlier in Sydney, 1962–63, Queensland had bowled out the New South Welshmen for 82, the lowest ever total by NSW in Sydney. NSW were a powerful batting side in that 1963–64 season, including such men as Simpson, O'Neill, Booth, Benaud and Grahame Thomas. The teenage Doug Walters was 12th man. NSW was described by Jack Reardon in the Brisbane *Courier Mail* as being able to "bat down to number 12". Reardon then suggested that the game "could be a battle of the batsmen, because Queensland is also strong in that department". The Queenland captain, Ken Mackay, after inspecting the pitch, told reporters: "It seems a typical 'Gabba wicket, and should last the match out."

The Queensland team included the internationals Mackay, Burge and Grout, and Test candidates Ray

Above: Bob Simpson of NSW, who scored 359 against Queensland in 1963–64. Inset: Peter Burge, who hit 283, the highest score by a Queenslander in the first 100 years of the Shield, in the same game, but ended on the losing team.

Reynolds, Sam Trimble and Tom Veivers. Reynolds and Trimble were the opening batsmen, both right-handers — the former aggressive, the latter watchful. Veivers was an off-spinning all-rounder who had plied his trades for Queensland since 1958–59.

Even without the medium pace of Walters, Benaud had a wide variety of bowling talent to call upon. The NSW side included five front-line spin bowlers; the leg breaks of Richie Benaud, Peter Philpott and Bob Simpson, the "offies" of Terry Lee, and the left-arm wrist spin of Johnny Martin. Benaud had also the option of the part-time turn of Norm O'Neill and Brian Booth. Opening the bowling were Frank Misson and Gordon Rorke.

Only three wickets fell on the opening day. Reynolds scored a brisk 121 after Trimble had been caught behind and Des Bull run out. Peter Burge at stumps was unbeaten on 97, Graham Bizzell was 36. Benaud had tried everything during the day, crowding the batsmen at times despite the scoreboard, on other occasions reverting to the safety-net of defence. The bowlers now and then had trouble with the new no-ball rule, which required the front foot to be kept behind the batting crease. Benaud himself was no-balled three times during the day, while Rorke at times appeared to lose his run-up and his pace.

The following day Burge went on to the highest first-class score ever made by a Queenslander. His 283 took 447 minutes, and he struck 42 fours and a six. He was out in crazy circumstances, run out after Wally Grout miscued a simple catch to O'Neill. Burge and Grout set off for a token single, as the ball hung timidly in the sky. Unfortunately O'Neill did not catch it, but compensated quickly and had the ball back to keeper Doug Ford before Burge could make good his ground.

Burge was a big, rugged man, who had first played for Queensland against South Australia in 1952–53, his sole appearance of that season. In his next Shield match, he scored his maiden century, against NSW in Brisbane, reaching 103. He remained a prolific component of the Queensland batting order for more than a decade, and in 1963–64 was in the peak of his form. Few Australians have driven the ball with more power, or been more assured and decisive playing the hook and pull shots. When he retired in 1968, no-one had scored more Shield runs for Queensland, or belted more than his 22 centuries.

Lee finished with three wickets, and there were three run outs; skipper Benaud was strangely ineffective. Burge and Bizzell added 190 for the fourth wicket, Burge and Ken Mackay (16) put on 53, and then Burge and Veivers (17) added 83. Grout was run out a single after Burge fell at 591, and the last two wickets fell to Lee at 613. The innings had gone on for 604 minutes. Mackay admitted later he had planned his declaration for 10 minutes later.

NSW had 46 minutes to survive on the second evening, but lost two wickets. Thomas was lbw to Peter Allan for two, and right on stumps O'Neill was caught at second slip. Simpson at the close was 32 not out.

On the Sunday rest day, Mackay told reporters: "We are in an excellent position. It's comforting to have those runs on the board." But he added words of caution. "New South Wales still have some great batsmen to come. We will have to dig them out, because the wicket will remain slow and easy today. But it's nice to have some runs to play with. We can afford to try out certain things."

On the third day the weather was perfect and only one wicket fell — Brian Booth caught at mid-on off Veivers for 121. Simpson batted all day, never less than remorseless, to reach 227, and Philpott was with him at stumps on 32. There was no suggestion of a chance in Simpson's batting this day. He later suggested he had never concentrated better, and admitted he had set himself the goal of achieving a huge score. The chance to underline his claims to succeed Benaud as national captain was in the back of his mind. This was the first time he had scored a double century for NSW.

The next day he went on to 359, the first triple century scored in the Shield since the War. In all, he batted for ten-and-a-half hours, and was not dismissed until after the first-innings win had been achieved. At 304 he might have been caught by Ken Mackay at short mid-on, but that apart, he was faultless until suiciding against the spin of Col Westaway. This stumping was the 206th dismissal of Grout's Queensland's career, a new state record. Simpson's main support came from Benaud who scored a powerful 80 — the pair adding 158 for the fifth wicket.

NSW passed the Queensland score five-down. Simpson was seventh out at 632, and the innings went on to 661. Benaud did not ask him to field when Queensland batted again for the last five overs of the match, but even so the NSW opener was on the ground for all but the final 70 minutes of the game.

One feature of the match was the bowling of Veivers, who sent down 53.2 eight-ball overs for 3–160. He troubled all the batsmen, and Simpson was more than cautious at various stages against him. One interested observer at this match was Dudley Seddon, the NSW representative on the Australian selection committee, and he must have been impressed by Veivers' skill and persistence. Six weeks later the Queensland spinner was chosen in the Test side for the first time.

In the seasons since this unique match, no team has scored more in a Shield innings than 661 and no individual has made more than 359. When Simpson flew back into Sydney he told pressmen: "I've never been so tired in my life." Not surprising — especially as he had run 141 singles during the game. It was an innings from a different era, more in keeping with the run-getting orgies of the 1920s.

The game set the trend for a fascinating season of Shield cricket, highlighted by batting feats. Two weeks after the match in Brisbane, NSW defeated Western Australia outright in Sydney as decisively as any Shield team could ever imagine. WA made 420, but were passed one down by Thomas, who made 127, Philpott who remained not out on 38, and the remarkable Simpson, who was unbeaten on 247 when Benaud declared as soon as NSW won first-innings' points. The Simpson-Thomas opening stand was worth 308 runs, breaking an ancient NSW record established by Victor Trumper and Reggie Duff. After W.A had been bowled out for 266, Benaud opted for a different opening partnership, this time Booth and O'Neill, and they put on 127. Philpott came in at number three once more, and with Booth, who reached 169, won the game without further loss.

A week later Burge scored his second double century of the season, 205 against WA in Brisbane. By season's end Burge had a Shield season's batting average of 171.25. Simpson's final average was *only* 112, good enough for no better than fourth spot. Booth averaged 127, and Benaud 113.50. In Adelaide, in the week between Christmas and New Year, Trimble and Reynolds added 259 for the opening wicket, only nine short of the Queensland record. Trimble would score five centuries during the Shield season, including a marathon, unbeaten 252 in Sydney.

But none of these players topped the Shield batting aggregate. That honour went to South Australia's import from Barbados, Gary Sobers, who scored 973 runs. Sobers also took the most wickets, 47, a figure only Grimmett of all South Australians had beaten to that time. Rex Sellers, a leg spinner who had made a comeback after missing the previous season, took just one wicket less than Sobers — and the pair spearheaded their state to their first Shield triumph since 1953.

At season's end an era closed with the retirement of Richie Benaud. Bob Simpson became the new NSW and Australian captain, but was unable to match his predecessor in the entertainment or victory departments. NSW's only Shield successes in the seasons between 1963–64 and Simpson's retirement in 1968 was in 1964–65 and 1965–66. He developed a reputation for reliability rather than flair. But in many ways this was more a reflection on the quality of his teams, rather than an indictment of his enterprise or daring. Simpson, it must be remembered, never had Harvey to score his hundreds, or Davidson and Benaud to get his wickets. He was a cricketer who recognised the importance of his runs and the means of best using his skill for the sake of his team. Few batsmen have been better equipped to set themselves to do the job that he grafted away at for years.

# 51

## DAZZLING DOUG

There have been few Sheffield Shield seasons which have matched the excitement of the campaign of 1964–65. But for a brief tour by Pakistan, the interstate matches were the only first-class cricket played in Australia, and the Shield rose to the challenge, producing a thrilling season in which the champion state was not found until the final ball was bowled. It was a year of firsts, sparkling cricket and controversy. Here is a little of what went on:
• Nineteen-year-old NSW all-rounder Doug Walters produced one of the great performances of the competition's history. In Adelaide, he became the youngest ever Shield player to score a double century, sharing an Australian record second-wicket partnership of 378 with Lynn Marks, and then took 7–63 in South Australia's first innings.
• Shield cricket was played for the first time on a Sunday. A conference involving the representatives of

each state ruled that if both states involved in a Shield match were in favour of Sunday cricket, then such cricket could be played. Consequently both matches between Queensland and Western Australia included Sunday play.

• Victorian medium pacer Eddie Illingworth was called for throwing in Adelaide, twice by the renowned Test umpire Col Egar and once by umpire J. Ryan. Illingworth subsequently bowled in the match against WA at the MCG without problems but was not seen in first-class cricket again.

• NSW umpire Ted Wykes no-balled Western Australian off-spinner Keith Slater once, for throwing his faster delivery. Slater had been called once previously in the Shield, in 1957–58 against Victoria in Melbourne. This was the only time he was ruled against in 1964–65, during which he played in four matches, chiefly as an opening batsman, and took just one wicket.

• In the same match that he called Slater, Wykes sent Western Australia's former Surrey and England left-arm finger spinner, Tony Lock, back to the dressing room to wipe off what Wykes thought was an excessive amount of a healing substance on Lock's bowling hand.

• Victorian medium-pacer Alan Connolly took 9–67 off 22.3 overs against Queensland in Brisbane, which remains the best bowling figures against Queensland in the Sheffield Shield.

• With two weeks remaining in the first-class season, any state of NSW, Victoria, South Australia or Western Australia could have won the Shield. Defending champions South Australia, under the aggressive and popular leadership of Les Favell but now without Gary Sobers, were on 32 points, On 24 points were Western Australia, who were two in front of Victoria. Lurking on 20 points were the New South Welshmen.

In the second last week of the season South Australia would play NSW in Adelaide, and Victoria would travel to Brisbane. A week later NSW would play Western Australia in Perth to complete the season. An outright win was worth 10 points, a first innings win four points, a draw two points, a loss of any kind no points, unless an outright loss followed a first innings win, in which case the reward was four points. An outright win after trailing on the first innings was also worth four points.

Thanks mainly to the controlled swing and seam of Connolly, Victoria were much too good for the Queenslanders, and won by an innings and 49 runs. One consolation for Queensland was the performance of Wally Grout, who broke Don Tallon's 1938–39 record for the most dismissals by a keeper in one Shield year. The Victorian captain Bill Lawry scored his fourth Shield century of 1964–65 in this match, to finish with a Shield season's batting average of 98.5.

Because the Australian team to tour the West Indies was departing for Jamaica in the week between NSW's matches in South Australia and Western Australia, skipper Bob Simpson, Brian Booth, Grahame Thomas and Norm O'Neill were unable to accompany their NSW teammates on the western tour. Then the first two choices as replacement leader, opening batsmen Warren Saunders and Bill Watson, told selectors they were unavailable. Finally Barry Rothwell was appointed captain, and keeper Brian Taber and Lynn Marks nominated as a makeshift opening pair, but before the squad left for Adelaide, paceman Graham Corling dropped out injured and Les Ellis was drafted.

The side was given little chance in Adelaide, especially as the South Australians were able to call upon their three Australian team members, wicketkeeper Barry Jarman, the country's leading all-rounder Neil Hawke, and the erratic but gifted left-arm wrist spinner David Sincock. Also in their side was the 21-year-old grandson of Victor Richardson, Ian Chappell, who had already scored two Shield centuries in the summer and made his Test debut against the touring Pakistanis.

Although Taber fell within 11 minutes of the match's first ball, by stumps NSW were firmly in charge. Marks, the son of Alex, a NSW batsman between 1929 and 1937, and brother of Neil, who played two first-class seasons until his career was stifled by an operation to repair a hole in the heart, batted all but the final 10 minutes of the day for 185. Both his father and brother had previously scored centuries against South Australia.

Doug Walters was unbeaten at stumps on 195, having started with a rush, his opening fifty coming in little more than an hour — most of them from Sincock full tosses. He was a little lucky, dropped three times, but in between produced a wonderful mixture of pulls, cuts and drives to both sides of the ground.

After he was finally dismissed, just five runs short of Bradman's record Shield score by a New South Welshman in Adelaide, Keith Butler in the *Advertiser* wrote: "Walters' innings, despite his three chances, was magnificent. It is doubtful whether there has been more spectacular or better placed driving on the offside for many years."

By stumps on Day 3, South Australia were 7–348, still 254 runs behind the NSW total despite Chappell's excellent century. NSW had been superb in the field, two catches off Walters' bowling, by

*Doug Walters, who in Adelaide in February 1965 produced the best all-round performance by a teenager in the competition's history.*

Taber and George Griffiths, being quite extraordinary. The keeper made many lengths to his left to intercept a Chappell leg glance, and soon afterwards Griffiths at short leg turned contortionist to hold a firm drive by Jarman. With Victoria's success in Brisbane confirmed, South Australia, because of their inferior average, needed points from the NSW game to win the Shield. The prayers were for rain, or a miracle batting performance from Hawke and his tailenders.

Hawke was in the final match of the best all-round season by a native South Australian since the days of George Giffen, and NSW were without their injured fast bowler Dave Renneberg, but the miracle did not happen. In fact had Taber not missed a difficult stumping chance offered by his opposite number Jarman when South Australia were 6–158 in their second innings NSW may have won outright. In the day's first half hour, while Hawke, on 89, watched stunned from the bowler's end, Walters grabbed 3–2 in 7 deliveries to finish the dreams of a draw. Just before tea, when debutant off spinner Michael Hill dismissed Alan Shiell with his first ball in Shield cricket to have the home team six-down, all looked lost for South Australia, as it probably would have been had Taber not fumbled. Jarman smashed 60 in less than an hour, added 89 for the seventh wicket with Hawke, and prevented the outright result. Even so, South Australia were out of the Shield race, the destination of the trophy now down to three alternatives.

Western Australia would have to beat NSW outright without their three Australian players, Graham McKenzie, Laurie Mayne and skipper Barry Shepherd. Lock took over the captaincy. And it was the cagey Surrey man who helped his side to an almost respectable total after Rothwell won the toss and sent the locals in. Peter Kelly was caught in the slips off Renneberg in the opening over, and WA were 3–17, then 5–44, then 8–115 before Lock helped "Jock" Irvine get the innings total to 184. By stumps NSW were 1–90, Walters and Marks on their way to another crucial second-wicket stand.

The next day Walters went to 57, Marks to 75, but the day's star was the lion-hearted all-rounder Des Hoare, who worked Western Australia back into the Shield. Hoare, a tall aggressive fast-medium bowler, had played for Australia in the Adelaide Test of the 1960–61 West Indies series, and here he took 8–98 from 30.4 overs, never refusing Lock's pleas for another extra effort. His eighth wicket was his 200th in first-class cricket. Rothwell closed just before stumps at 302, giving Walters just enough time to shatter the stumps of Hartley Joynt with the final ball of the day.

Walters had another wicket with the first delivery of the new morning, bowling the 20-year-old John Inverarity. For the second time in the match, W.A fell to 5–44 and then, five minutes after lunch, to 6–90 when Hoare was out after a slugging 32. Gordon Becker then rushed out to score the first century by a West Australian wicketkeeper in first-class cricket. Suddenly the fence was reachable, and balls that had been beating the bat were instead lofted to the outfield. He reached 50 in 55 minutes, and 100 in 112 minutes.

When number 11 Jim Hubble came out the score was 9–215, Becker on 76, and the overall lead 97. Somehow Becker fashioned a partnership of 58, Hubble scoring no more than a single. Becker was finally out for 130, bowled by an inswinger from Walters, who finished with 5–92. Rarely has a more heroic innings been played in the history of the competition. Two years later Becker toured South Africa with Bob Simpson's Australian team, and remained the West Australian keeper until Rod Marsh moved behind the stumps in 1969–70.

Had Inverarity held Walters in the slips before the New South Welshman had scored in the season's final innings, WA may have won. As it was Walters was there until the end, driving Kelly through the covers for two to get his state home by five wickets. It was a wonderful triumph for the inexperienced team, and for the stopgap captain, Rothwell, who had been clever and innovative in everything he did. And for Walters, still a teenager but the key figure in the victories in Adelaide and Perth.

Walters would remain an integral part of the NSW, and within two years, the Australian side until 1981. But strangely he would play in only one more Shield championship-winning side, and that in 1965–66. NSW were on the threshold of the leanest period in their cricket history. A new power in the game was emerging in the west. The performance of Western Australia in getting within five wickets of the Shield in 1964–65, was their best return since their successful debut season. Within three years they would be champions, and in the years following would remain a prime supplier of talent for Australia's cricket teams.

# 52

## TWO MORE TEN-FORS

In the first 73 years of the Sheffield Shield's life, only one bowler, Tim Wall of South Australia, was able to perform one of cricket's rarest feats — the taking of all 10 wickets in one innings. Then, in the space of just three seasons in the 1960s, Wall's performance was matched twice — by two men whose total Test experience would amount to a solitary game.

First up was Queensland's Peter Allan, a fast bowler who in three seasons of pennant cricket in Melbourne between 1960 and 1963 was not considered highly enough by the Victorian selectors to win a place in a solitary Shield match. In fact, in his third season in Melbourne, Allan was dropped to second grade by his club, Fitzroy — a decision that prompted the fast bowler to return to Brisbane.

In the second week of January 1966, Allan took 10–61 against none other than … Victoria, in Melbourne. His feat was duplicated 21 months later in Perth, when the Western Australian swing bowler, Ian Brayshaw, captured all 10 Victorian first-innings wickets, for 44 runs.

Allan was a right-hand fast medium bowler, who played 47 Shield matches for Queensland between 1959 and 1968. His only Test appearance came in the first match of the 1965–66 Ashes series, but he did win a place on the 1965 tour of the West Indies under Bob Simpson. He was a bowler with more stamina and persistence than class, but during that one magical innings at the MCG everything went right, and he wrote his name in Shield history as only one man had done before.

On the opening day of the game 14 wickets fell after Queensland had won the toss and batted. Both sides were without their Test stars — Grout, Burge and Veivers (Queensland); Lawry and Cowper (Victoria). The Queenslanders collapsed against the spin attack of Keith Stackpole and Keith Kirby, and the last nine wickets tumbled for just 57 runs, after Des Bull and Bill Buckle had added 111 for the second wicket.

In 65 minutes before stumps, Allan grabbed four wickets — Graeme Watson, Ian Redpath, Jack Potter and Stackpole — for 32 — runs that came mainly off the edge of the bat, as Victoria rushed to 4–76. Watson was caught by Sam Trimble at short leg, skying a hook; Redpath prodded too late at a fast one; Potter snicked an outswinger to the keeper, Lew Cooper; Stackpole was dropped behind, and then bowled fending meekly at one that smashed the middle stump.

The next day Allan was devastating, and limited Victoria to 130, 51 short of first-innings points. He bowled continuously through the innings, and swung the ball in a manner few Shield bowlers had ever been able to at the MCG.

On that remarkable second morning Victoria did not lose a wicket until the score reached 100. But then four wickets fell within 14 balls, all to Allan with the scoreboard locked on 100. Ray Jordon was bowled for 27; Paul Sheahan, John Swanson and John Grant were all caught jabbing at outswingers, Sheahan by the keeper, the other two by Bob Crane in the slip cordon. David Anderson and Kirby kept Allan at bay for a while, even managing a five after an unsuccessful shy at a run out, but after Anderson was caught by Graham Bizzell, Kirby was taken by an excited Trimble to give Allan his 10. He had taken the last six wickets for just 14 runs, including the overthrows, to complete the performance of his life.

After the innings Allan confessed to *The Australian's* correspondent that he was all but finished soon after dismissing John Grant, the eighth wicket to fall. "I spoke to my captain Sam Trimble, and said I would bowl another over and that would be it," he explained. "But in the next over I took the wicket of Anderson and it was only then I realised I had the chance of taking ten wickets. Naturally I found new life and wanted to get the tenth."

Just as Tim Wall had struggled the next time he bowled after his 10–36, Peter Allan was a different bowler when the Victorians faced him again. And just as NSW had come back to defeat South Australia despite Wall's record haul, so too did Victoria recover to win outright points from the Queenslanders. Even an opening stand of 169 between Trimble and Bull, who batted right through the innings for 167, could not save the visitors. At one stage it seemed Victoria would be chasing a huge tally, but in the end the target was 387, which they managed — with three wickets and time to spare.

In the fourth innings Allan bowled like a tired man, finishing with 0–63 from 11 listless overs. When the innings started, Allan lasted only four overs, belted from the bowling crease by Redpath and Watson, who took 16 from his fourth over. The hundred stand came in 93 minutes and both batsmen eventually went on to centuries, Redpath to a superb 180, his first score over 20 since being dropped (as Allan had been) from the Australian team after the first Test. While Allan would never tread the Test boardwalk again, Redpath remained a key batsman for Victoria and Australia until his retirement in 1976.

While Peter Allan had the advantage of bowling at a Victorian batting line-up weakened by the demands of Test cricket, Ian Brayshaw had no such luxury. In fact before the match, Victoria v WA in season 1967–68, the former Australian leg-spinner Doug Ring suggested that the Victorians had a batting line-up capable of destroying the world record score of 1,107. Nine of the 12 who travelled to Perth had Shield centuries in their batting account, and six of the first seven in the batting order possessed Australian caps.

Lawry, the Victorian captain, played down Ring's comments, but admitted his side was: "The best balanced team we have had for a few seasons."

The West Australians were led by the affable English professional, Tony Lock, in his first campaign as WA skipper. Lock had captained the side before, but only as a stop-gap, and he led a bowling attack that relied heavily on his crafty left-arm spinners, and the pace of Graham McKenzie. In support was the fast-medium Jim Hubble, an Australian bowler in South Africa the summer before, the erratic legspin and googlies of Tony Mann, and the 25-year-old Brayshaw, an efficient and controlled right-hander of no more than medium pace, who had played in 16 Shield matches, for the modest return of 36 wickets.

Brayshaw's greatest claim to fame was a Shield century, 104 on the SCG no. 2 in November 1966. The No.1 ground had still not recovered from an operation performed after the rugby league season.

Brayshaw managed only one scoring shot, a boundary, when Western Australia batted first against Victoria and were dismissed for 161. At stumps the visitors were 2–35. Redpath had played across the line of a late outswinger and been bowled, the left-handed Ken Eastwood caught in the gully having miscued a drive. Lawry was 2 not out, after 59 minutes without a stroke.

The innings disintegrated in the second over of the next day. Cowper, who had added only a single to his overnight 6, ignored three sharp Brayshaw outswingers and was then bowled by the inswinger. Potter, looking for a single, played around an outswinger and was bowled, and then Stackpole was surprised by the bounce of one that came in at him, and lobbed a catch to mid-off.

Watson set about the bowling as if none, rather than five of his teammates had floundered. Lawry was Lawry, cautious and dogged, a man who had rejected his attacking strokes for the good of his side. Together they steadied the ship, and had all-but reached lunch when Watson lost concentration. First he hooked wildly at McKenzie, and was almost caught by Brayshaw down near the fine-leg fence. Then he chased a wide Brayshaw outswinger, and sliced to second slip, where John Inverarity grasped a diving catch, gashing an elbow on the sprigs of first slip Ross Edwards in the process.

The last four wickets fell for 48 after lunch. The key wicket was Lawry, brilliantly caught down the leg side by Gordon Becker, who leapt at an inswinger which had been helped on its way. Then Ray Jordon was caught behind as well, lucky to hit a pearler that pitched on the off-stump line and only swung after the batsman had fashioned his defensive stroke. Grant then drove unsuccessfully at another inswinger, and Alan Connolly edged a slog to second slip.

Brayshaw controlled his swing beautifully. Like Wall and Allan, this was the inspired performance of a career. He was fortunate on only two counts. His colleagues' fielding was world class — the catching of Becker and Inverarity superb. And McKenzie was desperately unlucky, the perfect foil on a day when his efforts entitled him to more of a dividend. These realities in no way diminish the achievement of Brayshaw, who set a standard for swing bowling at the WACA that future Western Australian swing bowlers such as Bob Massie, Mick Malone and Terry Alderman could only strive to emulate.

Brayshaw had one thing from the match to set him apart from Tim Wall and Peter Allan. His bowling led to an outright victory. In the home side's second innings he made nought, lbw to Watson, and then, when three wickets would have equalled the state record for the most wickets taken in a first-class match, he managed two. One though was the crucial dismissal of Lawry, amazingly bowled around his legs as he ignored one that swung in from well wide of his pads. The fourth innings hero was Lock, who took five wickets, three of them in the first over after the final tea session, as WA headed on to a 136-runs victory.

Brayshaw continued to play Shield cricket for more than a decade, rarely rated a Test candidate, but never less than a key member of his state XI. He managed 10 wickets in a Shield match once more, in January 1978 when he took 4–73 and 6–29 against Victoria in Perth. He also took 5–26 (and scored 42 and 45) in his final Shield match, in Melbourne at the end of that season.

As were Peter Allan and Tim Wall before him, Brayshaw was a fine Shield cricketer, good enough for sports historian, Jack Pollard, in 1982 to call him "probably the best all-rounder to play for Western Australia". Yet it seems ironic that he, and his two fellow members of the "ten-for" club, managed a feat in interstate cricket that was beyond such champions as Grimmett, O'Reilly, Miller and Lillee. Such is cricket's way.

# 53

## WINNING THE LES FAVELL WAY

'm sure much of the Favell influence brushed off on me. Les was an inspiring captain, as well as an aggressive batsman. He used to love the challenge of beating or scoring points against the strong NSW teams of the sixties. On one occasion, I recall, NSW captain Richie Benaud set us a fairly stiff target to win on the final day of a Shield game at the Adelaide Oval. Typically Favell decided to take up the challenge, and turned to his opening partner Neil Dansie saying: "Come on Nod, let's get away to a quick start." Favell started in stirring fashion, hitting 12 runs off the first over against the new ball. After he had disposed of his third four in that over he turned to Dansie at the other end, and within earshot of the NSW fast bowler, loudly said: "You'd better get in for your chop quickly Nod, because this fellow won't be on for long."
— *Ian Chappell, from his book* Chappelli *(1976)*

Les Favell was a South Australian cricketer from 1951 to 1970. From 1959 until his retirement he was his state's leader, a tough, assertive captain with his eye always on a win, his actions always intended to support and encourage his comrades. He was the epitome of the inspiring leader, a man convinced that having his team playing to win was much more effective than waiting for opponents to lose.

Favell was born in Sydney, exactly one year before Richie Benaud, but at 22, after appearances in the NSW Colts side, recognised that the path to further riches was blocked by the enormity of cricket talent that abounded in NSW. He moved to Adelaide in the winter of 1951, and won selection in the South Australian side for a Shield match against NSW after Graeme Hole was chosen for a Test against the touring West Indies. Favell would probably have been 12th man, but a century for his club, East Torrens, on the Saturday preceding the NSW match won him his starting place, and he responded with a match double of 86 and 164. SA captain Phil Ridings' declaration in this match set NSW 281 to win in little more than four hours. In his autobiography *By Hook or by Cut*, Favell wrote: "Disappointingly they never really went after the runs." In fact the visitors, captained by Sid Barnes, finished just a tense 14 runs short. Even in his first game, Les Favell's aggressive instincts were hard to please.

Favell was on his way — on a road that would lead to 19 Tests, tours to the West Indies, South Africa, India, Pakistan and New Zealand but, sadly, never to England. His was the fifth Australian wicket to fall on the exciting final day of the first Tie in Test cricket, against the West Indies in Brisbane in 1960. Two seasons earlier in Adelaide he had hit the run that won back the Ashes from Peter May's Englishmen. His sole Test century came in India on the 1959–60 tour, a disappointing return for one so talented. His cavalier approach was perhaps too colourful for Test cricket, but it thrived in the Shield, where many an umbrella field was decimated as Favell went for the bowling well before the first drinks break.

He was a short man, no more than 5ft 7in (170cms) tall, and in his early career seemed even shorter as he crouched waiting for the fast men. Later he stood up straighter at the crease. His hooking was as brave as his captaincy, and his fielding reflected his experience in interstate baseball. He was an honest and blunt leader — and if his captaincy had a fault it was only that his strategies and aggression did not always fit the teams he now and then asked to justify his racy declarations.

In his book *Bowled Over*, the former South Australian and Australian all-rounder Neil Hawke told a story that captured the Favell approach. Hawke was involved in a South Australia-Victoria match at the MCG. Favell was batting, and was in full cry. The Victorian opening bowler Colin Guest had to leave the field because of boot trouble, and play was halted as the game waited for the 12th man Ian Law.

"I was standing outside the changing room doors when I saw Ian appear around a corner still in his street shoes," wrote Hawke. "Realising his problem I dashed down the path onto the field. Lawry, Favell and the other players stared at me in bewilderment. Bill guided me to mid-wicket and Meckiff ran into bowl to Favell. The ball was short, and quick as a flash Les was in position to play his favourite hook stroke. He mistimed it slightly, and the ball floated back over my head. I turned, ran with it and jumped forward to take a spectacular catch as it plummetted towards the turf.

"The Victorians were elated and with Guest ready to return to the field, I had to walk off with Favell. To the amusement of the spectators, I headed off towards another gate before rejoining Favell, who managed

*Below: Les Favell, Sydney-born but a favourite at the Adelaide Oval. He led South Australia to Shield championships in 1963–64 and 1968–69. Left: The remarkable West Indian Gary Sobers, a key figure in Favell's `63-64 side. In only three Shield seasons, Sobers took 128 wickets, and scored 2,247 runs.*

a wry grin. In the dressing room he demanded an explanation and said that I would be the last player he would send out as a substitute. When things had cooled down later he concluded that I was probably the only one in the team who could have caught it and he would have kicked my arse if I hadn't. The thought had never crossed my mind."

Favell never expected more than their best from his players, and no more than a fair go from the umpires, his opponents and Dame Fortune. In his last season as captain he refused to recall WA's John Inverarity, after Inverarity was bowled by a ball that was deflected in mid-pitch by an errant swallow. The bird lay on the ground, Inverarity drifted from the field, and the umpires asked the South Australian captain if he intended to recall the unfortunate batsman. Favell had been fielding at short backward square and saw nothing of the bird colliding with the ball.

"I'm not going to call him back," said Favell, "because I didn't see anything, but if you want to recall Inverarity that's fair enough, I won't complain."

Inverarity did come back, went on to 89, and Favell did not complain. It was his job to win cricket matches, not worry about the past, or what he did not see. The swallow, and the ball that killed it, were placed in a perspex case and presented to the SACA.

Favell won two Shields as captain of South Australia, in 1963–64 and 1968–69. His 1963–64 team was built around the extraordinary gifts of another aggressive cricketer, Gary Sobers. In his first Shield season, in 1961–62, Sobers had struggled with the pressures and challenges of the competition, but in his latter two years he flourished, the pivotal figure in a side that also included a young Ian Chappell.

By 1968–69, Chappell was the best batsman in Australia, the latest to wear the "new-Bradman" tag. Also in the side was Ian's younger brother Greg (who led the South Australian batting aggregates that season), the all–rounder Eric Freeman, and the former Western Australian spinners Terry Jenner and Ashley Mallett. Favell placed great responsibility on his two spin bowlers, who responded with 26 and 39 wickets respectively. One striking example of Favell's captaincy came in Brisbane that season. At that stage of his career Greg Chappell rarely bowled, and when he did he trundled down slow leg breaks. But Favell had faced some medium pace from his young batsman in the nets and been troubled by the bounce and occasional late swing Chappell's high action could generate. Favell resolved to try his new medium pace in the Brisbane humidity.

The experiment was a great success, Chappell's figures reaching 3–13 as the local batsmen jabbed catches into the slip cordon. When, two summers later, Ian Chappell grabbed a key wicket in his first Test match as captain by using Ken Eastwood, an untried "chinaman" bowler who had proved difficult to read in practice, perhaps many of the plaudits should have gone to Les Favell.

Favell's captaincy was never better than in a match against Queensland at the Adelaide Oval in January 1968. The first day of this match, a Friday, was washed out, and for much of the Saturday it seemed the second day would go the same way. Just before 3 o'clock the umpires decided play could begin, a cruel ruling, as Sunday was a rest day. The decision would leave one side batting on a soaked wicket for two hours, while the other could wait to Monday when the conditions would inevitably be much improved.

Favell lost the toss, and hurled the offending coin 40 metres towards the members stand in disgust. Two wickets fell in the first over, seven in the first 14, before Favell declared at 7–40, hoping to get the Queenslanders in for a 35 minutes while the pitch was still a despot. But for once his bowlers were poor, and Queensland lost only 1–22 from 11 inaccurate overs.

On the Monday, the South Australian fought back, but only after losing their new-ball bowler Allan Frost in ridiculous circumstances. Frost, undoubtedly inspired by Favell's rousing pre-match team-talk, charged up to bowl the first ball of the day, lost his footing, and crashed onto the pitch. He was taken to hospital with concussion, a jarred shoulder and grazed forehead, and was not released until the following morning. In the early overs the batsmen defended grimly while Favell attacked, and only 12 runs came in the first hour, while two wickets fell. The Queensland 100 did not come until the 64th over, and when the innings ended at 130, after 252 minutes of excellent bowling and puerile batting, the South Australians were back in the game.

At stumps, after 115 minutes, they were 3–126. Favell was 43 not out. The next morning he set his side the task of scoring 150 in the opening session, which would leave the Queenslanders with a target of 187 in 220 minutes. The assignment was achieved with extraordinary precision, the last wicket of the innings falling in the session's final over, after 153 runs had been added. The captain had set the mood, racing to 69 before being unluckily caught. Greg Chappell also scored 69, and Mallett belted a livewire 20 at the end.

The run chase in the afternoon was an exciting one, the crucial moment coming when Hawke grabbed two wickets in the first over after tea. Queensland had gone to the break needing 84 with seven wickets in hand. Favell gave the responsibility for the win to his two spinners, and they came through, Jenner taking three wickets, Mallett four. The final wicket, a run out of Peter Allan, was a team affair between the two, Mallett at point firing a perfect throw to Jenner at the bowler's end to beat the diving batsman.

Few captains could have fashioned a victory out of a first innings total of 40, no matter what the circumstances. But Favell was not one to hear of defeat until all the options had been explored. He retired having scored more runs for South Australia than any other batsman, more Shield runs than anyone bar Bradman, having made more Shield appearances than any other cricketer, and having built a reputation for attacking captaincy unrivalled in the history of the competition. He died far too early, in June, 1987. More than 7000 cricket followers had attended a testimonial match organised in Adelaide after it was revealed he was ill.

In the foreword to Favell's autobiography, published in 1970, Sir Donald Bradman wrote:

"I can remember only too well the feeling in cricket circles when I first migrated (from Sydney to Adelaide). Victoria and New South Wales were regarded with some awe; their players endowed with some special skills and this feeling of inferiority was a real psychological handicap to South Australian players. Thanks to men like Les Favell, this attitude has been dissipated and today South Australians face the men of the major states with confidence…

"To his everlasting credit Les Favell played in every match, a one-day or five-day game, with the same aggressive and attractive approach. He never scorned a challenge, rather did he welcome it. The most frequent criticism heard of Les during his career was that his batting was too risky. What a pity all players didn't have the same fault."

# 54

## A GENTLEMAN FROM SURREY

In the winter of 1962, officials of the Western Australian Cricket Association were discussing the prospects of finding an overseas import capable of taking the spot filled by the gifted West Indian Rohan Kanhai during the previous season. Eventually the debate centred on the name of Graham Anthony Richard Lock, of Surrey and, until most recently, England.

Of the 11 members of the England side that had played in the fourth Test against Pakistan at Trent Bridge in late July 1962, only Lock had not been in the M.C.C. squad for the Australian tour that was subsequently announced. When soon afterwards he was approached by the WACA, he grabbed the offer eagerly, and transferred his allegiance to the west of Australia, to play the first of what were to be nine highly significant seasons in the Sheffield Shield.

Lock was a left-arm finger spinner, who had been bowling in county cricket since 1946. He had been troubled now and then by umpires, some of whom questioned the legality of his bowling action, but had overcome these distractions, and shaped a marvellous career in first-class cricket — a career that had yielded 164 Test wickets in 44 matches. He had become renown too as the bowling partner of the great off-breaker, Jim Laker, for county and country.

Lock's first match for Western Australia was against the English team from which he had been dropped. He started with 4–68 against his former colleagues, and then took 3–36 and 0–37 for a Combined XI against the same opposition. The preliminaries completed, he settled down to make the West Australians a competitive force in Australian cricket. His first season was personally satisfying — 32 wickets at 29.59 — but his only real bowling support came when the fast man Graham McKenzie was not involved in Test matches. The season ended with WA above only Queensland on the Shield table, having lost six of their eight matches outright.

*The two leading Western Australian bowlers of the 1960s. Above: Tony Lock, who arrived from England in 1962 to change the face of cricket in the west. Right: Graham McKenzie, the lion-hearted paceman, who stood a class apart from other Australian fast bowlers in the eight seasons between the retirement of Alan Davidson and the emergence of Dennis Lillee.*

Lock returned to Britain to play another season of county cricket. He then became a permanent resident of Perth, but had a frustrating season in 1963–64, when he played only three matches, after the South African fast bowler Peter Pollock broke his arm with a flier at the start of the summer. He was captain in two of these matches, as regular skipper Barry Shepherd was now a Test cricketer, but could not inspire his side to even one outright victory, and the state finished at the foot of the Shield table, with just one first innings win on the ledger.

Things turned dramatically the following season — when Western Australia finished just an outright win away from the Shield. Lock returned to county cricket in 1965, with Leicestershire, and played three seasons there, always returning to Perth for the Shield. In 1965–66, WA finished second again, just four points from the champions, NSW. In this season they won all four of their matches away from Perth, and Lock took 41 wickets, the most in the competition. He topped the Shield aggregate again in 1966–67, becoming the first man since the war to take more than 50 wickets in one season, but his state struggled without their three Australian representatives, away in South Africa.

Murray Vernon captained Western Australia in 1966–67, after Shepherd had transferred to Sydney, but when Lock returned from Leicester after his third season there, he was appointed WA skipper. He immediately set about reviving the cricket fortunes of the west, adopting an aggressive approach, and instilling a discipline and resolve that had been lacking in the cricketers of the state.

Lock's first match as captain saw Ian Brayshaw take his remarkable 10-wicket haul against Victoria. In the second innings Lock took 5–36 as Western Australia won by 136 runs. Jack Lee in the *West Australian* noticed a marked improvement in the team's approach. "Lock's aggressive captaincy, his policy of quick bowling changes, and his obvious enthusiasm at the fall of each wicket provided a spur that induced the WA players to give perhaps their best display of bowling and fielding in first-class cricket." he wrote.

This was the first win in a season of triumph; it was the first time WA took out the Shield after playing a complete program of matches. Five matches were won outright, by a group of players who responded to the urgings of their captain, and produced performances of excellency that became commonplace in the seasons that followed. Lock asked his players to do only what was good for the team, and never to seek personal glory at the expense of others. He encouraged an "us-against-them" philosophy that was later enthusiastically adopted by his successors. His haul of 42 wickets in 1967–68 was topped by just one bowler, Alan Connolly of Victoria, and by the end of the season Lock had taken more wickets for Western Australia than any other bowler.

After the defeat of Victoria, NSW were beaten in Perth by 76 runs, largely because of the bowling of McKenzie, who took nine wickets, and the batting of Vernon, who scored a gutsy 133 on the first day. Western Australia did not play again for two months, when South Australia came west. The locals found Les Favell and the Chappell brothers in their best batting form, and the WA players performed exactly like men who had not played big cricket for eight weeks, and were beaten, by 95 runs. Against Queensland in Perth, first innings points were taken after Lock captured five wickets — but Des Bull and Lew Cooper, with only the injured Keith Dudgeon to come, batted out a dramatic last half hour to avert an outright loss.

Western Australia then began their eastern tour, aware that a productive trip could win the competition. In Adelaide they were thrashed by an innings, Greg Chappell and Barry Jarman belting centuries. But within a week things were turned around, and NSW fell, after John Inverarity and Jock Irvine scored hundreds, and McKenzie and fellow fast man Laurie Mayne ran through the NSW batting. In Brisbane Queensland were conquered by 144 runs, Lock taking 4–33 and 5–45. This result set up a "final" in Melbourne — as before the match, Victoria were two points ahead on the competition table, with just this game to go. The match crowned a fabulous season for Lock and his men, who through the batting of Inverarity and the new opening batsman, Ron Bowe, established control on the first day and never let go. Inverarity went on to 173, the innings ended at 405, and Victoria could do no better in reply than 196. Lock enforced the follow-on, and bowled superbly, taking five wickets as Victoria crumbled again for 227.

In his biography of Lock, *Put Lock On!*, author Kirwan Ward quoted the Englishman on this successful season: "When the crunch came," Lock said, "all I did really was what came naturally. The notion that Aussies all reject discipline is wrong; they'll accept it when it makes sense. We had good discipline without strain and without any sort of parade-ground stuff, but when we relaxed, well, we really relaxed, all of us, together. When we beat Victoria in that vital match at the MCG and won the Shield, the papers began calling Western Australia 'Locky's Mob'. It sounded great because I knew then that we were a real team."

While in Melbourne, Lock was asked by English authorities if he could go the West Indies to reinforce the M.C.C. team touring there. Lock agreed, and travelled to the last two Tests of his career. Before leaving Australia, Lock had to travel back to Perth with the Shield, to be met by an extraordinary reception.

Thousands greeted the team at the airport, and radio microphones and television cameras were every-where, all of them, it seemed aimed at the Englishman who had made it possible.

The following season WA slipped to second, behind Les Favell's South Australians. In many ways this side was even stronger than that of the previous season, the batting bolstered by the dynamic rungetting of another English import, Colin Milburn (who had played for WA in 1966–67), while Inverarity, Irvine and Derek Chadwick all scored important runs. McKenzie was superb when not on Test duty, while Mayne took 33 wickets, sufficient to win him a place in the Australia team to tour India and South Africa. Lock took 46 wickets himself — to become for the third time in four seasons the competition's leading wicket-taker.

The season's highlight was a fantastic double century hammered by the 18-stone (114kgs) Milburn in Brisbane. In six minutes less than four hours on the first day he smashed 243, including 38 fours and four sixes. Milburn had scored over 500 runs in his first Shield season, but never had he produced anything like this. With Chadwick, who scored 91, he added 328 for the first wicket, and broke Bob Simpson's record for the highest score by a West Australian batsman in the Shield. Between lunch and tea he scored an amazing 181 runs. The leg-spinner Bob Paulsen's first four overs cost 50 runs, and one Peter Allan over went for 21 (two sixes, three fours, one single). He was dropped three times, twice by the unfortunate Geoff Gray, who grabbed a blistering blow as it sailed for the fence, but was forced into the pickets, chest first, by the power of the shot and spilt the chance. Soon after Gray tried to catch a cover smash at boot level and all but broke his wrist.

In the next English season Milburn was severely injured in a car accident. He lost the sight of his left eye, and rarely played first-class cricket again. He died in 1990, aged 48.

Tony Lock played two more seasons before retiring. WA finished second and third in those years and Lock took his Shield bowling aggregate to 302 wickets from 63 matches. In his final season the side included such names Lillee, Massie, Marsh and Edwards, men who were to become key members of the national team during the next great era of Australian cricket. Statistically Lock's contribution to Western Australian cricket is enormous, but in many ways it is inappropriate to measure his performance in this way. In nine seasons Western Australia became a threat rather than threatened. Lock gave the players a belief in them-selves, and a confidence in their ability to succeed. The difference between Western Australian cricket in 1962 and 1971 was one thing more than the emergence of men such as John Inverarity, Ian Brayshaw, Ross Edwards, Dennis Lillee, Rod Marsh and Bob Massie. The difference was Tony Lock.

# 55

# JOHN BENAUD'S BOOTS

Of all the disputes between players and officials in the 100-year history of the Sheffield Shield there is no other that seems more absurd in hindsight than the matter of John Benaud's boots. And yet in many ways the battle of the boots was an extremely significant event in the modern game. The story is one that began with a breakthrough in cricket boot design. The new boots won the support of a number of Shield and international players, but not the approval of the Executive Committee of the NSW Cricket Association, which saw in the new footwear a reason for sloppy ground fielding, dropped catches, and lost wickets. The Association issued a directive to its Shield players: adhere to traditional boot designs or face the consequences. The serious consequences for the NSW captain turned out to be three weeks on the sidelines, banned because he chose to bat once too often in the outlawed footwear. That ban was later lifted, and by the start of the following season, the new boots were the preferred choice for most of the NSW and Australian team.

The NSW captain at the centre of the storm was John Benaud, Richie's younger brother, and a splendidly aggressive batsman. He was in his first season as a Shield captain, having taken over from Brian Taber who was touring India and South Africa with Bill Lawry's Australian team. NSW started the 1969–70 season slowly, but outright wins over Queensland and South Australia in early January had NSW challenging the competition leaders. Perhaps Benaud's best captaincy exhibition had been in Melbourne, where he scored a powerful second-innings century, and led a counter attack that reduced Victoria to 8–102 chasing 181 for maximum points. The home side eventually scraped home by one wicket, despite the brave efforts of Benaud and his men.

The boots saga had its genesis a season earlier, when the sporting goods manufacturer, Adidas, responded to the approaches of two prominent members of the Australian team, Doug Walters and Ian

*John Benaud batting against the spin of Tony Lock at the SCG in 1970–71.*

Chappell, and produced a lightweight cricket shoe. Chappell had remembered that Gary Sobers had scored many of his Shield runs batting in ripple-soled shoes. The English all-rounder Barry Knight, who worked with Adidas, took the new design idea back to England for the 1969 season, where the boot, once developed, was used by many players at Knight's home county, Leicestershire, — including the England captain Ray Illingworth and the Western Australian fast bowler Graham McKenzie.

The shoe was cut down below the ankle, and featured a revolutionary "ripple-soled" rubber heel instead of the conventional sprigged heel. Adidas at first produced the shoe with the trademark of three coloured stripes prominent on the sides. However the Board of Control objected to this and the stripes were toned down to traditional white.

The shoes quickly found favour with Australian cricketers. Many of the team in South Africa wore them, and in NSW as many as 10 of the players in the state side used the boot in some or all of their games. Tony Steele wore the new footwear when belting 158 and 152 in the wins over Queensland and South Australia. But there were members of the NSWCA Executive Committee who believed that the boots were reducing the effectiveness of the NSW fielding, and in some cases the batting and bowling as well.

On January 19, five days before the start of a key Shield match against Victoria, the Association announced it was banning the use of the rubber-heeled boots in first-class matches. In future NSW players would be wearing boots with a minimum of six spikes in the sole and three in the heel. Benaud immediately expressed astonishment at the decision. The NSWCA secretary, Mr Alan Barnes, when asked whether the NSW players would have to purchase new boots, commented: "Don't make me cry."

The edict left little time for the players to break in new boots. The following day Benaud said of the situation: "We are playing very good cricket now, and I'll be very annoyed if this decision plays any part in the outcome of this game. The more I think about the ban, the more ridiculous and stupid it seems. Why the Association didn't make the southern tour in a fortnight's time the ultimate date is hard to follow. If it wasn't so serious it would be laughable."

The controversy reached a head during the NSW second innings against Victoria — a game which which ended in a first-innings win for NSW. In the first innings, five players wore the boots, arguing that their replacement footwear was causing blisters. The NSWCA insisted that the players comply with their ruling, and all but Benaud did so when NSW batted again. The actions of the Association led to four pairs of the now-banned boots being left outside the home dressing room, under a sign which read: "4 SALE SLIGHTLY USED ENQUIRE WITHIN". The sign and boots were removed when an SCG Trust official told the players it was illegal to sell anything at the ground without a licence.

That night Benaud was suspended indefinitely from all Shield and grade matches under the jurisdiction of the NSWCA. The response from newspaper critics was almost uniform. Most felt Benaud was ill-advised to take the stand he did — but no-one could understand the heavy-handed strategy of the Association. The former NSW and Australian all-rounder Peter Philpott summed it up well: "It has been a badly handled affair by the executive, who have made a mountain out of a molehill. At the same time Benaud has not handled the matter in mature fashion. Unfortunately the only loser in the whole sorry mess is cricket itself."

In a back page story in *The Sun* newspaper, Benaud stated that his protest was not with the ban itself, but its timing. The former NSW captain wrote: "Surely anyone with pretensions to commonsense knows it is unrealistic to ask a cricketer or any sportsman for that matter to suddenly switch to gear which he has not used for a season, or in my case, not at all."

Benaud revealed that he had sought a meeting with Alan Barnes and the chairman of the NSWCA Executive, Syd Webb, on the Sunday of the Shield match, and told them he would be batting in the banned boots, because his new pair had blistered his feet. He guaranteed the two officials he would comply with the ban on the southern tour. He also revealed that Webb, who was 70 years old, had told him at that meeting that the ban would not be relaxed, had called him "a silly boy", had twice called him "Richie", and had suggested it was "immaterial" that complying with the ban might result in an inferior performance.

Webb would come out of the affair extremely badly, painted as an official totally out of step with the players and the game of that time. This was in many ways unfortunate, as Webb had been a champion of players' rights in an earlier era. But here he was the ogre, the man carrying the fight for the Association in the face of an increasingly hostile press. *The Sun* carried a backpage editorial headlined: "A MISERABLE ACTION". In the *Daily Mirror*, the veteran journalist Pat Farrell ran a story, based on an interview Webb had given Farrell at Canterbury racecourse, which did little for the cricket official's image. Webb was quoted as saying: "Unanimous congratulations we got from the Board for what we did over Benaud — The truth is he was no good at all as a captain."

Webb's subsequent denial of these and other remarks accredited to him, and the failure of the NSWCA to seek Farrell's record of the interview with Webb, led to Richie Benaud resigning as a life member of the Association. John Benaud's suspension was lifted on February 16, too late for him to go on the southern tour where NSW did not play well, losing matches in Perth and Adelaide. The meeting at which Benaud's ban was lifted was a somewhat rowdy affair, with Webb undergoing a torrid cross-examination from some angry club delegates. In a letter read at the meeting, Benaud wrote: "My main consideration was that the NSW team should do as well as possible in the Sheffield Shield. That was and still is my hope for the future." Four months later the NSWCA lifted the ban on the ripple-heeled boots, stipulating only that the boots worn by NSW cricketers had to be white.

This was little less than a complete comedown for the Association, which had little alternative after tests had suggested that the new boots were probably superior, and definitely not inferior, to the heavier boots of old. It was shown that cricketers who dropped simple catches or slipped in the field were probably guilty of poor technique or concentration, rather than a misguided choice of footwear.

John Benaud retired from first-class cricket following the 1973 Australian tour of the West Indies. He captained the state in four matches in 1972–73, scoring two Shield centuries in his last three seasons. His actions in the boots fiasco were a forerunner to the more drawn-out disputes involving players and officials that developed in the 1970s. In many ways the affair was inconsequential — the subject of the battle a trivial one, but it marked the arrival of a new atmosphere in Australian cricket, one in keeping with the times. Not since the days of Hill, Noble, Trumper and Armstrong had the players of the game been so prepared to speak out, and loudly, if they felt an injustice was being done.

# THE MODERN ERA

# Introduction by David Hookes

Sheffield Shield cricket traversed a spectacular rollercoaster journey during the decades of the 1970s and '80s. That the strength of the Australian Test team has always and will always be directly proportional to the potency of the country's domestic competition was very apparent.

The stunning transformation which came to the national side under the aggressive, brash, positive leadership of Ian Chappell reflected the strong Shield competition of the 1970s.

The '70s produced a staggeringly high proportion of wonderfully gifted, combative players, men willing to take on the might of the opposition head-on. And not only did they take on their rivals — they forced the issue of a lack of financial security by rebelling and joining World Series Cricket.

The effect of the best players being banned from Shield cricket was devastating. Suddenly many tyros found themselves representing their states, without the correct skills and mental approach, with all cricketing facets at an embryonic stage. State caps, jumpers and blazers, for so long a treasured and hard earned reward, were handed to some players who were no better than good, honest club cricketers.

Following cricket's most popular settlement in 1979 there was a five-year hangover period while States procrastinated on the business of resurrecting their teams' fortunes on and off the field. At the same time there was a lack of agreement on the points system used to determine the winners of each match, and ultimately the winner of the Shield.

In my view Shield matches must simulate as closely as possible Test matches and young players must be educated in the rigors of performing mentally and physically at the highest level.

For much of the modern era NSW played their home matches on an SCG pitch that was Australia's one true, slow turner, with the opening bowlers often used for only two or three overs before the slow bowlers were introduced into the attack. Despite this, NSW's Geoff Lawson was Australia's most successful opening bowler in the years following the retirement of Dennis Lillee. The left-handed Michael Whitney was the country's hardest worker on the cricket ground, perhaps not blessed with the natural ability of some of his fast bowling peers, but with a heart as big as his beloved SCG.

In the 1980s the spinners provided NSW with a unique and varied attack. Bob "Dutchy" Holland trundled old-fashioned leg spinners that bewildered the modern players of spin bowling, as they remained transfixed at the popping crease. Murray Bennett provided left-arm orthodox spin while off-spin novice Greg Matthews injected genuine enthusiasm and a passionate love of his State, and attracted a cult following.

From 1988 to 1992 Lawson was Australia's most exciting first-class captain, prepared to "make" the game from the first ball, declare when necessary to set up a match and adhere to the adage of "you have to give a bit to get a bit".

Queensland continued in vain to search for its elusive Holy Grail, and the consistently poor post-Christmas performances mystified the northerners and their opponents.

Having the advantage of wonderful winter weather, Queensland is always better prepared than other States at the beginning of the season and invariably achieves good early results. The wheels begin to fall off as the season approaches the halfway mark and the pressure on the side mounts from sponsors, from within the team and from all of Queensland, with expectations that a side that has chased imports from interstate and overseas should be able to grab the ultimate trophy.

The most convivial of hosts and the most cordial of opponents, Queensland might consider adopting some of the West Australians' healthy arrogance and "them versus us" attitude.

Tasmania, the competition's non-mainland state, has been shrouded in civil wars among their three associations, all of which fought, scrapped and bitched about hosting Shield matches in their respective towns, Launceston, Devonport and Hobart. It was not until the '90s that Hobart, and the well-appointed Bellerive ground, hosted all Tasmania's home matches. Such a complex administration was not conducive to high-quality cricket and further, the continued influx of imports to the Apple Isle was not a success in terms of winning matches.

Victorians believe Australian cricket is only strong when Victorian cricket is strong. Their aggressive arrogance often blinds their judgment.

Lack of success for the Vics in the period under review was a direct result of poor team selection which often resulted in a most unbalanced side. Far too often, Victoria was top heavy with a bowler or batsman, and its inability to handle on-field pressure saw it too often clutch defeat from the jaws of victory.

Mediocre medium-pace bowlers were often preferred to spin bowlers and one of the most disappointing results in the last 20 years was Victoria's Sheffield Shield victory in 1990–91, achieved primarily without a slow bowler. The attack of four fast bowlers was vindicated by the ultimate result, and the non-use of a spinner was explained by the Victorian coach who declared: "Spin bowling is dead".

South Australia maintained its dubious reputation as a half-way house for wayward interstate players. The fact of only two Shields won — 1975–76 and 1981–82 — for a State boasting the finest practice facilities and geographical locations of its club grounds in the land testified to a lack of planning in the local competition. Often players were selected without substantial club performances, and interstate cricketers appeared to be offered an unusually easy path into the State team. Slow, low, ill-prepared pitches created a dearth of fast bowlers and the Shield team suffered through lacking a genuine fast bowler.

The 1975-76 Shield was won with a combination of aggressive captaincy, youthful ignorance and a balanced attack of two fast bowlers and two quality spinners. The 1981–82 Shield was won by aggressive, fast-scoring batting, which allowed a relatively inexperienced attack to bowl out the opposition twice.

South Australia had eight coaches in 10 years, the last three from interstate and has had three captains in the past three seasons. The recent lack of continuity follows the loss of Greg Chappell to Queensland in the early '70s and the defection to Victoria in the early '90s of Darren Lehmann and Paul Nobes — two young batsmen who may have dominated the South Australian line-up for the remainder of the 20th century.

Perhaps the critical loss of players and instability in leadership personnel may coerce SACA administrators into aligning the lack of on-field success with the problems I have mentioned. South Australian cricket chiefs must address the situation of aggressively promoting the locals and encouraging home-grown products into the Shield team.

Sheffield Shield's bench mark for the past 15 years has been Western Australia because of two factors — their on-field dominance and off-field professionalism.

The John Inverarity dynasty coincided with a number of outstanding cricketers, two of whom (Rod Marsh and Dennis Lillee) formed the most lethal opening bowler/wicket-keeper combination in the history of cricket.

At one stage the Australian Test team contained seven West Australians yet the state side managed to win the Shield in the same season!

Tired of losing consistently through the 1960s, Inverarity instilled a healthy hatred of the eastern states and his players were fed a diet of "them versus us" philosophy. Teams crossed the Nullabor filled with trepidation and arrived in Perth to find playing conditions foreign and difficult to combat. Young West Australians were introduced to State squad practice where professionalism was arguably greater than any other state and the fresh players were quickly taught "perfect practice makes perfect" The team had a match plan which was followed without question. Players understood their role within the match-plan formula and the teams' record became the envy of their opponents.

Currently state rivalry is healthy and willing and while players maintain pride in their own state teams performances the system will continue to prosper.

The two most promising batsmen of the early '90s, Darren Lehmann and Michael Bevan may well be proven to have the ability to shape Australia's cricket future leading into the 21st century. Both possess the typical brash Australian aggressiveness so evident over the past 100 years and synonymous with matchwinning champions.

The lack of consistent Test wicket-taking wrist spinners since Richie Benaud's retirement has been of immense concern in cricket's corridors of power and led eventually to an intensive Australia-wide search for the next Benaud.

In 1992, after just a handful of first-class matches a portly, peroxide-blond Victorian tyro, Shane Warne was prematurely promoted into the Test team but yielded the unflattering figures of 1/159 from 45 overs against India. However, he showed he could handle the pressure at international level.

His captain Allan Border's words of encouragement before he gave him the ball for the first time in Test cricket were: "Don't do a Watkins on us Shane." (John Watkins was the leg-spinner plucked from obscurity in 1972-73 to play against Pakistan. He is remembered only for his brief wayward spell of bowling.)

Warne survived, and as he hones his craft in the labyrinth of Shield cricket let us hope he becomes a hero to youngsters wishing to emulate his deeds and become world-class leg-spinners. The history of the Shield is littered with heroes and wonderful deeds, of mavericks who strove for success and fame, of men who may have failed in their quest for long-time glory and honour but at least played a handful of matches for their States and were proud to don the cap.

A fine legacy has been left by a century of cricketers. It is now up to the contemporary generation to ensure the greatest game prospers and gives youngsters the chance to follow their dreams and stride onto first-class arenas with dignity and pride.

# 56

## SPRINGBOK SENSATION

In 1968 the South African opening batsman, Barry Richards, won a position with the Hampshire county cricket club in England. His first innings was at Sussex, and he started with a duck, bowled by the lethal fast man, John Snow. His first home match, against Glamorgan two weeks later, yielded four runs in two innings.

Despite the start that he had, Richards developed into one of Hampshire's greatest players, forming a dynamic opening partnership in later years with the West Indian Gordon Greenidge. In his first season in county cricket he scored more than 2,000 runs and was named one of *Wisden's* five cricketers of the year. Early in 1970 he made his Test debut, against Australia, and scored 508 runs in a four-Test series.

Richards was selected to go on the 1970 South African tour of England, but the trip was cancelled after vehement and sustained protests at the apartheid policies of the South African government. Richards could surely not have believed at this point that his Test career was over, after just four matches. Seeking experience and income, he accepted an offer to play cricket in South Australia in 1970–71, upsetting those back home who believed he should have stayed and supported the South African equivalent of the Sheffield Shield, the Currie Cup.

Richards came to South Australia on a complicated agreement. Coca-Cola supplied him with a car and a salary. The Prospect cricket club organised accommodation. Apart from playing, he was required to do promotional work, join the after-dinner speaking circuit, and to co-ordinate cricket coaching classes. Additionally, in the most highly publicised segment of the deal, Coke sponsored him — one dollar for every first-class run scored, and 10 dollars for every wicket taken. This was to prove a very expensive exercise for the soft drink conglomerate.

Things started much as they had at Hampshire. Richards' first innings for South Australia came in a one-day match against Victoria, and he was caught behind for nought. His Shield debut came against Western Australia in Adelaide, and he scored seven — caught at leg slip off Graham McKenzie — and 44 not out in a meaningless fourth innings that ran just 10.2 overs. The South African made almost as much money from his bowling, taking 3–29 in WA's second innings.

Against the Ray Illingworth's touring M.C.C. team, Richards smashed a superb 224. Then in Melbourne he made 51 and 42, edging Alan "Froggy" Thomson to keeper Ray Jordon in the first innings, and Alan Connolly to Jordon in the second. Thomson was, at that time, the great fast bowling hope in Australia, a man with an eccentric windmill action that ended with the ball being let go at fair speed off the "wrong foot". Thomson took seven wickets in the first South Australian innings, was rushed into the Australian Test team, but did little except frustrate the purists with his technique. By season's end a genuine fast bowler, Dennis Lillee, had emerged from the west. Thomson was hardly heard of again.

Lillee was in the West Australian side that faced Richards and company a week after the Victorian match. The WA bowling lineup was excellent, one of the strongest it had ever put on the field to that time. Lillee would bowl the second over, after McKenzie, Australia's best fast bowler. At first change was Ian Brayshaw, always a danger in Perth with his knowledge of the crafty WACA windshifts. Supporting were three spinners, the left-handed master Tony Lock, the bouncing leg breaks and wrong 'uns of Tony Mann, and the studious left-arm slows of John Inverarity. Behind the stumps was Rodney Marsh, still recovering from the shock of being selected as Australia's new wicketkeeper.

Ian Chappell won the toss, decided to bat, and at stumps Richards was 325 not out.

The following breakup of Richards' innings reveals something of the consistent, brutal quality of his batting.

| Runs | Minutes | Fours | Sixes |
|------|---------|-------|-------|
| 50 | 70 | 7 | |
| 100 | 125 | 13 | |
| 150 | 176 | 21 | |
| 200 | 209 | 28 | 1 |
| 250 | 268 | 30 | 1 |
| 300 | 317 | 39 | 1 |

In all he hit 44 fours and one six in the day, and faced 322 deliveries. He was the third man to score 300 in one day in an Australian first-class match, and the second, after Bill Ponsford, to do so in the Shield. Only five men in the history of first-class cricket anywhere had scored more runs in one day (the most ever is 345 by Charlie Macartney for Australia against Nottinghamshire in 1921). Richards smashed the record for the highest score by a Shield batsmen against WA, previously held by Bob Simpson at 247 (not out). The previous best by a South Australian against Western Australia was 195 by Gary Sobers. At stumps South Australia were 3–513. The runs had come as follows: 135 in the 110-minute pre-lunch session; 211 in the two hours between lunch and tea; and 167 in the 100 minutes before stumps. Ian Chappell had scored 129, in a partnership of 308 that ran for 170 minutes. Chappell, according to Jack Lee in the *West Australian*, "did not suffer greatly in comparison, and more than matched Richards in grace and style, if not in power and efficiency."

Lee observed: "Richards produced every shot in the book except the mishit." He enthused over the Springbok's batting having "more than a touch of the ruthless efficiency that was the hallmark of Australia's greatest batsman of all-time, Sir Donald Bradman".

Richards, a fraction more than 180cms in height, stood erect at the crease, and used a lengthy backlift as if to emphasise his high grip of the bat. He thought nothing of lofting the ball away from the infield, even over the turning heads of cover and mid-off. He hooked in the air, encouraging captains and bowlers, but rarely, if ever, was he trapped at fine leg. The legendary Australian cricket writer, Ray Robinson, suggested that Richards often left onlookers feeling that they had just been shown how the game should be played.

Lock tried everything, even C-grade full-tosses and long hops, but Richards concentration was as superb as his timing. If Lillee or McKenzie dropped short, Richards had them through point like a shot, or pulled them wide of the man at mid-on, a fieldsman whose role with the WA paceman operating was usually to hand the ball back to the bowler, not chase it to the fence. The cover field was taunted, the ball inevitably just out of reach. To Lock's left-arm spinners, the South African was always down the wicket, flaying the varied offerings that had been defeating Australians for years. The Englishmen's 11 overs cost 96 runs, Lillee's 16 went for 102.

In his 1978 book *The Barry Richards Story*, the South African wrote: "Somehow I managed to sustain for a complete day the sort of form that usually materialises only in short, glorious moments." For the first 15 minutes he did little but check out the line, and the pace and bounce of the wicket. Then he had McKenzie past point for four, and was on his way.

Richards recalled playing and missing at the first ball of the day, an outswinger from McKenzie. Rod Marsh turned to first slip Inverarity and snarled: "Geez, I thought this bloke was supposed to be able to play a bit." When Richards straight drove the last ball of the day, from Lillee, to the sight-screen, Inverarity turned to his weary keeper and said: "I suppose he can play a bit."

Richards was dropped once, an easy opportunity to a startled Brayshaw at mid-on when he was 169. This was a rare blemish by the W.A fieldsmen, who were almost as faultless as the batting, and were applauded by the press the following morning. Marsh gave what Jack Lee called "a brilliant display", stumping Ian Chappell cleverly off Lock, and diving at the feet of the slip cordon to hold an edge from Greg Chappell. The next day, Richards went to 356, when he was lbw to Mann, trying to place a fulltoss through the leg-side in a manner that suggested the ball would have pitched outside the line. He had batted for 42 minutes on the second morning, and struck another four boundaries. After he was dismissed the next five wickets fell for 22, before Ian Chappell declared at 9–575.

Western Australia were then bowled out for 289 and 175, only Inverarity, in the first innings, and Irvine, in the second, getting past 50. Richards earned another 10 dollars when he had Marsh caught by Ian Chappell off the last ball of the third day. The South African's summer was now in full swing, and he continued merrily on, finishing with 1145 runs for the Shield season, at 104.09.

One memory of Richards concerns his match in Sydney, where he scored 178, and attracted a healthy crowd to the Cricket Ground, even though an Ashes Test was being played in Melbourne, and televised into Sydney homes. NSW won the match on the first innings, 7 (declared) for 441, to 316. On the last day NSW batted again, and were bowled out for 133, the final wicket falling just before stumps. Throughout that final session the spectators continually barracked their own batsmen, especially the NSW captain Brian Taber. What they wanted was a declaration, however token, so that South Australia would have to bat again. On that final afternoon, the barrackers cared not at all for the outright points, or even the Sheffield Shield. All they wanted was one more glimpse of the batting of Barry Richards.

# 57
# BUILDING A DYNASTY

When Tony Lock first signed to play with the Western Australian team in 1962, he joined a side solidly installed in a position at or near the foot of the Sheffield Shield ladder. A decade later, the teamsheet he handed to his successor as WA captain, John Inverarity, included the names of many of the finest cricketers in the country. By the end of Inverarity's first season as leader, Western Australia, Sheffield Shield champions for the third time, had six players in the 17–man squad to tour England, and was clearly the dominant cricket force in the country.

Inverarity was the son of Mervyn Inverarity, who played for WA between 1925 and 1940. John made his debut, as a teenager, in the 1962–63 season, scoring 11 and 52 against South Australia. A crucial 173 at the MCG in the final match of the 1967–68 season — an innings that played a critical role in WA winning the match, and the Shield, confirmed his spot in the Australian team to tour England that winter, and in the following Australian summer he scored four Shield centuries, establishing himself as the key batsman in his state. However his international career was stifled when the Australian selectors preferred the batting potential and fielding gifts of the stylish Victorian right-hander Paul Sheahan for the Tests against the West Indies, and the power of fellow West Australian Jock Irvine for the tour of India and South Africa.

Inverarity consoled himself with his role as Lock's trusted lieutenant. When Lock retired after the 1970–71 season, Inverarity had the resources and the intelligence to push the development of Western Australian cricket up another notch. He had already scored more centuries for his state than any other cricketer, and quickly rivalled Ian Chappell for recognition as the Shield's most effective commander. Chappell was the captain of South Australia, the 1970–71 Shield champions, and Australia — a tough, intuitive leader of men, a captain who led from the front, and was not afraid to fight for his team. Invariably, in return they fought for him.

Before the 1971–72 season, the means of points allocation for the Shield was altered, with "bonus" points being introduced. Rather than teams gaining points for first-innings victories, they were rewarded for taking wickets and scoring runs in the first 65 overs. A point was won for every second first-innings wicket taken, and for every 25 runs scored after 150 in the first innings. The intention was to make less likely the chances of a boring first-innings stalemate, and to increase the likelihood of an exciting finish on the final afternoon. One side-effect was that captains began declaring innings closed rather than risk conceding additional bowling points. In one match in Melbourne in late December, NSW captain Brian Taber declared at 9–67. This was not a closure designed to get the Victorians in on a minefield. Taber reasoned that the runs his last pair of John Gleeson and Steve Bernard were unlikely to score were not worth the cost of an extra bonus point to his opponents. Victoria eventually won that match by an innings and 250 runs — their most decisive victory over NSW since 1926–27.

The 1971–72 season started for Western Australia with a demolition of Queensland in Perth. The pace quartet — Dennis Lillee, Graham McKenzie, Bob Massie and Graeme Watson — did the damage with the ball, and Watson, Inverarity and Ian Brayshaw scored the runs as the match was won by an innings. Watson, who scored 145, was "out" in bizarre circumstances. He hit a powerful cut into the gully, where Don Allen came up with the ball. Watson believed he had been caught, and left the wicket, but at stumps the umpires told the scorers to amend their books to show Watson as "retired, out". The catch, in their opinions, had not been taken. Western Australia finished with 19 points, Queensland 2.

Three weeks later, Inverarity set Victoria 235 minutes to score 278 on the final afternoon. In the end the declaration proved too cautious, but only just, as the final batting pair of Richie Robinson and Alan Thomson had to survive the final 10 minutes to avoid outright defeat.

Victoria were crushed again in early December, and then rain ruined a contest in Sydney that W.A might still have won. Bob Massie's second innings bowling figures were unusual — 7 overs; 5 maidens; 6 runs; 3 wickets. Doug Walters and Kerry O'Keeffe had to bat out the final hour after NSW had slumped to 6–43. In Brisbane, victory was taken by 10 wickets despite the third day being lost to the weather. Watson scored another century, but the star was Lillee, who took 10 wickets, including a hostile 6–24 on the first day. Lillee had, by this time, established his reputation as the quickest and most lethal fast bowler in Australia.

*John Inverarity, captain of Western Australia for much of the 1970s, the decade in which W.A. became the dominant force in Australian cricket.*

By the end of 1971, Inverarity and his men had cleared away at the top of the Shield table. From five matches they had three outright wins, the better of two draws, and had adapted better to the bonus points system than any of their opponents. However a rival was soon to emerge. South Australia had played only two matches, a rain-sodden draw with Queensland, and a comfortable victory over Victoria. Their threat to Western Australia became much more vivid when they defeated the Shield front-runners in a low-scoring struggle in Adelaide. Their hero was the off-spinner, Ashley Mallett, who took 6–64 and 7–58 to win his side a 25-run victory. South Australia then travelled to the east, first to Brisbane, where they were narrowly defeated, and then to Sydney, where they fashioned a crucial victory after all had seemed lost. Trailing by 42 on the first innings, they fought back to have NSW 7–91. Then Shield debutant, the left-handed Gary Gilmour, smashed a remarkable century in a session. South Australia needed 263, and made them, but only after nightwatchman Jeff Hammond batted for 269 minutes for 53, and last pair, Kevin McCarthy and Mike Hendricks somehow found the final 49 runs required.

In Perth, Doug Walters scored a superb 163 as NSW controlled a high-scoring draw. Ross Edwards and Inverarity also scored hundreds on a pitch too true for either side's good. A week later in Adelaide, Ian Chappell spearheaded an exciting run chase against NSW that led to a two-wicket victory. The South Australians were now very much in the Shield driving seat. On 82 points, they led WA by eight. Two matches remained in the Shield season — Western Australia v South Australia in Perth, followed a week later by Victoria v South Australia in Melbourne.

South Australia had to do little more than avoid outright defeat in Perth to retain the trophy. Western Australia's chances were hindered when Lillee announced two days before the start that he could not play because of a back injury. The left-handed Sam Gannon was called up as his replacement. Even with Lillee out, as many as 13 of the players involved in the match featured in newspaper columns discussing selections for the upcoming tour to England.

Ian Chappell won the toss, batted, and watched his team struggle slowly to 8–228. He made a typically forthright 52, and Ken Cunningham 56, but his colleagues disappointed against WA's four-pronged pace attack. South Australia won two batting points from the day, WA three bowling points. By stumps on day two, Inverarity was firmly in control. His team was 3–223, chasing 255. The runs had been scored in front of a record Sunday cricket crowd at the WACA ground of 9,331. The key innings was from the captain, who batted with enterprise and aggression for 87 in 130 minutes. Inverarity had developed a reputation in previous seasons as something of a stonewaller, as he had perceived that his value to his team lay in placing a high value on his wicket. As the WA batting line-up strengthened, he allowed himself a more aggressive approach, and now, at a crucial time, he took command. The base on which the innings was built was opener Ken McAulley's unbeaten 85, scored in more than four hours.

The next morning the game changed. McAullay was lbw to Terry Jenner after just seven minutes. At 245, Marsh sliced Hammond to Ian Chappell. In the same over Bob Meuleman hit a catch to Jenner at short leg. Three runs later Ian Brayshaw was caught in the gully. Inverarity allowed the total to creep past 250, and then declared three runs behind, rather than give his opponents any more bonus points.

McKenzie bowled an over to Ashley Woodcock for four runs, and then Peter Herbert was caught at short leg off Massie. In the following over, Woodcock was missed, a chance to Inverarity at slip. Two balls later Ian Chappell hooked to Gannon at fine leg, but again the chance went astray. McKenzie could only watch in despair. He had been Australia's leading fast bowler since the retirement of Alan Davidson in 1963, but his colleagues Lillee and Massie were in front of him now, and he needed wickets if he was to make a fourth trip to England.

Massie was bending the ball remarkably at times, and with the total at 52 he swung one through Chappell. South Australia could never edge clear. Woodcock fell one short of his fifty. Greg Chappell was caught in the gully for 22. The sixth wicket, Jenner, edging the off-spinner Paul Nicholls via the pad to Brayshaw at backward short leg, fell at 157. Mallett and Cunningham then became involved in another revival, adding 50 in even-time. Cunningham had developed something of a reputation as a fighter of South Australian lost causes. He was a tough left hand batsmen, good enough to score a hundred in each innings against WA in 1966–67, and a useful swing bowler. Here he swung and cut his way to his second half century of the game, and brought his side back into the game.

With the score on 209, McKenzie found the strength to get one up at Mallett's chest. The ball rose above the blade, and squeezed the batsman's bowling hand against the handle. The bat spun from his grasp, as he waved his hand in pain, and fell on his stumps, a wretched hit-wicket. Four runs later Cunningham skied Nicholls to Brayshaw at mid-off, then McCarthy and Hammond edged catches to the wicketkeeper. Western Australia needed 221 to win.

The runs were gathered comfortably, with five wickets to spare. Watson and McAullay added 101 for the first wicket — the highlight a huge six by McAullay into the new "Test match" stand. Watson fell within three runs of his partner, but then Edwards and Brayshaw added 55. Marsh fell immediately, creating tension, but Brayshaw and Inverarity pushed and nudged the score towards 200. A cut for four by Inverarity off Mallett, and then nine from one Hammond over took the total to 215. When Inverarity lobbed Mallett to mid-wicket it was the final wicket to fall.

Ian Chappell agreed his team had been outplayed by a better side. Even so, South Australia were still in the box seat, needing just seven points from their final match to win the Shield. The game at the MCG attracted enormous interest in Western Australia. Channel 7 in Perth arranged for a direct telecast of all four days, while the ABC provided coverage for regional viewers. It turned out to be a thriller. On the first day 16 wickets fell, including all 10 of South Australia — bundled out without gaining a batting point. They now needed an outright win, and led by their captain, who scored a fighting second-innings 106, they all but achieved it, losing in an exciting finish by just three wickets.

This was the first of five Sheffield Shield victories for Western Australia in the 1970s. In four of those five successful seasons they were led by Inverarity. In 1975 he accepted a teaching appointment in England, but returned two years later to lead the side again during the years of World Series Cricket. In his absence, WA was captained by Rod Marsh. Another teaching opportunity took Inverarity to Adelaide, where he played Shield cricket between 1979 and 1985, as captain in 1980–81. When he finally retired he had scored more Shield runs than any other man, and built a glowing reputation as both captain and cricketer.

# 58

## GREG CHAPPELL, QUEENSLANDER

In the winter of 1973, the Queensland Cricket Association wrote to Gregory Stephen Chappell, then of South Australia, asking him to travel north to take over the captaincy of their Sheffield Shield team. The invitation was an outrageously broad one and at first Chappell deflected the overtures. A persuasive phone call from the incumbent Queensland captain, wicketkeeper John Maclean, helped change things. The northern state needed Chappell's runs, and Maclean was far keener to be vice-captain of a competitive team, than leader of a side with no future. Chappell flew to Brisbane, to meet with a committee that had been established to co-ordinate his transfer. They offered a career opportunity and handsome salary with an insurance company, relocation costs, six months accommodation, and a three-year contact.

The SACA were unwilling, or unable, to match the Queensland offer. In South Australia, he would have to wait until the retirement of his elder brother Ian before he could be captain of his state, and without leadership experience in the Shield, it was unlikely he could be the next Australian captain. Greg Chappell had ambitions for that Australian captaincy. He took the middle ground — declining the three-year deal with the QCA, and instead opting for a 12-month trial. Within 12 months he had signed a five-year contract and South Australia had lost him forever.

Greg Chappell first played for South Australia in 1966–67. In seven seasons he had scored almost 4,000 runs, including 10 centuries — four of them in 1969–70 when he made his highest Shield score for his native state, 156 not out in Brisbane (he made 129 in the first innings of that game). By 1970–71 he was in the Test side, and started with an impressive century, batting seven. In England in 1972 he made his reputation, carving out graceful and confident Test centuries at Lords and The Oval. By the time he signed for Queensland he was not far from being the best batsman in the world.

Queensland in 1972–73 had finished last in the Shield race, many runs and many wickets from fourth placed Victoria. The Queenslanders had never won a Sheffield Shield, never even threatened since NSW edged them out in 1956–57. Within a season Greg Chappell made them contenders. He was assisted by another high-priced import, Pakistan's opening batsman, Majid Khan. From the gun they turned the side around. In the first two matches Majid scored 107 and 89 (against NSW), 4 and 100 (against Victoria); Chappell's contribution was 38, 36, 180 and 101. NSW avoided outright defeat by two wickets, the match with Victoria went down to the wire — Queensland needing seven runs and Victoria three wickets when time ran out.

The game against South Australia in Brisbane attracted great publicity. For the Chappell brothers this was something of a personal duel — Ian scored 70 and 126 fighting a losing cause, Greg smashed 56, and took 4–47 bowling medium pace in the South Australian second innings, as Queensland won by nine wickets. A week later Western Australia fell in Brisbane by 192 runs, and Queensland were leading the Shield. The WA game attracted a record Shield crowd for a Sunday — 9,201 Greg Chappell fans.

Of Chappell's impact, the young Queensland all-rounder Phil Carlson said: "He's the best cricketer in Australia. And he's playing for us. He is getting the players around him performing. Batting with Greg makes an enormous difference. It's so much easier with someone at the other end as good as he is. Greg is super-confident. He doesn't think there's anyone better than him. And there isn't."

Chappell was probably the most elegant Australian batsman since Archie Jackson and Stan McCabe. He was so superb off his pads that Shield attacks resolved never to pitch on his leg stump. His backlift was high, his follow-through graceful, especially when the cover or on-drive was racing to the fence. As a fieldsman he was supreme — ranking with Bobby Simpson as the best catcher in the slip cordon Australia has ever had. His captaincy lacked the lead-from-the-front bravado that was his brother's strength; he relied more on his runs than his intuition, but had many rewarding days for both Queensland and Australia, and invariably won the support of the key players under his command.

His greatest challenge was to teach the Queensland cricketers how to win. In 1974, in an interview in *Cricketer* magazine, he said: "As you practice bowling and batting, a side must also practice winning, and that is something Queensland hasn't had much chance at in the past few years. This was similar to Australia up until 18 months ago (Australia went 11 Tests without a win between January 1970 and June 1972). Queensland, and Australia, had forgotten how to finish a game, how to win. And Queensland has been in the position to win many times, but hasn't had the experience.

"They've thought: 'Great, we're in a position to win, so we'd better not lose,' and with that sort of attitude you do lose."

*Greg Chappell batting for Queensland at the SCG in the final Shield match of the 1973-74 season. The keeper is the NSW captain, Brian Taber, the slip fieldsman Gary Gilmour.*

*Greg Chappell during his farewell first-class match, the 1983–84 final against Western Australia in Perth.*

Dennis Lillee is congratulated by his Western Australian teammates after taking a wicket during the 1983–84 final.

Queensland went on the road in January, first to Melbourne, where they almost threw away a contest they had already won. Chappell had scored 115 of 227, after Victoria declared at 9–182. Victoria crashed again, and by stumps on day three Queensland required just 95, with nine wickets in hand. With seven wickets remaining they needed just 24, but only Chappell prevented an absurd loss, being 53 not out when victory was reached, with only two wickets left. In Adelaide, outright points were won more comfortably, after the captain scored 158 not out and 72. His Shield season batting average now stood at 123.5. On the same day, in Sydney, Victoria won outright, in their final match of the season. Queensland, with matches against Western Australia and NSW remaining, trailed the Victorians by 17 points.

The match in Perth coincided with the third Test against New Zealand in Adelaide. Without Chappell, the Queenslanders were thrashed by nine wickets, only Trimble in the first innings and Majid in the second getting past 50. While Chappell and his wife were in Adelaide, their home in Brisbane was devastated by cyclonic floods. Unsettled, but determined, Chappell was back for the final fling at the Shield, and sent the New South Welshmen in after winning the toss. Three wickets fell in the first two overs, another with the score at 24, but NSW recovered to 249, opener Marshall Rosen making 94, number-six Rick McCosker 56.

Then the Queenslanders ran into a tornado of a different kind. Jeff Thomson had bowled fast enough in his debut season, 1972–73, to win his first Test cap. A broken bone on his foot slowed him for a while, and he could not win back his place in the NSW XI for the first seven matches of the following season. Thomson was the fastest and most dangerous man in Sydney grade cricket, slinging the ball from behind his back after a short, slow jog to the wicket. On the first afternoon against Queensland he took two wickets in 5.1 overs, and the next day went on to 7–85 as Queensland tumbled to 205. Chappell was caught off the glove, chancing his arm at an attempted hook off a rapid riser. Majid was unsettled by the bounce, but caught driving at the leg-spin of Kerry O'Keeffe. Bill O'Reilly called Thomson "the most lethal bowler in Australian cricket". Within weeks Chappell was organising his transfer to Brisbane, all too late for the state's Shield hopes in 1973–74.

Two days later Queensland were defeated, by 167 runs. Chappell batted bravely for 44, under a cloud of concern for his wife, who had been taken to hospital after suffering a miscarriage. His Shield aggregate for the season went to 1013, from 13 innings (four of them centuries); he thus became the first Queenslander to go past the thousand. In the same innings Sam Trimble became the second highest runscorer in the Shield's history, overtaking Les Favell. Only Bradman remained to be beaten.

In the seasons ahead, Queensland would continue to import players, men such as Ian Davis, Viv Richards, Allan Border and Kepler Wessels, in the frustrating chase for the Shield grail. Chappell, the Australian captain from November 1975, was always the focus; with the best batsman in the competition in their ranks the Queenslanders were always in with a chance. But the elusive victory was not to be. Something always came up, be it the weather, the draw, the luck, or now and then an ill-timed inept performance. Greg Chappell would persist until the Shield final against Western Australia in 1984, missing only the years of World Series Cricket, and score 13 more centuries, some remarkable, all memorable, but none the one he so desperately wanted. The hundred that won the Sheffield Shield.

# 59

## SAM! SAM! SAM!

Greg Chappell produced perhaps the most extraordinary of all his Sheffield Shield innings in the opening match of the 1975–76 season. It was a performance of rare quality. With Queensland needing 165 in 18 overs to defeat NSW outright at the 'Gabba, Chappell belted 86 in 55 balls, and the target was achieved with nine deliveries to spare. When he departed, caught on the fence trying to hit Doug Walters for six, the required run rate had been reduced to just 4.7 runs per over, nearly half of the original asking rate.

And yet, when the crowd of more than 4,000 gathered outside the home dressing room after the match, it was not the name of Greg Chappell they were chanting. Their hero was Sam Trimble, who had lived through many a Queensland disappointment. Trimble had batted through the innings, for 66 from 72 balls — the greatest day of his cricket life.

Trimble was born in NSW, in Lismore on the far north coast on August 16, 1934. In 1957, the NSW selectors left him out of the State Colts team, and he decided to throw his lot in with Queensland. Brisbane, he reasoned, was a lot closer than Sydney, and if he failed, the journey home would be that much shorter. He made his Shield debut, batting three, in December 1959, scoring 1 and 17 against Victoria, and stayed in the Queensland side until late in the 1975–76 season. Over that period he scored 22 Shield centuries, many of them slow, laborious affairs, though none as tedious as a 539–minute 177 against the M.C.C. in 1970. Many thought that innings cost him his final chance at a Test cap. When the selectors decided to sack Bill Lawry for the final match of that series, the choice came down to Trimble and the Victorian opener Ken Eastwood. Trimble had played for Australia on the 1965 tour of the West Indies (not in a Test), but Lawry was pushed out for being too stolid, and Trimble would have been more of the same. The selectors went for Eastwood, who had a dismal match, and Trimble was never again thought of as a possible Australian player.

He was a batsman of little style, concentrating on defence as much as any Shield cricketer ever had. In many ways this was a reflection of the poor sides he stonewalled for — for however slow he might have been, his was the most prized Queensland wicket in the years following the retirement of Peter Burge. Perhaps his greatest game was against Victoria in 1963–64, when he scored a hundred in each innings, becoming the first Queenslander to do so in a first-class match since Leo O'Connor achieved the feat in the second Shield game Queensland ever played. Despite Trimble's efforts, the match was lost. Bob Cowper led Victoria to a fabulous victory, scoring a freewheeling, unbeaten 88 as 237 runs were smashed in 112 minutes and 23.2 overs, to win the day, by four wickets with three minutes to spare.

The Queensland win over NSW at the Gabba in October 1975 was just as exciting and amazing as that unlikely Victorian victory. Three days earlier there had appeared little chance of a result of any kind. So dreadful was the Brisbane weather that the QCA called off the first day's play 18 hours before the toss was scheduled to be made, when the ground director, Brisbane City Council alderman Clem Jones, informed the umpires the field would be unfit for play. A Sydney invention — a roller with a perforated steel drum covered by three inches of foam — imaginatively called the "Super Sopper" — was flown up in an effort to get play started. Before its arrival, little hope was held for the second day, but play started only 40 minutes late, and NSW had reached 5–240 by the close. Test opener Rick McCosker was undefeated on 109.

The next day Walters declared at 7–250. Trimble was out in the first over for a duck, and Queensland struggled to 7–127, before Chappell took command. He scored a majestic hundred, declared at 9–227, and then took an impossible catch, diving low to his right at first slip to grab a lightning snick from Jeff Thomson's bowling. NSW were 3–38 at stumps.

The NSW batting on the final day was dreadful. Alan Turner batted 84 minutes for 21, Kerry O'Keeffe 89 minutes for 20, and worst of all, Stuart Webster blocked, jabbed and groped for 140 minutes for just 16. Webster managed just one single from his first 52 balls. In 292 minutes, NSW scratched together just 141 runs, and were finally all out just after tea.

Leading the chase, Chappell showed his hand from the first ball, when he hit Test bowler Gary Gilmour over mid-on for four. From the third over of the innings he took 22. Then he charged the fast man Len Pascoe, probably the third quickest bowler in the country after Lillee and Thomson, and smashed the ball back over the bowler's head. The 41–year-old Trimble scampered for singles, giving his captain as much strike as possible. Dave Colley, a Test bowler three years earlier, was nearly decapitated by a stirring straight drive. Walters was swung for a huge six into the crowd at deep mid-wicket, and conceded 32 in his first two overs. That six broke Chappell's bat. "What a way for a bat to go!" he said later. All Gilmour on the boundary could do was watch, open-mouthed, as the ball sailed over the 'Gabba dog track. One straight blast struck the umpire at the bowler's end, Tom Warwick, in the small of his back.

The crowd of over 4,000 took up the chant of "Chappell! Chappell!" or "Trimble! Trimble!", depending on which of their heroes was on strike. Fifty was passed in the fifth over, in 28 minutes, the 100 in two balls less than 10 overs, 24 minutes later. After the match, Chappell called his innings "my proudest for Queensland". It ended when he tried to put Walters into the spectators beyond mid-on, but holed out to Colley. The opening onslaught was worth 146 spectacular runs. Thomson came in to slog, but was bowled immediately. Then Martin Kent arrived to keep Trimble company to the finish.

The crowd roared "Sam! Sam! Sam!" as the winning hit was made. He had played in a manner none thought possible. Originally it seemed he was there to poach the singles, but then he caught the hitting bug — and for an afternoon was a superstar. Later he shifted the congratulations to his captain. "When you are batting with Greg it's a bit easier. They tended to concentrate on him and forget about me." He was mobbed by happy teammates as he ran from the field.

Trimble's 66 had him within 413 of Sir Donald Bradman's record for the most runs scored in the Shield. Tantalisingly close, the veteran Queenslander was not to be the man to break Sir Donald's record. His form deteriorated, and with two matches left in the season he was dropped, after his last six innings yielded just 60 runs. Continual rain, which seemed to follow the Queenslanders, and the relentless form of Ian Chappell's South Australians meant that Trimble would not go out with a Shield winner's blazer. For all the glory and joy of that fabulous afternoon in October 1975, Sam Trimble would no doubt gladly have swapped that memory for just one Shield championship.

# 60

# A STATE ON STRIKE

Of all the long summers of Sheffield Shield cricket, the most controversial was 1975–76. It was a bitter season, one of disputes between players and players, players and umpires, players and selectors, players and officials. Many of these events involved the Shield champions, South Australia, and their leader, Ian Chappell. In a sensational four months the following incidents occurred:

• In a match between South Australia and NSW in Adelaide, Chappell dropped his cricket trousers to adjust his thigh pad, which had become loose. Unfortunately the exercise was captured by news photographers, and the sight of Chappell baring his backside to the public was printed throughout the newspapers of Australia the next day. In the same match he bowled an over of head high full tosses, in protest at the failure of his opposing captain Doug Walters to declare the NSW innings. Chappell was later warned by the SACA over the second incident, and also for swearing on the field. Three other South Australian players, the Test spinners Ashley Mallett and Terry Jenner, and the exciting young paceman, Wayne Prior, were also reported by the umpires for swearing.

• In the South Australia-Victoria match in Melbourne, Chappell was reported for abusing the umpires, both on the field and in the dressing rooms. He admitted to telling the umpires to "get stuffed" and was later severely reprimanded by the Australian Cricket Board. Chappell later expressed regret for his actions.

• The Victoria v Western Australia match in Perth featured a series of running exchanges between Lillee, WA captain Rod Marsh and Victorian all-rounder Trevor Laughlin. Earlier in the game Max Walker, a capable, but limited late-order batsman, had been struck in the face by a Lillee bouncer. Walker was taken to hospital.

• During the South Australia-Western Australia match at the Adelaide Oval, Mallett flung his bat at the

*The South Australian captain, Ian Chappell, batting against NSW at the SCG in 1975-76. Chappell scored a century. This was the first match after the South Australians had threatened to go on strike, in protest at the workings of their state's selection committee.*

ground, apparently in disgust, after receiving a series of bouncers from Lillee.

• Against Victoria in Adelaide, Mallett repeated his bat-throwing escapade when struck on the thigh, fingers and forearm by the fast bowler Alan Hurst. Chappell and Hurst had words after Mallett was hit for the third time. After the match, Mallett, recalling similar incidents that occurred at the ground during the bodyline Test series in 1932–33, commented on the Hurst's tactics: "There was only one team playing cricket out there. I can take one bouncer an over, but not four as he was bowling."

The Victoria-South Australia clash was the match of the season, a tense contest won by a fantastic second innings effort by Chappell, who batted for more than seven hours for 171, as the home side made a gallant fourth-innings rally to win by two wickets. Chappell, in on the third afternoon at 1–37, was not dismissed until only six runs were needed for victory, at 7–358. The win virtually guaranteed the Shield for Chappell and his men, who had mounted a remarkable revival after finishing a dismal last in the previous two seasons.

Chappell was a great cricket captain, considered by some to be an even better leader than Bradman or Benaud. He was fortunate to play under a leader as innovative as Les Favell, from whom he discovered the value of playing adventurous, attractive, aggressive cricket. Lillee wrote of Chappell's captaincy: "Chappell was a born leader and the players liked his style. He led by example. He understood that everyone was different. He was master of situations and made every member of the side feel like a part of what was happening." Chappell led South Australia to two Shield titles, scored 22 centuries in the competition, and on five occasions scored three hundreds in a Shield season.

In February 1976, *Cricketer* asked Ian Chappell how he wanted to be remembered. This was Chappell's reply:

"Just as someone who tried to play cricket as it was meant to be played. As someone who gave everything he had to the game and tried to win as often as possible. Not only as someone who enjoyed himself but who also made it enjoyable for the others around him — not only the spectators but the other players as well. In other words, putting your own personality on the game. I love playing, I enjoy playing, and I enjoy winning."

Of the Shield victory in 1975–76, Ashley Mallett wrote in his book *Spin Out*: "It was a great, total team effort. The team spirit was tremendous and, of course, this was something started by Chappell, something which became self-generating. Everyone helped each other. There was no jealousy, or selfishness between any of the players in the side that year."

The team was a combination of the experience of Chappell, Mallett, Jenner and Ashley Woodcock, and the precocity of young batsmen such as Gary Cosier, David Hookes, Rick Darling and the belligerent fastman, Prior. Chappell scored 840 runs, to lead the Shield aggregates, Cosier did enough to make the Test side. Mallett and Prior led the bowling, with 38 and 33 wickets respectively. Five matches were won outright, as the Shield was gained comfortably from the nearest rivals, Queensland.

Unfortunately much of the fervour that was generated by the team's success was stifled by events that occurred following the defeat of Victoria in Adelaide. Put in simplest terms, on February 23, 1976, the team went on strike. The dispute arose from the South Australian selectors' decision to select a 13-man squad to travel to Sydney and Brisbane for the final matches of the season. It had never been thought necessary to send 13 men on this tour before. The selectors were men of great standing and experience in South Australian cricket; Phil Ridings, Les Favell and Geff Noblet. In naming their 13 they had sacked opener Rick Drewer from the team. Drewer had been out of form, and only 12th man for the Victoria match.

Ian Chappell was disappointed with the squad. He did not argue with the decision to omit Drewer, but was angry that money was to be wasted on what he saw as an unnecessary 13th man. The selectors' logic was that as Prior had missed the Victorian game with an injured ankle, they had chosen the all-rounder Bob Blewett as an insurance policy if Prior's injury flared again. Chappell believed Prior was fit, and the extra man would be going on little more than an all-expenses-paid cricket holiday.

There had been ill-feeling between the SACA officals and some senior players since Chappell and Mallett had written provocative articles in the April 1975 issue of *Cricketer* under the headline: "The Tragedy of South Australia". In his essay Mallett was highly critical of the SA selectors. The carpeting of Chappell, Mallett, Jenner and Prior early in the season for what appeared trivial incidents did not help matters, and the conflict reached a climax with the players' strike.

The squad for the eastern tour had been selected on the third evening of the match against Victoria, while Chappell was in the early stages of his match-winning innings. That night Chappell had rung Ridings and asked why he had not been consulted as to the make-up of the side. Ridings explained that this had not been possible because Chappell had been batting at the time. Chappell voiced his protest at the selection of a 13th man, and told Ridings that if Prior convinced him of his fitness at the nets the next morning, he (Chappell) would not be available to captain, or play in the two remaining Shield matches.

The next day, while Chappell was playing his epic innings, senior players were organising a team meeting to be held after the game was concluded. At that meeting the players opted to withdraw from the eastern tour, as a unit, unless the decision to select a 13th man was rescinded. Later that evening, the SACA informed the players that a new squad would be selected the following day. Any player who wanted to change his mind had until the next morning to do so.

The younger players were advised by their senior colleagues to make themselves available, which they did. Gradually the strike dissolved. The younger players called Woodcock, and asked him to try to get their captain to change his mind. Chappell fielded pleas from Woodcock and Mallett, before a call from Blewett, asking if his withdrawal would make any difference, finally convinced Chappell he should travel with his team. Chappell explained to Blewett the dispute was not over him personally, rather a protest at what the players saw as a waste of money. Later that morning Woodcock rang the SACA and informed them that he, Mallett, Jenner and Chappell would be available to tour. The storm having abated, the originally selected squad travelled east, where they played two washed out draws to ensure the Shield returned to Adelaide.

The strike drew extensive coverage in the press throughout the country. The weekly *National Times*, which usually concerned itself with political or sociological issues, ran a lengthy piece on the drama. Much play was made of the thrifty ways of the SACA (one story suggested the Association had given the players — all 12 of them — $50 for celebratory drinks after the Victorian match), but in the main the players' action was painted in a less than favourable light.

The SACA later took no disciplinary action against the players, and the affair died a tame, uneventful death. Before the next season, Les Favell resigned as a state selector, and Chappell moved to Melbourne, to play pennant cricket with the North Melbourne club. Jenner retired after the first Shield match of the season, Mallett after being dropped from the Australian team. Woodcock lost form, and played only four matches. South Australia went back to the basement, finishing a poor last in the Shield.

This dispute, like the ripple-heeled boots fiasco in Sydney six seasons earlier, appears years later to have been a ridiculous conflict over a minor issue. The major difference between the two was that whereas the boots affair was brought to a head by the administrators, in Adelaide, the discontent was highlighted by the players. What both incidents showed was that in this turbulent era of cricket in Australia the relationship between the sport's leading players and its key officials had all but reached the bankruptcy stage. A major explosion was imminent. The South Australian players strike was the forerunner to a rebellion of a much bigger kind — the turmoil and extravagance of World Series Cricket.

# 61

## LILLEE AND MARSH

Dennis Lillee's first scalp in the Sheffield Shield was the wicket of Queensland captain Sam Trimble, caught at short leg by Derek Chadwick on the first day of November, 1969. Lillee was a young, fast, none-too-subtle bowler, who charged off a long, angled run with arms swinging about in an illogical fashion. His second wicket came much later in the day, when Keith Dudgeon was caught behind. His keeper was Rodney Marsh, who, with the retirement of Gordon Becker, had taken over as WA first choice custodian.

Marsh had beaten Lillee into the Shield by a season. In 1968–69 Marsh had played four matches as a batsman, with limited success, although he did keep wickets for a portion of the South Australian second innings in Adelaide. There he snared his first Shield catch as a keeper, Ken Cunningham, off the bowling of Laurie Mayne. However the match in Brisbane at the start of the 1969–70 season was his genuine debut as his state's wicketkeeper. It is not drawing too long a bow to suggest that he and Lillee started out along their cricketing paths together.

In his 1975 autobiography *You'll Keep*, Marsh recalled early days at the WACA Ground, watching the great Queensland and Australian keeper Wally Grout in action. "Though I didn't know as much then about the mechanics of wicketkeeping as I do now," Marsh wrote, "I can still say he's the best keeper I've seen. Though I didn't want to model my keeping on Wally's, I set myself to be his equal with the gloves." Grout holds the record for the most catches and most dismissals by a keeper in one Shield innings — eight, in the first Western Australian innings against Queensland in February 1960. When Marsh finally retired, this was one of the few keeping records he had not claimed.

In Marsh's first season as keeper he dismissed 28 Shield batsmen, 21 caught and seven stumped. Eight of them came from Lillee's bowling. The tearaway fast bowler had 30 dismissals, and won selection in the Australian team that made a short tour of New Zealand at the tailend of the season. Marsh missed out, the keeper's spot going to the young Queenslander John Maclean. This side was no more than a "second XI"; the cream of Australia's cricketers were in South Africa at the time, taking a thrashing from the Springboks.

The first choice Australian keeper then was Brian Taber, from NSW. Taber had equalled Edward Pooley and Don Tallon's world record of 12 dismissals in one first-class match in NSW's game in Adelaide in December 1968, but did not have a happy series in South Africa. For the 1970–71 Ashes campaign the selectors decided to replace him, not with the second string from the tour, the Victorian Ray Jordon, or Maclean — but with Marsh, largely because, it was generally accepted, Marsh had superior credentials with the bat.

In 1969–70 Marsh's performances had been impressive, but there was speculation about how far the beefy bloke from the west could go in big-time cricket. Marsh had responded to the comments about his shape and athleticism with a dedicated fitness campaign that had him in better trim than ever before. In the sixth match of his first Test series, Marsh was joined by Lillee, always a fitness fanatic, who won his cap largely through the dual components of pace and promise. He had taken 7–36 against South Australia the previous summer, but had struggled on WA's eastern tour early in 1970–71. With the return of Graham McKenzie to the state side he had been obliged to bowl the second over, but when McKenzie returned to Test duty, Lillee once more had the breeze at his back, and his form and confidence returned.

The summer of 1971–72 was the making of the pair. In the eastern states, and especially in Sydney, a media campaign was mounted for the return of Taber to the Australian side. Marsh, who had worked with such determination in the off-season on his skills and his fitness, responded in the manner of a champion, and by the end of the season had established himself as the best keeper in the country. In the Shield he took 22 catches in six matches. Lillee emerged the dominant bowler in the country, and took 24 Shield wickets, including returns of 6–24 and 4–46 against Queensland, and 5–75 against Victoria. His run-up was now straighter, though still very much a charge at the batsman, but he was beautifully balanced in his delivery stride and mustered speed unmatched by any other top-line bowler in the world.

In the years that followed the sight of Marsh leaping and diving to pull in Lillee's fastest deliveries was one of the most stirring in Australian cricket. It is difficult to believe there has ever been a more effective keeper standing back to fast bowlers than Rod Marsh. Such was the plethora of quality fast and fast-medium bowlers who played for Western Australia in the '70s — Lillee, McKenzie, Massie, Watson, Brayshaw, Malone, Alderman, Clark, Gannon — that it was nigh impossible for Marsh to build any reputation as a keeper to spin bowlers. But occasionally he would produce a stumping, such as the one that dismissed Ian Chappell the day Barry Richards cut loose at the WACA in 1970–71, that suggested he would not have been out of place in the years when legends such as Carter, Oldfield and Tallon were plying their trade.

Lillee's career was all-but ended by a crippling back injury in 1973. He did not bowl a ball in 1973–74, but eventually made it back — with a more sober, less frenzied delivery, after a battle with injury as brave as any in the history of the game. In his comeback game, in Adelaide, he bowled 28 overs for 4–82 and 3–40, without ever generating the pace that had made him famous — although Ian Chappell commented that he had hit the bat harder than any bowler he had faced the previous season. In Melbourne he took four wickets from 37 overs, in Sydney four wickets from 45 overs. The match against NSW was dominated by batsmen, with five centuries scored, two by the Blues' Rick McCosker, and one each by Wally Edwards, Bruce Laird and Marsh, who, from number three, hammered the local bowlers for an unbeaten 168, his highest Shield score. This match ended in a fabulous fashion, WA making a gallant but unsuccessful chase for 180 in the final 15 overs. They finished 29 short, with two wickets left, after John Inverarity called off the chase in the penultimate over.

Gradually Lillee worked back to something close to his fastest speed. His comeback was crowned by a sequence of magnificent performances in the Test series, where he and Jeff Thomson came together to blast the Ashes from the Englishmen. It became fully apparent that not only was Lillee a fabulously gifted paceman, he was also an artful, highly intelligent exponent of the art of fast bowling. Marsh was his aggressive comrade, and the pivotal figure in a superb bowling and fielding team. In the Shield, Marsh had his best day of the season against NSW in Perth, when he took six catches on the first day, including the

*Above: The belligerent batting style of Rodney Marsh, the best wicketkeeper/batsman to appear in the Shield since Don Tallon. Inset: Dennis Lillee bowling against NSW in 1971.*

top five men in the order. He played in all eight matches for WA, dismissing 43 batsmen, a Shield record, as his state won the trophy for the third time in four years.

The following season Marsh, now the Western Australian captain, had his best ever return from a first-class match. In the Shield game against Victoria in Perth he held 11 catches, equalling the world record established by Surrey's Arnold Long in 1964. Six of the catches came from Lillee's fast bowling. The match was won on the final day by a spirited 76 by…inevitably…Marsh, as WA scraped home by four wickets.

Later in the season Lillee produced his most lucrative performance of the competition, 7–41 and 5–72 against South Australia in Adelaide, as the eventual Shield champions were defeated in three exciting days. On the first day South Australia were bowled out for 87, but clever bowling by the off-spinner Ashley Mallett brought his side back into the game. Lillee, with Mick Malone, had South Australia out quickly again, but Mallett and the slow-medium Gary Cosier reduced WA to 6–62, chasing 150, before Kim Hughes and Ian Brayshaw stopped the rot and got their side over the line.

The Lillee and Marsh story rolled on. In 1976–77, Lillee twice took 10 wickets in Shield games, and Marsh had a wonderful match against South Australia, scoring 104 and taking 10 catches. Then came World Series Cricket, and the Shield had to make do without their champions, Marsh, Lillee and the rest. When they returned in 1979 the Shield saw less of them, as the hectic schedule of Tests, tours and one-day internationals took precedence.

In 1984 Rod Marsh and Dennis Lillee announced their retirements — going out in appropriate fashion as key figures in a Shield championship-winning side. With the regular WA captain, Kim Hughes, continually on Test duty, Lillee took over as leader that season. During the season he passed Tony Lock's record of 302 Shield wickets for WA In the Shield final against Queensland in Perth his rival skipper was Jeff Thomson. Also in the Queensland side (and playing his final first-class match) was Greg Chappell.

Lillee's brief reign as captain was not without its controversy. In Brisbane he had a heated discussion with the umpires over the taking of a drinks break during a rain-affected pre-lunch session. There had earlier been much acrimony over a rejected appeal for a catch behind. The umpires had ruled that no drinks break would be taken, but Lillee literally ignored them. He was reported by the umpires to a players' disciplinary committee, who exonerated him. The umpires then appealed to the ACB, who rejected the original verdict and suspended Lillee for two Shield matches and fined him $1,000. Lillee took his case to the Supreme Court and won an injunction that allowed him to play grade cricket in Perth. Later the court ruled that the suspension should stand, which meant that Lillee missed the last two matches of the regular season (when Marsh took over as captain), but returned for the Shield final.

The final was a match that Queensland might have won, especially after they batted first for 7 (declared) for 431 and gained a first-innings lead of 68. But the WA bowlers fought back on the fourth day, and the fourth-innings requirement was a modest 223. At 5–138 the fate of the Shield was still in the balance, but Marsh came out to join the diminutive former Test opener Bruce Laird, also in his last Shield match, and the pair added 61 to secure the victory. Marsh was out for 45, but Laird remained unbeaten on 54 when the winning run was struck, to complete WA's seventh Shield triumph in 13 seasons.

For Rod Marsh this was the end; but Dennis Lillee was not quite finished. In 1987–88 he made a shock return to the Shield, playing five matches for Tasmania, for 15 wickets, including a dividend of 4–99 against South Australia in Devonport. It was a long way from the glory days, and his image was tarnished by a peculiar episode involving the great English all-rounder Ian Botham who was in Australia trying to do what many others had been unable to do before him — win the Shield for Queensland. Lillee and Botham were alleged to have caused substantial damage to a dressing room in Launceston, and were later fined by the ACB. This was not Botham's only mishap that season. He was also disciplined for using offensive language in a Shield match in Melbourne, and again following incidents on a plane taking the Queensland team to Perth for that year's final. Botham had signed a three-year deal with the QCA, but did not return for the final two years of the contract.

Lillee's wicket-taking record for WA was surpassed by Terry Alderman during the 1989–90 season. But no-one, least of all Alderman, the superb fast-medium seamer, would claim that he was a superior bowler. Lillee was undisputably the best of his time, and perhaps the best fastman of them all. No bowler has ever combined pace, skill, intelligence, courage, and passion in quite the unique way he did. Through it all, Marsh was his ally, providing support and guidance, and his own special skills. Marsh could fairly claim to have achieved his ambition of being the equal of the great Wally Grout. Many would suggest he might have reached a mark even slightly higher. He and Lillee were two of the greatest competitors and cricketers to walk onto a Sheffield Shield ground — but more important than that, they were a team, the most effective bowler-keeper pairing in the modern game.

# 62

## HURRICANE HOOKES

When David Hookes strode onto the Adelaide Oval to face the Victorian bowlers on February 4, 1977, he brought with him a Shield career batting average of 23.64, from 15 innings; highest score 54. In 1976–77 he had scored 35 Shield runs, at 8.75, in a season interrupted by university studies. In his most recent Shield match, a month earlier in Perth, he had scored one and three.

Four hours later he departed in triumph, having accomplished his maiden first-class century in a stunning display of power and timing. He scored 163, including 10 fours and seven sixes. It was the beginning of a run of scoring unprecedented in the competition's history. In six innings, against Victoria, Queensland and NSW over three successive weeks, David Hookes scored five hundreds, all of them dazzling, all of them special. The runs were scored while the Australian team was in New Zealand, playing a two-Test series. Within a month Hookes was in that Australian side, playing in the Centenary Test match at the MCG, purely on the weight of his runs. Australian cricket was probably still not quite sure what to think about him.

On the morning of the South Australia-Victoria Shield match in February, the Victorian opening bowler Colin Corstorphin had to withdraw with a back injury. After a hasty conference between senior players and officials, it was decided that the all-rounder Brendan McArdle would be brought from Melbourne. For almost the first two sessions the Victorians were effectively one man short as McArdle did not arrive at Adelaide airport until just before 3pm. He dashed to the ground, quickly changed, and on running onto the oval, was placed by his captain, wicketkeeper Richie Robinson, on the wide mid-on boundary, for the flighty leg breaks of Colin Thwaites.

McArdle's first role in the match was to fetch the ball from deep in the grandstand, as Hookes hit Thwaites for a huge six to bring up his fifty. The next two balls went the same way, as did the fifth. McArdle could not have dreamed that Sheffield Shield cricket was about this. In all 29 runs came from the over, and in 14 balls Hookes went from 49 to 85.

Hookes had taken 113 minutes to reach his first 50, as if he was trying to rid himself of a reputation for throwing away promising situations. In the previous season, his first in the Shield, he had been dismissed nine times, from eleven starts, between 15 and 54. Once past 50 against Victoria he went berserk, and the hundred was claimed in just 36 extra minutes. In a stand of 116 for the sixth wicket with wicketkeeper Russell Vincent, Hookes scored 90.

In the second innings he was bowled by a grubber for only nine, as South Australia disintegrated for just 86, to lose by an innings. For the team, the heady days of the season before had been long forgotten. Three men captained the side during the season, none with success, and rumours were about that Greg Chappell was to be enticed back to his home state. This came to nothing and instead the state's one Test batsman, the former Victorian Gary Cosier, eventually transferred to Queensland. Just about all the South Australian cricket fans had to cheer were the runs of David Hookes.

Hookes and the short Adelaide Oval boundaries at cover and mid-wicket added up to a marriage made in cricket heaven. He faced staring intently over his right shoulder as the bowler approached, feet straddled slightly wider than the norm. In form he was ruthless on anything wide outside the off stump and timed the ball as well as anyone in the game. He captured many of his runs off the back foot, and could hook the fastest bowlers. Most of all, it seemed, he loved to swing slow bowlers away over the leg side fence.

His hundred in the first innings against Queensland was a characteristically powerhouse affair, especially between lunch and tea, when he smashed 94 runs. He had been in at 3–14, after Queensland paceman Colin Cooke ran through the top order. Hookes reached his fifty in 57 minutes, his hundred in two hours, and slowed only when struck with an attack of cramps after tea. His last 22 runs took an hour and he was finally dismissed for 185 after 260 sensational minutes.

In the pre-lunch session of the final day he scored another century, this time in 91 minutes off 82 balls. In two overs from the Sri Lankan-born leg spinner Malcolm Francke he smashed 35 runs. All up he hit 11 fours and two sixes. This innings was the first glowing feature of one of the Shield's most thrilling days. South Australian captain Bob Blewett set the Queenslanders 263 to win in 152 minutes plus 15 overs.

When the last hour arrived the target was 103, with seven wickets still in hand. In the sixth last over, the fifth wicket, Queensland skipper John Maclean, was lost, with 34 still wanted. Two more wickets fell

*The young Allan Border, batting for NSW in 1976–77.*

Australia. Thoroughly ravaged by the generous Packer offers, WA dipped deep into their extraordinary cricket reservoir, and somehow found men capable of retaining the Shield in 1977–78 and of influencing Australian cricket in the years that followed. They were fortunate that John Inverarity had returned from England to reclaim the captaincy. Without Lillee and Malone, the pace bowling became the responsibility of Wayne Clark, Terry Alderman and Sam Gannon. Rod Marsh was replaced by Kevin Wright. Laird's place at the top of the batting order was filled by the left-handed Graeme Wood. Bruce Yardley and Tony Mann remained to provide the spin, Kim Hughes and Craig Serjeant the runs in the middle order.

Against NSW and Border, WA were without Hughes, Wood and Yardley, all required in Brisbane for the first Test against Mike Brearley's Englishmen. Hilditch, playing his first game in Perth, was the NSW captain. Inverarity, who had been playing at the WACA from almost the time Hilditch was born, won the toss, sent NSW in, and watched his bowlers humble the young batsmen for just 166. Border batted 114 minutes for 26, Hilditch 160 for 44. Three of the NSW batsmen were struck agonising blows. Steve Rixon, the rejected Test keeper, batted at number three, but smashed his left hand. David Johnston, at number five, fractured a knuckle. Bob Vidler, at number seven, broke a forearm. Johnston carried on, while Vidler left the field but later came back to reach 38 not out. When the innings ended all three were taken away for x-rays, and ruled out of the match.

Inverarity declared WA's first innings at 9–283, 40 minutes before stumps on the second day. Hilditch took 12 from the first over of the second innings, and he and Dyson survived to the close, and then continued the next morning, grafting 128 for the first wicket before the captain was bowled by Alderman. Dyson and Border carried on, Dyson in a helmet, Border a cap, to 191 before Dyson ran himself out seeking a single to Geoff Marsh at mid-off. Then came something of a collapse. Graeme Beard had batted eight in the first innings. Now he was in at number four, but hit a full toss straight to Inverarity at mid-on. Graeme Hughes, the first man in almost 50 years to play cricket and rugby league for NSW, was confused by Mann, and departed, lbw. Lawson, who had batted nine on the first day, came out at six, and stayed with Border for the last 69 minutes of the afternoon.

At stumps Border was 66, after 227 minutes of stoic defence, and NSW 4–269. He had refused to play at anything remotely wide of the off stump, unless the ball was poor enough to demand a square cut. He relied on nudges through the leg side field, and his superb concentration, to get him to tomorrow. Ken Cassellas in the *West Australian* wrote the next morning: "He looks sure to play for Australia this summer."

The next day Border went on to 135, before offering an exhausted edge to the wicketkeeper. He had batted for another 162 minutes, continuing on with Lawson for more than an hour, and then with another fast bowler, Greg Watson, for 96 minutes. When Border was finally out, the outright result was gone, but the West Australians did not need David Hourn, as inadequate a batsman as had played for NSW, to come out and strike 22 runs in 23 ridiculous minutes. When Watson was caught, at 7–408, Hilditch closed the innings, his only remaining batsmen having their arms in slings or plaster casts.

A week later Border scored another century, against Victoria in Sydney, and before the season was over had hit a third, off the Tasmanians. He was the only man to score three Shield centuries that season. The following summer, Greg Chappell gave him the number three spot in the national side, and the stiff international schedule kept him to just one Shield appearance for NSW. In Brisbane he scored a sparkling 200 in what proved to be his last match for his home state. A lucrative offer co-ordinated by Brisbane businessmen lured Border north, on the same road travelled by Jeff Thomson six years earlier. He scored a century in his first match for his new home, 106 against NSW at the 'Gabba, but his impact on the Shield in the years that followed was limited by a never-ending sequence of Tests, one-day internationals and overseas tours.

He played only 60 of Queensland's 123 Shield matches between 1980–81 and 1991–92. Between 1983–84 and 1988–89 he was captain, and in those years, led his side into three Shield finals — but like Greg Chappell before him, never to the trophy. For much of his cricket career he was as dominant a figure in the Australian batting order as had been only Bradman, and perhaps Trumper, before him. At the same time, his influence on the Shield can be judged less significant, solely because of commitments that resulted from the exacting schedules drawn up in post-WSC days. It is ironic that while World Series Cricket did not take Border from the Sheffield Shield, the aftermath did.

# 64

## FLAT JACK

The first ever first-class cricket match played in Australia, on February 11 and 12, 1851, was won by Tasmania, by three wickets over Victoria at the Launceston racecourse. However, forty years later, when the Sheffield Shield was being devised, no one thought of inviting the Tasmanians. They were left with no more than the visits of interstate second elevens and international touring teams to satisfy their hunger for top grade cricket. If the state did produce a cricketer of quality, such as Jack Badcock, Doug Ring or Max Walker, he was quickly lost to the mainland. It was not until nearly 130 years after that historic first match that the best of contemporary Tasmanian cricketers at last got their chance in a Sheffield Shield match.

When the island state was finally invited to come and play, in 1977–78, it was on a provisional basis much in the manner of the Western Australian entry thirty years before. Three games were played at home, one in Melbourne, and one in Perth. The first season was without an outright win, but not without its encouraging signs. The home matches were shared between the capital city, Hobart, and the provincial centres, Launceston and Devonport, and all attracted healthy crowds. This concept, of promoting the competition in country areas, was later adopted by the associations of the mainland states, with some success.

In that first season the Tasmanians were permitted two overseas imports. These men were the crafty veteran Lancashire off-spinner "Flat" Jack Simmons, who was appointed captain, and the former England batsman Jack Hampshire. Also in side was the occasional WA Shield pace bowler Dennis Baker, the first of a stream of interstate imports to fill the Tasmanian Shield side in the years that followed. During the season Hampshire scored two centuries on his way to almost 500 runs, and the gritty right-hander Roger Woolley, brought into the side for the home matches, managed 49 and 55 against South Australia, and a stirring century against Queensland, becoming the first Tasmanian-born batsmen to score a Shield century for his home state. Of the skipper, *Wisden* wrote: "The principal value of Simmons lay in long experience and his leadership; he achieved little with bat or ball."

Twelve months later, *Wisden* was much more positive in assessing the skipper's contribution. "It is doubtful if a state has so successfully called for a greater personal effort in the Sheffield Shield competition than Tasmania did of their stalwart captain, Jack Simmons," was the almanack's summary. His side was in a fighting mood early in the season, earning creditable draws in Adelaide and Brisbane, and a stunning victory in the interstate one-day competition, the Gillette Cup. Simmons' form in these matches was inspiring. He scored a gutsy 103 from number eight against South Australia, and snared seven Queensland wickets for 59 in the first innings at the 'Gabba — the best figures of his career. In the one-day final against Western Australia, he scored a crucial, unbeaten 56, and then took 4–17 from 10 overs as WA crumbled to be all out for 133.

The match in Queensland marked the debut of a short but stocky 17-year-old batsman David Boon, who scored a tidy 22 batting six — and turned out to be a personal nightmare for Woolley, who was dismissed by the first ball he faced in both innings. In the Gillette Cup semi-final, played while Tasmania were in Brisbane, Woolley managed a third duck.

The selectors persevered with Woolley for the match against Western Australia, although had he not also been the side's keeper this loyalty may not have been so forthcoming. Boon was unfortunate — relegated to 12th man. On the day before the match the Australian Cricket Board announced that the Tasmanians would remain in the Shield on a trial basis for a further two seasons, a decision which rocked many in the state, who had believed that full membership of the Shield "club" had been rightly earned. However there had been some criticism of the Tasmanians on the mainland, not least from the South Australian captain Bob Blewett, who before the match between the two states in Adelaide, had publically questioned whether Tasmania had any right to be in the competition at all.

In Devonport for the WA match, the chairman of the Tasmanian selectors, Bob Ingamells, said of the ACB ruling: "They've treated us as though we're not even part of Australia." Simmons commented: "Surely the improvement we've shown in the past two years warrants our full admission. The only way to answer the ACB is to win our first Shield match and show them just how wrong they were."

After two days play things looked fairly grim for Simmons and his men, with WA at 2–40 in their second innings, having already built a first-innings lead of 124. John Inverarity had scored a typically gritty century on the first day, then declared overnight and watched his fast-medium attack of Wayne Clark, Terry Alderman and Graeme Porter rip through the local batting. Only the burly allrounder Tony Benneworth, who hit out for 42, managed to curb the Western Australians. At one stage Tasmania had been 8–80. Later that evening Simmons told reporters: "Don't give up on us yet. It's a long shot but we can still win. We've got a good chance of getting the runs, don't you worry about that."

When Inverarity closed his second innings not long after tea on the third day, he left the Tasmanians ample time to score 356. The locals' response was encouraging, an opening stand of 51 in little more than an hour between Gary Goodman and Mick Norman. When Goodman was dismissed just before stumps, caught-and-bowled by Inverarity, Simmons sent Benneworth in to hold the fort, which he did, but only just. The WA captain would spend much of the final day rueing the catch he dropped from the big Tasmanian in the dying minutes of the third afternoon.

Norman was out early on the final day, but Benneworth remained, to hammer his second valuable innings of the match. He was hampered by a shoulder he had damaged in the Gillette Cup final, but still swung lustily for 75. At lunch Tasmania were 4–147, soon after 5–160, and then when Benneworth skied Tony Mann to Ric Charlesworth at cover point, 6–187.

Simmons came out to join Woolley, who had been doing little to suggest he was running back into form. In the first innings the keeper had struggled to 23, scarcely a confidence booster, and now he was batting, in the words of Simmons, "like an old woman". The captain himself was little better, and Inverarity moved in for the kill. Western Australia needed the outright points to get back in the Shield race.

There is nothing an out-of-touch cricketer needs more than an overdose of good fortune, and gradually Woolley edged himself back into form. Simmons was the cagey pro, his many seasons told him batting badly was much better than not batting at all. At tea the partnership was worth 61, the requirement for the win 109 in an hour plus 15 eight-ball overs. There was no suggestion that Tasmania would not be going for the win. Simmons and Woolley came out after the break to swing, drive and run their way to a remarkable and unlikely victory.

Simmons was soon lofting the Western Australian bowlers into the outfield, and encouraging his partner to dash for singles. Woolley was now superb, driving the spinners easily and powerfully, and emphasising to the faster men how little remained in the Devonport wicket. When the 15 overs began the target was 51, and after two maidens, Inverarity played his last card, the part-time leg breaks of Kevin Prindiville. He, like Simmons, was interested in no less than a win.

Unfortunately Prindiville's line was as poor as his length, and Woolley helped himself to a succession of long hops and half trackers that pitched outside the leg stump. Fourteen runs came from the over that effectively decided the match. A succession of twos took Woolley to 99, and brought the scores level — before Simmons edged Clark through to the vacant fine leg fence for the winning run, with six overs still remaining. The stand had been worth 172 in 179 exciting minutes. Only five other Shield sides since the Second World War had scored more than 350 runs in the fourth innings to win.

After the game Simmons and his jubilant team were presented live on national television, as 2,000 happy local supporters remained at the ground. Inverarity was generous in defeat. "We're a side that always has a go," he commented. "Tasmania did the same out there today and did it well. Good luck to them." His side would come back to win its last two matches outright, but finish only second, well behind the new Shield champions, Victoria.

Simmons did not return to Tasmania after the 1978–79 season, which ended disappointingly after the fervour of Devonport. Matches against Victoria and NSW were lost by an innings. It would not be until 1982–83 that Tasmania would become a fully fledged member of the Sheffield Shield. Simmons continued on in first-class cricket with Lancashire until he retired, aged 48, in 1989. He was one of *Wisden's* five Cricketers of the Year in 1985, more for his overall contribution to the game than his performances in the 1984 season, though in that year he had his most lucrative season for the county, taking 63 wickets. In Tasmania he is remembered with great affection. In the years that followed the state imported a vast number of quality Test cricketers from interstate and abroad, men of the calibre and experience of Michael Holding, Richard Hadlee and Dennis Lillee. None were more popular than "Flat" Jack Simmons.

*The leading run-scorer in the first 100 years of the Sheffield Shield — David Hookes.*

*The great Queensland fast bowler Jeff Thomson, bowling on the third day of the thrilling 1984–85 final at the SCG, a match eventually won by the last NSW partnership.*

# 65
## STRAIGHT HIT

Victoria v NSW matches in the 1970s were often highly dramatic, turbo-charged affairs, very definitely in line with the tradition of intense competition which had started back in 1856. But something was *extra* special about these games in this turbulent decade of cricket in Australia — as men such as Walters, McCosker and Lawson battled with Redpath, Walker, and John Leehane.

John Leehane? He was talented right-arm fast bowler who led the Victorian attack in their successful Shield season of 1979–80, and a batsman of extremely modest means, with a career highest score in the Shield of seven. His moment of real Shield glory ironically however came with the bat — and it concerned the last ball bowled in a match between the competition's most traditional rivals in the 1970s. Leehane struck a thundering blow to the MCG boundary which would, when competition points were added up three months later, prove to be the shot that won his side the Shield.

Here are a few of the other extraordinary chapters that were written in the Victoria-NSW cricket story in the decade of the '70s:

• In 1971–72 the two matches were both won by an innings. In Sydney, Bruce Francis and Doug Walters scored big hundreds, as NSW hammered the Victorian bowling for 497, but at the MCG, the New South Welshmen could make only 9 (declared) for 67 and 105 as Victoria won their biggest victory over the traditional rivals since 1926.

• In 1972–73 both matches went down to the wire. In Melbourne the home side lost all but their last two wickets in scoring the 355 needed to win outright. A week later Victoria required 388 for maximum points but fell 23 runs short, after reaching 6–309. In the Melbourne match Doug Walters scored 133 in the NSW second innings; in Sydney he was dominant, belting 43 and 176 with the bat, and then taking 6–51 to ruin Victoria's victory charge on the final day.

• The match in Melbourne in 1974–75 was the 200th between the two states. It developed into an intriguing celebration of the anniversary, with NSW firmly in control for the first two days, but perilously close to surrendering on the final afternoon. NSW number three Rick McCosker had scored his fourth straight Shield century — the most prolific sequence since Bradman in 1938–39 — as NSW won a first innings lead of 205. But Victorian captain Ian Redpath scored 146 to lead a revival, and on the final day his bowlers reduced NSW to 9–90 before time ran out.

• The 1978–79 match in Sydney featured a remarkable bowling spell by the left-arm wrist spinner David Hourn, who destroyed a Victorian innings that at one stage had reached 2–262. In the final hour of the day, Hourn took the last eight wickets, for 17 runs in 36 balls, to finish with 9–77. The match ended in a tame draw, but the return fixture a week later was not decided until the final over, when NSW scraped home by three wickets.

None of them however compared with the extraordinary finish to Leehane's match in Melbourne in late-December 1979. It was a game that was extremely slow to reach its climax — in fact for the first two days the headlines spoke not of excitement but of tedium. "CHRISTMAS BORE AT THE MCG" sniffed *The Sydney Morning Herald*. "DREARY NSW PLODS ON" declared *The Age*.

NSW had crawled their way to 5–217 on the first day, and struggled on to 261 all out. Victoria had been no more attractive in fashioning their reply, which finished 11 runs short. At stumps on day three NSW were 183 runs in front, with five wickets in hand. Still there had been little action. On the third day, as NSW tried to put itself in a dominant position, John Dyson survived for 201 minutes, for 71. When Peter Toohey slammed 21 in even time late in the afternoon, it was the first time in the match a batsman had actively sought to dominate. The next day, Christmas Eve, Walters was assertive as NSW reached 9 (declared) for 234, setting the home side 246 runs in 205 minutes and 20 overs.

After Graham Matthews was caught behind in the first over, Dav Whatmore and David Broad added exactly 100 in quick time to set up the exciting final session. Whatmore ran to 88, before he became the fourth wicket to fall, at 146, hitting the leg spinner Bob Holland to mid-wicket. Jeff Moss and Graham Yallop pushed the score to 182 before both fell, Moss lbw to Holland as he tried to pull, Yallop bowled driving over a Geoff Lawson yorker. At 6–182 Victoria needed 64 in 19 overs for the outright win.

In came Trevor Laughlin, a burly all-rounder, who batted left-handed and was renowned for his hitting. He had played Test cricket during the WSC years, and with some success in the one-day internationals in 1979–80. Strangely against NSW he adopted a more cautious role, as first Ray Bright and then Max Walker hit lustily for the win. Both fell to big hits, and when Walker was out, swinging unsuccessfully at Lawson, Victoria needed 11, and Laughlin had only the marginal talents of numbers 10 and 11, Jim Higgs and Leehane, to keep him company to the finish.

Higgs had, perhaps unfairly, developed a reputation as one of Australia's poorest ever batsmen, a status chiefly earned on the 1975 tour of England, when he failed to score a single first-class run. Higgs was a fine leg spin bowler, but scarcely has a big-time cricketer looked less certain at the crease, or had less power in his drives. As his career unfolded Higgs had worked hard at building a defence that had to be penetrated. Even then, he was never a batsman who could be labelled intimidating. Leehane batted after Higgs. Not many other first-class batsmen did.

Higgs hung on until the final ball of the second last over, while six runs were added, one of them his own, before he aimed a hopeful swing at Lawson and miscued to Ian Davis at mid-off. Laughlin had either miscounted, miscalculated, or knew something no-one else at the ground did, and ran through, losing the strike for the last over. McCosker had perservered with Holland through the final overs, but had been weighing up the value of keeping his leg spinner on. Now, with Leehane on offer, he had no hesitation in handing him the ball for the final over.

Leehane aimed hopful swings at the first two balls, but could not connect. To the third he swung again, missed, but obscured the keeper, Steve Rixon, and the ball ran away for a precious bye. Laughlin was on strike, to the relief of the home supporters, who were fully aware that just one big safe hit could win their state the game. McCosker and Holland conferred, seeking the appropriate balance of aggression and caution. The fourth ball was well up, and Laughlin played it safely down to the fieldsman on the long on fence, who dashed in to prevent a second run. Three to win.

Leehane and Laughlin met in mid-wicket, before Leehane swiped ridiculously and unsuccessfully across the line at the penultimate ball. So far he had faced four balls without once getting bat on ball. He again walked up the pitch to confer with his senior partner. Their conversation was lengthy, as Holland prepared for the vital ball. McCosker did not have to change his field. All he needed was the right delivery.

"You can't play him from the crease," Laughlin told Leehane in mid-pitch. "The only chance we have got is if you go down the wicket and hit him straight."

Leehane had been aiming at the mid-wicket boundary, but now he accepted the advice and swung straight, and true, catching the ball in the unmarked middle of his bat. The ball sailed into the outfield, and crashed against the sightscreen, as NSW fieldsman Trevor Chappell made a desperate but vain sprint from long-on to get to the ball. The two batsmen met in mid-pitch, watching, but not believing the arc of the ball to the boundary, and then ran, arm-in-arm to their colleagues in the dressing room.

The outright win was worth 10 points. At season's end Victoria finished with 130 points, nine more than their closest rivals South Australia.

# 66

# END OF AN ERA

As the key members of Ian Chappell's superb Australian side of the mid-1970s gradually departed from the Sheffield Shield, it was surprising, and a touch ironic that only one, Rod Marsh, managed to make his exit as a winner. The men who had combined to make Australia such a successful Test side could not find that elusive farewell season of Shield glory. The first to leave big-time cricket was Ian Redpath, whose final season for Victoria, in 1975–76, was a dismal one, his side entrenched on the bottom of the table.

*Ian Chappell, in the unlikely role of wicketkeeper, appeals for lbw against the Victorian batsman Jeff Moss during the SA–Victoria match at the MCG in 1979–80. In the final week of the season, the two sides met again in Adelaide, in the match that decided the competition.*

Ross Edwards had played in many victorious WA outfits, but his last year in Shield cricket was as a NSW player, in 1979–80 — a season in which the Blues ended up third. Ashley Mallett retired from first-class cricket after being dropped from the Australian side in 1976–77. That season South Australia finished last. He returned to the Shield after playing in World Series Cricket, and continued until the end of the 1980–81 season, with South Australia again at the bottom of the ladder.

Doug Walters retired after being left out of the Australian side for England in 1981. His state's final Shield season started full of promise, but nosedived near the end, and was finally scuttled by a dreadful batting performance at home against the lowly-rated Tasmanians. Max Walker's final full Shield season was in 1980–81, when Victoria could do no better than fourth, and he was dropped midway through the following season, when his state ran a conspicuous last. Rick McCosker handed over the captaincy of NSW to the much younger Dirk Wellham in 1983–84, and retired at the end of that season, with NSW a distant fourth.

Dennis Lillee, Greg Chappell and Marsh were all supposed to be playing their last Shield match in the final of 1983–84, won by Lillee and Marsh's Western Australia over Chappell's Queensland. But Lillee made a comeback in 1987–88, and ended his Shield career with the perennial cellar-dwellers Tasmania. In Jeff Thomson's final two seasons, 1984–85 and 1985–86, he played for Queensland in the Shield final, both times ending a loser, both times in heartbreaking circumstances.

And what of the captain? Ian Chappell's final Shield game came in March 1980, the last game of the season, between the two sides at the top of the Shield table. Chappell's South Australia led the competition on 115 points, their opponents Victoria were on 111. The match was played on the Adelaide Oval, scene of many Chappell triumphs. Everything was made for a happy ending, but it was not to be.

For Chappell the season was a mixture of what had made him such a significant and splendid cricketer, and equally what had made him such a rebellious and controversial figure. His captaincy was inspiring, assured and effective, his batting outstanding. But his prickly nature brought him into conflict with the umpires, and inevitably the Board. Following an umpires' report of events in the South Australia-Tasmania match in Devonport, Chappell was suspended for three weeks, having been found guilty of using abusive language.

Attendance figures for the Shield in the summer of 1979–80 dropped significantly, as the cricket calendar became more and more clogged with international fixtures. The early matches were played with the Australian team members still in India completing a six-Test series. And before the Shield season was over the Test players were on their way to Pakistan. Lillee and Marsh played only two matches for Western Australia, Kim Hughes none at all. Greg Chappell scored more than 400 runs for Queensland, in three games. Allan Border appeared just once for NSW. And yet while the patrons stayed away, the sponsorship support of the competition boomed, a range of companies jostling for position to be involved.

When Victoria and South Australia met to decide the destiny of the Shield in 1979–80, there was more than just the trophy up for grabs. A win for South Australia would push their season's takings to $70,000 — $30,000 from their major sponsor, the Adelaide Building Society, $20,000 from the local radio station 5DN, $14,000 from the national cricket sponsor, Benson and Hedges, and $6,000 from the members of the Adelaide Oval. The Victorians were in a position to net as much as $79,000, through a variety of sponsorships and incentives. At the start of the season the Victorian team sponsor, Federation Insurance, had offered $10,000 bonuses to any Victorian player who scored 650 Shield runs or captured 45 Shield wickets. Coming into the final match, the left-hander Jeff Moss had 612 runs, and Max Walker had 39 wickets. The side had already picked up a $5,000 bonus for winning the McDonald's Cup one-day competition.

On the first day Moss scored 85 to get his money — which he promptly donated to the team fund. At stumps, after Chappell had sent them in, Victoria were 4–258. The crowd was the best Friday attendance at the Oval for almost a decade, proof that interest in the Shield still prospered. The following day Victoria declared at 5–365, having gained five batting points. South Australia had two bowling points. Their lead in the Shield was now reduced to a single point.

Two days later, Ian Chappell was faced with one of the most intriguing captaincy decisions of his career. Bowling bonus points were now awarded after the 1st, 3rd, 5th, 7th and 9th wickets to fall in the first 100 six-ball overs. When the sixth South Australian wicket fell at 229, Chappell's side had three batting points, Victoria had three bowling points. South Australia were still one point clear on the Shield table. Chappell had the option of declaring, and setting his side the task of avoiding an outright loss to take the trophy. Instead he gambled on the ability and nerve of his leg-spinning all-rounder Peter Sleep, and was rewarded handsomely. Sleep had been the cause of Chappell's dismissal — run out for 112 — late on the second day, but now he repaid his captain's faith with an assured innings. When the seventh wicket, Trevor Robertson, fell at 235 the Shield was all tied up. Sleep was joined by Geoff Attenborough;

four years earlier they had been the men involved in the final run out that completed the second tie in Shield history. Now they needed to get to 250 before the completion of the 100th over.

With four overs to go the target was 11. As Walker prepared to bowl the 100th over, the score was 245. Sleep took two from the first ball with an educated "french" cut, and then four from the fourth ball, with a pull over mid-wicket. The shot was met with chaotic scenes in the outer, the members, and the SA dressing room. Most believed the Shield had been won. Attenborough was out in the 101st over, as was Mallett, but Sleep combined with Wayne Prior to add 53 for the final wicket, and keep the Victorian lead to 61.

The Victorians, never beaten, went for quick runs, and at stumps were 6–182. Overnight their captain Dav Whatmore declared, leaving South Australia all day to get 244 and the Shield. Chappell, inevitably, would have nothing of playing for the draw, and set out after the win. The morning session was encouraging for the locals. Opening bat John Nash fell early, but Chappell and John Inverarity, steadied the ship, and by lunch had reached 1–90.

After lunch everything went hopelessly wrong for South Australia, and wonderfully right for Victoria, and especially for their often-maligned leg spinner Jim Higgs. In his six overs after lunch he took five wickets for nine runs, as South Australia collapsed to 6–118. Within three minutes of the resumption he had Chappell caught behind, off the glove. Inverarity then deflected a chance to short leg, and Jeff Crowe jumped out to one that drifted down the leg side and was stumped. Sleep lost his middle stump not offering at a top spinner, and Jeff Hammond's across-the-line swipe went no further than the wicketkeeper.

The end came quickly. Walker came back to dismiss Bob Zadow, his only second-innings wicket, leaving him two short of the $10,000 bonus. The fast-medium Shaun Graf chipped in to dismiss Mallett and Attenborough, and the final wicket fell, appropriately, to Higgs, Robertson skying an abortive sweep for Whatmore to dash from slip to take the catch. South Australia were all out for 160, before tea, as astonishing a collapse by the home team as the Adelaide Oval had seen in years.

The Victorian team returned to Melbourne, to be met by a fleet of Rolls Royces hired to transport the players to a civic reception. For Chappell there was the disappointment of a loss to close his career. Without his leadership and aggression South Australia slipped back to the foot of the Shield table in 1980–81. And without his style, and his runs, the Shield lost one of its finest batsmen. He was the central character in an era of cricket in Australia of extraordinary controversy and success, a man prepared to fight for his team, his players, and his victories, whatever the cost. If any cricketer from the 1970s earned the right to go out a winner, it surely was Ian Chappell.

# 67

# THE CLOSEST FINAL

The closest Queensland ever came to winning the Sheffield Shield was in 1984–85. Few better cricket matches have been played than that season's final, staged at the SCG, and won in dramatic fashion by NSW's last-wicket partnership over a brave and desperate Queensland attack.

Many times on the fateful final day, on March 19, 1985, Allan Border's team from the northern state sat on the edge of glory. But the glory went again to their opponents, and especially to the last NSW pair. After the match the jokes and jibes about Queensland never winning the Shield seemed more appropriate than ever.

Perhaps what hurt most was that the final should never have been played in Sydney anyway. The home ground advantage had been stupidly and illogically thrown away two weeks before. At that time, with only the last series of matches in the regular season remaining, Queensland were on top of the Shield table. All that was required was an outright win against the lowly-placed South Australia in Adelaide, or anything but an outright win by NSW against Victoria at the SCG, and the final would be played at the Gabba.

For the first three days everything went well. With only three sessions remaining in both matches, South Australia were struggling, just 73 runs on, with three second-innings wickets remaining, while in Sydney, Victoria had started confidently after NSW captain Dirk Wellham boldly gave them seven hours to get 269 for outright points.

On the final day in Adelaide, a day which closed the first-class career of that renowned Shield campaigner John Inverarity, South Australia fought courageously, but into the final session Queensland needed just 63 with seven wickets in hand. At the last drinks break at the SCG, Victoria were 6–230. Even if South Australia could hold out for a draw, it seemed the Victorians would ensure the final was in Brisbane.

Then things began to go horribly wrong. Queensland collapsed while Victoria suicided. South Australian off-spinner Tim May finished with 6–24 as Queensland lost their remaining wickets for 50. In Sydney, the visitors amazingly stonewalled, and then surrendered against the left-arm spin of Murray Bennett, and were all out 25 runs short.

How quickly a season can change. The loss of the home ground advantage was a huge setback for the Queenslanders, who now needed an outright win away from home, rather than anything better than an outright loss at the 'Gabba. But they welcomed back their internationals Border, Robbie Kerr and Kepler Wessels, who had missed the final Shield round because of the World Championship of Cricket, a festival of one-day internationals held to celebrate the 150th anniversary of the founding of Victoria. NSW were also strengthened, opener Steve Smith, keeper Steve Rixon and their prized import, the Pakistan captain Imran Khan, returning.

The local slow bowlers, Bennett, the veteran leg-spinner Bob Holland and the off-breaking all-rounder Greg Matthews, were expected to hold the key. The SCG square had been criticised all summer, not least by the touring West Indians who had been spun out by Holland and Bennett in the fifth Test two months before. NSW had not conceded more than 260 in any one innings at home, despite being without, due to injury, their left-arm paceman Mike Whitney for the entire season, and Australia's number-one quick, Geoff Lawson, for most of it. Imran's imput had been crucial, as had the emergence of David Gilbert, who would, after many of the country's best fast men signed to play "rebel" cricket in South Africa, eventually be chosen to tour England with Border's 1985 Australian team.

The Queenslanders at full strength were an imposing team, perhaps the best eleven in the state's history. The side was built around the runs of Border, Kerr and Wessels, and the intimidating pace attack of Jeff Thomson, Craig McDermott, Carl Rackemann and John Maguire. The underrated googly bowler Trevor Hohns provided the spin, and keeper Ray Phillips exuberance and polish behind the stumps. They had won four of the first five matches outright, to lead the table clearly, before international commitments took a toll. McDermott would miss the final through injury.

For four days the 1984–85 Shield decider provided tough, skilful sport, but gave few indications of the theatre to come. Queensland scored 374 in their first innings — Hohns 103 — and NSW replied with 318, including the slowest half century in the state's history, 50 off 208 balls in 292 minutes by former Test opener John Dyson. A highlight was the poise and daring of the 19-year-old NSW batsman, Steve Waugh, who made an impressive 71 and dominated an eight-wicket stand of 55 with Bennett, who made only 10.

Queensland lost two wickets late on the third day, but the next morning began to consolidate before Imran struck a vital blow, breaking a Border-Phillips fourth wicket partnership in bizarre fashion, just when it seemed the Queensland captain was taking command. Dyson was moved from first slip to nearly third slip, leaving a peculiar gap between Dyson and the wicketkeeper. Almost immediately Border slashed a wide one straight to Dyson. 4 for 116. From there the innings folded. The last six wickets were lost for just 47, Imran finished with 5–34, NSW needed 220 to win.

In the fourth day's final session the game swung once more. NSW lost three wickets — Dyson and Rixon to Thomson, Smith to Rackemann, setting the stage for one of the great days in the Shield's lifetime.

Wellham and Matthews went early in the final morning — the captain embarrassed by an outrageous slower ball from Thomson, Matthews given out controversially after an appeal for a catch at the wicket. But Peter Clifford, NSW's leading run-getter all season, remained. Twenty-five-years old, solid and batting in glasses, Clifford proved the man for the occasion. He added 40 with Imran (out playing an absurd slog) and 33 with Waugh. But immediately after the teenager edged the superb Rackemann behind, Bennett, usually so dependable, pushed the same bowler straight to Border at short leg. Clifford was on his own — 8–175. Queensland were closer to the Shield than they had ever been.

Later in 1985 Bob Holland would register five Test ducks in a row. Twenty years earlier he had spun his leg breaks at Mike Smith's Englishmen. He was now 38-years-old, a mediocre batsman but a cunning and perceptive cricketer, and he and his younger colleague edged towards their target. Clifford kept going,

*The gallant Queensland paceman, Carl Rackemann, gazes sadly at the presentation after the 1984-85 final. Rackemann had bowled one of the most inspiring spells ever seen on the SCG, yet still finished on the losing side.*

scoring two to his partner's one, and coping superbly with the pressure.

Others were not. Wessels appeared to deliberately shoulder Clifford in a childish mid-pitch clash. With 20 runs needed, Border stood beside the wicket and abused Clifford after a defensive jab almost popped the ball onto the stumps. But while his teammates panicked, Rackemann powered on, bowling one of the bravest and most sustained spells of modern times. At the end he would leave the field in tears, his extraordinary effort totally unrewarded.

Holland defied Rackemann and Thomson for 58 minutes while 34 runs were scored, 10 of them his own. He could have been caught backward of square where a Glenn Trimble swan dive all but reached the lofted result of a crude swipe. Clifford might have been run out going for an absurd third run to get the strike. Then Rackemann finally broke through. Holland slicing to the gully after Border opted for the second new ball.

Eleven to win, or 10 to tie. Fast bowler Gilbert strode out, to help Clifford to the Shield.

"Don't stuff it up for me. I've been waiting all year for this," Gilbert told Clifford when he reached the wicket. He had been dismissed only once in Shield cricket all summer, and was averaging more than 80 as a batsman for the season.

Gilbert pushed a single through the gully. Then Clifford took over, driving Rackemann for three past cover, and Thomson for three more, almost to the sightscreen. Rackemann bowled a maiden, the last ball searing beyond the outside edge. Thomson got one past Gilbert, but then overpitched and Gilbert drove him past Wessels at mid-off. They ran two, and, as the tiny crowd roared in celebration, a third to level the scores. Gilbert danced around like a centre forward at Wembley, Clifford waved his bat at the pandemonium in the home dressing room. The Queenslanders stood motionless, scarcely believing what had happened to them.

In the next over, Gilbert, unjustly, lofted Rackemann towards the boundary at long-off to win the match. The gallant Queenslander slumped in the middle of the pitch, hands on knees, while his fieldsmen consoled him. The batsmen raced to the pavilion where they were met by supporters, journalists and teammates. Clifford was 83 not out, having played one of the most famous innings in Shield history.

Allan Border called the game: "A tribute to cricket." Wellham admitted to being resigned to losing many times on the final day. Rackemann described the loss as "like being hit in the guts".

The Brisbane *Courier Mail*, in its editorial the next day, declared that: "Probably no cricket match since the famous Tied Test of 1961 (sic) has produced more nail-biting, palm-sweating, heart-stopping tension than this season's Sheffield Shield final…For those of us who might have been seduced by the attractions of the pyjama game, the Queensland and NSW teams yesterday reminded us that the traditional game, played under the traditional rules with the traditional gear, generates its own suspense. We have only two reasons to lament: that the game was played in front of such a disappointingly small crowd, and that Queensland did not win."

# 68

# BEING A COMMENTATOR ISN'T EASY

Twelve months after the unforgettable 1984–85 Shield final, the competition once more came down to a classic last-day NSW-Queensland battle at the Sydney Cricket Ground. This epic was without its Test men, missing in New Zealand for a three-match series, but certainly not without its drama. On the last, captivating day, Queensland persisted throughout, in search of the 10 second-innings wickets required to claim the elusive trophy. At different stages, NSW looked certain to win, lose and draw. In the end the season came down to a tense final half hour which was as thrilling and absorbing a climax as any cricket broadcaster has ever had to describe.

Queensland had batted for most of the first two days, and despite a NSW revival were still able to set

*Below: NSW captain Dirk Wellham grimly walks from the SCG after running himself out on the tense final afternoon of the 1985–86 final.*
*Right: NSW paceman Mike Whitney, a nervous number 11, and part-time commentator, during the dramatic last half hour.*

225

the Shield champions 275 to win the match outright. To retain the Shield NSW needed no more than a draw, but on the final day the home captain, Dirk Wellham, adopted an aggressive approach, and when he and Mark Waugh became involved in a lucrative fifth-wicket stand, it appeared the competition would be won comfortably. At 182 Waugh was dismissed by the part-time bowling of the Queensland captain, the South African Kepler Wessels. Two runs later NSW keeper Greg Dyer, who had saved a potential disaster in the NSW first innings with a stirring, unbeaten 88, was ridiculously run out, and the season was in the balance once more.

Wellham found another fighting comrade in the off-spinning all-rounder Peter Taylor, in the side only because Greg Matthews was in New Zealand with the Australian team. Ironically, 10 months later Taylor would replace Matthews in the Test XI. Here Taylor played an intelligent hand, refusing to let the circumstances stifle his attacking game, and with his captain he pushed his side towards the Shield.

With 10 overs left NSW needed just 21. Then Wellham chanced his life on a dangerous third run, and was caught short of his ground. Next over, Taylor drove outside a half volley from the left-arm fast bowler Dirk Tazalaar, and was lbw. The Queenslanders, after seasons of having Dame Fortune work against them, now made plans to welcome her aboard. The new men at the batting crease were seasoned professionals, the former Test spinners, Murray Bennett and Bob Holland. Thoughts of an outright win had been jettisoned. The two late-order batsmen settled down to the task of seeing out the final overs.

Every defensive stroke was cheered, every over gratefully farewelled. In the NSW dressing room, the uneasy silence was broken by the sound of the telephone. Closest to the receiver was number 11, Mike Whitney, all padded up, gloves and bat by his side, waiting nervously for the inevitable crisis. He grabbed at the phone, to hear the voice of coach Bob Simpson, calling from Dunedin where he was overseeing the Australian tour. Simpson wanted to know where the Shield was heading, and Whitney obliged, first giving an expert summary of the day's play, and then moving into ball-by-ball mode, providing a slightly less mellow, slightly more larrikin version of Alan McGilvray, as Bennett and Holland inched closer and closer to the final ball.

Whitney was calling the game for not just Simpson, but also for Matthews, Steve Waugh and Dave Gilbert, the NSW players in the Australian squad. The commentary continued for two overs before Whitney could stand it no more, and handed the "microphone" to his captain for the final 10-minute stonewall to the line.

Wellham took over with aplomb, and provided a slightly different, certainly more positive view of proceedings for the listeners in New Zealand. He appeared to have more confidence in his number 11 than the previous commentator, but doubted he would be needed. His two late-order batsmen were capable with the bat, and sensible men. In the middle Wessels rung the changes, but it now appeared almost certain that Queensland were to be the bridesmaids again.

In the penultimate over, Holland faced Jeff Thomson, who was bowling the final over of his extraordinary career. Sadly the champion's last desperate effort was not enough, and not long after, when the match's second last ball was safely parried with NSW still just eight-down, the home dressing room exploded into turmoil, as triumph was shared, and moves were made to the boundary fence in preparation for a rush onto the field. The phone was left dangling towards the floor, the shouts from New Zealand left blissfully unanswered. Bob Simpson and his fellow listeners across the Tasman were left with no more than well-educated guesses as to the fate of the Shield.

# 69

## KING OF THE ADELAIDE OVAL

The most fabulous Shield innings of the modern era was played by David Hookes. On October 25, 1982, at the Adelaide Oval, Hookes blasted a century against Victoria in 43 minutes, off just 34 balls. Time-wise it was the fastest century ever scored by an Australian in first-class cricket. In terms of balls faced it was the fastest first-class hundred of all time.

On that magic day, Hookes, in his second season as his state's captain, had opened the South Australian second innings in an angry mood. His opposing captain, Graham Yallop, had all-but ruined the match with some absurdly negative strategies, having his batsmen crawl along at an unimaginative pace, and delaying his declaration until South Australia required 272 from an hour and 20 overs.

The statistics of what followed are quite awesome. Regular opener Rick Darling took the first ball of the innings from Rod McCurdy. The first ball Hookes faced was from the other opening bowler, Peter King, and he belted it over mid-wicket for six. Three more fours came from the over. King's only two overs in the innings cost 38 runs. Hookes reached his fifty in 17 minutes, having faced 17 balls and smashed nine fours and two sixes — 48 in boundaries. An incredible 94 runs came from the first six overs, 83 of them to Hookes. When Hookes was out, for 107, scored from 40 balls in 55 minutes, the score was 122. Darling was out later for 11.

Hookes peppered the short boundaries at mid-wicket and cover in astonishing fashion. His three sixes all went over the advertising at mid-wicket, while six of his fours were struck to the fence between backward square and wide mid-on. He was murderous on anything wide of the off stump, and seven fours went to the point or cover boundary. During the conquest Yallop made sure to man the outfield, but Hookes' blazing was so sure that he only missed the fence twice with shots that pierced the infield. He hit only one three in the 107, the shot that took him from 99 to 102.

Later Hookes commented: "I was upset at the way Yallop had captained the side for the past two days. I thought we'll just have a go for a while and see what happens." Perhaps the greatest irony of the day was that in humiliating the Victorian bowlers as he did, he probably vindicated the outlandish caution Yallop displayed.

When Hookes reached 99, Yallop instructed McCurdy to stall for time. It took the fast bowler all of two minutes to undo and retie his shoelaces, as Hookes threw his bat on the ground and raged to umpire Tony Crafter at square leg. Only 11 six-ball overs were bowled in the first hour of the final session. Hookes was finally out when he miscued McCurdy to Brad Green at deep mid-off. The run chase was not called off until the seventh wicket fell at 204, though Hookes had held back John Inverarity and Andrew Hilditch to kill the final overs if required. This however was not necessary, as soon after the seventh wicket fell the umpires offered the batsmen the opportunity to leave the field because of the fading light.

Four seasons later Hookes played another extraordinary innings, of a different kind. Against Tasmania at the Adelaide Oval he scored 306, the highest score by a native South Australian since Clem Hill had hit 365 against NSW at the turn of the century. Hookes and the wicketkeeper/batsman Wayne Phillips, who scored 213, added an undefeated 462 for the fourth wicket, in 299 minutes from 84.3 overs, and broke every single Australian partnership record.

This was more a slaughter than a partnership. Both were batsmen perfectly suited to the Adelaide Oval, and the Tasmanian "attack" had been ravaged by injury. Phillips was also left-handed, and just as powerful and certain on the square cut and back foot drive. Together the pair added 200 off 28 overs on the last session of the second day, when Hookes was his most lethal, and then 181 off 32 overs on the following morning, when Phillips outscored his captain by 103 to 76.

The first record the pair defeated was the South Australian fourth-wicket Shield partnership record. Then came the South Australian fourth-wicket record. Then the South Australian Shield partnership record. Then the record South Australian partnership. Then the Shield fourth-wicket record was broken. Then the record Shield partnership. Then the Australian fourth-wicket record. Then the Australian partnership record. As every new landmark was reached, the Adelaide Oval ground announcer broadcast the news to the throng. Later the Tasmanian captain David Boon commented: "It sounded like a history lesson".

Hookes' triple century came from 330 balls, included 41 fours and two sixes and occupied 398 minutes. Phillips faced 253 balls, and played at every one of them. He struck 30 fours and a six. The only chance

*David Hookes, during his incredible century against Victoria at the Adelaide Oval in October 1982.*

between them was one offered by Phillips. Hookes ended the innings at lunch, declaring at 3–643. The shell-shocked Tasmanians, who had made 240 in the first innings, made 257 the second time around.

David Hookes' Shield career continued until 1991–92. In his second last match he lifted his Shield batting aggregate past John Inverarity's previous record. It was a record that had seemed his for the taking at the start of the season, when he required 416 runs, and even more so after he took 75 off the West Australians in Adelaide in November and then 156 from NSW a month later. But the runs slowed, and he hit his way past 50 only once after the New Year. When he walked to the wicket for the second innings of the match against Victoria in Adelaide, he was still 44 runs short, with just a match in Perth remaining in what he had confirmed would be his final season.

The Hookes who batted this day was not the explosive dynamo who had demoralised the Victorian attack 10 seasons before. This time he scored from only 26 of the 105 balls he faced, and had to endure more than two hours before two successive boundaries off Simon O'Donnell, one through mid-wicket, the next through the covers, gave him the record. The crowd gave him a standing ovation, and later Hookes told *The Advertiser's* Alan Shiell: "It was quite an emotional, draining moment. I just felt I'd finally got the record off my back. The crowd reaction was nice. I've never been one for long acknowledgements, but to look through clouded eyes and see the people standing....it was a very proud moment."

Hookes played one more match, an anti-climax in Perth, before calling his Shield career quits. For more than a decade since the retirement of Ian Chappell he had been the most recognisable figure in South Australian cricket. As captain for nine seasons from 1981–82 he had been successful, controversial and unorthodox, and had made South Australia's Shield matches as interesting and competitive as they could possibly have been. He was unswervingly loyal to his players and to his philosophy of the game — but would sometimes fight for what he believed in to beyond the point of no return. Even so, his temperamental moments occurred less often than his timely declarations, and once in a while he would produce his speciality, the thing that separated him from all the rest: the innings that no-one else in the game could play.

# 70

# BOON AND MARSH INC.

The revival in fortune of the Australian team in the late 1980s had much to do with the emergence of two tough, skilful batsmen from the Shield's youngest states. Tasmania's David Boon and Geoff Marsh from Western Australia came together in the national team in 1985–86, for the first Test of the three-match series against India. Just five weeks earlier the champion New Zealand paceman Richard Hadlee had reduced Australia to one of its most devastating Test losses, a painful innings humiliation in Brisbane. Resilience was required at the top of the order. Boon and Marsh were the men to provide it.

Marsh had first appeared in the Sheffield Shield in 1977–78, Boon a season later. Boon, from Launceston, was something of a schoolboy prodigy, and made the Australian under-19 team to tour England in 1977 in remarkable circumstances. In a selection trial at the MCG he scored a century from number nine to edge out Dirk Wellham for the final batting place. He was only 16 at the time. Marsh, from the WA country town of Wandering, was vice-captain on the tour, and topped the batting averages.

From the year Tasmania were given their place in the Shield, Boon was identified as the cricketer who would provide the state's first home-based Australian cap, especially after his first century — 114 against a full-strength Victorian attack in Hobart in December 1980. In fact it turned out that the first Tasmanian Shield player to win an Australian cap was Roger Woolley, who beat Boon by a little more than a season.

Marsh's quest for a Test place was less assured, and he was obliged to battle in the Shield for eight long seasons before he played a Test. In 1979–80 he scored just 37 runs in six Shield innings, and lost his place in the team. The next season he did not play in the Shield at all. In 1981–82 he won back his spot for the fourth WA match of the season (as a replacement during the absence of Test stars), failed twice

*Two of the most sensible and reliable Australian cricketers of the 1980s and early '90s — Tasmania's David Boon (below) and Geoff Marsh of Western Australia.*

against Tasmania, but managed a plucky second-innings 67 at home against Victoria, and then turned the corner, with a powerful 176 in Sydney. By the end of the season he was sixth on the first-class averages, with 545 runs from five Shield matches. The long wait was over, and his career was thoroughly on its way.

With Tasmania only playing five Shield matches per season for their first five years in the competition, Boon was less likely to impress the national selectors than his rivals from the mainland. Despite this, he rejected offers from officials in Perth, Sydney and Melbourne, and took his chances when Tasmania's schedule was expanded in 1982–83. Against WA he was unlucky to fall for 99; in his next match in Brisbane he scored 115 and 57 not out; before the summer was out he had another century, against South Australia. In 1983–84 he scored more than 650 Shield runs, including 227 in one superb performance in Melbourne, and by the following season his international career was underway.

Marsh scored a confident century against NSW in 1983–84, in Rod Marsh's farewell to the SCG, and then another hundred in the Shield final. But his Test call-up did not come until 1985–86. With Kim Hughes and Greg Shipperd in South Africa on a "rebel" tour, Marsh was promoted to number three in the WA lineup, and thrived, scoring successive centuries against Victoria and Queensland. In his debut Test, in Adelaide, he scored 5 and 2 not out — while Boon scored his maiden Test century. In the third Test, Marsh was promoted to open the batting with his Tasmanian colleague, and the pair combined for 217, Boon scoring a century, and Marsh 92. The following year against England the combination struggled, with Boon in poor form. After a brief R & R in the Shield, Boon was recalled for the 1987 World Cup in India. From this point, until Mark Taylor forced the Tasmanian down to number three in 1989, the firm of Boon and Marsh Inc. were firmly established as Australia's opening partnership.

Both cricketers have produced sterling performances when given the opportunity for the Sheffield Shield sides. Boon's most memorable effort came in 1987–88 — centuries in both innings as Tasmania won a match crucial to Queensland's chances of hosting that season's final. For Marsh his greatest day with the bat was in 1989–90, when he smashed the South Australian bowling for 355 not out, the highest score ever by a Western Australian in first-class cricket.

In February 1988, Queensland were riding high, atop the Shield ladder. For their match with Tasmania, they were without the battle-weary Craig McDermott, but still boasted an attack that included the internationals Carl Rackemann, John Maguire and Ian Botham, plus the left-handed pace of Dirk Tazalaar (later to share that season's Shield player of the year award with NSW's Mark Waugh) and the leg breaks and googlies of Trevor Hohns. Tasmania to this stage had not registered a Shield point all season. In fact they were on minus .2 of a point, having been penalised for bowling their overs too slowly on the final day against South Australia in Adelaide. They had not once gained outright points in their last 44 Shield starts. To Rackemann's first ball of the match, Boon jabbed — and the resultant edge flew straight to Queensland captain Allan Border at third slip. Border had been snaring these chances for years, but this one went down. David Boon went on to 108, as Tasmania reached 5–334 by stumps. During the innings Boon overtook Woolley as Tasmania's leading runscorer in the Shield.

A short, squat man, Boon was the epitome of calm and confidence at the batting crease. His stance, his preparation, and his demeanour were all designed to have him right behind the line of the most lethal of bowlers. In the late '80s no Australian batsman hooked the fast bowling with greater surety. He was the man most likely to score runs when they were most needed. His value to Tasmanian cricket is inestimable. No Tasmanian-born cricketer so far has got anywhere close to what he has achieved in Shield and international cricket.

His first innings century had come from 203 balls. His second innings 143 took just 165, and included 23 fours and a six. He was the first Tasmanian to score a century in both innings of a Shield match. He and fellow opener Glenn Hughes put together century partnerships in both innings. On the final day, after Tasmanian captain Brian Davison had set Queensland the unlikely target of 409 in 83 overs, the Queenslanders fell for 314, after reaching 1–221. A week later they lost again in Melbourne, and then were beaten in the final in Perth — to thus lose another Shield they might well have won.

Marsh's epic 355 came in December 1989. He had returned from the Ashes tour entrenched as Australia's vice-captain (a position he had first taken in 1986–87 after Boon was dropped). An injury in the WACA nets on the eve of a Test against New Zealand — a Rackemann yorker broke the big toe on his left foot — put him out of cricket for a month however, and left him to make his return through the Shield ranks as Australia headed into a Test match against Sri Lanka in Hobart.

At stumps on the first day of the Shield game in Perth, after David Hookes had won the toss, WA were 0–283. Marsh was 170, Mike Veletta 96. Marsh had batted with a specially designed guard on his left foot, and after a typically watchful start — at one stage he faced 28 balls without scoring — had pummelled the

South Australians, driving and cutting with all his trademark assurance. Like Boon, his stance was designed to suit his own technique, the bat brought straight back well before the bowler reached his delivery stride. On the leg side he relied on drives and glances, but to anything outside the line of the off-stump he could be merciless, and his cover and off drives were economical and sure. Patience was his trademark, occasionally frustratingly so, but his record in one-day matches showed that rapid runs were far from beyond him.

His century against South Australia took 240 minutes, the third 50 came in a little more than an hour. The next day he and Veletta went on to 431, the highest opening stand in the competition's history. Veletta was finally out for 150, and the score ran on to 563 before Graeme Wood declared, with Marsh just one short of Barry Richards' record score for the ground. In all the innings went for 628 minutes, Marsh hit 53 fours and two sixes, and did not offer a chance until he began to look for short cuts near the end.

For the young South Australia keeper Darren Berry, the match was something of a landmark. During the WA innings he conceded one bye — just enough to break a sequence of 2,446 runs scored against his side without a bye being conceded. When South Australia batted Berry was one of five wickets to fall for 63, before Paul Nobes and Michael Bevan both scored hundreds in a partnership of 221. Bevan was making his debut. In the South Australian second innings, he was out for just two, bowled by Marsh, the WA batsman's first first-class wicket.

In 1991–92, Marsh became the third man, after Lillee and Wood, to captain WA to success in the Sheffield Shield final. In the same season he lost his place in the Test side, and doubts were expressed as to his future in the big-time. For Border, the thought of international cricket without his trusty lieutenant appalled him, and he fought a spirited and public battle to keep Marsh in the team. For Boon, the cricket caravan journeyed on and on. His impact on the Shield has been limited only by the demands of the Australian team, and the shortcomings of his teammates. In an era where cricket spent much of its time in the fast lane, Boon and Marsh were two men who stayed true to the Australian tradition of producing sensible, professional cricketers. They were quality products of their own time — and would have been *exactly* that in any of cricket's eras.

# 71

## CYCLONE CRAIG

In the winter of 1983, 18-year-old Queenslander Craig McDermott was a member of the Australian under-19 team that toured England. The team was captained by Mike Veletta, later to score 262 for Western Australia in the 1986–87 Shield final, and the touring squad included seven other future Shield players, and two other future Test players, Ian Healy and Tony Dodemaide. McDermott had injury problems on the tour, and bowled in only one "Test", the first in Nottingham. In December McDermott made his Shield debut, against Victoria in Brisbane. Queensland captain Jeff Thomson gave him the first over, and he had the left-hander Gary Watts dropped from his very first ball. He finished the innings with 4–75 — a much more than promising debut. Later in the season he bowled at the West Indians in a one-day match, and earned praise from Clive Lloyd, who labelled him potentially the best paceman in the country.

By December 1984, McDermott was in the Test side, opening the bowling against the West Indians. It had been an astonishingly swift rise to the top. Next came an England tour, where, with Geoff Lawson slowed by injury, McDermott became the country's leading paceman, and captured 30 Test wickets. As a result of that outstanding campaign he was chosen as one of *Wisden's* five cricketers of the year. During the series he had become the youngest Australian to take eight wickets in one Test innings. *Wisden*, never a publication to make outlandish prophesies, suggested he would soon be leading the Australian attack "with the same devilish intent as Lillee".

But something went wrong. Instead of pacing in the footsteps of Lillee, McDermott became one of the

*Mark Waugh of NSW, the most stylish batsman to appear in the Shield since the retirement of Greg Chappell.*

*Western Australia's Mike Veletta, who in the 1986-87 final batted for 766 minutes for 262, the longest individual innings ever played in the Shield.*

*One of Queensland's many expensive overseas imports, Ian Botham, pictured during the 1987–88 final in Perth.*

David Boon, who in the seasons since Tasmania's entry into the Shield in 1977–78, has established most of his state's Shield batting records, including most runs, most centuries and highest score.

country's most frustrating cricketers, as much out of the Test side as in it. He appeared to lose something in trying to correct a follow-through problem which had him trampling on the batsmen's portion of the pitch. In 1985–86 he played just three Shield matches (international commitments kept him from the remainder) for 14 wickets, and his first-class bowling average for the season ballooned to almost 40.

When the Australian team for the first Test of the 1986–87 Ashes series was chosen, McDermott was not in it — the pace bowling spots going to Bruce Reid, Merv Hughes and Chris Matthews. Lawson was recalled for the second Test, then jettisoned. McDermott came back for the fourth Test, but bowled badly, and lost his place once more. In the Shield however he found excellent form, and took 44 wickets in nine matches, including 6–89 against Victoria at Wangaratta, and seven and nine-wicket match hauls, against NSW and Victoria respectively, at the 'Gabba.

In October 1987 he was a key member of the Australian team that won the World Cup in India. There were many signs that all would be well with his career — clearly his recuperation in the Shield had been good for him. Back in Australia he played in all five Test matches in 1987–88, for 20 wickets. In the Shield he had two superb matches, taking seven wickets against Victoria in Queensland's first match of the season, and 10 wickets against NSW in Newcastle, including seven in the second innings, when NSW collapsed for 83. But in his three other Shield matches he collected only five more wickets, and only one in the final, which was won by Western Australia.

Season 1988–89 was a personal disaster, as he appeared to lose firstly his rhythm and pace and eventually his place in the Queensland side. He played in the first and third Tests against the West Indies, but whatever line or length he bowled seemed inevitably to be the wrong one. It seemed absurd that a career that had promised so much could be on the skids. In the fiery debate that followed the non-selection of that season's leading wicket-taker, Mike Whitney of NSW, in the 1989 team for England, nobody mentioned that Craig McDermott, still just 23 years old, had been left out as well. He was, at that moment, no better than the seventh best fast bowler in the country.

McDermott resolved to find the key, to re-prove himself. From his earliest days he had believed passionately in the value of being perfectly fit. While Alderman, Lawson, and Hughes were bowling Australia to a remarkable 4–nil Ashes triumph in England, McDermott made ready for their return. He trained with the iron man champion Trevor Hendy and reached a level of fitness he had not thought possible. During the season that followed he reaped the benefits of his preparation, and took 54 wickets, bowling many lengthy spells; but still he could not win back his Test place, as the men from the England tour continued as the front-runners.

His best performance of the season came against Tasmania in Brisbane, when he blasted the visitors out for just 105, taking 8–44 from 22 consistently dangerous overs. His first two wickets came on the opening day, Jamie Cox unluckily caught at short leg after deflecting a fast one onto his boot, and the former West Australian, Greg Shipperd, bowled jabbing at a rapid off-cutter. At stumps on the rain-shortened day his figures were 2–23, Tasmania were 3–69. The second day was lost entirely, as the remnants of cyclone "Nancy", ripped the covers off the square, exposing the pitch to the elements.

The next day the Tasmanians were struck with a cyclone of a different kind, as McDermott achieved the best ever bowling figures by a Queenslander in a home Shield match. Charging in with the wind at his back, and aiming at a pitch with just a little give, McDermott was all but unplayable. He rarely lost his line, and in the main kept the ball up at the batsman. But when he bowled his bouncer he made it count, always at the bat handle. His last six wickets all came from catches behind the wicket, three of them to Steve Storey in the gully, and two to keeper Peter Anderson.

Queensland hustled early in the chase for first-innings points, but lost seven wickets as Dave Gilbert bowled with much fire from McDermott's end. At 7–85, the result was in the balance, but McDermott joined Storey in an unbroken 24–run stand (the highest of the innings) to edge the home side in front. Captain Greg Ritchie declared as soon as the Queenslanders reached the lead, and in the 68 minutes before stumps, Tasmania lost two wickets, one of them, Shipperd, to McDermott.

How quickly did McDermott bowl? Peter Clifford, the man whose batting won NSW the 1984–85 Shield final, but now a Queenslander, watched the expressions on the Tasmanian batsmen's faces throughout the innings from the safety and comfort of short leg. Afterwards he told Robert Craddock of the Brisbane *Courier-Mail*: "I faced Jeff Thomson here and he was about as quick as that. Greg Shipperd nicked a ball to slip, said 'oh no' and took one step before the ball reached Greg Ritchie (the first slip). That's how far back they were standing."

The pitch improved on the final day, and Tasmania managed to hold out for a draw. Largely through McDermott's endeavours, Queensland grafted their way to the Shield final, but on the spinner's dream that was the SCG their pace-oriented attack was no match for the NSW Test-strength batting line-up, and they were defeated comfortably.

The 1989–90 season proved pivotal in McDermott's career. It was, incredibly, only the second time he had participated in anything like a full season of Sheffield Shield cricket, and he used the opportunity to harness natural gifts that had always been in him. Notwithstanding that the glitter of a crowded international program had taken the limelight away from the Shield, the interstate competition remained the ultimate training ground for future Test cricketers. At the end of it McDermott's career was ready for its second take-off.

The following summer he was the best bowler in the country, took 41 wickets in six Shield matches, and won back his Test place. By 1991–92 Craig McDermott was the spearhead of his country's pace attack, having finally and fully realised the promise of nearly a decade before.

# 72

## TWIN PEAKS

Before the emergence of the gifted Waugh brothers, the Shield had hosted only two sets of twins on its playing fields. In December 1923, Norm Walsh made his Shield debut for South Australia, scoring 2 and 3 against NSW. His Shield career ended five matches later, with a highest score of 33 from 12 innings. Five years later, his twin brother Laurie Walsh began his Shield career with a duck, bowled by Eddie Gilbert in Brisbane. In the second innings he scored 23. He then travelled to Sydney, where Hal Hooker had him lbw for nought in the first innings. He made 18 in the second — and that was his first-class career.

In November 1931, a tall, gangling slow-medium bowler named Lisle Nagel played his first Shield match for Victoria, and in the second innings took six South Australian wickets. Twelve months later, Nagel took 8–32 for an Australian XI against Jardine's Engishmen in Melbourne, and found himself in the Australian side for the first Test. His Test career amounted to no more than that one match, and his Shield career was done with by December 1933. Victoria's Shield match in Adelaide in 1932–33 took place just days before Nagel's only Test appearance. He and the other Victorian Test players, Ponsford, Woodfull and Ironmonger, were unavailable, and chosen among their replacements was Vernon Nagel, Lisle's twin brother. He took one wicket in 14 overs, and did not play in Shield cricket again until the first week of 1936, when he scored a duck and didn't take a wicket in 25 overs against South Australia. That was the end of his Shield career.

Steve Waugh played Shield cricket for the first time in 1984–85, as a number nine batsman, and first change bowler. He had only limited success, but did score a vital 94 against Victoria, and an excellent 71 in the final against Queensland. The next season he was joined in the Shield by his younger (by four minutes) brother, Mark, who was chosen with another promising batsman, Mark Taylor, to open the NSW batting. The highly successful pair from the previous season, John Dyson and Steve Smith, had joined the "rebel" tour to South Africa, creating the opening. Mark Waugh did not have a happy time, and while his brother was doing enough to win his first Test cap, he was dropped from the side. By season's end, however, he was back — in the unlikely role of Mike Whitney's new ball partner, and a number six batsman.

In the seasons that followed the two brothers' careers took substantially different paths. What was always clear was that both were richly talented cricketers, but while Steve was given an extended trial in the Test side, Mark was obliged to bide his time, paying his dues in grade cricket, and then in the Sheffield Shield. In 1986–87, Mark played only one Shield match, but the following year he found a rich seam of success, and was a joint winner (with Dirk Tazalaar) of the Shield's player of the year award. By 1989 he was on the threshold of joining his brother in the Australian side, considered by many to be unfortunate to miss the last batting spot on that year's tour to England.

The Waugh boys were cricketers of extraordinary talent, and contrasting styles. Both superb fieldsmen,

*Despite the constant demands of international cricket, Craig McDermott has taken more Shield wickets for Queensland than all bar Jeff Thomson and Geoff Dymock.*

Mark as good and versatile in the field as anyone of his generation; both capable, and clever medium pace bowlers, with an ability to disguise their changes of pace that would have been more appropriate in the armoury of a spinner. At the batting crease, Steve almost always appeared the more earnest, Mark more the free spirit.

Rarely has a cricketer crashed the ball through the covers off the back foot with more certainty than Steve, or driven the ball wide of mid-on with greater style or consistency than Mark. When Steve was at his best, cricket followers agreed there was no finer batsman, no better player to watch in full cry. Then Mark would come out, drive and cut his way to 50, and everyone would think again. That they played in the same team seemed somehow unfair. That they came from the same family was astonishing.

In December 1990, the twins combined for one of the greatest partnerships in the competition's history. Purely in terms of runs it was *the* greatest — 464 runs, breaking the previous record of 462 set by David Hookes and Wayne Phillips at the Adelaide Oval four seasons before. The runs were made in a style in keeping with the champions of the competition's history, scored in 407 minutes of exhilarating cricket. During the devastation of the WA attack, which included the international pacemen Bruce Reid, Terry Alderman, Ken MacLeay and Chris Matthews, both men went past their previous highest scores in first-class cricket.

*The amazing Waugh twins, Steve (left) and Mark, toast their record-shattering partnership against Western Australia in Perth in December 1990.*

They came together at 4–137. Reid had just dismissed Mark Taylor and Trevor Bayliss, and Mark O'Neill had fallen to MacLeay. At this point Geoff Marsh could not have been regretting his decision to send the New South Welshmen into bat. At stumps NSW were 4–375, Mark Waugh was 128, having batted for 244 minutes. Steve, arriving at the crease 38 minutes after his brother, was 112. It was the second time the pair had both scored hundreds in the same Shield innings, the previous occasion being against Victoria in Sydney in December 1987.

In many ways the situation was made for the brothers. The pitch was almost white, just about devoid of grass. The outfield was lightning fast; any shot through the infield went like a bullet for four. But neither had gone past 50 in a Shield innings at the WACA before, nor had they been in the best of form, and the scoreboard suggested they had to be careful, at least early on. They were quickly in command, brilliantly so; the opening fifty of their stand came up in even time. The second fifty took just half an hour…and history was on its way.

The next morning the Waughs continued on at the same rate as the afternoon before. At lunch NSW were 4–497, Mark 183, Steve 169. After the break they headed on towards 600, as Marsh tried the illogical and the unorthodox to try and break the stand. Alderman was reduced to bowling slow-medium from a short run, and then keeper Tim Zoehrer took off the pads to bowl five overs of reasonable leg breaks, with Mike Veletta keeping. The twins were unaware that when the total reached 600 they would have the Australian record stand. Twelfth man Michael Bevan came out to relay that news, and once the milestone was reached, Geoff Lawson declared. Mark Waugh was 229, Steve Waugh 216.

Apart from the Hookes-Phillips record, many other landmarks had been reached. They included:
• A world record for the fifth wicket in first-class cricket, breaking the old figure of 405, set by Don Bradman and Sid Barnes in the second Ashes Test of 1946–47.
• The partnership was the first by two NSW batsmen to go past 400. The previous highest was 397 by Warren Bardsley and Charles Kelleway against South Australia in December 1920.
• The NSW total was the highest by that state in a Shield match against Western Australia, and the highest by any team playing WA at the WACA.
• Steve and Mark became the first brothers to score double centuries in the same first-class match.
• Both men achieved their highest first-class score.
• Mark, who had played for the English county Essex during the Australian winter, became the 10th Australian to score 3,000 first-class runs in one calender year.

In an article written for the Association of Cricket Statisticians in England, Greg McKie, detailed some revealing figures about the record stand. Although Mark batted for 38 more minutes than Steve (445 to 407), he faced only four more balls. Mark struck 35 fours and a six, Steve 24 fours. The most expensive over was bowled by Reid, who conceded 12 runs off the opening over of his third spell. Three overs went for 11, the first by off-spinner Wayne Andrews and last by Matthews and Zoehrer. Astonishingly, amidst the carnage Alderman managed to bowl five consecutive maiden overs. Steve's first 50 was reached more rapidly than Mark's, but Mark was quicker from 50 to 100. From 100 to 150 Steve was more aggressive, but Mark again was the faster to 200.

But this was an event about more than statistics. The two batted in a manner which was the envy of their contemporaries. Rod Marsh thought their batting superior to that of Barry Richards the day the South African scored 325 in a single day at the WACA. That, coming from the man who was behind the stumps for every ball that Richards faced, was supreme praise.

When Western Australia finally batted, Lawson asked Steve Waugh to open the bowling, which he did, sending down three overs for seven runs. WA were eventually bowled out for 314. Lawson enforced the follow-on, and the match remained in the balance until the final session, when MacLeay and Zoehrer became involved in an extraordinary counter attack, adding 249 in 128 minutes to confirm the draw. They actually scored faster than the Waugh brothers, and each finished with unbeaten centuries.

It must be remembered that when this amazing Waugh partnership took place Mark had not yet played in a Test match. His debut was still a month away, but when it finally came he took his chance boldly and brilliantly — compiling a century of class and grace that left observers wondering only why he had been forced to wait so long. Sadly he was in the side as a replacement for his brother, dropped from the team after 42 consecutive appearances. It was not until later that year that the twins played together in the same Test match. By the final Test of the 1991–92 Test series against India, neither brother was in the side. Those who had seen the pair slaughter the WA attack in December 1990 could not have believed it was so.

# 73

# A COMEBACK OF THE BRAVEST KIND

As Victorian cricket fans celebrated their state's victory in the 1979–80 Sheffield Shield they could surely not have contemplated the awaiting reality — that the trophy would not be won again until 1991. They could not have envisaged that when the concept of a Shield final was introduced in 1982–83, that their state would appear in just *one* of the first eight finals, and that unsuccessfully. For a state with as proud a cricketing tradition as Victoria, the results of the '80s were little short of sporting heresy.

In 1989–90 Victoria had finished last, for the second year in a row. They had provided two players, the flamboyant batsman Dean Jones and the irrepressible and tenacious fast bowler Merv Hughes, to the international season — plus their captain Simon O'Donnell to the one-day matches, but had played without much spirit, and done little to suggest a rosy future. For the new season they were bolstered by the return of the skilful young wicketkeeper Darren Berry from the Cricket Academy in Adelaide, and by the signing of the exciting South Australian left-hander Darren Lehmann.

O'Donnell was in his third year as Victoria's captain. His was as inspiring a story as existed in Australian sport. After playing a crucial role in Australia's World Cup victory in India in 1987, O'Donnell was found to be suffering from a form of cancer and in urgent need of treatment. He tackled his problem and the therapy with a brand of courage that won respect from all Australians. Ultimately he beat the disease so thoroughly that he was able to return to the cricket field as early as 1988. On his comeback he was handed the Victorian captaincy, which he probably did not need, but certainly did not reject.

He was not a leader in the mould of the tacticians such as John Inverarity, or Dirk Wellham. Rather he was a man capable of inspiring others by his bravery and bravado. He was arguably the finest one-day cricketer in the country; only the Waugh twins could match his ability to influence a limited-over game through his batting, bowling and fielding. His bowling was not quite fast enough to be intimidating, but his strength and his persistence made him more than brisk. As a batsman he was extremely strong, striking his drives with formidable power. His technique had been found out at Test level, but he was still a batsman to be feared, a man who through his confidence and daring could turn a game.

Occasionally in the Shield he produced an innings of rare quality, such as the hundred he smashed on a bowler's wicket at St Kilda against NSW in early November 1986. It was the same with his bowling — an example the performance at the SCG in November 1988, when he dismissed Steve Waugh, Mark Waugh and Steve Smith for ducks and took six wickets in all, as NSW collapsed to 8–71 after Victoria had been reduced to 175 all out.

At the end of the 1989–90 season, Victorian state coach Ian Redpath had not sought re-appointment. His replacement was the former Shield batsman, Les Stillman. Another ex-Victorian cricketer, Paul Hibbert, became the new chairman of selectors. Whether these changes were the catalyst for the improvement in the Shield side's fortunes was not easily gauged, but after a depressing batting performance in Brisbane, Victoria thrashed a weakened NSW by nine wickets at St Kilda, and had the better of a draw with Tasmania. They then almost beat South Australia by an innings in Adelaide, and went to Perth and brought off the near-impossible, beating the Western Australians outright.

Jamie Siddons, a right-handed batsman of rare talent, was having a superb season. He had scored a brilliant 245 against NSW, coming in at 3–41, and would score another double century later in the summer against South Australia. Lehmann was slow to start, but found his best form with a dynamic hundred against his former state, followed by another century in Perth. Behind the stumps Berry was outstanding; ultimately he finished the season with 46 dismissals. The bowling was led by the young pacemen Paul Reiffel and Damien Fleming. Against Tasmania at St Kilda, Reiffel had a fabulous game, smashing 86 with the bat and taking 10 wickets with the ball. When Hughes appeared he was outstanding, but Dean Jones' contribution was negligible. Late in the season, with Hughes in the West Indies with the Australian team, the former international medium-pacer Tony Dodemaide re-appeared, and took 20 wickets in the last three games.

In the final game of the regular season, Victoria had to defeat Queensland outright at home to host the final. An outright win for Queensland would have taken the final to the 'Gabba. A draw — and the season's decider would be at the SCG. It all came down to Queensland needing 193, with time of no concern.

*Simon O'Donnell, Victoria's successful captain in 1990–91.*

*Jamie Siddons, whose fourth-innings century for Victoria in the 1990-91 final, turned a match that had to that point been dominated by the bowlers.*

They adopted an unlikely defensive approach, did not score a run in the first seven overs (during which Peter Cantrell was run out) and were eventually dismissed for a dismal 79. The final would be at the MCG, which had been off-limits for Shield games for the entire season while a massive new grandstand was being constructed.

The NSW team that came to Melbourne was without its five Australian players, all in the West Indies, and two others out injured. But they included the Shield's most exciting batsman, the gifted 21-year-old left-hander Michael Bevan. Bevan had scored a century on his Shield debut in 1989–90, for South Australia while studying at the cricket academy at Adelaide. When he returned to Sydney for the following season he at first struggled to make the Blues' star-studded line-up, but once in the side he went on a batting rampage, belting hundreds in five consecutive Shield games, one against each of the states. And he hammered them in the style of a budding champion, treating slow and fast bowling with equal contempt.

That he was to struggle the following season became one of the mysteries of the Shield.

Also in the NSW side was a left-hander of a different kind, the veteran Steve Small, a gutsy, unorthodox opening bat with a bizarre technique, superlative "eye", and lots of runs to prove how good a player he was. Small's basic style was to stand at the crease and crunch anything that deserved crunching, and some that didn't. He favoured the offside with a passion, and was more than prepared to back away to thrash the ball through the covers. His style had won few plaudits from the purists or the selectors, but considerable attention from statisticians who kept their eyes on the seasons' batting aggregates. In 1990–91 he scored more than 1,000 first-class runs — the least likely, but most prolific of all the NSW batsmen.

The first scheduled day of the final was lost to the Melbourne weather. The playing conditions were such that an extra day was then added. When the match finally began, O'Donnell sent the visitors in, and by stumps NSW had struggled to 8–198. Small batted typically, for 82 in 87 balls, but his young colleagues had floundered against the four Victorian fast bowlers and the left-arm spin of Paul Jackson. Small had been the fifth wicket to fall, at 103, after which wicketkeeper Phil Emery and debutant Randall Green had added 73. Three late wickets had tilted the match back Victoria's way.

The next day, after NSW had reached 223, the local batsmen collapsed, all out for just 119. The NSW fast attack of Wayne Holdsworth, Phil Alley and captain Geoff Lawson had prevailed. Holdsworth and Alley were as great a contrast as two opening bowlers could be. Holdsworth, tiny for a paceman, no taller than 5ft 8ins (173cms), fired the ball at the Victorians via a right-handed, slinging delivery based on the same concept as Jeff Thomson's famous action. The 6ft 8 (203cms) Alley used every millimetre of his left-handed delivery as he took three wickets in his first spell, two of them in his first over.

NSW had no time to bat on the second evening — but collapsed the following day, the swing of Dodemaide and determination of O'Donnell being too much for them. Small and Brad McNamara had the Blues at 0–50, but only Bevan of the remaining batsmen fought past 15, as the game changed once more. The target for Victoria was 239, a considerable assignment considering the dominance of bat over ball to that point.

At stumps the chase had reached 2–102. The two wickets fell to Holdsworth in the first 27 runs, after which Siddons and the little opener Wayne Phillips combined in the most significant partnership of the match. The following day, after the first three hours were lost to rain, the Victorians ran to the Shield in a style that belied the regular fall of wickets of the previous sessions. Holdsworth was still blisteringly fast, and Lawson as crafty as ever, but Siddons was outstanding, and Phillips determined, as the target was reached without the further loss of a wicket. Early on Siddons was uncertain, but as the total increased he grew in confidence, and built a century as important as any he would score. The key partnership endured for nearly five tense hours, as Lawson tried anything to contrive a breakthrough.

Afterwards O'Donnell called the game as tense as any he had played in, more draining even than the World Cup final. Lawson was gracious in defeat, and refused to blame the pitch for his batsmen's low scores. The bowling, not the conditions, had been the problem. The last word was with little Phillips, an unglamorous but highly effective player, who had batted right through the five-and-a-half hours of the final's fourth innings for 91, and provided the platform for Siddons to win the game. "Fantastic!" he told *The Age's* Greg Baum, when asked what it felt like to be a part of a Shield win. "A lot of guys play a lot of cricket and don't play in winning Shield teams."

# 74

## A MODERN MIRACLE

In the pages of this book there are stories of remarkable games of cricket — of extraordinary performances that have led to seemingly impossible victories. But has there ever been a comeback to rival the effort of South Australia to win the home match against Queensland in February 1992? The South Australian batsmen were given the task of scoring 506 for outright points. And they got them, with four wickets in hand!

Queensland came into the match as they had most Shield matches played in February over the preceding seasons — as the competition frontrunners. In all of those years they found a way to throw away their lead. This time they were at full strength, and included seven current or past Test players — Allan Border, Craig McDermott, Dirk Wellham, Carl Rackemann, Ian Healy, Peter Taylor and Greg Ritchie — plus the highly credentialled Stuart Law, who had scored 1,087 Shield runs the season before, the most ever by a Queenslander in a single Shield season. The South Australian side was a promising blend of experience and scarcely tested enthusiasm. The skipper was Jamie Siddons, who had transferred to Adelaide after helping Victoria win the Shield final the year before, and the team included the three veterans David Hookes, Andrew Hilditch and Peter Sleep, and the former Test off-spinner Tim May. The batting featured two highly promising sons of former Shield players, Jamie Brayshaw and Greg Blewett; the bowling was led by the highly rated young all-rounder Joe Scuderi, and the quick, but injury prone former Victorian Denis Hickey. Behind the stumps was the second season tyro Tim Nielsen, rated with the Victorian Darren Berry as the most promising gloveman in the country.

South Australia batted disgracefully in the first innings for 130, after Queensland had made 334. McDermott and Rackemann were too much for them. Rackemann, the fourth first-choice Queensland captain in four seasons (after Border, Ritchie and Trevor Hohns), declared his second innings at 4–301, 12 minutes after lunch on the third day, leaving South Australia 580 minutes — which under the conditions of the Shield in 1991–92 meant 154 overs — to get 376 more than they had managed to muster in their first innings.

Rackemann had a slight thigh strain, and McDermott had already bowled a vast number of overs in the season, but the chances of a home victory still looked slightly less than zero. No team had gone that far in a fourth innings to win a match since 1896, when Cambridge University beat a Marylebone Cricket Club "Club and Ground" team at Lord's. In that match the Cambridge captain had insisted that Albert Trott, the M.C.C.'s leading bowler, be taken off because he was intimidating the Varsity batsmen. This, suggested *Wisden*, "militated against the seriousness with which the result was regarded by the public." Two other sides had scored more than 500 in the fourth innings to win a first-class match, one of them a South African Universities XI that defeated Western Province in Stellenbosch, near Cape Town in 1978–79. Coincidentally two century-makers from that successful Universities side, Peter Kirsten and Adrian Kuiper, were in Adelaide, as members of their country's World Cup squad, on the day South Australia achieved their record score. The previous highest successful fourth innings score in a Shield match had been NSW's 6–446 in Adelaide in 1926.

After Rackemann declared, Hilditch and Blewett batted with a purpose that had been totally absent in the first innings. At stumps the South Australians were 0–204, Hilditch on 93, Blewett 97. Hilditch had been dropped once, a difficult return catch to Border. "NOW JUST 302 TO GO" grinned the Adelaide *Advertiser* headline. Asked what the odds should be, Hilditch commented: "We're a chance, but it's a long shot."

Blewett was out immediately the next morning, caught behind by Healy off McDermott. Brayshaw came out, and batted badly against the spin of Border and Taylor, scoring just three from his first 50 balls. Hilditch was much less assertive than he had been on the previous afternoon, but the pair survived, and when Rackemann brought McDermott back with the second new ball, the pair saw the immediate danger through. At lunch the score was 1–276.

Twelve minutes after resuming, Hilditch edged McDermott to Healy, and it was 2–283. Twenty four runs later, Brayshaw drove over a well-pitched delivery from the former NSW paceman Greg Rowell and was bowled. South Australia held its collective breath for another blaze of glory from David Hookes, but the left-hander stayed just 15 minutes, before slicing McDermott to the slip cordon. Border had spilt a similar chance two balls before... but not this time. Two runs to Siddons later, Scuderi was lbw to McDermott for nought, and left ruefully, studying the inside edge of his bat. The fightback had slumped to 5–316.

To date, Jamie Siddons had not had as lucrative a season as he would have wished in Adelaide. In Melbourne he had been felled by a bouncer from former teammate Merv Hughes that struck him on the face, an incident which had typified a season which was more down than up. Twelve months earlier he had been on high on the waiting list of those in line for Australian selection; now he had dropped away. But this day he was quickly in form against McDermott and company, and found a trusty ally in Sleep, veteran of many a lost cause on the Adelaide Oval. Early on Sleep was fortunate, Ritchie at slip being slow to react to an edge off McDermott. The pair saw off the gallant fast bowler, and set about creating a platform for a final-session charge to the line.

Twice more before tea chances were missed, and each time the culprit was Ritchie. First Siddons was missed off Taylor, and then Sleep off the same bowler. At tea South Australia had reached 355. There were 33 more overs scheduled to be bowled. Another 151 runs were needed for the win.

Experienced patrons in the members bar shook their heads. Revivals of this kind always fall short...it is generally the way of the game. All agreed Siddons and his side had done remarkably well to get as far as they had. In the Queensland dressing room, the talk was of staying calm, waiting for wickets to fall. There was no mention of past failures, of previous winning positions thrown away, but the thought was there. Disasters had occurred too many times before.

After tea Siddons and Sleep were magnificent. They came out determined to go for the win — and promptly set about the bowling. Rackemann asked nothing more of his bowlers than he asked of himself, and bowled himself into the ground. McDermott and Taylor were brave, but wearily ineffective. As word spread of the happenings at the Oval, office workers from the city streamed in to watch the final hour. By 5.30pm the crowd had ballooned to more than 5,000. The offical attendance for the day was 1,900.

Siddons and Sleep added 152 in almost even time before the captain fell for 87, bowled by Rackemann. South Australia needed 38 to win with 8 overs to go. With seven overs left the requirement was exactly five per over. The fact that a chase for 506 could come down to a "limited-over" equation of this kind was extraordinary. Sleep and Nielsen took seven off the 148th (seventh last) scheduled over of the innings. 28 needed in six. Then it was 22 off five... 16 off four. With every run the crowd yelled and clapped its support. Throughout it all, Sleep was remarkably calm. He had been the fieldsman who threw the last two batsmen out for the tie against Queensland in 1977. He had been the batsman who scored a century under trying circumstances in the final match of 1979–80. He was the bowler who had taken the match-winning wicket in an Ashes Test with the last ball of the match's second last over. In many ways he had seen all this before, but never in quite such unique circumstances.

Four runs came from the fourth last over. McDermott was running rather than charging in, the petrol all but drained from his tank. Late in the third last over he felt a twinge as his body finally gave up on him. Even so his over cost only three runs. Nine now needed in two.

Taylor had toiled manfully without luck throughout this incredible day. The best "one-day" slow bowler Australia has had, he knew what to do, but his body was not in quite the condition to do exactly what was required. At 10 minutes past six, and in his 42nd over, Taylor could not counter the marauding batsmen. Eight runs came from the second last over, as the crowd went close to berserk. Men in double breasted business suits who had not been to the Shield in years were now remembering why they should never have stayed away. McDermott informed Rackemann he could not bowl the final over, so the captain elected to bowl it himself, and set about trying to prevent the single necessary for the historic win.

Sleep, on strike, needed four for his hundred, though that landmark did not interest him at all. Lance Campbell in the *Advertiser* would later describe his innings as "probably the best non-hundred hundred ever made." Rackemann brave to the last, kept Sleep at bay for the first three balls. For the first time all day, Sleep was in a quandary, and he went to his partner to discuss the gambles that were needed. The fourth ball was shorter, and Sleep propped it up and behind, on the leg-side, for Nielsen, Carl Lewis-like, to sprint through for the winning run. The crowd roared its appreciation. Sleep, blade of the bat in his left hand, waved his arms heavyweight champion-style above his head. The Queenslanders were generous in defeat, quick to congratulate Sleep and Nielsen on their hour of triumph.

It was a victory quite amply described by the task they had completed. One hundred and fifty one runs had been scored in the final two hours and 16 minutes, from 32.4 overs, by a team that had already scored over 350 runs in the innings. To call it a "miracle" win is not to stretch it too much. Captains at any level will always quote the time-honoured maxim that it is harder to chase runs than to score them first. This is true no matter how plumb the wicket, or how many internationals are in the bowling side. The effort of the South Australians was one of the most unlikely in the lifetime of the Shield. The Queenslanders could only shake their heads and conclude that it could only happen to them.

# 75

# HENRY LAWSON

As NSW off-spinner Peter Taylor prepared to bowl the final over of the 1988–89 regular season all sorts of possibilities existed as to the makeup and location of the Shield final. NSW (on 16 competition points) needed two wickets, for an outright victory (and six points) over Queensland, and a place in the final at the WACA. Queensland (20 points) needed nine runs to win outright, to secure the final for the Gabba. South Australia (also on 20 points, and with a superior quotient to Queensland), had just been beaten by Tasmania in Adelaide, and prayed for a draw, which would leave them in the final in Perth. Western Australia (24 points) were safely in the final, but required a NSW outright win or a draw in Sydney for the final to be played in Perth.

Taylor could not find the wickets he sought in that fateful over, but the Queensland batsmen, Ian Healy and Dirk Tazalaar, could score only five. This resolved, Western Australia went on to more than comfortably handle South Australia in the final, with the towering Tom Moody in spectacular form — scoring hundreds in each innings.

NSW in 1988–89 were captained in the latter part of the season by the fast bowler Geoff Lawson, who had been elevated to the position after wicketkeeper Greg Dyer had been controversially sacked following a bitter dispute in Adelaide — a dispute which centred, ironically, on Lawson. The young South Australian left-hander Darren Lehmann had been run out attempting a comfortable single, following a collision with the bowler, Lawson. Many felt Dyer should have refrained from removing the bails with Lehmann spread-eagled on the pitch. He did not, and the Adelaide Oval members gave the NSW team, and especially Dyer and Lawson, a very hot reception when they left the field soon afterwards at the tea break. When the NSW side was announced for the following match, Dyer was not in the side, and Lawson was the new captain.

If Lawson came to the job in unfortunate circumstances, it did not affect him, and he took to the position with relish, adopting a positive, aggressive approach that won him great favour with the NSW faithful. He believed that the idea of the game was to win, and every strategy he adopted, every move he made, was crafted for the purpose of reaching an outright result. He appreciated that in a four-day match it was not always possible to simply rely on your batsmen scoring more runs and your bowlers taking more wickets. Things sometimes had to be hurried along, gambles occasionally had to be taken. Lawson realised that in the Sheffield Shield of the 1990s a captain had to be prepared to lose occasionally if he wanted to win more often.

Geoff Lawson had first come into the NSW Shield team in 1977–78, his rise accelerated by the absence of Gary Gilmour and Len Pascoe who had signed with World Series Cricket. By the time the WSC players returned, Lawson, nicknamed "Henry" after the celebrated poet, was an Australian player, and he held his place in the Shield side comfortably. By 1982–83, with Lillee sidelined through injury, Lawson was leading the Australian attack. At the end of that season he helped NSW to their first Shield success in 17 seasons, in the first ever Shield final, in Perth. At lunch on the final day of that game the home side were 4–180 chasing 293, with Kim Hughes and Rod Marsh in imposing form. But after the break Lawson quickly dismissed both batsmen; then the medium pace cutters of Trevor Chappell cleaned up the tail, and NSW won by 54 runs.

Seven years and many wickets later, Lawson was the state's leader when NSW won the right to host the Shield final, against Queensland. Unluckily Lawson could not play, sidelined by an arm injury, but Test opener, Mark Taylor, took over in devastating fashion, scoring a hundred in each innings as NSW won easily, by 345 runs. The side Lawson guided to the championship that season was an extremely powerful one, especially at home, where the outstanding off-spinning allrounder Greg Matthews was as effective as any bowler in the land. The batting was led by Mark Waugh and the underrated first wicket, Trevor Bayliss; the bowling featured the persistence and skill of the highly popular Mike Whitney.

In the seasons between these two finals, the preparation put in by Shield players had become much more intense. Whitney estimated that the players in 1982–83 had put in perhaps 60% of the work of those of 1989–90. This is not to suggest, he stressed, that the players of 1982–83 were not dedicated or fit. Far from it. Some, such as Trevor Chappell were fitness fanatics. But attitudes had been modified, and the art

*Geoff "Henry" Lawson, who at the end of the first 100 years of the Sheffield Shield had taken more Shield wickets than any other fast bowler, and more than any bowler except the leg-spinner Clarrie Grimmett.*

of cricket preparation had taken a new, more intense direction. Of Geoff Lawson the captain, Whitney said: "He always went for the win. I've never played under anyone else who would do that."

On some occasions Lawson and controversy went arm-in-arm in the quest for outright points. More than once he became involved in confrontations with the equally aggressive captain of South Australia, David Hookes, never more so than in an incident in Sydney in February 1989, in which the two had traded insults on the field and in the press after an attempt to contrive an exciting final day had gone haywire.

Lawson had taken the unusual step of phoning Hookes during the lunch interval of the third day to discuss a "deal". NSW at that point trailed by 122 runs with four first-innings wickets in hand. The suggestion from Lawson was that NSW's two not out batsmen, Matthews and Peter Taylor, would be presented with easy runs to create a situation where Lawson would declare, not too far behind the SA total, leaving Hookes to later set NSW a reasonable target for outright points on the final day. Consequently Hookes kept an attacking field and an unguarded boundary while the batsmen flailed away — but was appalled when Lawson delayed his declaration until after NSW had won first-innings points. Hookes believed he had been betrayed, and registered his protest by having his bowlers aim well wide of the stumps. Later Lawson claimed he had never guaranteed he would declare, but that his phone call was an expression of interest rather than a commitment. It was a peculiar, unnecessary affair that did the competition no good.

In December 1991 Lawson attracted further jibes when he forfeited his side's first innings against Tasmania. On this occasion the criticisms seemed unfair. The match had been severely interfered with by rain, and all Lawson was doing was trying to give his state an opportunity to win outright points. Unfortunately this was a gamble that came unstuck. After Tasmania were bowled out a second time, NSW were dismissed 48 runs short.

During that 1991–92 season, Lawson's last in the Shield, one of his team produced an all-round performance the like of which had not been seen since the days of George Giffen. In the match against Queensland at the SCG, Greg Matthews scored 85 not out and 67 with the bat, and took 6–63 and 5–70 with the ball. No man had managed to combine twin half-centuries with twin five-wicket hauls since Giffen in 1902–03. Matthews, who had been dropped from the Test side at the start of the season, finished the year with 49 Shield wickets, the best season's haul by a NSW spinner since Bill O'Reilly in 1939–40.

Matthews was the key figure in NSW reaching the Shield final in Lawson's farewell season. The match was staged at the WACA, scene of many a battle between the two states, and for five days ebbed and flowed as few Shield contests ever had. It was, despite the colour and flourish of that season's World Cup staged in Australia and New Zealand, the cricket match of the summer, proof yet again that with the leading actors on stage, the Sheffield Shield show can be as inviting as any.

The opening day of the final belonged to the locals, with Tom Moody, Wayne Andrews and Tim Zoehrer hammering half centuries as WA reached 5–295. Next day the WA total reached 396. Then the Waugh brothers, aided by some miserable fielding, drove and cut NSW to 2–208. Both twins went on to centuries (Mark 163, Steve 113), the third time in succession that they had both scored at least hundreds in the same innings against WA at the WACA — but NSW lost their final five wickets for 15, and had their first-innings advantage restricted to just 19 runs.

Lawson must have been hoping for a lead closer to 200, but he and Whitney charged in when WA batted again, and effectively dismantled the top order. Geoff Marsh, facing his second ball, gloved Lawson through to the keeper, Phil Emery. Next over, Mike Veletta was bowled by a Whitney leg-cutter, for his second duck of the match. With the total on three, Moody jabbed Lawson to Steve Small at short leg. Suddenly the first-innings lead was looking more like 1900. The exciting young batsmen, Damien Martyn and Justin Langer, steadied things in the last session, but Martyn (57) fell to Wayne Holdsworth before the close. With the home side at 4–99, and two days remaining, the important cards appeared to be held by the New South Welshmen.

This final however was a match of many hands. The next morning, after Whitney had removed the night-watchman Jo Angel and the dangerous Andrews before the score reached 130, Langer and Zoehrer combined in a 191–run partnership to swing the game back to the west. Langer, in his seventh first-class match, scored 149 and Zoehrer, so often an effective batsman against NSW, reached 81. Whitney came back with the second new ball to take four quick wickets, and end the innings. Before stumps NSW lost Mark Taylor, but Small and Steve Waugh took NSW to 1–71 by the close. The final-day requirement was 255.

The score reached 157 before the second-wicket partnership was broken, Waugh falling to Reid for 68. Then came perhaps the most crucial play of the match. Marsh brought back Angel to bowl at Small and Mark Waugh. In two overs the freewheeling batsmen took Angel for 20 runs, as the victory target loomed larger and larger. Marsh had a dilemma. To persist with his young bowler, or revert to the vastly

*Geoff Lawson's bowling partner in many a Shield batttle — the brave and highly popular Michael Whitney.*

more proven Test men, Reid and Terry Alderman? Marsh gave Angel another over, and Small lofted him to be caught at mid-wicket — out two short of his hundred. Later Marsh commented: "You have to persevere with young blokes. Once they're in the Shield side you can't protect them."

Small's dismissal precipitated a collapse that settled the issue. Seven wickets fell for 53 runs, and only a rollicking stand of 26 between Holdsworth and Whitney for the season's last wicket limited the final margin to 44 runs. Lawson suggested later the match was one of the five best of his career. At the after-match presentation the WA crowd gave him a standing ovation.

Lawson retired as the greatest wicket-taker of all the great Shield wicket-takers since the second World War. In a century of summers only Clarrie Grimmett had taken more than his 367 wickets. During his career he had been at different times superb, controversial, brave, frustrating and colourful, just as the competition itself had been all of these things. As the Sheffield Shield entered its 101st year the challenge for NSW, and the Shield, was to find more cricketers of the style of "Henry" Lawson.

*Western Australia's Tom Moody, who in the 1988–89 final passed 150 in both innings.*

*The Victorian side of 1990–91 celebrate their state's first Shield triumph for over a decade.*

A triumphant South Australian, Peter Sleep, after
his state had scored 6-506 to defeat Queensland
in February, 1992.

# Epilogue by
# Sir Donald Bradman, A.C.

Having written dozens of introductions in my time I found the request to do an epilogue rather appealing. The difference is somewhat akin to that between looking forward to a tasty breakfast and the contentment after a gourmet meal.

I found my challenge of reading and commenting upon *A Century of Summers* very satisfying in that it revived memories on the one hand and vastly improved my knowledge on the other.

Initially the book very correctly surveys how the Australian Sheffield Shield competition came into being. That is fairly well documented though it came as a shock to me to learn that the crucial motion for the Shield to go ahead was only carried by six votes to five.

Also little is known about the attempt by Victoria and NSW, just after World War I, to end the competition.

That the move was frustrated made me feel a sense of pride that South Australia, guided by my old friend the late Bernie Scrymgour, should have led the fight to retain this binding link with England.

The younger generation of Australians as we approach the 21st century can well do with a reminder of how much we owe to the mother country for our heritage.

Australia, in 1891, was in a deep depression and cricket's future not by any means assured when Lord Sheffield made his magnificent donation of 150 pounds (some say guineas) thereby enabling the creation of the Sheffield Shield (made incidentally by a Polish migrant then living in Melbourne) and the birth of the interstate competition bearing that name.

To the modern era, 150 pounds sterling may not sound much, but my enquiry to the Reserve Bank indicated that its worth in today's currency would be of the order of $14,500, and that puts a different complexion on the gift.

But it wasn't only the Sheffield Shield. The noble Lord personally financed the tour of Australia in 1891/92.

We don't know what that cost. But we do know what he paid Dr W.G. Grace to be a member of and captain of the side.

Grace was then 43 years old and approaching the end of his long reign as the dominant figure in cricket history (even though there were 33 centuries still to come from his bat).

His remuneration, as an amateur, was three thousand pounds sterling, worth some $290,000 in today's currency, plus the non-taxable fringe benefit of a free trip for his wife and two children.

Despite his reputation as the father figure of cricket, Grace apparently suffered many barbs from the press, including in one match against NSW, a charge that he told the umpire he (the umpire) was blind.

In 1948, Australia's Sid Barnes found a more subtle way of making such an inference. In one match in England a small dog ran onto the field. The mercurial Barnes chased and caught the dog and then attempted to hand it to the umpire with the remark "you only need the white stick now and you'll be set."

Up until 1891 the matches between NSW, Victoria and South Australia only took place spasmodically whereas with the creation of the Sheffield Shield competition, matches were arranged on a regular basis.

Strangely, Queensland was not a participant and was not admitted to the fold until the 1926/7 season.

Despite continued pleas for admission by West Australia, these were constantly rejected on economic grounds. And understandably so. Jet aircraft had not then been invented.

I feel a sense of satisfaction that I devised a formula which was agreed to by all States and enabled our western neighbour to participate, firstly on a restricted basis in 1947/8, then finally as a full and equal partner.

As I write these lines it is remarkable that Queensland, after nearly 70 years, despite heavy financial outlays to entice prominent overseas players to play for the State, has never won the Shield, whereas West Australia did so in her initial season and many times since.

That record is a tribute to the way cricket has been administered in the West and also to the splendid playing conditions which have always been a feature of cricket in Perth — not least among them the priceless asset of owning and controlling their own ground. In that regard they are the envy of every other State. And not overlooking their sound judgment in the recruitment of overseas players.

*A Century of Summers* naturally highlights people and events which are part of this momentous period. Amongst the notable features are the chapters dealing with the brilliant NSW quartet of Macartney, Kippax, Trumper and Jackson.

Sadly I did not have the pleasure of watching Victor Trumper bat.

Those who did seem unanimous in acclaiming him as the finest stylist of them all. Others have bettered his figures but cricket has a peculiar way of giving points for aesthetic grace and pleasure, assets this quartet referred to had in good measure.

Trumper died much too young and there is an old movie film depicting the thousands of mourners who attended his funeral, a tribute to the adulation showered upon him by friend and foe alike.

Regrettably my memories take in further sadness in relation to Macartney and Jackson. Watching the first Test I ever saw, at the Sydney Cricket ground in 1921, I was privileged to see Macartney make a glorious 170, an innings which was an inspiration to me.

In due course our careers were intermingled and we became staunch friends. Whenever I made a good score there would in the post next day, be a postcard from Charlie depicting on one side the loved photo of his cover drive and on the other the words "keep hitting them".

At his funeral my eyes grew dim as I watched his coffin disappear with his favourite cricket bat on top — something that nostalgically happened with another of cricket's shining lights, Les Favell, many years later.

I was regrettably closer to the scene as a pall bearer at the funeral of Archie Jackson, his cricket career having been cut down at the tender age of 23 when he was in the spring time of a talent which was the greatest I ever saw in one so young.

Alan Kippax was a graceful batsman whose batting, according to legend, was based on the Trumper he watched in his youth.

Jackson, allegedly, emulated Kippax. True or not, they were two of the most attractive players of all time.

As the statistics of Kippax's career show style was not the be all and end all. His name is honoured in *Wisden*, along with Hooker's, for the world's record 10th wicket stand of 307, made in Melbourne against Victoria in 1928/9, a record which may never be broken.

Before the stylists came the eminent tradesmen, including the notable George Giffen from South Australia, dubbed the Australian equivalent of W.G. Grace. Giffen's 271 and 16 for 166 in one match stands unrivalled in all first-class games.

When nearly 44 years of age, he made 81 and 97 not out and took 15 for 185. The chapter on Giffen's life is compelling reading.

Whilst being aware of great figures of the past I was suddenly confronted with a chapter headed "TOM HASTINGS". I had never heard of him. To my astonishment it was a story out of Disneyland.

This comparatively unknown was never quite good enough to command a regular place in the Victorian team and never quite bad enough to be pensioned off. The result was that in 21 years he could only muster 15 appearances for his State. In that time he astounded everyone by once going in at No. 11 and making a century — the only time it has been done in Australian first-class cricket.

Hastings was also involved when, at the end of a day's play, the umpire mistakenly gave the bowler one ball too many and Hastings was bowled by it.

One could hardly be more unlucky than that.

The chapter on Hastings is riveting and should be read over and over.

So indeed should be the chapter on Clem Hill. His father had so many children (16) that he could, in the modern era, have almost lived on pension income without having to work. Surely the revelation highlights the astonishing change in lifestyle.

Today Australia sees families of two and three as the norm, whereas a century ago the Hill example was common.

Clem Hill's father was merely emulating the precedent of Australia's first Test captain, Dave Gregory, one of a family of 13, and who himself had three wives and sired 16 children.

Further to the chapter on Clem Hill, I would think the author underrates Arthur Morris when he claims four left-hand batsmen in the persons of Hill, Sobers, Harvey and Border stand out from the rest. I say that because of Arthur's outstanding record and in particular his marvellous displays on the English tour of 1948. In five Tests he scored 696 runs at an average of 87; on the whole tour 1922 runs at 71.18.

I have written elsewhere that Arthur's form in 1948 was equal to anything I ever saw from a left hander.

Perhaps he doesn't figure quite so prominently in Sheffield Shield history but that was due to World War II taking several seasons out of his most productive years and because he retired relatively early.

Morris burst on the scene like a meteor in 1940 when he opened for NSW against Queensland and made a century in each innings — a feat unequalled on debut by any other player.

Personally, I loved reading about some of the early characters who graced the Sheffield Shield competition, men such as Jack Worrall, John Blackham, Hughie Trumble, Henry Moses (who, as a Trustee of the Sydney Cricket Ground befriended me), and the legendary "Harry" Donnan (the first of all Shield century makers and whose effort to alter my style of batting failed) and the redoubtable Ernie Jones.

There are still those who believe "Jonah" was the fastest bowler who ever played in the Shield. One who certainly believed it was Jones himself.

I say that because from his own lips I heard him say he could "kick his hat faster than Larwood could bowl".

I don't know about his pace but I do know he had an incredible physique simply oozing strength. I once shook hands with him, but once was enough. I thought every finger was broken.

J.C. Davis ("Not Out" of *The Referee*), with whom I briefly worked, was a good friend. He was responsible for one of the most moving stories in the book when he tells of the demise of "Jackie" Marsh.

Undoubtedly two of the many characters in Shield history were the aboriginals Marsh and Eddie Gilbert. The latter was incredibly fast for two or three overs. He very nearly decapitated me one day at the 'Gabba in Brisbane.

Neither achieved Test status, possibly because both were victims of being no-balled for throwing. Indeed Marsh was the first Sheffield Shield bowler to be dealt with in this way.

In 1902 Archie MacLaren, the English captain, refused to allow his team to play against Marsh in a match at Bathurst and Marsh was replaced.

Around that time questionable bowling actions were prevalent in England and a concerted campaign was mounted which resulted in a hasty end to the careers of quite a few bowlers.

Strange how history repeats itself. Australia had a similar experience in the late 1950s and early 1960s. I was deputed to go to London for the International Cricket Conference at which, in conjunction with the late Sir George Allen, I was partly responsible for a re-wording of the law. Remarkably no attempt had previously been made to define what constituted a throw, even though such a delivery was outlawed.

Eddie Gilbert had a short and most controversial time with Queensland.

The description of my first contest against him is colourful and draws heavily on imagination. My notable duck has made the headlines far more than my 233 against him in Adelaide, a score which included 157 runs between lunch and tea, the last 50 in 14 minutes.

There is no doubt the Queensland umpires were very lenient in interpreting Gilbert's bowling action.

I don't want to enlarge upon the Gilbert-Marsh controversy, but, as Davis so eloquently wrote, it was tragic how both these hapless souls ended their lives in such unhappy circumstances.

Harking back to Victor Trumper for a moment — it is incredible how one so universally loved could have fallen foul of the administrators as much as he did.

The story is spelt out of his years of feuding with the NSW Cricket Association. Then there was the famous row with the Australian Cricket Board when he was one of the big six who refused to tour England under the Board's auspices in 1912.

And perhaps more remarkable was his prominence in being one of the leaders who caused the football breakaway in NSW and the setting up of professional Rugby League — Trumper being the first treasurer of the newly created body.

Obviously no book on Sheffield Shield cricket could be complete without reference to its dominating figures. One of them was undoubtedly "Mary Ann" Noble.

Although his first-class career ended long before mine started I did have the pleasure of playing in a match with him and observing first hand how he bowled genuine out swerves due to extreme off spin (as distinct from using the position of the seam for swing).

He combined the use of his strong index finger with a distinctive body position and slightly round arm delivery and I promise you the result was most effective.

Noble was an extremely forceful character who at once gave the impression of being a strong leader — as he was.

I must refer to the incredible records of Bill Ponsford whose scoring in the 1920s was phenomenal.

The writer, who says "Ponsford was close to if not in — the champion class", underrates him. He was indeed a champion.

I ought to know because we had so many great partnerships together including the long standing 2nd wicket record of 451 against England at The Oval in 1934.

Nobody has yet beaten Ponsford's incredible 2454 runs at an average of 163.6, scored in Shield cricket between January 23, 1925 and January 3, 1928. As "Johnnie" Moyes wrote — "he scored his runs with remorseless certainty".

In the midst of a big innings I cannot remember any other player who looked so safe and secure, the only reservation being when he was opposed to bowlers of exceptional speed.

Clarrie Grimmett was the best slow leg spinner I ever saw and he always maintained that he would rather bowl against anyone other than Ponsford.

With it all Ponsford remained not only modest but positively shy, and I really believe his premature retirement in 1934, just before his 34th birthday, was largely because he could no longer put up with the publicity and notoriety surrounding his career.

My late and revered friend "Johnnie" Moyes, often talked to me about "Sunny" Jim Mackay and I found the comments on him most revealing and very sad. That J.C. Davis ranked him alongside Trumper is praise indeed.

Clarrie Grimmett occupies an honoured place in all Shield history. Born in New Zealand, where he played his early cricket, Clarrie gravitated to Sydney, Melbourne and finally Adelaide, where he settled permanently. Then in his early thirties he made up for lost time by carving out for himself a niche amongst the all-time greats.

A small round shouldered man he was often called "the gnome", but his strong sinewy fingers delivered more balls than any man in Shield history and brought him the record tally of 513 wickets. He was the most accurate slow leg spinner of all time and when he was playing for South Australia the bowling crease at one end seemed to belong to him as if by right. I doubt if we will see his like again.

Grimmett's perennial appearances for South Australia in the Shield were in striking contrast to the briefer tenure of Bill O'Reilly. The latter's first class career for NSW was relatively short and for various reasons, in the seasons 1934/5 to 1936/7, he only played three times for his State.

Because of such absences O'Reilly's bag of wickets is much lower than Grimmett's but the marvellous quality of his bowling shows up in his average of 17.10

per wicket — by far the lowest of any of the great bowlers.

Although only slow medium his bowling was accurately described by Hassett as "savage aggression". Attack was his creed and there was never any respite from his relentless accuracy.

Without doubt he was the best bowler I ever faced or saw and he must surely rank with S.F. Barnes as the two best of all time.

Although Tim Wall will never be classified as one of Australia's finest bowlers he can lay claim to perhaps the best single performance in Shield history with his 10 for 36 at Sydney in February 1933.

After lunch he took nine wickets for five in 5.4 overs on a perfectly docile pitch.

Out of a total of 113, Jack Fingleton and I made 99 and there were seven sundries.

I can truthfully say I was never troubled in the slightest by the bowling yet wickets fell like ninepins and when the NSW innings was clearly approaching its end I tried to take the initiative away from Wall only to mishit a simple hook shot.

Everything Tim did that day turned to gold and his name will forever be linked with that one marvellous performance.

Tim was a kind and gentle man. He lacked the fire and brimstone one usually associates with fast bowlers. Yet for half an hour that sunny February afternoon in Sydney, he was the brightest star of all.

And would you believe it — after his playing career had ended the doctors discovered that he was born with only one kidney. What would he have done with two!

In marked contrast to O'Reilly and Grimmett was the "wayward genius" of "Chuck" Fleetwood-Smith. He was more akin to Arthur Mailey who was once described as bowling like a millionaire. Massive spin but straying somewhat in accuracy characterised them both.

"Chuck" was an ambidextrous cricketer, batting right hand and bowling left.

Nobody spun the ball more and nobody was more capable of delivering that one unplayable ball.

In the 4th Test at Adelaide in 1937 he without question won the game for Australia by bowling Hammond with a superb delivery.

His Shield career was brief but brilliant. His life too was comparatively short, his closing years being tragic and sad.

*Wisden* records that he was born in 1910 — his birth certificate says 1908.

During the history of the Sheffield Shield competition there were two periods when play was suspended — during the First World War 1914-18 — and the Second 1939-45. Sadly some fine players lost their lives in those two conflicts. But on each occasion at the end of hostilities a services team was put together in

England and on returning to Australia those teams helped rejuvenate the Shield by producing cricketers of tremendous skill and character.

The star of the A.I.F. team was undoubtedly Jack Gregory, one of the most dynamic and exciting talents ever to play the game.

A wonderful athlete Jack won the 100 yards sprint, the 120 yards hurdles and the tennis cup for his squadron.

Against South Africa in 1921 he made a century at Johannesburg in 70 minutes, still the fastest in terms of time in all Test records.

For the AIF against NSW he opened the batting and made a century in each innings, opened the bowling and took eight wickets, and showed himself to be the world's best slip fieldsman. He went on to become a marvellous Shield personality.

The A.I.F. side threw up a future Australian captain in Herbie Collins, and other splendid players.

The second services side also honed the skills of another future Australian Test captain in the person of Lindsay Hassett, as well as that other mercurial Shield and Test star Keith Miller, who would vie with Gregory as to who was the greater crowd pleaser.

I played a lot of cricket with both these stars. They were tall, handsome and beautifully built — and superb cricketers.

Today's batsmen who resemble American grid-iron players would appear strange to Gregory who never wore even a cap; nor did he ever bother with batting gloves. Sadly Gregory's career was relatively short.

My first Test in 1928 was Gregory's last as he injured a knee going for a caught-and-bowled, and the mishap ended his career. Miller's exciting bursts of fast bowling were also curtailed by injuries — the bug bear of fast bowlers throughout the ages.

Perhaps at this point I might refer to one aspect of Shield cricket which has played quite a part in its history and development, namely the interchange of players between States.

With due modesty may I mention my own case first.

From 1929 to 1934 I had been employed in occupations not so much of my choosing as of economic necessity. These positions meant that I was virtually living, eating and breathing cricket all my wakened hours.

I was not a professional cricketer in that I did not earn my living playing cricket, and I never wanted to be a professional. But my ancillary jobs were too close for comfort and not to my liking. Moreover I was conscious that they in part were responsible for some of my mental and physical fatigue during that five year period.

Accordingly in 1934 when the chance arose to go to South Australia and earn a calling totally unconnected with cricket, together with a six year contract of security, I jumped at the opportunity, despite the enormity of the upset from a private and family point of view.

When I finally took up residence in my adopted State it

helped somewhat to redress the balance of cricket power vis a vis Victoria and NSW.

I suspect a somewhat similar background tipped the scales when Greg Chappell opted to go from South Australia to Queensland, and his presence was a wonderful fillip to the game in that State.

Other examples were perhaps more opportunist in that players on the fringe of selection thought their prospects would be enhanced by changing their domicile. Such a move was outstandingly successful for South Australia and Les Favell. Ashley Mallett and Terry Jenner from Perth to Adelaide also paid handsome dividends, as did Neil Harvey and Keith Miller from Victoria to NSW, whilst Bobby Simpson's shift from Sydney to Perth turned him from a promising batsman into a very great player almost overnight.

Many other names could be mentioned but the chief thrust of my observations is to emphasise the way cricket standards between states have been partially levelled out, which is highly desirable if the competition is to preserve its continuing interest for the public.

Similarly the states, with Victoria a notable exception, have all adopted from time to time the practice of having one overseas player in their ranks — the outstanding case being the world's finest all rounder, Gary Sobers, to South Australia.

By their very presence and example such players lifted the local standard, and in a modest way, attendances.

In the years that lie ahead we are likely to see many more moves of this type, with cricket the ultimate winner.

I found in my reading of *A Century of Summers* that to a large extent the book could be broken down into two parts, the second being the period after World War II.

Prior to that it was relatively easy to isolate individuals or events of special significance whereas the post war story, even though often splendidly descriptive, is so detailed that it is much harder to pick out items to highlight. It starkly reveals the wonderful panorama of gifted players who have adorned the Shield over the years.

As the text discloses, Sheffield Shield cricket after World War II commenced with Bill Johnston bowling and Keith Miller misfielding in the covers. Bill went on to become probably Australia's best left hand bowler and Keith proceeded to join the ranks of the many wonderful all rounders who became such a part of Australia's post war successes — men such as Davidson, Simpson, the Chappells, et al.

The state of Western Australia is rightly congratulated considering its Shield team started its inaugural season with such gusto and success.

Unfortunately I found a jarring note where it is suggested at one point that I was unhappy about WA's initial success. Frankly I think Morgan Herbert was misquoted in this matter but if not, the inference is untrue.

I, more than any other administrator, (as referred to elsewhere) was responsible for WA being admitted to the Shield competition. Moreover I coached its captain Keith Carmody as a lad in Sydney and I rejoiced to see one of my ex-pupils perform so well.

As a selector and as an administrator for much of the period, I saw a great number of the Shield matches in the post-war era and I think the author has shown great perception in his selection of players and events to highlight.

How lucky the Australian public have been, to be presented with cricket of such skill and character.

When for instance Tony Lock took back from the Eastern tour his victorious Shield side, a description is given of a reception in Perth much akin to the more recent triumph of the West Coast Eagles in the AFL and full credit is given to Tony for his aggressive leadership qualities.

The same pattern was adopted by Les Favell and Ian Chappell in SA and by Richie Benaud in NSW. In his own quiet but dignified way John Inverarity also stamped his character on the play.

Those present will never forget Colin Milburn's 181 between lunch and tea in Brisbane nor Barry Richards' 325 in a day at Perth.

The description of Queensland's nail biting loss just when they appeared to have won the Shield for the first time is quite exciting.

Contemplating my reading about Shield matches over the more recent years and having regard to the volume of cricket played I feared the possibility of a plethora of statistics which might have become boring. To my relief and enjoyment I discovered the reverse was the case. The narrative is racy and entertaining.

The deeds of David Hookes for instance are not enmeshed in just a mass of figures but are brought to life in a very exciting way. His wonderful century off 34 balls and his marvellous partnership with Wayne Phillips become living performances before your eyes.

In the same way the combination of Rod Marsh and Dennis Lillee is brought out as a part of living history instead of just a statistic.

I pictured in my mind's eye the staggering partnership of the Waugh brothers Steve and Mark in Perth with their record shattering 464 unconquered.

Cricket has thrown up at least four examples of twins who graced the fields of play. Perhaps least renowned were Laurie and Norm Walsh who played for South Australia.

They were both personal friends of mine and Laurie recounted how he went on an interstate trip during which he had the great pleasure in Melbourne of entertaining a female partner. The next season he was not in the side but his twin brother was, so Laurie duly passed over the lady's address and phone number. Norm did the right thing and took her out for an evening's entertainment and he swore the girl believed it was the same person on both occasions.

To those who think the standard of modern cricket has declined I would point out that in 1930 Stan

McCabe was selected for the Australian side to tour England without having scored a first-class century.

I reflected on this as I read about the scintillating hundreds made by two very attractive left handers, Michael Bevan and Darren Lehmann, still not deemed good enough to warrant a green blazer. It helped indicate the great reservoir of talent latent today in the Shield ranks.

In the chapter headed "FAREWELL TO THE DON", the author pays me a tribute which I appreciate and humbly acknowledge.

I would have preferred not to have played at all after returning from England in 1948 but could scarcely refrain from playing in my own testimonial match, which the Board generously arranged.

And having done that I could hardly do other than play in the benefit matches for Alan Kippax/Bert Oldfield and for Arthur Richardson.

Sadly my physical condition and my form really did not warrant my participation and I regretted not doing better in both games. The truth is that my best days in the Shield were prior to 1940 and though I played again after the War I did so more for patriotic than personal reasons.

I was glad to read the eulogistic remarks about Phil Ridings. As a South Australian I saw, more than most people, the work Phil put into his cricket (with perhaps less reward than he deserved) firstly as a player and secondly as an administrator.

In the latter context few people served the game so long and so capably. The same can be said for Alan Davidson and, in his special domain, Bobby Simpson.

In many ways I think it is a pity more leading players don't turn their hands towards administration because the experience of the heat and burden of the day in the middle undoubtedly gives one a "feel" for the game which many non performers lack.

As an example I would refer to Richie Benaud.

He was not an overnight star — indeed the selectors, with patience and foresight, persevered with him when they could not have been blamed had they given him a spell. They were rewarded by his eventual blossoming into a great all-rounder but I think even more so by what I would describe as his "captaincy flair", and by his acute perception of what was good for cricket and for public entertainment.

Who will ever forget the tied Test in Brisbane? It was the attitudes of the captains that day which were responsible for the thrilling cricket.

Cricket is competing against alternate forms of entertainment to a greater degree than ever before, and in a social era whereby the turn of a knob is enough to signal dissatisfaction with the fare being offered.

I fully understand Richie's inability to combine administration with his present occupation and would like to express my appreciation for his balanced and sensible contributions on our TV screens.

I don't think I am being pessimistic but I am certainly being realistic when I say that our legislators cannot afford to be complacent about the future.

There was a time when the gate money taken at Sheffield Shield matches was enough to make the competition self supporting and viable.

Those days are gone. The game now depends on revenue from other sources such as TV and sponsorship. And it would seem that before long cricket will be denied the freedom to accept sponsorships from whatever source it pleases. Despite such problems I believe it to be imperative that a full Sheffield Shield programme be played every year — otherwise the feed stock will dry up.

Back in 1954-55 a restricted program was played. It proved a disaster in every way and I hope the lesson has been learned.

This book details how we once had an incentive points system of scoring in Shield cricket. I believe it was a great success and that we would be wise to bring it back. No system can be devised which will please everybody and the change away from the incentive points system was, I believe, made on emotional grounds, and was a big mistake.

Our administrators should not shirk from being innovative and from using the Shield competition as a testing ground. I'm even radical enough to think we should revert to eight ball overs (despite any resistance from the M.C.C.) because such a move would be better for the game and the public prefer it. We did it in the 1920s and it proved successful.

And we should press on relentlessly to get a reversion to the back foot no-ball law, because the front foot rule is a failure and disastrous for spectators. And for good measure have another look at restricting the on-side field to five, as we once did with good results.

When limited overs games first started I led the van in advocating restrictions on field placing. Many people objected to my view.

They were of course short-sighted. Once they saw a match with the farcical situation in a tight finish of every fieldsman including the wicket keeper on the fence, there was a clamour for change. Nobody in his right mind would now revert to unrestricted field placings.

We should not shrink from sensible evolution in our great Shield competition. Let us encourage our players to stamp their authority and character on what posterity has handed down.

The major cricketing countries have domestic competitions from which they draw their Test players. England has its County Championship and there are a number of minor leagues (such as the Lancashire League) but these are usually confined to weekend fixtures. Seldom (with S.F. Barnes the big exception) has a player been selected for England in an international game unless a regular County player.

In Australia, although the selectors are not bound by Sheffield Shield status, it has also been rare for a player outside those ranks to be chosen for Tests or a touring party. And any such departures have not been notably successful.

From my own observations, and from opinions passed on to me, I believe the Australian Sheffield Shield competition sets a higher standard of play than any other of its kind in the world.

In recent years heavy inroads have been made into the Shield programme by the concentration of Tests and limited over games.

This is an aspect which will need careful handling in the future because it is imperative to retain a strong Sheffield Shield for the introduction of competent players into the Test arena.

Cricket is still our greatest game. It behoves us all to make sure it is preserved for all time.

*Left: Don Bradman wearing the colours of NSW.
Above: Bradman congratulated by his Queensland opponents after breaking Bill Ponsford's Shield-record highest score in January, 1930.*

# Statistics

***Compiled By Ian Russell — As at 30 September, 1992***

## 1. SHIELD CHAMPIONS

| | |
|---|---|
| 1892-93 | Victoria |
| 1893-94 | South Australia |
| 1894-95 | Victoria |
| 1895-96 | NSW |
| 1896-97 | NSW |
| 1897-98 | Victoria |
| 1898-99 | Victoria |
| 1899-00 | NSW |
| 1900-01 | Victoria |
| 1901-02 | NSW |
| 1902-03 | NSW |
| 1903-04 | NSW |
| 1904-05 | NSW |
| 1905-06 | NSW |
| 1906-07 | NSW |
| 1907-08 | Victoria |
| 1908-09 | NSW |
| 1909-10 | South Australia |
| 1910-11 | NSW |
| 1911-12 | NSW |
| 1912-13 | South Australia |
| 1913-14 | NSW |
| 1914-15 | Victoria |
| 1919-20 | NSW |
| 1920-21 | NSW |
| 1921-22 | Victoria |
| 1922-23 | NSW |
| 1923-24 | Victoria |
| 1924-25 | Victoria |
| 1925-26 | NSW |
| 1926-27 | South Australia |
| 1927-28 | Victoria |
| 1928-29 | NSW |
| 1929-30 | Victoria |
| 1930-31 | Victoria |
| 1931-32 | NSW |
| 1932-33 | NSW |
| 1933-34 | Victoria |
| 1934-35 | Victoria |
| 1935-36 | South Australia |
| 1936-37 | Victoria |
| 1937-38 | NSW |
| 1938-39 | South Australia |
| 1939-40 | NSW |
| 1946-47 | Victoria |
| 1947-48 | Western Australia |
| 1948-49 | NSW |
| 1949-50 | NSW |
| 1950-51 | Victoria |
| 1951-52 | NSW |
| 1952-53 | South Australia |
| 1953-54 | NSW |
| 1954-55 | NSW |
| 1955-56 | NSW |
| 1956-57 | NSW |
| 1957-58 | NSW |
| 1958-59 | NSW |
| 1959-60 | NSW |
| 1960-61 | NSW |
| 1961-62 | NSW |
| 1962-63 | Victoria |
| 1963-64 | South Australia |
| 1964-65 | NSW |
| 1965-66 | NSW |
| 1966-67 | Victoria |
| 1967-68 | Western Australia |
| 1968-69 | South Australia |
| 1969-70 | Victoria |
| 1970-71 | South Australia |
| 1971-72 | Western Australia |
| 1972-73 | Western Australia |
| 1973-74 | Victoria |
| 1974-75 | Western Australia |
| 1975-76 | South Australia |
| 1976-77 | Western Australia |
| 1977-78 | Western Australia |
| 1978-79 | Victoria |
| 1979-80 | Victoria |
| 1980-81 | Western Australia |
| 1981-82 | South Australia |
| 1982-83 | NSW |
| 1983-84 | Western Australia |
| 1984-85 | NSW |
| 1985-86 | NSW |
| 1986-87 | Western Australia |
| 1987-88 | Western Australia |
| 1988-89 | Western Australia |
| 1989-90 | NSW |
| 1990-91 | Victoria |
| 1991-92 | Western Australia |

*Notes:*
*1. No competition took place between 1915 and 1919 because of World War I.*
*2. No competition took place between 1940 and 1946 because of World War II.*
*3. Bonus points were awarded for first innings performances between 1971-72 and 1980-81.*
*4. A Sheffield Shield Final was first played in 1982-83 (see section 11)*

## 2. TEAM RECORDS

### Summary of Seasons

| *State* | *No. of Seasons* | *1st* | *2nd* | *3rd* | *4th* | *5th* | *6th* |
|---|---|---|---|---|---|---|---|
| NSW | 90 | 40 | 24 | 15 | 8 | 3 | - |
| Queensland | 60 | - | 12 | 14 | 22 | 12 | - |
| South Australia | 90 | 12 | 17 | 34 | 8 | 18 | 1 |
| Tasmania | 15 | - | - | 1 | 3 | 2 | 9 |
| Victoria | 90 | 25 | 32 | 18 | 7 | 3 | 5 |
| Western Australia | 45 | 13 | 5 | 8 | 12 | 7 | - |

### Summary Of Games Played

| *State* | *First Season* | *Played* | *Won* | *Lost* | *Drawn* | *Tied* |
|---|---|---|---|---|---|---|
| NSW | 1892-93 | 587 | 263 | 150 | 173 | 1 |
| Queensland | 1926-27 | 464 | 111 | 171 | 181 | 1 |
| South Australia | 1892-93 | 578 | 165 | 257 | 155 | 1 |
| Tasmania | 1977-78 | 125 | 12 | 48 | 65 | - |
| Victoria | 1892-93 | 579 | 219 | 163 | 196 | 1 |
| Western Australia | 1947-48 | 353 | 117 | 98 | 138 | - |

| | |
|---|---|
| Total matches played: | 1343 |
| Outright results: | 887 |
| Draws: | 454 |
| Ties: | 2 |

*Notes:*
*1. All results in this table are outright results. Results on the first innings have not been included.*
*2. There have been three matches abandoned without a ball being bowled. All three were scheduled between Queensland and Victoria, and have not been included in these tables.*

| New South Wales | *Played* | *Won* | *Lost* | *Drawn* | *Tied* |
|---|---|---|---|---|---|
| v Queensland | 123 | 51 | 25 | 47 | - |
| v South Australia | 176 | 100 | 46 | 30 | - |
| v Tasmania | 25 | 11 | 4 | 10 | - |
| v Victoria | 181 | 68 | 54 | 58 | 1 |
| v Western Australia | 82 | 33 | 21 | 28 | - |
| Total | 587 | 263 | 150 | 173 | 1 |

| Queensland | *Played* | *Won* | *Lost* | *Drawn* | *Tied* |
|---|---|---|---|---|---|
| v NSW | 123 | 25 | 51 | 47 | - |
| v South Australia | 118 | 33 | 44 | 40 | 1 |
| v Tasmania | 25 | 8 | 2 | 15 | - |
| v Victoria | 116 | 30 | 46 | 40 | - |
| v Western Australia | 82 | 15 | 28 | 39 | - |
| Total | 464 | 111 | 171 | 181 | 1 |

| South Australia | *Played* | *Won* | *Lost* | *Drawn* | *Tied* |
|---|---|---|---|---|---|
| v NSW | 176 | 46 | 100 | 30 | - |
| v Queensland | 118 | 44 | 33 | 40 | 1 |
| v Tasmania | 25 | 9 | 1 | 15 | - |
| v Victoria | 176 | 42 | 88 | 46 | - |
| v Western Australia | 83 | 24 | 35 | 24 | - |
| Total | 578 | 165 | 257 | 155 | 1 |

| Tasmania | *Played* | *Won* | *Lost* | *Drawn* | *Tied* |
|---|---|---|---|---|---|
| v NSW | 25 | 4 | 11 | 10 | - |
| v Queensland | 25 | 2 | 8 | 15 | - |
| v South Australia | 25 | 1 | 9 | 15 | - |
| v Victoria | 25 | 3 | 7 | 15 | - |
| v Western Australia | 25 | 2 | 13 | 10 | - |
| Total | 125 | 12 | 48 | 65 | - |

| Victoria | Played | Won | Lost | Drawn | Tied |
|---|---|---|---|---|---|
| v New South Wales | 181 | 54 | 68 | 58 | 1 |
| v Queensland | 116 | 46 | 30 | 40 | - |
| v South Australia | 176 | 88 | 42 | 46 | - |
| v Tasmania | 25 | 7 | 3 | 15 | - |
| v Western Australia | 81 | 24 | 20 | 37 | - |
| Total | 579 | 219 | 163 | 196 | 1 |

| Western Australia | Played | Won | Lost | Drawn | Tied |
|---|---|---|---|---|---|
| v New South Wales | 82 | 21 | 33 | 28 | - |
| v Queensland | 82 | 28 | 15 | 39 | - |
| v South Australia | 83 | 35 | 24 | 24 | - |
| v Tasmania | 25 | 13 | 2 | 10 | - |
| v Victoria | 81 | 20 | 24 | 37 | - |
| Total | 353 | 117 | 98 | 138 | - |

## Highest Team Scores

| Total | Match | Ground | Season |
|---|---|---|---|
| 1107 | Victoria v NSW | Melbourne | 1926-27 |
| 918 | NSW v Sth Australia | Sydney | 1900-01 |
| 821 (7 wkts) | Sth Australia v Qld | Adelaide | 1939-40 |
| 815 | NSW v Victoria | Sydney | 1908-09 |
| 807 | NSW v Sth Australia | Adelaide | 1899-00 |
| 805 | NSW v Victoria | Melbourne | 1905-06 |
| 802 | NSW v Sth Australia | Sydney | 1920-21 |
| 793 | Victoria v Queensland | Melbourne | 1927-28 |
| 786 | NSW v Sth Australia | Adelaide | 1922-23 |
| 770 | NSW v Sth Australia | Adelaide | 1920-21 |
| 761 (8 wkts) | NSW v Queensland | Sydney | 1929-30 |
| 724 | Vic v Sth Australia | Melbourne | 1920-21 |
| 713 (6 wkts) | NSW v Victoria | Sydney | 1928-29 |
| 713 | NSW v Sth Australia | Adelaide | 1908-09 |
| 708 | NSW v Victoria | Sydney | 1925-26 |
| 705 | NSW v Victoria | Melbourne | 1925-26 |

Notes:
The highest scores for other states are:

| | | | |
|---|---|---|---|
| Queensland | 687 v NSW | Brisbane | 1930-31 |
| Tasmania | 592 v Sth Australia | Adelaide | 1987-88 |
| Western Aust | 654 v Victoria | Perth | 1986-87 |

## Lowest Team Scores (Completed Innings)

| Total | Match | Ground | Season |
|---|---|---|---|
| 27 | South Australia v NSW | Sydney | 1955-56 |
| 31 | Victoria v NSW | Melbourne | 1906-07 |
| 35 | Victoria v NSW | Sydney | 1926-27 |
| 41 | WA v South Australia | Adelaide | 1989-90 |
| 43 | Victoria v South Australia | Melbourne | 1895-96 |
| 49 | Queensland v Victoria | Melbourne | 1936-37 |
| 50 | Western Australia v NSW | Sydney | 1951-52 |
| 51 | Western Australia v NSW | Perth | 1950-51 |
| 52 | Queensland v WA | Perth | 1982-83 |
| 54 | Queensland v Victoria | Brisbane | 1932-33 |
| 54 | WA v Queensland | Brisbane | 1972-73 |

Note:
The lowest totals by other states are:

| | | | |
|---|---|---|---|
| NSW | 66 v Victoria | Melbourne | 1894-95 |
| Tasmania | 76 v NSW | Hobart | 1991-92 |

## Highest Match Aggregates

| Runs | Wkts | Result |
|---|---|---|
| 1929 | 39 | NSW (642 and 593) beat South Australia (475 and 219) by 541 runs, Sydney, 1925-26 |
| 1911 | 34 | NSW (815 and 4-141) beat Victoria (468 and 487) by six wickets, Sydney, 1908-09 |
| 1752 | 34 | Queensland (577 and 5-300) beat NSW (287 and 588) by five wickets, Sydney, 1926-27 |
| 1716 | 40 | South Australia (349 and 519) beat NSW (276 and 572) by 20 runs, Sydney, 1907-08 |
| 1683 | 40 | Victoria (310 and 724) beat South Australia (246 and 403) by 385 runs, Melbourne, 1920-21 |

Note:
Since 1930 matches have been limited to four days (excluding Shield finals since 1982-83, which ran for five days). The highest match aggregate since 1930 is:

| | | |
|---|---|---|
| 1568 | 34 | SA (528 and 6-257) beat NSW (347 and 8 (dec) 436) by four wickets, Adelaide, 1965-66 |

## Lowest Match Aggregates (Completed Matches)

| Runs | Wkts | Result |
|---|---|---|
| 417 | 30 | SA (199 and 0-10) beat Victoria (165 and 43) by 10 wickets, Melbourne, 1895-96 |
| 430 | 30 | NSW (217) beat Tasmania (76 and 137) by an innings and four runs, Hobart, 1991-92 |
| 431 | 30 | Queensland (238) beat SA (97 and 96) by an innings and 45 runs, Brisbane, 1976-77 |
| 460 | 30 | Victoria (8 (dec) 182 and 2-49) beat Western Australia (126 and 103) by eight wickets, Melbourne, 1950-51 |

Note:
The lowest match aggregate in a match where 40 wickets fell is:
| | | |
|---|---|---|
| 537 | 40 | NSW (127 and 151) beat Victoria (88 and 171) by 19 runs, Sydney, 1893-94 |

## Largest Margins of Victory

*By an Innings Margin:*

| | |
|---|---|
| Innings and 656 runs | Victoria (1107) defeated NSW (221 and 230), Melbourne, 1926-27 |
| Innings and 605 runs | NSW (918) defeated South Australia (157 and 156), Sydney, 1900-01 |
| Innings and 527 runs | NSW (713) defeated South Australia (97 and 89), Adelaide, 1908-09 |

*By a Runs Margin:*

| | |
|---|---|
| 685 runs | NSW (235 and 8 (dec) 761) defeated Queensland (227 and 84), Sydney, 1929-30 |
| 638 runs | NSW (304 and 770) defeated South Australia (265 and 171), Adelaide, 1920-21 |
| 571 runs | Victoria (304 and 649) defeated South Australia (149 and 233), Melbourne, 1926-27 |

## Closest Margins of Victory

| | |
|---|---|
| 6 runs | NSW (306 and 5 (dec) 390) defeated South Australia (376 and 314), Adelaide, 1963-64 |
| 7 runs | NSW (154 and 248) defeated Western Australia (233 and 162), Sydney, 1960-61 |
| 7 runs | SA (5 (dec) 279 and 177) defeated Victoria (7 (dec) 275 and 174), Melbourne, 1975-76 |
| 8 runs | NSW (280 and 475) defeated Queensland (356 and 391), Brisbane, 1926-27 |

Note:
There have been 14 instances of victory by one wicket. The occasion on which most runs were added for the last wicket is: South Australia (216 and 9-263) defeated NSW (258 and 220), Sydney, 1971-72, when M Hendricks and KJ McCarthy added an unbeaten 49 for the final wicket

## Tied Matches

Victoria (244 and 197) v NSW (281 and 160), St Kilda, 1956-57
South Australia (431 and 7 (dec) 171) v Queensland (8 (dec) 340

## Victory After Following-on

South Australia (212 and 330) defeated NSW (337 and 148) by 57 runs, Adelaide, 1892-93
NSW (108 and 450) defeated Queensland (307 and 224) by 27 runs, Brisbane, 1965-66

## Most Outright Wins in Succession

| | | |
|---|---|---|
| 13 | NSW | 1903-04 to 1906-07 |

## Most Matches Without Outright Defeat
27 (16 wins, 11 draws) Western Australia    1975-76 to 1978-79

*Note: This sequence of undefeated matches was ended by Western Australia's loss to Tasmania at Devonport in January, 1979 - Tasmania's first win in the Sheffield Shield.*

## Most Outright Losses in Succession
16    Sth Australia    1920-21 to 1924-25

*Note: In the match immediately before the commencement of this sequence, South Australia followed-on after trailing NSW by 611 runs on the first innings. The match was abandoned due to rain. Prior to this draw, South Australia lost ten successive matches between 1914-15 and 1920-21.*

## Most Matches in Succession Without Outright Victory
40 (20 losses, 20 draws) Tasmania    1983-84 to 1987-88

## 3. APPEARANCE RECORDS
### Most Games For Each State

| State | Games | Player | Career |
|---|---|---|---|
| NSW | 103 | GF Lawson | 1977-78 to 1991-92 |
| Queensland | 123 | SC Trimble | 1959-60 to 1975-76 |
| Sth Australia | 121 | LE Favell | 1951-52 to 1969-70 |
| Tasmania | 76 | DC Boon | 1978-79 to 1991-92 |
| Victoria | 101 | RJ Bright | 1972-73 to 1987-88 |
| WA | 108 | RJ Inverarity | 1962-63 to 1978-79 |

### Most Games

| Games | Player | Career |
|---|---|---|
| 159 | RJ Inverarity (WA, SA) | 1962-63 to 1984-85 |
| 123 | SC Trimble (Qld) | 1959-60 to 1975-76 |
| 121 | LE Favell (SA) | 1951-52 to 1969-70 |
| 120 | DW Hookes (SA) | 1975-76 to 1991-92 |
| 117 | PR Sleep (SA) | 1976-77 to 1991-92 |
| 109 | GM Wood (WA) | 1977-78 to 1991-92 |
| 108 | AMJ Hilditch (NSW, SA) | 1977-78 to 1991-92 |
| 107 | HN Dansie (SA) | 1949-50 to 1966-67 |
| 105 | TV Hohns (Qld) | 1972-73 to 1990-91 |
| 103 | GF Lawson (NSW) | 1977-78 to 1991-92 |
| 101 | GS Chappell (SA, Qld) | 1966-67 to 1983-84 |
| 101 | RJ Bright (Vic) | 1972-73 to 1987-88 |
| 100 | KD Mackay (Qld) | 1946-47 to 1963-64 |
| 99 | DM Wellham (NSW, Tas, Qld) | 1980-81 to 1991-92 |
| 94 | SJ Rixon (NSW) | 1974-75 to 1987-88 |
| 94 | GM Ritchie (Qld) | 1980-81 to 1991-92 |
| 91 | IJ Brayshaw (WA) | 1960-61 to 1977-78 |
| 91 | KD Walters (NSW) | 1962-63 to 1980-81 |
| 91 | TM Alderman (WA) | 1974-75 to 1991-92 |
| 90 | KH MacLeay (WA) | 1981-82 to 1991-92 |

*Note:*
*Most games by players before 1940 were:*

| | | |
|---|---|---|
| 79 | CV Grimmett (Vic, SA) | 1923-24 to 1939-40 |
| 77 | VY Richardson (SA) | 1919-20 to 1936-37 |

## 4. GROUND RECORDS

### Grounds Used

| Ground | Home State | No. of Games | Seasons Used |
|---|---|---|---|
| Adelaide Oval | SA | 286 | 1892-93 to 1991-92 |
| Melbourne Cricket Ground | Vic | 266 | 1892-93 to 1991-92 |
| Sydney Cricket Ground | NSW | 281 | 1892-93 to 1991-92 |
| Exhibition Ground, Brisbane | Qld | 13 | 1926-27 to 1930-31 |
| Brisbane Cricket Ground (The Gabba) | Qld | 214 | 1931-32 to 1991-92 |
| W.A.C.A. Ground, Perth | WA | 180 | 1947-48 to 1991-92 |
| Junction Oval, St Kilda | Vic | 20 | 1955-56 to 1990-91 |
| Sydney Cricket Ground No. 2 | NSW | 1 | 1966-67 |
| T.C.A. Ground, Hobart | Tas | 12 | 1977-78 to 1986-87 |
| N.T.C.A. Ground, Launceston | Tas | 17 | 1977-78 to 1989-90 |
| Devonport Oval | Tas | 19 | 1977-78 to 1989-90 |
| Oakes Oval, Lismore | NSW | 1 | 1979-80 |
| Kardinia Park, Geelong | Vic | 4 | 1980-81 to 1981-82 |
| Newcastle Sportsground | NSW | 9 | 1981-82 to 1989-90 |
| Princes Park, Carlton | Vic | 2 | 1984-85 |
| Manuka Oval, Canberra | NSW | 1 | 1984-85 |
| Wangaratta Showground | Vic | 1 | 1986-87 |
| Bellerive Oval, Hobart | Tas | 15 | 1987-88 to 1991-92 |
| Lavington Sportsground, Albury | NSW | 1 | 1989-90 |

### Highest Score and Best Bowling at Each Ground

| Ground | Total | Batsman | Match | Season | Total | Bowler | Match | Season |
|---|---|---|---|---|---|---|---|---|
| Adelaide Oval | 365* | C Hill | SA v NSW | 1900-01 | 9-40 | EL McCormick | Vic v SA | 1936-37 |
| MCG | 437 | WH Ponsford | Vic v Qld | 1927-28 | 10-61 | PJ Allan | Qld v Vic | 1965-66 |
| SCG | 452* | DG Bradman | NSW v Qld | 1929-30 | 10-36 | TW Wall | SA v NSW | 1932-33 |
| Exhibition Ground | 275* | FC Thompson | Qld v NSW | 1930-31 | 7-35 | H Ironmonger | Vic v Qld | 1929-30 |
| The Gabba | 359 | RB Simpson | NSW v Qld | 1963-64 | 9-67 | AN Connolly | Vic v Qld | 1964-65 |
| W.A.C.A. Ground | 356 | BA Richards | SA v WA | 1970-71 | 10-44 | IJ Brayshaw | WA v Vic | 1967-68 |
| Junction Oval | 249 | KC Wessels | Qld v Vic | 1982-83 | 7-81 | MG Hughes | Vic v Qld | 1987-88 |
| SCG No. 2 | 122 | G Goffet | NSW v WA | 1966-67 | 4-63 | JF Martin | NSW v WA | 1966-67 |
| T.C.A. Ground | 198 | RF Jeffery | Tas v Qld | 1979-80 | 8-41 | LS Pascoe | NSW v Tas | 1981-82 |
| N.T.C.A. Ground | 176 | GM Watts | Vic v Tas | 1987-88 | 8-95 | PM Clough | Tas v WA | 1983-84 |
| Devonport Oval | 220 | KC Wessels | Qld v Tas | 1981-82 | 7-59 | MA Holding | Tas v Vic | 1982-83 |
| Oakes Oval | 85 | KC Wessels | Qld v NSW | 1979-80 | 5-33 | GR Beard | NSW v Qld | 1979-80 |
| Kardinia Park | 173 | KC Wessels | Qld v Vic | 1981-82 | 4-12 | TM Chappell | NSW v Vic | 1981-82 |
| Newcastle | 143 | PS Clifford | NSW v Tas | 1984-85 | 7-54 | CJ McDermott | Qld v NSW | 1987-88 |

| Ground | Total | Batsman | Match | Season | Total | Bowler | Match | Season |
|---|---|---|---|---|---|---|---|---|
| Princes Park | 118 | MD Taylor | Vic v Tas | 1984-85 | 4-89 | WM Clark | WA v Vic | 1984-85 |
| Manuka Oval | 76 | J Dyson | NSW v WA | 1984-85 | 4-42 | GF Lawson | NSW v WA | 1984-85 |
| Wangaratta | 141 | GM Ritchie | Qld v Vic | 1986-87 | 6-89 | CJ McDermott | Qld v Vic | 1986-87 |
| Bellerive Oval | 223 | GR Marsh | WA v Tas | 1988-89 | 7-46 | GJ Rowell | Qld v Tas | 1991-92 |
| Lavington | 100* | ME Waugh | NSW v Vic | 1989-90 | 4-13 | GRJ Matthews | NSW v Vic | 1989-90 |

## 5. BATTING RECORDS

### Most Runs in a Career

| Runs | Batsman | Career | M | Inn | NO | HI | 100 | 50 | Average |
|---|---|---|---|---|---|---|---|---|---|
| 9364 | DW Hookes (SA) | 1975-76 to 1991-92 | 120 | 205 | 9 | 306* | 26 | 44 | 47.77 |
| 9341 | RJ Inverarity (WA, SA) | 1962-63 to 1984-85 | 159 | 275 | 32 | 187 | 23 | 45 | 38.44 |
| 8926 | DG Bradman (NSW, SA) | 1927-28 to 1948-49 | 62 | 96 | 15 | 452* | 36 | 20 | 110.19 |
| 8762 | GS Chappell (SA, Qld) | 1966-67 to 1983-84 | 101 | 173 | 20 | 194 | 27 | 42 | 57.27 |
| 8647 | SC Trimble (Qld) | 1959-60 to 1975-76 | 123 | 230 | 13 | 252* | 22 | 40 | 39.85 |
| 8269 | LE Favell (SA) | 1951-52 to 1969-70 | 121 | 220 | 4 | 164 | 20 | 43 | 38.28 |
| 7665 | IM Chappell (SA) | 1961-62 to 1979-80 | 89 | 157 | 13 | 205* | 22 | 45 | 53.22 |
| 7613 | AMJ Hilditch (NSW, SA) | 1977-78 to 1991-92 | 108 | 192 | 11 | 230 | 18 | 32 | 42.06 |
| 7084 | PJP Burge (Qld) | 1952-53 to 1967-68 | 83 | 138 | 12 | 283 | 22 | 30 | 56.22 |
| 6904 | GM Wood (WA) | 1977-78 to 1991-92 | 109 | 174 | 25 | 186* | 20 | 32 | 46.33 |
| 6692 | HN Dansie (SA) | 1949-50 to 1966-67 | 107 | 196 | 6 | 185 | 17 | 32 | 35.22 |
| 6615 | WM Lawry (Vic) | 1955-56 to 1971-72 | 85 | 139 | 14 | 266 | 17 | 38 | 52.92 |
| 6520 | AR Border (NSW, Qld) | 1978-79 to 1991-92 | 81 | 137 | 12 | 200 | 16 | 34 | 52.16 |
| 6471 | RB Simpson (NSW, WA) | 1952-53 to 1977-78 | 78 | 133 | 21 | 359 | 17 | 28 | 57.77 |
| 6341 | KD Mackay (Qld) | 1946-67 to 1963-64 | 100 | 162 | 22 | 223 | 14 | 31 | 45.29 |
| 6285 | DM Wellham (NSW, Qld, Tas) | 1980-81 to 1991-92 | 99 | 159 | 21 | 167 | 11 | 44 | 45.54 |
| 6274 | C Hill (SA) | 1894-95 to 1922-23 | 68 | 126 | 6 | 365* | 18 | 27 | 52.28 |
| 6096 | AF Kippax (NSW) | 1919-20 to 1934-35 | 61 | 95 | 8 | 315* | 23 | 14 | 70.07 |
| 6096 | GM Ritchie (Qld) | 1980-81 to 1991-92 | 94 | 154 | 14 | 213* | 14 | 34 | 43.54 |
| 6014 | VY Richardson (SA) | 1919-20 to 1936-37 | 77 | 146 | 7 | 203 | 18 | 27 | 43.27 |
| 5861 | GN Yallop (Vic) | 1972-73 to 1984-85 | 76 | 136 | 9 | 246 | 18 | 32 | 46.15 |
| 5854 | RN Harvey (Vic, NSW) | 1946-47 to 1962-63 | 76 | 122 | 6 | 231* | 16 | 24 | 50.46 |
| 5787 | MRJ Veletta (WA) | 1983-84 to 1991-92 | 83 | 144 | 15 | 262 | 16 | 30 | 44.86 |
| 5746 | PR Sleep (SA) | 1976-77 to 1991-92 | 117 | 193 | 34 | 146* | 12 | 29 | 36.13 |
| 5630 | J Dyson (NSW) | 1975-76 to 1988-89 | 82 | 150 | 16 | 241 | 11 | 29 | 42.01 |
| 5602 | KD Walters (NSW) | 1962-63 to 1980-81 | 91 | 157 | 16 | 253 | 17 | 24 | 39.73 |
| 5535 | AL Hassett (Vic) | 1932-33 to 1952-53 | 58 | 97 | 10 | 229 | 18 | 28 | 63.62 |
| 5519 | GR Marsh (WA) | 1977-78 to 1991-92 | 80 | 138 | 10 | 355* | 16 | 23 | 43.11 |
| 5482 | DC Boon (Tas) | 1978-79 to 1991-92 | 76 | 134 | 4 | 227 | 15 | 26 | 42.16 |
| 5413 | WH Ponsford (Vic) | 1922-23 to 1933-34 | 43 | 70 | 5 | 437 | 21 | 14 | 83.27 |
| 5372 | G Shipperd (WA, Tas) | 1977-78 to 1990-91 | 87 | 147 | 18 | 200* | 13 | 25 | 41.64 |
| 5281 | JD Siddons (Vic, SA) | 1984-85 to 1991-92 | 73 | 121 | 11 | 245 | 15 | 25 | 48.01 |
| 5280 | RB McCosker (NSW) | 1973-74 to 1983-84 | 70 | 124 | 15 | 168 | 17 | 26 | 48.44 |
| 5235 | DF Whatmore (Vic) | 1975-76 to 1988-89 | 85 | 150 | 17 | 170 | 10 | 31 | 36.60 |
| 5222 | IR Redpath (Vic) | 1961-62 to 1975-76 | 76 | 132 | 11 | 261 | 11 | 27 | 43.16 |
| 5036 | RB Kerr (Qld) | 1981-82 to 1989-90 | 79 | 135 | 7 | 201* | 15 | 24 | 39.34 |
| 5008 | DM Jones (Vic) | 1981-82 to 1991-92 | 61 | 102 | 7 | 243* | 16 | 19 | 52.71 |
| 4997 | WW Armstrong (Vic) | 1899-00 to 1921-22 | 59 | 106 | 7 | 250 | 17 | 17 | 50.47 |
| 4943 | BC Booth (NSW) | 1954-55 to 1968-69 | 81 | 128 | 14 | 177 | 10 | 25 | 43.36 |
| 4934 | BK Shepherd (WA) | 1955-56 to 1965-66 | 75 | 127 | 13 | 219 | 11 | 26 | 43.28 |
| 4916 | KD Meuleman (Vic, WA) | 1946-47 to 1960-61 | 70 | 114 | 13 | 234* | 13 | 25 | 48.67 |
| 4896 | MA Noble (NSW) | 1894-95 to 1908-09 | 51 | 81 | 9 | 281 | 19 | 17 | 68.00 |
| 4821 | RW Marsh (WA) | 1968-69 to 1983-84 | 86 | 139 | 9 | 168* | 6 | 23 | 37.08 |
| 4779 | KC Wessels (Qld) | 1979-80 to 1985-86 | 53 | 91 | 3 | 249 | 15 | 19 | 54.31 |
| 4749 | NC O'Neill (NSW) | 1955-56 to 1966-67 | 61 | 104 | 10 | 233 | 15 | 21 | 50.52 |
| 4716 | WA Brown (NSW, Qld) | 1932-33 to 1949-50 | 53 | 92 | 4 | 215 | 12 | 28 | 53.59 |
| 4646 | GA Bishop (SA) | 1982-83 to 1991-92 | 78 | 141 | 6 | 224* | 8 | 24 | 34.41 |
| 4613 | J Ryder (Vic) | 1912-13 to 1931-32 | 60 | 104 | 12 | 295 | 12 | 21 | 50.14 |
| 4608 | J Potter (Vic) | 1956-57 to 1967-68 | 73 | 120 | 14 | 221 | 12 | 24 | 43.47 |
| 4501 | PL Ridings (SA) | 1938-39 to 1956-57 | 76 | 131 | 12 | 186* | 9 | 21 | 37.82 |
| 4462 | MA Taylor (NSW) | 1985-86 to 1991-92 | 57 | 98 | 3 | 199 | 12 | 22 | 46.96 |
| 4330 | KG Cunningham (SA) | 1960-61 to 1973-74 | 76 | 133 | 10 | 203 | 6 | 24 | 35.20 |
| 4324 | PA Hibbert (Vic) | 1974-75 to 1986-87 | 71 | 121 | 9 | 163 | 8 | 21 | 38.60 |
| 4263 | R Edwards (WA, NSW) | 1964-65 to 1979-80 | 69 | 120 | 16 | 158 | 10 | 22 | 40.99 |
| 4171 | W Bardsley (NSW) | 1908-09 to 1925-26 | 47 | 77 | 8 | 235 | 15 | 14 | 60.45 |
| 4140 | WS Andrews (WA) | 1982-83 to 1991-92 | 76 | 115 | 12 | 139 | 5 | 28 | 40.19 |
| 4120 | RD Woolley (Tas) | 1977-78 to 1987-88 | 68 | 114 | 13 | 144 | 7 | 25 | 40.79 |
| 4067 | RM Cowper (Vic, WA) | 1959-60 to 1969-70 | 59 | 89 | 13 | 195* | 10 | 21 | 53.25 |
| 4038 | PM Toohey (NSW) | 1974-75 to 1983-84 | 64 | 109 | 10 | 158 | 11 | 18 | 40.79 |

## Most Runs For Each State

| State | Runs | Batsman | State | Runs | Batsmen |
|---|---|---|---|---|---|
| NSW | 6096 | AF Kippax | Tasmania | 5482 | DC Boon |
| Queensland | 8647 | SC Trimble | Victoria | 6615 | WM Lawry |
| South Australia | 9364 | DC Hookes | Western Australia | 6888 | RJ Inverarity |

## Highest Individual Scores

| Score | Batsman | Match | Ground | Season |
|---|---|---|---|---|
| 452* | DG Bradman | NSW v Queensland | Sydney | 1929-30 |
| 437 | WH Ponsford | Victoria v Queensland | Melbourne | 1927-28 |
| 365* | C Hill | South Australia v NSW | Adelaide | 1900-01 |
| 359 | RB Simpson | NSW v Queensland | Brisbane | 1963-64 |
| 357 | DG Bradman | South Australia v Victoria | Melbourne | 1935-36 |
| 356 | BA Richards | South Australia v Western Australia | Perth | 1970-71 |
| 355* | GR Marsh | Western Australia v South Australia | Perth | 1989-90 |
| 352 | WH Ponsford | Victoria v NSW | Melbourne | 1926-27 |
| 340* | DG Bradman | NSW v Victoria | Sydney | 1928-29 |
| 336 | WH Ponsford | Victoria v South Australia | Melbourne | 1927-28 |
| 325 | CL Badcock | South Australia v Victoria | Adelaide | 1935-36 |
| 315* | AF Kippax | NSW v Queensland | Sydney | 1927-28 |
| 306* | DW Hookes | South Australia v Tasmania | Adelaide | 1986-87 |
| 295 | J Ryder | Victoria v NSW | Melbourne | 1926-27 |
| 283 | PJP Burge | Queensland v NSW | Brisbane | 1963-64 |
| 281 | MA Noble | NSW v Victoria | Melbourne | 1905-06 |
| 277 | RB Simpson | NSW v Queensland | Sydney | 1967-68 |
| 275* | WH Ponsford | Victoria v South Australia | Melbourne | 1928-29 |
| 275* | FC Thompson | Queensland v NSW | Bris Exh. | 1930-31 |
| 271* | AF Kippax | NSW v Victoria | Sydney | 1925-26 |
| 271* | CL Badcock | South Australia v NSW | Adelaide | 1938-39 |
| 271 | RA Duff | NSW v South Australia | Sydney | 1903-04 |
| 271 | CE Pellew | South Australia v Victoria | Adelaide | 1919-20 |
| 267 | DG Bradman | South Australia v Victoria | Melbourne | 1939-40 |
| 266 | WM Lawry | Victoria v NSW | Sydney | 1960-61 |
| 264* | RG Flockton | NSW v South Australia | Sydney | 1959-60 |
| 263 | SB Smith | NSW v Victoria | Melbourne | 1982-83 |
| 262 | MRJ Veletta | Western Australia v Victoria | Perth | 1986-87 |
| 261 | IR Redpath | Victoria v Queensland | Melbourne | 1962-63 |
| 260* | AF Kippax | NSW v Victoria | Melbourne | 1928-29 |
| 260 | WB Phillips | South Australia v Queensland | Adelaide | 1981-82 |
| 259* | GB Stevens | South Australia v NSW | Sydney | 1958-59 |
| 258 | DG Bradman | NSW v South Australia | Adelaide | 1930-31 |
| 253 | DG Bradman | NSW v Queensland | Sydney | 1933-34 |
| 253 | CW Andrews | Queensland v NSW | Sydney | 1934-35 |
| 253 | AR Morris | NSW v Queensland | Brisbane | 1951-52 |
| 253 | KD Walters | NSW v South Australia | Adelaide | 1964-65 |
| 252* | SC Trimble | Queensland v NSW | Sydney | 1963-64 |
| 251* | DG Bradman | South Australia v NSW | Adelaide | 1939-40 |
| 251 | GS Sobers | South Australia v NSW | Adelaide | 1961-62 |
| 250 | WW Armstrong | Victoria v South Australia | Melbourne | 1911-12 |

*Note: The highest individual score by a Tasmanian is 227 by DC Boon, v Victoria in Melbourne, 1983-84*

## Most Centuries

| No. | Batsman | No. | Batsman |
|---|---|---|---|
| 36 | DG Bradman (NSW, SA) | 17 | HN Dansie (SA) |
| 27 | GS Chappell (SA, Qld) | 17 | RB Simpson (NSW, WA) |
| 26 | DW Hookes (SA) | 17 | WM Lawry (Vic) |
| 23 | AF Kippax (NSW) | 17 | KD Walters (NSW) |
| 23 | RJ Inverarity (WA, SA) | 17 | RB McCosker (NSW) |
| 22 | PJP Burge (Qld) | | |
| 22 | SC Trimble (Qld) | | |
| 22 | IM Chappell (SA) | | |
| 21 | WH Ponsford (Vic) | | |
| 20 | LE Favell (SA) | | |
| 20 | GM Wood (WA) | | |
| 19 | MA Noble (NSW) | | |
| 18 | C Hill (SA) | | |
| 18 | VY Richardson (SA) | | |
| 18 | AL Hassett (Vic) | | |
| 18 | GN Yallop (Vic) | | |
| 18 | AMJ Hilditch (NSW, SA) | | |
| 17 | WW Armstrong (Vic) | | |

*Notes:*

*1. The leading scorers of double-centuries (ie scores of 200 or more) are:*

| | |
|---|---|
| *13* | *DG Bradman* |
| *7* | *WH Ponsford* |
| *6* | *AF Kippax* |
| *6* | *RB Simpson* |
| *5* | *MA Noble* |
| *5* | *AL Hassett* |
| *5* | *PJP Burge* |

*2. The 26 centuries scored by Hookes are the most by one player for one state. His 17 centuries at the Adelaide Oval are the most by one player at one ground.*

*3. Bradman scored 17 centuries for NSW, 19 for South Australia*

## Most Scores Over 50

| No. | Batsman | 50-99 | 100-149 | 150-199 | Over 200 |
|---|---|---|---|---|---|
| 70 | DW Hookes | 44 | 15 | 9 | 2 |
| 69 | GS Chappell | 42 | 17 | 10 | - |
| 68 | RJ Inverarity | 45 | 18 | 5 | - |
| 67 | IM Chappell | 45 | 17 | 4 | 1 |
| 63 | LE Favell | 43 | 17 | 3 | - |
| 62 | SC Trimble | 40 | 17 | 3 | 2 |
| 56 | DG Bradman | 20 | 17 | 6 | 13 |
| 55 | WM Lawry | 38 | 13 | 2 | 2 |
| 55 | DM Wellham | 44 | 9 | 2 | - |
| 52 | PJP Burge | 30 | 14 | 3 | 5 |
| 52 | GM Wood | 32 | 15 | 5 | - |
| 50 | GN Yallop | 32 | 15 | 2 | 1 |
| 50 | AMJ Hilditch | 32 | 13 | 4 | 1 |
| 50 | AR Border | 34 | 11 | 4 | 1 |

## Centuries and Double-Centuries by State

| State | Centuries | Double-Centuries |
|---|---|---|
| NSW | 546 | 54 |
| Queensland | 311 | 19 |
| South Australia | 447 | 32 |
| Tasmania | 74 | 3 |
| Victoria | 494 | 44 |
| Western Australia | 249 | 12 |

Note: There have been 2121 centuries scored in the Shield. Of these 164 have been double-centuries.

## Centuries in Each Innings of a Match

Three times: DW Hookes (SA)

Twice: DG Bradman (NSW, SA), CJ Pinch (SA), LE Favell (SA), GS Chappell (SA, Qld), RB McCosker (NSW), GN Yallop (Vic), MA Taylor (NSW)

Notes:
1. The feat has been accomplished once by 27 players.
2. In successive matches in 1976-77, DW Hookes scored 185 and 105 v Queensland, and 135 and 156 v NSW. These four innings were all at the Adelaide Oval, within 11 days.

## Centuries by Era

| Years | Seasons | Matches | Centuries | Centuries Per Match |
|---|---|---|---|---|
| 1892-93 to 1914-15 | 23 | 133 | 205 | 1.54 |
| 1919-20 to 1939-40 | 21 | 208 | 421 | 2.02 |
| 1946-47 to 1957-58 | 12 | 189 | 276 | 1.46 |
| 1958-59 to 1969-70 | 12 | 240 | 385 | 1.60 |
| 1970-71 to 1980-81 | 11 | 238 | 294 | 1.23 |
| 1981-82 to 1991-92 | 11 | 335 | 540 | 1.61 |
| Totals | 90 | 1343 | 2121 | 1.57 |

Note:
The most centuries in one season is 56 (in 31 matches) in 1990-91. Other high totals include: 50 (in 20 matches) in 1963-64 and 38 (in 12 matches) in 1926-27.

## Centuries and Double-Centuries by Ground

| Ground | Centuries | Double Centuries |
|---|---|---|
| Adelaide Oval | 498 | 44 |
| SCG | 460 | 43 |
| MCG | 418 | 35 |
| The Gabba | 318 | 18 |
| W.A.C.A. Ground | 259 | 17 |
| Exhibition Ground | 28 | 1 |
| Bellerive Oval | 24 | 1 |
| Devonport Oval | 23 | 1 |
| T.C.A. Ground | 23 | - |
| N.T.C.A. Ground | 22 | - |
| Junction Oval | 21 | 4 |
| Kardinia Park | 9 | - |
| Newcastle | 8 | - |
| SCG no. 2 | 3 | - |
| Princes Park | 3 | - |
| Wangaratta | 3 | - |
| Lavington | 1 | - |
| Oakes Oval | - | - |
| Manuka Oval | - | - |

## Double-Century and Century in Same Match

| Scores | Batsman | Match | Ground | Season |
|---|---|---|---|---|
| 157* and 245 | WW Armstrong | Victoria v South Australia | Melbourne | 1920-21 |

## Century on Debut

| Batsman | Score | Match | Ground | Season |
|---|---|---|---|---|
| H Donnan | 120 | NSW v South Australia | Adelaide | 1892-93 |
| JJ Lyons | 124 | South Australia v NSW (2) | Adelaide | 1892-93 |
| W Bruce | 128 | Victoria v NSW | Melbourne | 1892-93 |
| JP O'Halloran | 128* | Victoria v South Australia (d) | Melbourne | 1896-97 |
| LOS Poidevin | 140* | NSW v South Australia | Sydney | 1900-01 |
| M Ellis | 118 | Victoria v South Australia | Melbourne | 1902-03 |
| EF Waddy | 129* | NSW v South Australia | Adelaide | 1904-05 |
| A Diamond | 164# | NSW v South Australia | Adelaide | 1905-06 |
| FA Tarrant | 105 | Victoria v South Australia | Melbourne | 1907-08 |
| RL Park | 104 | Victoria v South Australia (2) | Melbourne | 1913-14 |
| J Bogle | 200 | NSW v South Australia | Adelaide | 1919-20 |
| WH Ponsford | 108 | Victoria v South Australia | Adelaide | 1922-23 |
| HO Rock | 127 | NSW v South Australia (d) | Sydney | 1924-25 |
| LW Gwynne | 138 | NSW v South Australia | Adelaide | 1924-25 |
| LT Gun | 136* | South Australia v NSW (d) | Adelaide | 1924-25 |
| WC Alexander | 133 | South Australia v Victoria | Melbourne | 1925-26 |
| HC Steele | 130 | NSW v Queensland (2)(d) | Bris Exh. | 1926-27 |
| FC Thompson | 134 | Queensland v NSW | Bris Exh. | 1926-27 |
| LPD O'Connor | 196 | Queensland v NSW (2) | Bris Exh. | 1926-27 |
| EC Knowles | 144 | Queensland v Victoria (2) | Bris Exh. | 1926-27 |
| DG Bradman | 118 | NSW v South Australia (d) | Adelaide | 1927-28 |

| Batsman | Score | Match | Ground | Season |
|---|---|---|---|---|
| RM Levy | 129 | Queensland v Victoria (d) | Bris Exh. | 1928-29 |
| BW Hone | 137 | South Australia v Victoria (d) | Adelaide | 1928-29 |
| RN Nutt | 102 | NSW v South Australia (d) | Adelaide | 1931-32 |
| EW Lukeman | 118 | NSW v South Australia (d) | Adelaide | 1946-47 |
| SJE Loxton | 232* | Victoria v Queensland (d) | Melbourne | 1946-47 |
| LE Favell | 164 | South Australia v NSW (2)(d) | Adelaide | 1951-52 |
| M Fitchett | 108 | Victoria v Western Australia | Perth | 1951-52 |
| RE Briggs | 121 | NSW v Western Australia (d) | Perth | 1952-53 |
| BK Shepherd | 103* | Western Australia v Queensland (d) | Perth | 1955-56 |
| RB Lyons | 102 | Queensland v Victoria (d) | Brisbane | 1955-56 |
| NG Marks | 180 | NSW v South Australia (d) | Sydney | 1958-59 |
| IM McLachlan | 188* | South Australia v Queensland (2) | Adelaide | 1960-61 |
| RB Kanhai | 135 | Western Australia v South Australia | Adelaide | 1961-62 |
| D Chadwick | 129 | Western Australia v Queensland (d) | Brisbane | 1963-64 |
| JFC Loxton | 100 | Queensland v Western Australia (d) | Perth | 1966-67 |
| MJ Lucas | 107 | Queensland v NSW (d) | Brisbane | 1968-69 |
| GJ Gilmour | 122 | NSW v South Australia (2)(d) | Sydney | 1971-72 |
| Majid Khan | 107 | Queensland v NSW | Brisbane | 1973-74 |
| MF Kent | 140 | Queensland v NSW (d) | Brisbane | 1974-75 |
| KJ Hughes | 119 | Western Australia v NSW (d) | Perth | 1975-76 |
| JM Wiener | 106 | Victoria v Queensland (2)(d) | Brisbane | 1977-78 |
| MD Taylor | 107 | Victoria v Queensland (2)(d) | Melbourne | 1977-78 |
| CE Penter | 112 | Western Australia v NSW (d) | Sydney | 1979-80 |
| DM Wellham | 100 | NSW v Victoria (d) | Melbourne | 1980-81 |
| MD Haysman | 126 | South Australia v Queensland (d) | Adelaide | 1982-83 |
| SP O'Donnell | 130 | Victoria v South Australia (d) | Melbourne | 1983-84 |
| WJS Seabrook | 165 | NSW v Victoria (d) | Melbourne | 1984-85 |
| EJ Harris | 118 | Tasmania v South Australia (2)(d) | Adelaide | 1985-86 |
| MG Bevan | 114 | South Australia v W. Australia (d) | Perth | 1989-90 |
| MP Lavender | 118 | Western Australia v Victoria (d) | Melbourne | 1990-91 |
| ML Hayden | 149 | Queensland v South Australia (d) | Brisbane | 1991-92 |

# indicates retired. Diamond was told of the death of his brother in an accident in Sydney when he returned to the dressing room at the close of the second day, and withdrew from the match.
(2) indicates scored in second innings
(d) indicates first-class debut

Notes:
1. DG Bradman is the only player to score a century on Shield debut for two states. As well as his debut 118 for NSW in Adelaide in December 1927, Bradman scored 117 in his first innings for South Australia, against NSW at the Adelaide Oval in 1935-36.
2. WH Ponsford and DM Wellham are the only players to score a century on their Shield and Test match debut.

## Centuries Scored in Less Than An Hour

| Mins | Batsman | Match | Ground | Season |
|---|---|---|---|---|
| 43 | DW Hookes | South Australia v Victoria | Adelaide | 1982-83 |
| 58 | VT Trumper | NSW v Victoria | Sydney | 1905-06 |

Note: Hookes' century came off 34 balls - in terms of deliveries faced, the fastest century ever scored in first-class cricket

## Individual Innings Lasting More Than 10 Hours

| Mins | Score | Batsman | Match | Ground | Season |
|---|---|---|---|---|---|
| 766 | 262 | MRJ Veletta | Western Australia v Victoria | Perth | 1986-87 |
| 630 | 275* | FC Thompson | Queensland v NSW | Bris Exh. | 1930-31 |
| 630 | 359 | RB Simpson | NSW v Queensland | Brisbane | 1963-64 |
| 628 | 355* | GR Marsh | Western Australia v South Australia | Perth | 1989-90 |
| 621 | 437 | WH Ponsford | Victoria v Queensland | Melbourne | 1927-28 |
| 605 | 166 | G Shipperd | Western Australia v NSW | Perth | 1982-83 |

## Carrying Bat Through Completed Innings

| | |
|---|---|
| Three times: | WM Lawry |
| Twice: | W Bardsley, JW Burke, MRJ Veletta |

Notes:
1. Nineteen players have accomplished this feat on one occasion
2. The highest score by a batsman carrying his bat is 199 by N Claxton (out of an innings total of 378) for South Australia v Victoria, Melbourne, 1905-06

## 1000 Runs in a Season

| Runs | Batsman | Season | M | Inn | NO | HI | 100 | Average |
|------|---------|--------|---|-----|----|----|-----|---------|
| 1254 | GN Yallop (Vic) | 1982-83 | 10 | 18 | - | 246 | 4 | 69.66 |
| 1217 | WH Ponsford (Vic) | 1927-28 | 5 | 8 | - | 437 | 4 | 152.12 |
| 1145 | BA Richards (SA) | 1970-71 | 8 | 13 | 2 | 356 | 4 | 104.09 |
| 1109 | DM Wellham (NSW) | 1982-83 | 11 | 20 | 5 | 136* | 2 | 73.93 |
| 1096 | RB McCosker (NSW) | 1982-83 | 11 | 21 | 3 | 124 | 3 | 60.88 |
| 1091 | WH Ponsford (Vic) | 1926-27 | 5 | 8 | - | 352 | 5 | 136.37 |
| 1087 | SG Law (Qld) | 1990-91 | 10 | 18 | 4 | 142* | 3 | 77.64 |
| 1062 | DG Bradman (SA) | 1939-40 | 6 | 10 | 2 | 267 | 3 | 132.75 |
| 1060 | AD Ogilvie (Qld) | 1977-78 | 9 | 18 | 2 | 194 | 6 | 66.25 |
| 1038 | TM Moody (WA) | 1988-89 | 11 | 18 | 1 | 202 | 4 | 61.06 |
| 1015 | KC Wessels (Qld) | 1981-82 | 9 | 15 | - | 220 | 5 | 67.66 |
| 1014 | DW Hookes (SA) | 1987-88 | 10 | 18 | 1 | 132 | 3 | 59.65 |
| 1014 | GM Wood (WA) | 1987-88 | 11 | 16 | 3 | 186* | 3 | 78.00 |
| 1013 | GS Chappell (Qld) | 1973-74 | 7 | 13 | 2 | 180 | 4 | 92.09 |
| 1006 | J Dyson (NSW) | 1983-84 | 10 | 18 | 3 | 241 | 3 | 67.07 |
| 1005 | NC O'Neill (NSW) | 1957-58 | 8 | 14 | 2 | 233 | 4 | 83.75 |

Note: The highest batting average in a season is 300.66, by RB Simpson (WA) in 1959-60, who scored 902 runs in five matches.

## Partnership Records

| Wkt | Runs | Batsmen | Match | Ground | Season |
|-----|------|---------|-------|--------|--------|
| 1st | 431 | MRJ Veletta & GR Marsh | Western Australia v South Australia | Perth | 1989-90 |
| 2nd | 378 | LA Marks & KD Walters | NSW v South Australia | Adelaide | 1964-65 |
| 3rd | 390* | JK Moss & JM Wiener | Victoria v Western Australia | St Kilda | 1981-82 |
| 4th | 462* | DW Hookes & WB Phillips | South Australia v Tasmania | Adelaide | 1986-87 |
| 5th | 464*# | ME Waugh & SR Waugh | NSW v Western Australia | Perth | 1990-91 |
| 6th | 332 | NG Marks & G Thomas | NSW v South Australia | Sydney | 1958-59 |
| 7th | 335 | CW Andrews & EC Bensted | Queensland v NSW | Sydney | 1934-35 |
| 8th | 270 | VT Trumper & EP Barbour | NSW v Victoria | Sydney | 1912-13 |
| 9th | 232 | C Hill & EA Walkley | South Australia v NSW | Adelaide | 1900-01 |
| 10th | 307# | AF Kippax & JEH Hooker | NSW v Victoria | Melbourne | 1928-29 |

* indicates unbroken partnership
# indicates world record for that wicket in first-class cricket

## Highest Partnership for Each State

| State | Runs | Wkt | Batsmen | Opponent | Ground | Season |
|-------|------|-----|---------|----------|--------|--------|
| NSW | 464* | 5th | ME Waugh & SR Waugh | Western Australia | Perth | 1990-91 |
| Queensland | 388 | 1st | KC Wessels & RB Kerr | Victoria | St Kilda | 1982-83 |
| South Australia | 462* | 4th | DW Hookes & WB Phillips | Tasmania | Adelaide | 1986-87 |
| Tasmania | 258 | 4th | MD Taylor & DJ Buckingham | South Australia | Adelaide | 1987-88 |
| Victoria | 390* | 3rd | JK Moss & JM Wiener | Western Australia | St Kilda | 1981-82 |
| Western Australia | 431 | 1st | MRJ Veletta & GR Marsh | South Australia | Perth | 1989-90 |

# 6. BOWLING RECORDS

## Most Wickets in a Career

| Wkts | Bowler | Career | M | Balls | Runs | Best | 5/ | 10/ | Average |
|------|--------|--------|---|-------|------|------|----|----|---------|
| 513 | CV Grimmett (Vic, SA) | 1923-24 to 1939-40 | 79 | 28465 | 12796 | 9-180 | 48 | 13 | 25.29 |
| 367 | GF Lawson (NSW) | 1977-78 to 1991-92 | 103 | 20930 | 8744 | 6-31 | 12 | - | 23.82 |
| 366 | TM Alderman (WA) | 1974-75 to 1991-92 | 91 | 18037 | 8692 | 7-28 | 17 | 3 | 23.74 |
| 355 | JR Thomson (NSW, Qld) | 1972-73 to 1985-86 | 84 | 16939 | 8591 | 7-27 | 18 | 3 | 24.20 |
| 344 | AA Mallett (SA) | 1967-68 to 1980-81 | 77 | 20906 | 8173 | 7-57 | 19 | 2 | 23.76 |
| 338 | DK Lillee (WA, Tas) | 1969-70 to 1987-88 | 75 | 17814 | 8086 | 7-36 | 18 | 4 | 23.92 |
| 302 | GAR Lock (WA) | 1962-63 to 1970-71 | 63 | 20107 | 7210 | 7-53 | 15 | 2 | 23.87 |
| 297 | AN Connolly (Vic) | 1959-60 to 1970-71 | 71 | 18033 | 7745 | 9-67 | 12 | 4 | 26.07 |
| 273 | JW Martin (NSW, SA) | 1956-57 to 1967-68 | 77 | 17078 | 8703 | 8-97 | 12 | - | 31.87 |
| 266 | R Benaud (NSW) | 1948-49 to 1963-64 | 73 | 17948 | 7174 | 7-32 | 12 | 3 | 26.96 |
| 266 | G Dymock (Qld) | 1971-72 to 1981-82 | 75 | 17110 | 7223 | 6-79 | 8 | - | 27.15 |
| 262 | CJ McDermott (Qld) | 1983-84 to 1991-92 | 57 | 12362 | 6358 | 8-44 | 20 | 2 | 24.26 |
| 257 | CG Rackemann (Qld) | 1979-80 to 1991-92 | 70 | 15396 | 6797 | 7-49 | 8 | 1 | 26.44 |
| 252 | RJ Bright (Vic) | 1972-73 to 1987-88 | 101 | 22789 | 8833 | 6-61 | 10 | - | 35.05 |
| 246 | LO Fleetwood-Smith (Vic) | 1931-32 to 1939-40 | 40 | 11576 | 6034 | 9-135 | 25 | 8 | 24.52 |
| 246 | AK Davidson (NSW) | 1949-50 to 1962-63 | 62 | 13423 | 5195 | 7-31 | 10 | - | 21.11 |
| 244 | RR Lindwall (NSW, Qld) | 1946-47 to 1959-60 | 66 | 14084 | 5518 | 7-45 | 11 | 1 | 22.61 |
| 240 | JD Higgs (Vic) | 1970-71 to 1982-83 | 75 | 14961 | 7202 | 8-66 | 12 | 2 | 30.00 |
| 237 | GRJ Matthews (NSW) | 1982-83 to 1991-92 | 78 | 17460 | 6618 | 7-50 | 13 | 2 | 27.92 |
| 236 | CD Matthews (WA, Tas) | 1984-85 to 1991-92 | 54 | 12008 | 5744 | 8-101 | 17 | - | 24.33 |
| 235 | PR Sleep (SA) | 1976-77 to 1991-92 | 117 | 17807 | 9072 | 8-133 | 6 | - | 38.60 |

| Wkts | Bowler | Career | M | Balls | Runs | Best | 5/ | 10/ | Average |
|------|--------|--------|---|-------|------|------|-----|------|---------|
| 234 | TJ Jenner (WA, SA) | 1963-64 to 1976-77 | 87 | 17010 | 8124 | 7-127 | 8 | 1 | 34.72 |
| 234 | MG Hughes (Vic) | 1981-82 to 1991-92 | 66 | 14595 | 7069 | 7-81 | 8 | 2 | 30.21 |
| 232 | GD McKenzie (WA) | 1959-60 to 1973-74 | 73 | 16566 | 7322 | 6-100 | 7 | - | 31.56 |
| 231 | MR Whitney (NSW) | 1980-81 to 1991-92 | 71 | 13602 | 6652 | 7-75 | 9 | - | 28.79 |
| 229 | KH MacLeay (WA) | 1981-82 to 1991-92 | 90 | 17761 | 7033 | 6-93 | 5 | - | 30.71 |
| 220 | MHN Walker (Vic) | 1968-69 to 1981-82 | 62 | 15011 | 6476 | 6-49 | 11 | - | 29.94 |
| 215 | H Ironmonger (Vic) | 1914-15 to 1933-34 | 44 | 14594 | 5290 | 7-13 | 16 | 4 | 24.60 |
| 209 | E Jones (SA) | 1892-93 to 1902-03 | 39 | 12139 | 5508 | 8-157 | 19 | 4 | 26.35 |
| 208 | DR Gilbert (NSW, Tas) | 1983-84 to 1991-92 | 73 | 14152 | 6865 | 7-127 | 8 | - | 33.00 |
| 203 | WJ O'Reilly (NSW) | 1927-28 to 1939-40 | 33 | 10748 | 3472 | 9-41 | 18 | 7 | 17.10 |
| 202 | JRF Duncan (Qld, Vic) | 1964-65 to 1972-73 | 62 | 14024 | 5954 | 8-55 | 9 | 1 | 29.48 |
| 200 | AIC Dodemaide (Vic) | 1983-84 to 1991-92 | 66 | 13635 | 6141 | 6-80 | 8 | - | 30.70 |

## Most Wickets For Each State

| State | Wkts | Bowler | State | Wkts | Bowler |
|-------|------|--------|-------|------|--------|
| NSW | 367 | GF Lawson | Tasmania | 110 | DR Gilbert |
| Queensland | 328 | JR Thomson | Victoria | 297 | AN Connolly |
| South Australia | 504 | CV Grimmett | Western Australia | 366 | TM Alderman |

## Most Wickets in an Innings

| Total | Bowler | Match | Ground | Season |
|-------|--------|-------|--------|--------|
| 10-36 | TW Wall | South Australia v NSW | Sydney | 1932-33 |
| 10-44 | IJ Brayshaw | Western Australia v Victoria | Perth | 1967-68 |
| 10-61 | PJ Allan | Queensland v Victoria | Melbourne | 1965-66 |
| 9-30 | JPF Travers | South Australia v Victoria | Melbourne | 1900-01 |
| 9-40 | EL McCormick | Victoria v South Australia | Adelaide | 1936-37 |
| 9-41 | WJ O'Reilly | NSW v South Australia | Adelaide | 1937-38 |
| 9-50 | WJ O'Reilly | NSW v Victoria | Melbourne | 1933-34 |
| 9-52 | WP Howell | NSW v Victoria | Melbourne | 1902-03 |
| 9-67 | AN Connolly | Victoria v Queensland | Brisbane | 1964-65 |
| 9-77 | DW Hourn | NSW v Victoria | Sydney | 1978-79 |
| 9-83 | RG Holland | NSW v South Australia | Sydney | 1984-85 |
| 9-135 | LO Fleetwood-Smith | Victoria v South Australia | Melbourne | 1937-38 |
| 9-147 | G Giffen | South Australia v Victoria | Adelaide | 1892-93 |
| 9-180 | CV Grimmett | South Australia v Queensland | Adelaide | 1934-35 |
| 8-23 | WJ O'Reilly | NSW v Queensland | Sydney | 1939-40 |
| 8-31 | ES White | NSW v South Australia | Sydney | 1935-36 |
| 8-39 | H Trumble | Victoria v South Australia | Melbourne | 1898-99 |
| 8-41 | LS Pascoe | NSW v Tasmania | Hobart | 1981-82 |
| 8-42 | IW Callen | Victoria v Queensland | Melbourne | 1976-77 |
| 8-44 | CJ McDermott | Queensland v Tasmania | Brisbane | 1989-90 |
| 8-50 | RB Minnett | NSW v Victoria | Melbourne | 1914-15 |
| 8-51 | MA Polzin | Queensland v Victoria | Melbourne | 1989-90 |
| 8-52 | WA Johnston | Victoria v Queensland | Melbourne | 1952-53 |
| 8-55 | JRF Duncan | Queensland v Victoria | Melbourne | 1970-71 |
| 8-56 | AL Newell | NSW v Victoria | Sydney | 1897-98 |
| 8-56 | HR Gorringe | Western Australia v Queensland | Perth | 1952-53 |
| 8-57 | CV Grimmett | South Australia v NSW | Adelaide | 1927-28 |
| 8-58 | H Trumble | Victoria v NSW | Melbourne | 1898-99 |
| 8-61 | NJN Hawke | South Australia v NSW | Sydney | 1967-68 |
| 8-64 | EW Freeman | South Australia v NSW | Adelaide | 1970-71 |
| 8-66 | TR McKibbin | NSW v South Australia | Sydney | 1894-95 |
| 8-66 | JN Crawford | South Australia v Victoria | Adelaide | 1912-13 |
| 8-66 | JD Higgs | Victoria v Western Australia | Melbourne | 1974-75 |
| 8-74 | TR McKibbin | NSW v South Australia | Adelaide | 1896-97 |
| 8-77 | G Giffen | South Australia v NSW (1st innings) | Adelaide | 1894-95 |
| 8-79 | LO Fleetwood-Smith | Victoria v Queensland | Melbourne | 1936-37 |
| 8-81 | AA Mailey | NSW v South Australia | Sydney | 1920-21 |
| 8-84 | EA McDonald | Victoria v NSW | Sydney | 1921-22 |
| 8-84 | AG Hurst | Victoria v Queensland | Melbourne | 1977-78 |
| 8-86 | CV Grimmett | Victoria v South Australia | Adelaide | 1923-24 |
| 8-87 | AL Thomson | Victoria v NSW | Melbourne | 1969-70 |
| 8-93 | TR McKibbin | NSW v Victoria | Melbourne | 1895-96 |
| 8-95 | PM Clough | Tasmania v Western Australia | Launceston | 1983-84 |
| 8-97 | JW Martin | NSW v Victoria | Sydney | 1962-63 |
| 8-98 | DE Hoare | Western Australia v NSW | Perth | 1964-65 |
| 8-101 | CD Matthews | Western Australia v Queensland | Perth | 1987-88 |
| 8-106 | JV Saunders | Victoria v South Australia | Adelaide | 1902-03 |
| 8-109 | G Giffen | South Australia v NSW (2nd innings) | Adelaide | 1894-95 |
| 8-110 | G Giffen | South Australia v Victoria | Adelaide | 1902-03 |

| Total | Bowler | Match | Ground | Season |
|---|---|---|---|---|
| 8-111 | M Pierce | NSW v South Australia | Adelaide | 1892-93 |
| 8-111 | TR McKibbin | NSW v Victoria | Sydney | 1896-97 |
| 8-111 | LO Fleetwood-Smith | Victoria v South Australia | Melbourne | 1933-34 |
| 8-113 | LO Fleetwood-Smith | Victoria v NSW | Sydney | 1934-35 |
| 8-129 | H Trumble | Victoria v South Australia | Adelaide | 1898-99 |
| 8-133 | PR Sleep | South Australia v Victoria | Melbourne | 1978-79 |
| 8-148 | BJ Flynn | Queensland v NSW | Brisbane | 1953-54 |
| 8-157 | E Jones | South Australia v NSW | Sydney | 1896-97 |
| 8-287 | G Giffen | South Australia v NSW | Adelaide | 1899-00 |

## Economical Bowling Analysis (5, 6 or 7 wickets in an innings)

| Total | Bowler | Match | Ground | Season |
|---|---|---|---|---|
| 7-12 | KR Miller | NSW v South Australia | Sydney | 1955-56 |
| 7-13 | H Ironmonger | Victoria v Queensland | Melbourne | 1932-33 |
| 7-17 | LO Fleetwood-Smith | Victoria v Queensland | Melbourne | 1936-37 |
| 7-18 | CJ Hill | NSW v Queensland | Sydney | 1932-33 |
| 7-18 | LS Pascoe | NSW v South Australia | Sydney | 1979-80 |
| 6-6 | JC Scuderi | South Australia v Western Australia | Adelaide | 1989-90 |
| 6-12 | CR Miller | South Australia v NSW | Sydney | 1990-91 |
| 6-13 | AK Davidson | NSW v Western Australia | Sydney | 1951-52 |
| 6-15 | E Jones | South Australia v Victoria | Melbourne | 1895-96 |
| 5-8 | CG Macartney | NSW v Victoria | Melbourne | 1922-23 |

## Most Wickets in a Match

| Total | Bowler | Match | Ground | Season |
|---|---|---|---|---|
| 16-186 | G Giffen | South Australia v NSW | Adelaide | 1894-95 |
| 16-289 | CV Grimmett | South Australia v Queensland | Adelaide | 1934-35 |
| 15-96 | LO Fleetwood-Smith | Victoria v Queensland | Melbourne | 1936-37 |
| 15-125 | TR McKibbin | NSW v South Australia | Adelaide | 1896-97 |
| 15-185 | G Giffen | South Australia v Victoria | Adelaide | 1902-03 |
| 15-226 | LO Fleetwood-Smith | Victoria v NSW | Sydney | 1934-35 |
| 14-45 | WJ O'Reilly | NSW v Queensland | Sydney | 1939-40 |
| 14-87 | TM Alderman | Western Australia v NSW | Perth | 1981-82 |
| 14-98 | WJ O'Reilly | NSW v South Australia | Adelaide | 1937-38 |
| 14-189 | TR McKibbin | NSW v South Australia | Sydney | 1894-95 |
| 13-87 | HV Hordern | NSW v Victoria | Sydney | 1910-11 |
| 13-105 | EW Freeman | South Australia v NSW | Adelaide | 1970-71 |
| 13-110 | PJ Allan | Queensland v NSW | Sydney | 1968-69 |
| 13-111 | WJ O'Reilly | NSW v Queensland | Brisbane | 1933-34 |
| 13-122 | AA Mallett | South Australia v Western Australia | Adelaide | 1971-72 |
| 13-125 | JRF Duncan | Queensland v Victoria | Melbourne | 1970-71 |
| 13-135 | CV Grimmett | South Australia v Queensland | Brisbane | 1932-33 |
| 13-141 | AL Thomson | Victoria v NSW | Melbourne | 1969-70 |
| 13-149 | JC Reedman | South Australia v Victoria | Melbourne | 1904-05 |
| 13-153 | GE Tribe | Victoria v South Australia | Adelaide | 1946-47 |
| 13-155 | J Ryder | Victoria v South Australia | Melbourne | 1912-13 |
| 13-165 | AN Connolly | Victoria v South Australia | Adelaide | 1967-68 |
| 13-181 | H Ironmonger | Victoria v South Australia | Melbourne | 1914-15 |
| 13-194 | JV Saunders | Victoria v South Australia | Adelaide | 1902-03 |
| 13-240 | TR McKibbin | NSW v Victoria | Sydney | 1896-97 |
| 13-265 | M Pierce | NSW v South Australia | Adelaide | 1892-93 |

Note: The best match return by a Tasmanian is 11-183 by RL Brown, v South Australia in Adelaide, 1985-86

## Five or More Wickets in an Innings Most Times

| No. | Bowler |
|---|---|
| 48 | CV Grimmett (Vic, SA) |
| 25 | LO Fleetwood-Smith (Vic) |
| 20 | CJ McDermott (Qld) |
| 19 | E Jones (SA) |
| 19 | AA Mallett (SA) |
| 18 | G Giffen (SA) |
| 18 | JV Saunders (Vic) |
| 18 | WJ O'Reilly (NSW) |
| 18 | DK Lillee (WA) |
| 18 | JR Thomson (NSW, Qld) |
| 17 | TM Alderman (WA) |
| 17 | CD Matthews (WA, Tas) |
| 16 | H Ironmonger (Vic) |
| 15 | GAR Lock (WA) |

Note:
1. CV Grimmett achieved this feat once for Victoria and 47 times for South Australia.
2. The most times this feat has been achieved by a Tasmanian is 6, by CD Matthews.

## Ten or More Wickets in a Match Most Times

| No. | Bowler |
|---|---|
| 13 | CV Grimmett (SA) |
| 8 | LO Fleetwood-Smith (Vic) |
| 7 | G Giffen (SA) |
| 7 | WJ O'Reilly (NSW) |
| 5 | TR McKibbin (NSW) |

## Four Wickets in Four Successive Balls

| Bowler | Match | Ground | Season |
|---|---|---|---|
| JEH Hooker | NSW v Victoria | Sydney | 1928-29 |

*Note: Hooker took wickets with each of the three final balls of the Victorian first innings, and a wicket with his first ball in the second innings.*

## Hat-tricks

| Bowler | Match | Ground | Season |
|---|---|---|---|
| WW Armstrong | Victoria v NSW | Melbourne | 1902-03 |
| AJY Hopkins | NSW v South Australia | Sydney | 1903-04 |
| HI Ebeling | Victoria v Queensland | Melbourne | 1928-29 |
| CV Grimmett | South Australia v Queensland | Bris Exh. | 1928-29 |
| AK Walker | NSW v Queensland | Sydney | 1948-49 |
| JC Treanor | NSW v Queensland | Brisbane | 1954-55 |
| GF Rorke | NSW v Queensland | Sydney | 1958-59 |
| AK Davidson | NSW v Western Australia | Perth | 1962-63 |
| D Robins | South Australia v NSW | Adelaide | 1965-66 |
| RF Surti | Queensland v Western Australia | Perth | 1968-69 |
| W Prior | South Australia v NSW | Adelaide | 1975-76 |
| LS Pascoe | NSW v South Australia | Adelaide | 1980-81 |
| PM Clough | Tasmania v NSW | Hobart | 1982-83 |
| JR Thomson | Queensland v Western Australia | Brisbane | 1984-85 |
| DR Gilbert | NSW v Victoria | Sydney | 1984-85 |

## Most Runs Conceded in One Innings

| Runs | Wkts | Bowler | Match | Ground | Season |
|---|---|---|---|---|---|
| 362 | 4 | AA Mailey | NSW v Victoria | Melbourne | 1926-27 |
| 287 | 8 | G Giffen | South Australia v NSW | Adelaide | 1899-00 |
| 249 | 6 | JDA O'Connor | South Australia v Victoria | Melbourne | 1907-08 |
| 225 | 2 | A Jarvis | South Australia v NSW | Sydney | 1900-01 |
| 222 | 1 | AW Wright | South Australia v Victoria | Melbourne | 1907-08 |
| 220 | 2 | H Ironmonger | Victoria v NSW | Sydney | 1928-29 |

## Most Runs Conceded in a Match

| Runs | Wkts | Innings' Figures | Bowler | Match | Ground | Season |
|---|---|---|---|---|---|---|
| 394 | 10 | (4-192 & 6-202) | CV Grimmett | South Australia v NSW | Sydney | 1925-26 |
| 362 | 4 | (4-362) | AA Mailey | NSW v Victoria | Melbourne | 1926-27 |
| 345 | 3 | (3-190 & 0-155) | JD Scott | South Australia v NSW | Sydney | 1925-26 |
| 326 | 11 | (6-134 & 5-192) | NL Williams | South Australia v Victoria | Adelaide | 1928-29 |

## Most Balls Bowled in an Innings

| Balls | (O-M-R-W) | Bowler | Match | Ground | Season |
|---|---|---|---|---|---|
| 512 | (64-0-362-4) | AA Mailey | NSW v Victoria | Melbourne | 1926-27 |
| 498 | (83-17-249-6) | JDA O'Connor | South Australia v Victoria | Melbourne | 1907-08 |
| 493 | (82.1-42-98-5) | RW McLeod | Victoria v NSW | Melbourne | 1892-93 |
| 488 | (61-18-126-5) | LF Kline | Victoria v NSW | Sydney | 1956-57 |
| 463 | (77.1-7-287-8) | G Giffen | South Australia v NSW | Adelaide | 1899-00 |
| 451 | (75.1-16-190-7) | AL Newell | NSW v South Australia | Adelaide | 1893-94 |

## Most Balls Bowled in a Match

| Balls | (O-M-R-W) | Bowler | Match | Ground | Season |
|---|---|---|---|---|---|
| 848 | (106-14-394-10) | CV Grimmett | South Australia v NSW | Sydney | 1925-26 |
| 743 | (92.7-22-245-10) | DD Blackie | Victoria v South Australia | Adelaide | 1926-27 |
| 736 | (92-16-267-9) | CV Grimmett | South Australia v Victoria | Adelaide | 1924-25 |
| 720 | (120-58-152-11) | RW McLeod | Victoria v NSW | Melbourne | 1892-93 |
| 695 | (115.5-51-191-12) | G Giffen | South Australia v NSW | Adelaide | 1892-93 |

## Most Wickets in an Innings on Debut

| Total | Bowler | Match | Ground | Season |
|---|---|---|---|---|
| 8-86 (2) | CV Grimmett | Victoria v South Australia | Adelaide | 1923-24 |
| 8-111 (d) | M Pierce | NSW v South Australia | Adelaide | 1892-93 |
| 7-55 | HV Hordern | NSW v Victoria | Sydney | 1910-11 |
| 7-59 (d) | MA Polzin | Queensland v South Australia | Brisbane | 1986-87 |
| 7-75 (2)(d) | LC Mayne | Western Australia v NSW | Perth | 1961-62 |
| 7-85 | GE Tribe | Victoria v South Australia | Adelaide | 1946-47 |
| 7-101 | LO Fleetwood-Smith | Victoria v South Australia | Melbourne | 1931-32 |
| 7-133 | JL Wall | NSW v South Australia | Adelaide | 1921-22 |

*(d) indicates first-class debut*
*(2) indicates bowling figures achieved in second innings*

## Most Wickets in a Match on Debut

| Total | Bowler | Match | Ground | Season |
|---|---|---|---|---|
| 13-87 | HV Hordern | NSW v Victoria | Sydney | 1910-11 |
| 13-153 | GE Tribe | Victoria v South Australia | Adelaide | 1946-47 |
| 13-265 (d) | M Pierce | NSW v South Australia | Adelaide | 1892-93 |
| 12-191 | G Giffen | South Australia v NSW | Adelaide | 1892-93 |
| 11-103 (d) | MA Polzin | Queensland v South Australia | Brisbane | 1986-87 |
| 11-120 | LO Fleetwood-Smith | Victoria v South Australia | Melbourne | 1931-32 |
| 11-152 | RW McLeod | Victoria v NSW | Melbourne | 1892-93 |
| 11-256 | JL Wall | NSW v South Australia | Adelaide | 1921-22 |

*(d) indicates first-class debut*

## Most Wickets in a Season

| Wkts | Bowler | Season | M | Balls | Runs | Best | 5/ | Average |
|---|---|---|---|---|---|---|---|---|
| 60 | LO Fleetwood-Smith (Vic) | 1934-35 | 6 | 2164 | 1137 | 8-113 | 8 | 18.95 |
| 56 | CD Matthews (WA) | 1987-88 | 11 | 2553 | 1215 | 8-101 | 3 | 21.70 |
| 55 | J Garner (SA) | 1982-83 | 8 | 2419 | 976 | 7-78 | 4 | 17.74 |
| 54 | CJ McDermott (Qld) | 1989-90 | 10 | 1392 | 1375 | 8-44 | 4 | 25.46 |
| 52 | WJ O'Reilly (NSW) | 1939-40 | 6 | 1766 | 705 | 8-23 | 6 | 13.55 |
| 51 | GAR Lock (WA) | 1966-67 | 8 | 2392 | 1086 | 6-85 | 3 | 21.29 |
| 49 | CV Grimmett (SA) | 1934-35 | 6 | 2214 | 1043 | 9-180 | 5 | 21.28 |
| 49 | CV Grimmett (SA) | 1939-40 | 6 | 2478 | 1215 | 6-118 | 5 | 24.79 |
| 49 | AL Thomson (Vic) | 1969-70 | 8 | 2104 | 876 | 8-87 | 5 | 17.87 |
| 49 | AA Mallett (SA) | 1972-73 | 8 | 2551 | 893 | 5-41 | 3 | 18.22 |
| 49 | PR Reiffel (Vic) | 1990-91 | 10 | 2585 | 1053 | 6-57 | 3 | 21.49 |
| 49 | GRJ Matthews (NSW) | 1991-92 | 11 | 2686 | 1023 | 6-63 | 4 | 20.87 |
| 48 | DW Hourn (NSW) | 1977-78 | 9 | 2222 | 995 | 7-71 | 4 | 20.72 |
| 48 | CD Matthews (Tas) | 1991-92 | 10 | 2267 | 1066 | 6-89 | 6 | 22.21 |

Notes:
1. In 1896-97 TR McKibbin (NSW) took 44 wickets in four matches, at an average of 14.88.
2. The best average by a bowler taking at least 10 wickets in a season is 13.55 by WJ O'Reilly, as above.

## 7. WICKETKEEPING RECORDS

### Most Dismissals in a Career

| Total | Keeper | Career | Mat | Cght | Stpd |
|---|---|---|---|---|---|
| 346 | RW Marsh (WA) | 1968-69 to 1983-84 | 86 | 313 | 33 |
| 312 | JA Maclean (Qld) | 1968-69 to 1978-79 | 86 | 288 | 24 |
| 290 | TJ Zoehrer (WA) | 1980-81 to 1991-92 | 87 | 264 | 26 |
| 276 | ATW Grout (Qld) | 1946-47 to 1965-66 | 86 | 214 | 62 |
| 260 | SJ Rixon (NSW) | 1974-75 to 1987-88 | 94 | 219 | 41 |
| 250 | BN Jarman (SA) | 1955-56 to 1968-69 | 77 | 192 | 58 |
| 238 | RD Robinson (Vic) | 1971-72 to 1981-82 | 68 | 212 | 26 |
| 229 | RC Jordon (Vic) | 1959-60 to 1970-71 | 70 | 198 | 31 |
| 226 | RB Phillips (NSW, Qld) | 1978-79 to 1985-86 | 71 | 214 | 12 |
| 213 | KJ Wright (WA, SA) | 1976-77 to 1983-84 | 63 | 195 | 18 |
| 211 | HB Taber (NSW) | 1964-65 to 1973-74 | 64 | 179 | 32 |
| 207 | D Tallon (Qld) | 1933-34 to 1953-54 | 69 | 146 | 61 |
| 191 | CW Walker (SA) | 1928-29 to 1939-40 | 57 | 104 | 87 |
| 180 | WAS Oldfield (NSW) | 1920-21 to 1937-38 | 51 | 109 | 71 |

Note:
These figures do not include catches taken while fielding or bowling.

### Most Dismissals in an Innings

| Dismissals | Keeper | Match | Ground | Season |
|---|---|---|---|---|
| 8 (8ct) | ATW Grout | Queensland v Western Australia | Brisbane | 1959-60 |
| 7 (3ct, 4stp) | D Tallon | Queensland v Victoria | Brisbane | 1938-39 |
| 7 (6ct, 1stp) | HB Taber | NSW v South Australia | Adelaide | 1968-69 |
| 7 (7ct) | JA Maclean | Queensland v Victoria | Melbourne | 1977-78 |
| 7 (7ct) | JM Holyman | Tasmania v Western Australia | Hobart | 1990-91 |

Note:
Holyman was making his first-class debut.

## Most Dismissals in a Match

| Dismissals | Keeper | Match | Ground | Season |
|---|---|---|---|---|
| 12 (12ct) | D Tallon | Queensland v Victoria | Brisbane | 1938-39 |
| 12 (9ct, 3stp) | HB Taber | NSW v South Australia | Adelaide | 1968-69 |
| 11 (11ct) | RW Marsh | Western Australia v Victoria | Perth | 1975-76 |
| 11 (11ct) | TJ Nielsen | South Australia v Western Australia | Perth | 1990-91 |
| 10 (7ct, 3stp) | BN Jarman | South Australia v NSW | Adelaide | 1961-62 |
| 10 (9ct, 1stp) | RC Jordon | Victoria v South Australia | Melbourne | 1970-71 |
| 10 (10ct) | RW Marsh | Western Australia v South Australia | Perth | 1976-77 |

*Note: In the match where Marsh took 10 catches, he also scored 104, the only occasion in first-class cricket where a wicketkeeper has scored a century in the same match in which he completed ten dismissals.*

## Most Dismissals in a Season

| Total | Keeper | Season | Mat | Cght | Stpd |
|---|---|---|---|---|---|
| 52 | RB Phillips (Qld) | 1984-85 | 11 | 51 | 1 |
| 47 | TJ Zoehrer (WA) | 1987-88 | 11 | 43 | 4 |
| 46 | DS Berry (Vic) | 1990-91 | 11 | 46 | - |
| 45 | RW Marsh (WA) | 1974-75 | 8 | 40 | 5 |
| 44 | JA Maclean (Qld) | 1977-78 | 9 | 43 | 1 |
| 44 | RB Phillips (Qld) | 1983-84 | 11 | 41 | 3 |

*Note: Prior to the inclusion of Western Australia in the Shield in 1947-48, the best aggregates by a keeper in a season were:*

| | | | | | |
|---|---|---|---|---|---|
| 34 | D Tallon (Qld) | 1938-39 | 6 | 21 | 13 |
| 29 | CW Walker (SA) | 1939-40 | 6 | 16 | 13 |

## 8. FIELDING RECORDS

### Most Catches in a Career

| No. | Fieldsman | Career | Match |
|---|---|---|---|
| 189 | RJ Inverarity (WA, SA) | 1962-63 to 1984-85 | 159 |
| 128 | DW Hookes (SA) | 1975-76 to 1991-92 | 120 |
| 112 | IM Chappell (SA) | 1961-62 to 1979-80 | 89 |
| 110 | DF Whatmore (Vic) | 1975-76 to 1988-89 | 85 |
| 108 | GS Chappell (SA, Qld) | 1966-67 to 1983-84 | 101 |
| 100 | RB Simpson (NSW, WA) | 1952-53 to 1977-78 | 78 |
| 97 | VY Richardson (SA) | 1919-20 to 1936-37 | 77 |
| 96 | MRJ Veletta (WA) | 1983-84 to 1991-92 | 83 |
| 95 | IJ Brayshaw (WA) | 1960-61 to 1977-78 | 91 |
| 92 | R Benaud (NSW) | 1948-49 to 1963-64 | 73 |
| 90 | RB McCosker (NSW) | 1973-74 to 1983-84 | 70 |

*Note: These figures include any catches taken while acting as a substitute wicketkeeper*

### Most Catches in an Innings

| No. | Fieldsman | Match | Ground | Season |
|---|---|---|---|---|
| 5 | H Trumble | Victoria v South Australia | Melbourne | 1900-01 |
| 5 | PA McAlister | Victoria v South Australia | Melbourne | 1901-02 |
| 5 | KC Wessels | Queensland v South Australia | Brisbane | 1985-86 |

### Most Catches in a Match

| No. | Fieldsman | Match | Ground | Season |
|---|---|---|---|---|
| 7 | H Trumble | Victoria v South Australia | Melbourne | 1900-01 |
| 7 | EW Freeman | South Australia v Western Australia | Adelaide | 1971-72 |
| 6 | R Benaud | NSW v Victoria | Melbourne | 1954-55 |
| 6 | AJ Woodcock | South Australia v Western Australia | Adelaide | 1968-69 |
| 6 | DJ Rolfe | South Australia v Tasmania | Devonport | 1979-80 |
| 6 | CS Serjeant | Western Australia v Tasmania | Perth | 1981-82 |

### Most Catches in a Season

| No. | Fieldsman | Mat | Season |
|---|---|---|---|
| 23 | CS Serjeant (WA) | 9 | 1981-82 |
| 23 | JD Siddons (Vic) | 11 | 1990-91 |
| 19 | MA Taylor (NSW) | 10 | 1988-89 |
| 19 | SM Small (NSW) | 11 | 1991-92 |

*Note: GHS Trott took 13 catches in 4 matches for Victoria in 1892-93*

## 9. ALL-ROUND PERFORMANCES

### 2000 Runs and 100 Wickets in a Career

| Player | Career | Mat | Runs | 100 | Ave | Wkts | 5/ | Ave |
|---|---|---|---|---|---|---|---|---|
| WW Armstrong (Vic) | 1899-00 to 1921-22 | 59 | 4997 | 17 | 50.47 | 177 | 5 | 24.68 |
| R Benaud (NSW) | 1948-49 to 1963-64 | 73 | 3749 | 9 | 39.05 | 266 | 12 | 26.96 |
| IJ Brayshaw (WA) | 1960-61 to 1977-78 | 91 | 3771 | 1 | 30.17 | 167 | 7 | 24.53 |
| RJ Bright (Vic) | 1972-73 to 1987-88 | 101 | 2704 | 2 | 23.51 | 252 | 10 | 35.05 |
| PH Carlson (Qld) | 1969-70 to 1980-81 | 81 | 3825 | 5 | 29.42 | 113 | 5 | 23.58 |
| GS Chappell (SA, Qld) | 1966-67 to 1983-84 | 101 | 8762 | 27 | 57.27 | 105 | - | 28.74 |
| GG Cook (Qld) | 1931-32 to 1946-47 | 53 | 2584 | 1 | 29.03 | 101 | 2 | 36.31 |
| AK Davidson (NSW) | 1949-50 to 1962-63 | 62 | 2400 | 4 | 32.88 | 246 | 10 | 21.11 |
| AIC Dodemaide (Vic) | 1983-84 to 1991-92 | 66 | 2315 | 1 | 30.06 | 200 | 8 | 30.70 |
| G Giffen (SA) | 1892-93 to 1903-04 | 38 | 2318 | 4 | 36.22 | 192 | 18 | 29.56 |
| NJN Hawke (SA, WA) | 1959-60 to 1967-68 | 57 | 2001 | 1 | 29.86 | 175 | 9 | 30.80 |
| HSTL Hendry (NSW, Vic) | 1919-20 to 1932-33 | 52 | 3393 | 10 | 43.50 | 101 | 3 | 29.54 |
| TV Hohns (Qld) | 1972-73 to 1990-91 | 105 | 3965 | 2 | 30.50 | 188 | 8 | 39.11 |
| RJ Inverarity (WA, SA) | 1962-63 to 1984-85 | 159 | 9341 | 23 | 38.44 | 157 | 5 | 32.11 |
| TJ Jenner (WA, SA) | 1963-64 to 1976-77 | 87 | 2537 | - | 20.96 | 234 | 8 | 34.72 |
| C Kelleway (NSW) | 1907-08 to 1928-29 | 39 | 2304 | 9 | 40.42 | 126 | 3 | 27.37 |
| F Laver (Vic) | 1892-93 to 1911-12 | 60 | 2750 | 4 | 28.65 | 108 | 2 | 36.99 |
| SJE Loxton (Vic) | 1946-47 to 1957-58 | 66 | 3157 | 7 | 36.28 | 130 | 1 | 23.90 |
| KD Mackay (Qld) | 1946-47 to 1963-64 | 100 | 6341 | 14 | 45.29 | 122 | 5 | 37.56 |
| KH MacLeay (WA) | 1981-82 to 1991-92 | 90 | 2591 | 3 | 28.16 | 229 | 5 | 30.71 |
| AL Mann (WA) | 1963-64 to 1983-84 | 68 | 2106 | - | 23.66 | 181 | 5 | 31.65 |
| JW Martin (NSW, SA) | 1956-57 to 1967-68 | 77 | 2701 | 1 | 27.84 | 273 | 12 | 31.87 |
| GRJ Matthews (NSW) | 1982-83 to 1991-92 | 78 | 3777 | 7 | 37.02 | 237 | 13 | 27.92 |
| KR Miller (Vic, NSW) | 1939-40 to 1955-56 | 52 | 3803 | 13 | 56.76 | 109 | 3 | 25.86 |
| MA Noble (NSW) | 1894-95 to 1908-09 | 51 | 4896 | 19 | 68.00 | 158 | 7 | 22.65 |
| SP O'Donnell (Vic) | 1983-84 to 1991-92 | 53 | 2930 | 5 | 38.05 | 113 | 2 | 32.73 |
| RK Oxenham (Qld) | 1926-27 to 1936-37 | 46 | 2314 | 4 | 30.85 | 167 | 6 | 22.13 |
| PI Philpott (NSW) | 1954-55 to 1966-67 | 46 | 2148 | 4 | 36.40 | 143 | 7 | 29.62 |
| J Ryder (Vic) | 1912-13 to 1931-32 | 60 | 4613 | 12 | 50.14 | 127 | 7 | 27.69 |
| RB Simpson (NSW, WA) | 1952-53 to 1977-78 | 78 | 6471 | 17 | 57.77 | 103 | 3 | 39.06 |
| K Slater (WA) | 1955-56 to 1967-68 | 61 | 2027 | 1 | 22.03 | 112 | - | 44.26 |
| PR Sleep (SA) | 1976-77 to 1991-92 | 117 | 5746 | 12 | 36.13 | 235 | 6 | 38.60 |
| GS Sobers (SA) | 1961-62 to 1963-64 | 23 | 2247 | 9 | 57.61 | 128 | 8 | 24.27 |
| KD Walters (NSW) | 1962-63 to 1980-81 | 91 | 5602 | 17 | 39.73 | 110 | 4 | 32.81 |
| GD Watson (Vic, WA, NSW) | 1964-65 to 1976-77 | 60 | 2674 | 4 | 31.09 | 115 | 6 | 25.25 |

### Century and Five Wickets in an Innings

| Player | Runs | Wkts | Match | Ground | Season |
|---|---|---|---|---|---|
| G Giffen | 181 | 9-147 | South Australia v Victoria | Adelaide | 1892-93 |
| JF Giller | 116 | 7-51 | Victoria v South Australia | Adelaide | 1898-99 |
| MA Noble | 100 | 5-128 | NSW v Victoria | Sydney | 1898-99 |
| MA Noble | 155 | 6-91 | NSW v Victoria | Sydney | 1899-00 |
| MA Noble | 147 | 5-67 | NSW v South Australia | Adelaide | 1903-04 |
| WW Armstrong | 168* | 6-66 | Victoria v NSW | Melbourne | 1906-07 |
| JN Crawford | 163 | 8-66 | South Australia v Victoria | Adelaide | 1912-13 |
| RJB Townsend | 117 | 5-60 | South Australia v NSW | Adelaide | 1921-22 |
| FA O'Keeffe | 180 | 5-45 | Victoria v South Australia | Adelaide | 1921-22 |
| RK Oxenham | 117 | 5-72 | Queensland v NSW | Bris Exh. | 1929-30 |
| R Benaud | 158 | 5-88 | NSW v Queensland | Brisbane | 1953-54 |
| KD Mackay | 113 | 5-51 | Queensland v South Australia | Brisbane | 1958-59 |
| RB Simpson | 236* | 5-45 | Western Australia v NSW | Perth | 1959-60 |
| AK Davidson | 108 | 7-31 | NSW v Western Australia | Perth | 1961-62 |
| GS Sobers | 251 | 6-72 | South Australia v NSW | Adelaide | 1961-62 |
| GS Sobers | 107* | 5-69 | South Australia v NSW | Adelaide | 1962-63 |
| GS Sobers | 124 | 6-81 | South Australia v NSW | Adelaide | 1963-64 |
| JW Martin | 101* | 5-126 | NSW v Western Australia | Perth | 1963-64 |
| GS Sobers | 124 | 6-71 | South Australia v Victoria | Adelaide | 1963-64 |
| PI Philpott | 125 | 6-65 | NSW v Western Australia | Sydney | 1964-65 |
| NJN Hawke | 141* | 5-92 | South Australia v Queensland | Adelaide | 1964-65 |
| KD Walters | 253 | 7-63 | NSW v South Australia | Adelaide | 1964-65 |
| GR Davies | 112 | 6-43 | NSW v Queensland | Sydney | 1967-68 |
| KD Walters | 176 | 6-51 | NSW v Victoria | Sydney | 1972-73 |
| PH Carlson | 102* | 5-46 & 5-27 | Queensland v NSW | Brisbane | 1978-79 |
| SL Saunders | 125 | 5-114 | Tasmania v NSW | Sydney | 1983-84 |
| JC Scuderi | 110 | 7-79 | South Australia v NSW | Adelaide | 1991-92 |

## One Hundred Runs and Ten Wickets in a Match

| Player | Batting | Bowling | Match | Ground | Season |
|---|---|---|---|---|---|
| G Giffen | 43 & 181 | 9-147 & 2-88 | South Australia v Victoria | Adelaide | 1892-93 |
| G Giffen | 81 & 97* | 7-75 & 8-110 | South Australia v Victoria | Adelaide | 1902-03 |
| JN Crawford | 91 & 40 | 5-89 & 5-71 | South Australia v NSW | Sydney | 1913-14 |
| CJ Hill | 17 & 91 | 7-18 & 5-49 | NSW v Queensland | Sydney | 1932-33 |
| TJ Jenner | 59 & 47 | 4-43 & 7-127 | South Australia v Western Australia | Adelaide | 1973-74 |
| PH Carlson | 24 & 102* | 5-46 & 5-27 | Queensland v NSW | Brisbane | 1978-79 |
| JC Scuderi | 110 | 7-79 & 3-86 | South Australia v NSW | Adelaide | 1991-92 |
| GRJ Matthews | 85* & 67 | 6-63 & 5-70 | NSW v Queensland | Sydney | 1991-92 |

## Wicketkeeper's Double: Century and Five Dismissals in an Innings

| Keeper | Runs | Dismissals | Match | Ground | Season |
|---|---|---|---|---|---|
| LPD O'Connor | 160 | 5 (5c) | Queensland v Victoria | Melbourne | 1928-29 |
| D Tallon | 193 | 5 (4c 1s) | Queensland v Victoria | Brisbane | 1935-36 |
| GRA Langley | 141* | 5 (5c) | South Australia v Queensland | Brisbane | 1948-49 |
| BN Jarman | 196 | 5 (5c) | South Australia v NSW | Adelaide | 1965-66 |
| JA Maclean | 132 | 6 (6c) | Queensland v Victoria | Melbourne | 1972-73 |
| RW Marsh | 104 | 6 (6c) | Western Australia v South Australia | Perth | 1976-77 |
| RD Robinson | 120 | 5 (4c 1s) | Victoria v South Australia | Adelaide | 1980-81\ |

## Best All-Round Seasons: 500 Runs and 40 Wickets

| Player | Season | M | Runs | 100 | Avge | Wkts | 5/ | Avge |
|---|---|---|---|---|---|---|---|---|
| GS Sobers (SA) | 1962-63 | 8 | 701 | 3 | 53.92 | 46 | 4 | 22.60 |
| GS Sobers (SA) | 1963-64 | 8 | 973 | 5 | 74.84 | 47 | 2 | 27.59 |
| GRJ Matthews (NSW) | 1991-92 | 11 | 580 | 1 | 41.42 | 49 | 4 | 20.87 |

*Note: Other excellent all-round performances in restricted seasons are:*

| Player | Season | M | Runs | 100 | Avge | Wkts | 5/ | Avge |
|---|---|---|---|---|---|---|---|---|
| G Giffen (SA) | 1892-93 | 4 | 468 | 1 | 58.50 | 33 | 4 | 23.00 |
| MA Noble (NSW) | 1899-00 | 4 | 515 | 3 | 85.83 | 24 | 1 | 22.08 |
| R Benaud (NSW) | 1953-54 | 7 | 665 | 3 | 60.45 | 30 | 2 | 27.70 |
| NJN Hawke (SA) | 1964-65 | 7 | 502 | 1 | 62.75 | 32 | 4 | 24.06 |

# 10. PLAYER RECORDS

## Youngest Players

| Years | Days | Player | Date of Birth | Debut | Opponent | Ground |
|---|---|---|---|---|---|---|
| 16 | 249 | ID Craig (NSW) | 12 Jun 1935 | 16 Feb 1952 | South Australia | Sydney |
| 16 | 320 | FW Sides (Qld) | 15 Dec 1913 | 31 Oct 1930 | South Australia | Brisbane |
| 16 | 355 | RB Simpson (NSW) | 3 Feb 1936 | 23 Jan 1953 | Victoria | Sydney |
| 17 | 8 | KD Walters (NSW) | 21 Dec 1945 | 29 Dec 1962 | Queensland | Brisbane |
| 17 | 31 | SP George (SA) | 20 Oct 1970 | 20 Nov 1987 | Queensland | Adelaide |
| 17 | 53 | A Cotter (NSW) | 3 Dec 1884 | 25 Jan 1902 | Victoria | Sydney |
| 17 | 64 | VT Trumper (NSW) | 2 Nov 1877 | 5 Jan 1895 | South Australia | Adelaide |
| 17 | 82 | A Jackson (NSW) | 5 Sep 1909 | 26 Nov 1926 | Queensland | Bris Exh. |

## Oldest Players

| Years | Days | Player | Date of Birth | Final Day | Opponent | Ground |
|---|---|---|---|---|---|---|
| 51 | 298 | H Ironmonger (Vic) | 7 Apr 1882 | 30 Jan 1934 | NSW | Sydney |
| 50 | 217 | DD Blackie (Vic) | 5 Apr 1882 | 8 Nov 1932 | NSW | Sydney |
| 48 | 23 | CV Grimmett (SA) | 25 Dec 1891 | 17 Jan 1940 | NSW | Sydney |
| 45 | 339 | C Hill (SA) | 18 Mar 1877 | 20 Feb 1923 | Victoria | Adelaide |
| 45 | 202 | RK Oxenham (Qld) | 28 Jul 1891 | 15 Feb 1937 | South Australia | Brisbane |

*Note: The "Final Day" given is the last day of the player's final match.*

## Longest Careers

| Years | Days | Player | Career | Matches |
|---|---|---|---|---|
| 28 | 82 | C Hill (SA) | 1894-95 to 1922-23 | 68 |
| 24 | 358 | RB Simpson (NSW, WA) | 1952-53 to 1977-78 | 78 |
| 23 | 354 | H Carter (NSW) | 1897-98 to 1921-22 | 25 |
| 23 | 42 | B Yardley (WA) | 1966-67 to 1989-90 | 52 |

## Players Who Represented Three States

| Player | Career | Mat | NSW | Qld | SA | Tas | Vic | WA |
|---|---|---|---|---|---|---|---|---|
| GD Watson | 1964-65 to 1976-77 | 60 | 4 | - | - | - | 34 | 22 |
| GJ Cosier | 1971-72 to 1980-81 | 46 | - | 22 | 20 | - | 4 | - |
| TM Chappell | 1972-73 to 1984-85 | 63 | 45 | - | 14 | - | - | 4 |
| RJ McCurdy | 1980-81 to 1984-85 | 33 | - | - | 8 | 5 | 20 | - |
| DM Wellham | 1980-81 to 1991-92 | 99 | 59 | 10 | - | 30 | - | - |

## Imports

*Explanatory Note:*
*This table lists all players who represented another country in Test cricket before representing a state in the Sheffield Shield. Players are grouped by the country for whom they played Test cricket.*

### England

| Player | Mat | Shield Career |
|---|---|---|
| JN Crawford (SA) | 17 | 1909-10 to 1913-14 |
| GAR Lock (WA) | 63 | 1962-63 to 1970-71 |
| PJ Loader (WA) | 1 | 1963-64 |
| C Milburn (WA) | 16 | 1966-67 to 1968-69 |
| TW Graveney (Qld) | 6 | 1969-70 to 1971-72 |
| JH Hampshire (Tas) | 10 | 1977-78 to 1978-79 |
| RO Butcher (Tas) | 10 | 1982-83 |
| GC Small (SA) | 9 | 1985-86 |
| RM Ellison (Tas) | 8 | 1986-87 |
| VJ Marks (WA) | 11 | 1986-87 |
| IT Botham (Qld) | 11 | 1987-88 |

### India

| Player | Mat | Shield Career |
|---|---|---|
| RF Surti (Qld) | 32 | 1968-69 to 1972-73 |

### New Zealand

| Player | Mat | Shield Career |
|---|---|---|
| WR Playle (WA) | 16 | 1965-66 to 1967-68 |
| RJ Hadlee (Tas) | 4 | 1979-80 |

### Pakistan

| Player | Mat | Shield Career |
|---|---|---|
| DA Sharpe (SA) | 12 | 1961-62 to 1965-66 |
| Younis Ahmed (SA) | 5 | 1972-73 |
| Majid Khan (Qld) | 8 | 1973-74 |
| Imran Khan (NSW) | 6 | 1984-85 |

### South Africa

| Player | Mat | Shield Career |
|---|---|---|
| JAJ Christy (Qld) | 12 | 1934-35 to 1935-36 |
| BA Richards (SA) | 8 | 1970-71 |

### West Indies

| Player | Mat | Shield Career |
|---|---|---|
| WW Hall (Qld) | 16 | 1961-62 to 1962-63 |
| RB Kanhai (WA) | 7 | 1961-62 |
| GS Sobers (SA) | 23 | 1961-62 to 1963-64 |
| LR Gibbs (SA) | 8 | 1969-70 |
| IVA Richards (Qld) | 4 | 1976-77 |
| AME Roberts (NSW) | 2 | 1976-77 |
| AI Kallicharran (Qld) | 6 | 1977-78 |
| WW Daniel (WA) | 2 | 1981-82 |
| J Garner (SA) | 8 | 1982-83 |
| MA Holding (Tas) | 8 | 1982-83 |
| WW Davis (Tas) | 8 | 1985-86 |

*Notes:*
*1. The following players represented a state in Sheffield Shield cricket before representing an overseas country in Test cricket.*

| Player | Mat | Shield Career | Country Represented |
|---|---|---|---|
| JJ Crowe (SA) | 29 | 1977-78 to 1981-82 | New Zealand |
| KC Wessels (Qld) | 53 | 1979-80 to 1985-86 | South Africa* |
| NF Williams (Tas) | 6 | 1983-84 | England |
| BP Patterson (Tas) | 9 | 1984-85 | West Indies |
| GA Hick (Qld) | 10 | 1990-91 | England |

*\*KC Wessels also played Test cricket for Australia, from 1982-83 to 1985-86*

*2. Since admission to the Shield, Tasmania has had several overseas players. High profile imports who did not play Test cricket were:*

| Player | Mat | Shield Career | Country of Origin |
|---|---|---|---|
| J Simmons | 10 | 1977-78 to 1978-79 | England |
| BF Davison | 41 | 1979-80 to 1987-88 | Zimbabwe |
| FD Stephenson | 5 | 1981-82 | Barbados |

## 11. SHEFFIELD SHIELD FINALS

In 1982-83 the ACB introduced a final to decide the Shield champions. The final is played between the two leading teams after the 30 "home-and-away" matches. The leading team hosts the final, and wins the Shield unless defeated outright.

Results

| Season | Ground | Result |
|---|---|---|
| 1982-83 | Perth | NSW defeated Western Australia by 54 runs |
| 1983-84 | Perth | Western Australia defeated Queensland by 4 wickets |
| 1984-85 | Sydney | NSW defeated Queensland by one wicket |
| 1985-86 | Sydney | NSW drew with Queensland |
| 1986-87 | Perth | Western Australia drew with Victoria |
| 1987-88 | Perth | Western Australia defeated Queensland by 5 wickets |
| 1988-89 | Perth | Western Australia drew with South Australia |
| 1989-90 | Sydney | NSW defeated Queensland by 345 runs |
| 1990-91 | Melbourne | Victoria defeated NSW by 8 wickets |
| 1991-92 | Perth | Western Australia defeated NSW by 44 runs |

### Highest Totals

| Runs | Final | Season |
|---|---|---|
| 654 | Western Australia v Victoria | 1986-87 |
| 535 | Western Australia v South Australia | 1988-89 |

### Lowest Totals

| Runs | Final | Season |
|---|---|---|
| 103 | Queensland v NSW | 1989-90 |
| 119 | Victoria v NSW | 1990-91 |

### Highest Individual Scores

| Runs | Batsman | Final | Season |
|---|---|---|---|
| 262 | MRJ Veletta | Western Australia v Victoria | 1986-87 |
| 166 | KC Wessels | Queensland v NSW | 1985-86 |
| 163 | ME Waugh | NSW v Western Australia | 1991-92 |

### Century in Each Innings

| Scores | Batsman | Final | Season |
|---|---|---|---|
| 162 & 155 | TM Moody | WA v SA | 1988-89 |
| 127 & 100 | MA Taylor | NSW v Qld | 1989-90 |

### Best Bowling

| Total | Bowler | Final | Season |
|---|---|---|---|
| 8-101 | CD Matthews | WA v Queensland | 1987-88 |
| 7-75 | MR Whitney | NSW v WA | 1991-92 |
| 7-112 | CR Miller | SA v WA | 1988-89 |
| 6-54 | CG Rackemann | Queensland v NSW | 1984-85 |
| 6-65 | MR Whitney | NSW v Queensland | 1985-86 |

# Bibliography

Richie Benaud, *Willow Patterns*, London: Hodder and Stoughton, 1969
Richie Benaud, *On Reflection*, Sydney: Collins, 1984
Brian Booth, *Booth to Bat*, Sydney: Anzea Publishers, 1983
Sir Donald Bradman, *Farewell to Cricket*, London: Hodder and Stoughton, 1950
Ian Chappell, *Chappelli*, Melbourne: Hutchinson, 1976
Brian Crowley, *A History of Australian Batting 1850-1986*, Sydney: Macmillan, 1987
Brian Crowley, *A History of Australian Bowling and Wicket-keeping 1850-1986*, Sydney: Macmillan, 1987
Philip Derriman, *True to the Blue*, Sydney: Richard Smart Publishing, 1985
Philip Derriman (editor), *The ABC Australian Cricket Almanac*, Sydney: ABC Enterprises, 1991, 1992
David Dobson, *Records of Australian First-Class Cricket 1851-1989.*
Keith Dunstan, *The Paddock that Grew*, Melbourne: Cassell, 1962
Les Favell, *By Hook or by Cut*, Adelaide: Investigator Press, 1970
Jack Fingleton, *The Immortal Victor Trumper*, London: Collins, 1978
Bill Frindall, *The Wisden Book of Cricket Records*, London: Queen Anne Press, 1986
David Frith, *The Archie Jackson Story*, Ashurst, UK: Published by *The Cricketer*, 1974
George Giffen, *With Bat and Ball*, Melbourne: Ward, Lock and Co., 1898
Benny Green (compiler), *The Wisden Book of Cricket Obituaries*, London: Queen Anne Press, 1986
Greg Growden, *A Wayward Genius; The Fleetwood-Smith Story*, Sydney: ABC Enterprises, 1991
Chris Harte, *The History of the Sheffield Shield*, Sydney: Allen and Unwin, 1987
Neil Harvey, *My World of Cricket*, London: Hodder and Stoughton, 1963
Neil Hawke, *Bowled Over*, Adelaide: Rigby Publishers, 1982
E.M. Hutcheon, *A History of Queensland Cricket*, Brisbane: Published by Queensland Cricket Association, 1947
Dennis Lillee, *Over and Out*, Sydney: Metheun Australia, 1984
Alan McGilvray, *The Game is Not the Same*, Sydney: ABC Enterprises, 1985
Alan McGilvray, *The Game Goes On*, Sydney: ABC Enterprises, 1987
Adrian McGregor, *Greg Chappell*, Sydney: William Collins, 1985
Ken Mackay, *Slasher Opens Up*, London: Pelham, 1964
Ashley Mallet, *Spin Out*, Melbourne: Gary Sparke and Associates, 1977
Ashley Mallet, *Trumper - The Illustrated Biography*, Melbourne: Macmillan, 1985
Rod Marsh, *You'll Keep*, Melbourne: Hutchinson, 1975
Christopher Martin-Jenkins, *The Complete Who's Who of Test Cricketers*, Adelaide: Rigby, 1980
Keith Miller, *Cricket Crossfire*, London: Oldbourne Press, 1956
A.G. Moyes, *Bradman*, Sydney: Angus and Robertson, 1948
A.G. Moyes, *Australian Bowlers*, Sydney: Angus and Robertson, 1953
A.G. Moyes, *Australian Batsmen*, Sydney: Angus and Robertson, 1954
A.G. Moyes, *Australian Cricket: A History*, Sydney: Angus and Robertson, 1959
A.G. Moyes, *Benaud*, Sydney: Angus and Robertson, 1962
A.G. Moyes, *The Changing Face of Cricket*, Sydney: Angus and Robertson, 1963
M.A. Noble, *The Game's the Thing*, London: Cassell and Company, 1926

Norman O'Neill, *Ins and Outs*, London: Pelham, 1964
Ian Peebles, *Straight from the Shoulder*, London: Hutchinson, 1968
Jack Pollard (editor), *Cricket the Australian Way*, Melbourne: Landsdowne Press, 1968
Jack Pollard, *Australian Cricket, The Game and the Players*, Sydney: Hodder and Stoughton, 1982
Barry Richards, *The Barry Richards Story*, London: Angus and Robertson, 1978
Victor Richardson, *The Vic Richardson Story*, Adelaide: Rigby, 1967
Ray Robinson, *On Top Down Under*, Sydney: Cassell Australia, 1975
Irving Rosenwater, *Sir Donald Bradman*, London: B.T. Batsford, 1978
John Scott, *Caught in Court*, London: Andre Deutsch, 1989
Bob Simpson, *Captain's Story*, London: Stanley Paul, 1966
Peter Sharpman, *Trumper*, Sydney: Hodder and Stoughton, 1985
Kirwan Ward, *Put Lock On!*, London: Robert Hale, 1972
Ray Webster (compiler), *First-Class Cricket in Australia, 1850-51 to 1941-42*, Glen Waverley, Victoria: Ray Webster, 1991
R.S. Whitington, *The Quiet Australian; The Lindsay Hassett Story*, Melbourne: Heinemann, 1969
R.S. Whitington, *Time of the Tiger; The Bill O'Reilly Story*, Melbourne: Hutchinson, 1970
R.S. Whitington and George Hele, *Bodyline Umpire*, Adelaide: Rigby, 1974
R.S. Whitington, *Keith Miller, The Golden Nugget*, Adelaide: Rigby, 1981

## PUBLICATIONS OF THE ASSOCIATION OF CRICKET STATISTICIANS
International Cricket Year Book, 1988 to 1991
NSW Cricketers, 1855-1981
Queensland Cricketers, 1892-1979
South Australian Cricketers, 1877-1984
Tasmanian Cricketers, 1851-1982
The Cricket Statistician (quarterly journal)
Western Australian Cricketers, 1892-1983

## MAGAZINES, ANNUALS AND PERIODICALS
Australian Cricket
Australian Cricket Yearbook and Annual
Cricket: A Weekly Record of the Game
Cricketer
Cricket Year
NSW Cricket Association Yearbook
The Australian Cricketer
The Cricketer International: Quarterly Facts and Figures
Wisden Cricketers' Almanack

## NEWSPAPERS
Advertiser (Adelaide;) Australian Town and Country Journal (Sydney); Brisbane Courier (Brisbane); Courier Mail (Brisbane); Daily Guardian (Sydney); Daily Mail (Brisbane); Daily Mirror (Sydney); Daily Telegraph (Sydney); Evening News (Sydney); Hobart Mercury (Hobart); Observer (Adelaide;) South Australian Register (Adelaide); Sydney Mail (Sydney); The Age (Melbourne); The Argus (Melbourne); The Australasian (Melbourne); The Australian (Sydney); The Australian Star (Sydney); The Leader (Melbourne); The Referee (Sydney); The Sun (Sydney); The Sunday News (Sydney); The Sun Herald (Sydney); The Sunday Telegraph (Sydney); The Sydney Morning Herald (Sydney); The Sydney Sportsman (Sydney); The Times (London); The West Australian (Perth); Truth (Sydney).